BICYCLE RIDES
Los Angeles County

•• 83 Rides With Detailed Maps & Elevation Contours ••

BY DON AND SHARRON BRUNDIGE

Books by Don and Sharron Brundige:
Bicycle Rides: Los Angeles and Orange Counties (Out of Print)
Bicycle Rides: San Fernando Valley and Ventura County (Out of Print)
Bicycle Rides: Orange County
Bicycle Rides: Los Angeles County
Bicycle Rides: Inland Empire
Bicycle Rides: San Diego and Imperial Counties
Bicycle Rides: Santa Barbara & Ventura Counties
Mountain Biking L.A. County (Southern Section)
Outdoor Recreation Checklists

Published by B-D Enterprises
122 Mirabeau Ave.
San Pedro, California 90732-3117
e-mail: bnyduk@aol.com

Printed by Moore Graphics Services, San Diego, California
First Printing - April 1989
Second Printing (revised) - August 1991
Third Printing (revised) - May 1995
Fourth Printing (completely revised and expanded) - June 2000

Photography by Don and Sharron Brundige (unless noted otherwise)
Custom Photo Work by The Foto Factory in Torrance

All rights reserved
Library of Congress Catalogue Number 99-097150
ISBN 0-9619151-8-8
Copyright © 1989, 1991, 1995, 2000 by Don and Sharron Brundige
Published in the United States of America

We want to hear from you!

Corrections and updates will make this a better book and are gratefully appreciated. Publisher will reply to all such letters. Where information is used, submitter will be acknowledged in subsequent printing and given a free book (see above) of choice.

Front Cover: Long Beach Shoreline Park Inside Title Page: La Mirada Creek Park
Back Cover: Elysian Park (upper); Old Ridge Route Road (lower)

TABLE OF CONTENTS

71 Trips and 85 Rides

DEDICATION

To our dear friend Nels M. Ostrem
the eternal optimist
who had already devised a thousand ways to sell this book

ACKNOWLEDGMENTS

We offer our thanks to family, friends and bicycling acquaintances who gave us ideas, advice and plenty of encouragement while developing this biking book. This includes a "thank you" to the state, county and city agencies and individuals who offered their services and publications. Kudos to Sam Nunez, Susan Cohen, Jill Morales, Karen Profet, Walt and Sally Bond, Rich Davis, Anders Ljungwe, Jim Cradduck and the folks we met on the road, for sharing the tours. We also show particular gratitude to our venerable crew that was kind enough to review and comment on our original manuscript: Jill Morales, Al Hook, and Walt and Sally Bond. Thank you Jackie Broom and Alex Moi for helping us through so many computer crises.

We specifically wish to acknowledge the following individuals and/or organizations who provided some excellent ideas for bicycle trips in the original book: Joel Breitbart of the City of Los Angeles; the folks at CALTRANS District 07; the Department of Transportation of the City of Los Angeles; Al Kovach of the City of Torrance; the Recreation Department of the City of Arcadia; the Public Works Department of the City of Pasadena; the Parks and Recreation Department of the City of Burbank; the Cities of Glendale and La Mirada; and Noelia Chapa of the City of La Habra Heights.

Finally, we want to thank contributors to our 2000 edition: the East Area Administrative Office for their help in directing us around Elysian Park; Pete Weisser at the California Department of Water Resources for providing updated information about the California Aqueduct; Ron Milan of the Los Angeles County Bicycling Coalition (LACBC) for acquainting us with the latest additions to marked City of Los Angeles bikeways; Will and Kathi Decker of the *Southern California Bicyclist* magazine for keeping us on our toes to update our tours; and both Cary Green and Dick Farrar, local cycling enthusiasts, for providing corrections/updates to some of our previous ride descriptions.

INTRODUCTION

As with all our books, we wanted to provide a trip guide that concentrates on trip navigation, contains a large number of well-documented trips, provides the necessary trip maps and elevation contours, and is reasonably priced. Hopefully, again, we have succeeded!

This guide has been developed based on biking trips developed or revisited in 1999-2000. It is a total update/revision of *Bicycle Rides: Los Angeles County*. Because of new construction, new or modified traffic flow, changes of park and facility names and other effects of time, this book has over 20 completely new maps and both map and route description changes to a majority of the original trips. Also, 21 new trips in the East County, San Fernando Valley, Canyon Country and High Desert. region have been added. Finally, there are numerous new photos in highly scenic areas scattered throughout.

There are over 1100 <u>one-way</u> bike miles described! The document identifies 71 trips which blanket Los Angeles County. Trips of exceptional length or complexity are broken down into segments or "rides." There are a total of 83 rides described. Each ride is written to be as complete and self-standing as possible. The authors and riding buddies used 18-speed bicycles, although the vast majority of trips can be ridden with bikes having a lesser number of gears.

A cross section of trips is provided. There are some short-length family trips on separated bikepaths, many longer exploratory and workout trips for more experienced bikers on various quality bike routes, and a few "gut-buster" trips on open roadway for the most physically fit and motivated cyclists. The trip domains include cities, parks, beaches, harbors, rivers, lakes, valleys, canyons, mountains and desert. The trips vary from extremely scenic to somewhat monotonous (e.g., certain stretches of the concrete "wastelands" along the Class I river routes). There is a little something for everybody!

The strong emphasis in this book is "getting from here to there." This navigation is provided using detailed route descriptions in terms of landmarks, mileage, elevation contours and a quality set of trip maps. Scenery, vistas and scenic or historic landmarks and sightseeing attractions are regularly noted for each trip, although detailed information about these features must be sought out in other publications. Public restrooms and sources of water are identified on those few trips where these facilities are available. Pleasant rest spots are also pointed out. Finally, "wine and dine" spots are noted for two specific circumstances: 1) where places to eat along the route are scarce; and 2) where the establishment is too unique or exceptional not to mention.

HOW TO USE THIS BOOK

There are two ways to use this book: one way is for the person who wants to enjoy the research along with enjoying the bike ride, and another way for the biker who is just anxious to get out there "amongst em."

For the "anxious biker," follow Steps l through 5 below and split!

1. Check the "BEST OF THE BEST" trip summary noted on the inside cover for candidate trips or use the "Master Trip Map" in the "TRIP ORGANIZATION" section to select areas of interest for the bike ride. Note the candidate trip numbers. (Another option is to select a trip based on landmarks and sightseeing attractions referenced in the "INDEX.")

2. Go to the "Master Trip Matrices" in the "TRIP ORGANIZATION" section and narrow down the number of candidate trips by reviewing their general features.

3. Read about the individual trips and select one. Make a photocopy of the trip(s) of interest subject to the copyright limitations noted on page ii.

4. Read and understand the safety rules described in the "GENERAL BIKING CONSIDERATIONS" section and review the "CHECKLIST" section.

5. See you later. Enjoy the ride!

For the more methodical folks, continue reading the next chapter. By the time you're through, you'll understand the trip description and maps much better than the "anxious biker."

TRIP ORGANIZATION

This bike book is organized by trip number. Extended length trips are broken down into trip segments by ride number, which is the trip number plus a letter. Thus, Trip #6 is the "Palos Verdes Peninsula Loop," while Ride #6A is the "Palos Verdes Drive North" segment. Trip numbers are in a general sequence governed by whether the tours are coastal, river, inland or special tours. Refer back to the "TABLE OF CONTENTS" for the entire trip list.

The "Master Trip Maps" show the general trailhead location of trips using a circled reference number (i.e., ⑦ refers to Trip #7). Extended length trips are identified by circled numbers at both beginning and terminal points.

The "Master Trip Matrices" provide a quick reference for selecting candidate trips and for more detailed reading evaluation. The matrices are organized by trip number. The key trip descriptors provided in those matrices are briefly explained in the footnotes at the below of the last matrix (page 12). A more detailed explanation of those descriptors is provided in the "TRIP DESCRIPTION/ TERMINOLOGY" section which follows.

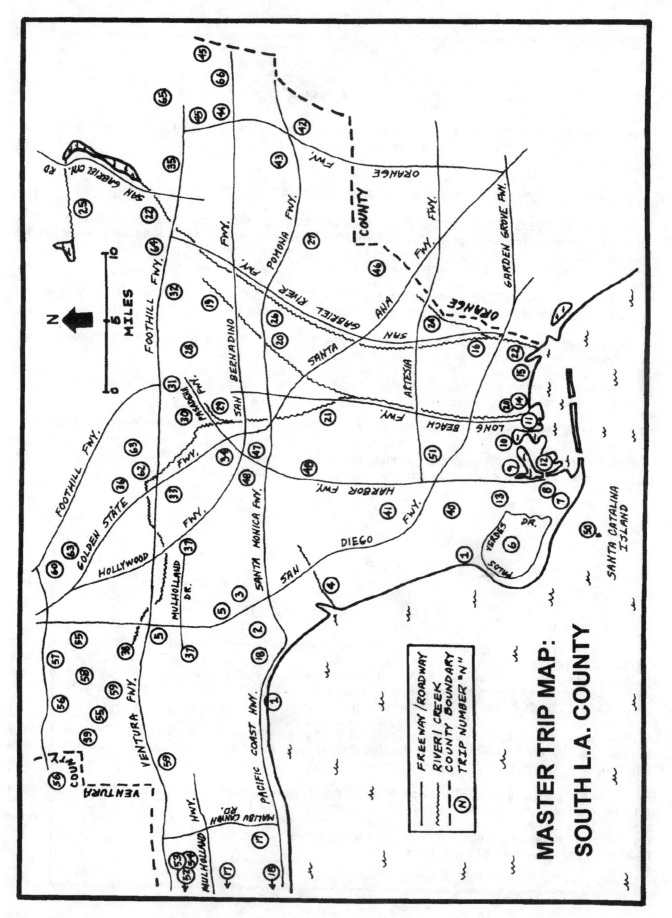

MASTER TRIP MAP:
SOUTH L.A. COUNTY

FREEWAY/ROADWAY
RIVER/CREEK
COUNTY BOUNDARY
N TRIP NUMBER "N"

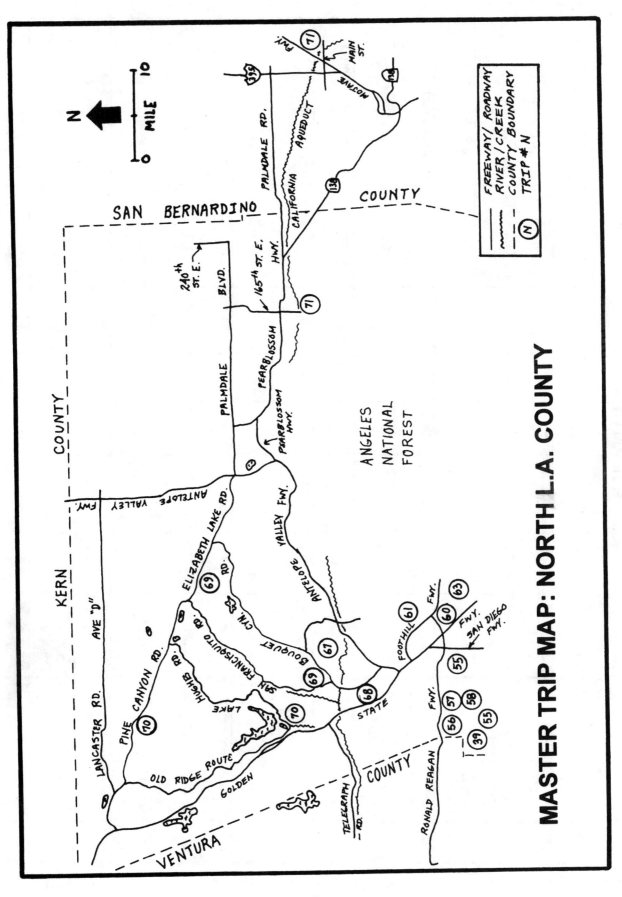

MASTER TRIP MAP: NORTH L.A. COUNTY

MASTER TRIP MATRIX

TRIP NO.	GENERAL LOCATION	LEVEL OF DIFFICULTY			ROUTE QUALITY			TRIP CHARACT.[2]	COMMENTS
		L.O.D.[1]	MILES	ELEV.	BIKE TRAIL (%)	BIKE LANE (%)	OTHER (%)		
1	Redondo Beach-Pacific Palisades	M (1-w) M-S (r/t)	22.0 (1-w)	Flat	90	10	-	S, L, S/A, M	South Bay Bike Trail
1A	Redondo Beach-Manhattan Beach	E	5.4	Flat	80	20	-	S, L, S/A	Southern Segment
1B	Manhattan Beach-Marina Del Rey	E	7.3	Flat	100	-	-	S, L, S/A	Middle Segment
1C	Marina Del Rey-Pacific Palisades	E	9.3	Flat	80	20	-	S, L, S/A	Northern Segment
2	Santa Monica	E (1 loop) M (2 loops)	6.4 11.9	Flat Flat-Mod.	10 40	90 60	- -	S, L, S/A	Santa Monica Loops
3	Westwood	M	6.7-7.5	Flat-Mod.	10	70	20	S, L	Westwood Loops (2 options)
4	Marina Del Rey-Culver City	E (1-w) M (r/t)	6.6 (1-w)	Flat	100	-	-	M	Ballona Creek Bikeway
5	Westwood-Encino	S (1-w) S-VS (r/t)	7.3 (1-w)	Steep	-	50	50	S, E	Old Sepulveda Blvd. (Sepulveda Pass)
6	Palos Verdes Peninsula	S-VS	23.2	Steep	20	80	-	S, L, S/A, E, M	Palos Verdes Peninsula Loop
6A	Rolling Hills	M (1-w) M-S (r/t)	5.8 (1-w)	Mod.	70	-	30	S, L, E	Palos Verdes Drive North
6B	Palos Verdes Estates	M (1-w) M (r/t)	5.1 (1-w)	Mod.	-	20	80	S, L	Palos Verdes Drive West
6C	Rancho Palos Verdes	M (1-w) M (r/t)	5.7 (1-w)	Mod.	-	-	100	S, L, S/A	Palos Verdes Drive South
6D	Miraleste-Rancho Palos Verdes	S (1-w) S-VS (r/t)	6.6 (1-w)	Steep	10	-	90	S, E	Palos Verdes Drive East

1,2 See footnotes on page 12

MASTER TRIP MATRIX

TRIP NO.	GENERAL LOCATION	LEVEL OF DIFFICULTY			ROUTE QUALITY			TRIP CHARACT.[2]	COMMENTS
		L.O.D.[1]	MILES	ELEV.	BIKE TRAIL (%)	BIKE LANE (%)	OTHER (%)		
7	San Pedro	M (1-w) M (r/t)	6.2 (1-w)	Mod.	30	60	10	S, L, S/A	Cabrillo Beach, Point Fermin
8	San Pedro	E (1-w) E (r/t)	6.2 (1-w)	Flat	10	-	90	S, L, S/A	L. A. Harbor Main Channel, Ports O' Call
9	Los Angeles Harbor	E (1-w) E-M (r/t)	9.6 (1-w)	Flat	10	—	90	S, L	East and West Basins
10	Long Beach Harbor	M (1-w) M (r/t)	13.1 (1-w)	Flat	-	-	100	S, L	Cerritos and Back Channels
11	Long Beach Harbor	E (1-w) E-M (r/t)	8.4 (1-w)	Flat	-	-	100	S, L, S/A	Southeast Basin
12	Los Angeles Harbor, Long Beach Harbor	E (E)	6.0 (12.8)	Flat	-	-	100	S, L	Terminal Island Loop (with excursion trip)
13	Harbor City	E (E)	4.5 (5.5)	Flat	60	-	40	S, N	Harbor Regional Park Loop (with campus excursion)
14	Long Beach	E (E)	7.6 (9.0)	Flat	90	-	10	S, L, S/A	L.B. Shoreline Park Loop (with excursion trip)
15	Long Beach, Naples	E (E)	10.9 (12.9)	Flat	50	20	30	S, L	Belmont Shore, Naples Loop (with Marina Park excursion)
16	Long Beach	E	4.3	Flat	100	-	-	S, N, S/A	El Dorado Park Loop
17	Santa Monica Mountains	VS	43.8	Steep-Sheer	-	30	70	S, N, L, E, M	PCH-Topanga Canyon-Mulholland Hwy. Loop
18	Santa Monica-Port Hueneme	M-S (1-w) S-VS (r/t)	44.7 (1-w)	Mod.-Steep	-	80	20	S, N, L, S/A, E, M	Bicentennial Coastal Route
18A	Santa Monica-Malibu	M (1-w) M (r/t)	10.5 (1-w)	Mod.	-	-	100	S, N, L, S/A	Southern Segment

1,2 See footnotes on page 12

MASTER TRIP MATRIX

TRIP NO.	GENERAL LOCATION	LEVEL OF DIFFICULTY			ROUTE QUALITY			TRIP CHARACT.[2]	COMMENTS
		L.O.D.[1]	MILES	ELEV.	BIKE TRAIL (%)	BIKE LANE (%)	OTHER (%)		
18B	Malibu-Sycamore Cove	M-S (1-w) S (r/t)	20.1 (1-w)	Mod.-Steep	-	100	-	S, N, L, S/A, E	Middle Segment
18C	Sycamore Cove-Port Hueneme	M (1-w) M (r/t)	13.7 (1-w)	Mod.	-	70	30	S, N, L	Northern Segment
19-20	El Monte-Long Beach	M (1-w) S (r/t)	28.1 (1-w)	Flat	100	-	-	S, N, L, M	Rio Hondo-L.A. River Bike Trail
19	El Monte	E (1-w) M (r/t)	8.2 (1-w)	Flat	100		-	S, N, L, M	Upper Rio Hondo River Trail
20A	Downey	E (1-w) M (r/t)	9.0 (1-w)	Flat	100	-	-	S, N, L, M	Upper Lario Trail (Rio Hondo & L.A. Rivers)
20B	Long Beach	E (1-w) M (r/t)	10.9 (1-w)	Flat	100	-	-	S, L, M	Lower Lario Trail (Los Angeles River)
21	Southgate-Bell	E (1-w) E (r/t)	5.6 (1-w)	Flat	95	-	5	M	Los Angeles River (northern segment)
22	Seal Beach-Azusa	M-S S (r/t)	39.0 (1-w)	Flat	100	-	-	S, N, L, S/A, M	San Gabriel River (shore to mountains)
22A	Seal Beach-Long Beach	E (1-w) E (r/t)	5.6 (1-w)	Flat	100	-	-	S, N, S/A, M	Ocean to El Dorado Park
22B	Long Beach-Downey	E (1-w) M (r/t)	9.7 (1-w)	Flat	100	-	-	S, N, S/A, M	El Dorado Park to Wilderness Park
22C	Downey-Pico Rivera	E (1-w) M (r/t)	7.7 (1-w)	Flat	100	-	-	S, N, L, M	Wilderness Park to Whittier Narrows/Legg Lake
22D	Pico Rivera-Irwindale	E (1-w) M (r/t)	11.4 (1-w)	Flat	100	-	-	S, N, L, M	Whittier Narrows/Legg Lake to Santa Fe Dam
22E	Irwindale-Azusa	E (1-w) M (r/t)	7.5 (1-w)	Flat	100	-	-	S, N, L, M	Santa Fe Dam to San Gabriel Canyon

1,2 See footnotes on page 12

8

MASTER TRIP MATRIX

TRIP NO.	GENERAL LOCATION	LEVEL OF DIFFICULTY			ROUTE QUALITY			TRIP CHARACT.²	COMMENTS
		L.O.D.¹	MILES	ELEV.	BIKE TRAIL (%)	BIKE LANE (%)	OTHER (%)		
23	Sea to Mountains to Sea	VS	83.5 (1-w)	Flat	90	5	5	S, N, L, S/A, M	San Gabriel-Rio Hondo-L.A. River Loop
24	Long Beach-Cerritos	E (1-w) M (r/t)	14.0 (1-w)	Flat	100	-	-	S, L, M	San Gabriel River-Coyote Creek
25	Angeles National Forest	M (River) S (Dam)	13.4 (15.0)	Flat (Sheer)	100	-	-	S, N, E	West Fork, San Gabriel River (plus Cogswell Reservoir)
26	Pico Rivera	E	11.2	Flat	100	-	-	S, N, L	Whittier Narrows, Legg Lake Loop
27	Hacienda Heights	M	5.6	Mod.	-	100	-	S	Hacienda Heights Loop
28	San Marino	M	6.8	Mod.	-	-	100	S, L	San Marino City Loop
29	Montecito Heights	E	7.5	Flat	50	50	-	S, N, L	Arroyo Seco Bike Trail (loop)
30	Highland Park	E	7.6	Mod.	10	80	10	S, N, L, S/A	Highland Park City Loop
31	Pasadena	E-M (1-w) M (r/t)	6.8 (1-w)	Mod.	20	80	-	S, N, L	Kenneth Newell Bikeway
32	Arcadia	M-S	29.4	Mod.	-	100	-	S, L, M	Arcadia City Loops
33	Griffith Park	M-S (M)	8.8 (8.2)	Mod.-Steep (Mod.)	-	100	-	S, L, S/A	Griffith Park Loop (easier up and back option)
34	Elysian Park	M-S (E)	6.4	Mod.-steep (Mod.)	-	-	100	S, L, S/A, E	Elysian Park Loop (without Angel's Point Road)
35	Glendora	M	8.3	Mod.	-	100	-	S	Glendora Bikeway (loop)
36	Burbank	M-S	14.8	Steep	-	100	-	S, L, E	Burbank City Loop
37	Encino-Universal City	S (1-w) S-VS (r/t)	13.0 (1-w)	Steep	20	80	-	S, L, E, M	Mulholland Drive

1,2 See footnotes on page 12

MASTER TRIP MATRIX

TRIP NO.	GENERAL LOCATION	LEVEL OF DIFFICULTY			ROUTE QUALITY			TRIP CHARACT.[2]	COMMENTS
		L.O.D.[1]	MILES	ELEV.	BIKE TRAIL (%)	BIKE LANE (%)	OTHER (%)		
38	Encino	E	9.1	Flat	95	5	-	S, L	Sepulveda Dam Bikeway (loop)
39	Chatsworth	E	6.3	Flat	20	-	80	S, L	Chatsworth Tour, Brown's Creek Bikeway (loop)
40	Torrance	M	14.3	Flat	5	55	40	S	Torrance Tour (loop)
41	Gardena	E	12.2	Flat	40	-	60	S, N	Gardena Tour, Dominguez Channel (loop)
42	Diamond Bar	M	10.4	Mod.	60	-	40	S	Diamond Bar Loop
43	Walnut, City of Industry	M	12.9	Mod.-Steep	-	40	60	S, E	San Jose Hills (loop)
44	Pomona, San Dimas	M	8.9	Mod.	30	20	50	S, N, L, S/A	Bonelli Park, Puddingstone Reservoir (loop)
45	San Dimas, La Verne, Claremont	M	22.3	Mod.	-	-	100	S, L, S/A	Baseline Road, San Gabriel Mountain Foothills (loop)
46	La Mirada	E	10.0	Flat-Mod.	30	65	5	S, N	La Mirada City Loop (loop)
47	Los Angeles Civic Center	M	9.8	Mod.	-	35	65	S, L, S/A	Skyscraper Tour (downtown Los Angeles loop)
48	Central Los Angeles	M	9.8	Mod.	100	-	-	S, L, S/A	L.A. Bikeway System, Exposition Park, USC Campus
49	South Bay-Central L.A.-L.A. River-Long Beach-Palos Verdes Peninsula	S	71.7	Mod.-Steep	50	10	40	S, L, S/A, M	Tour de Los Angeles (loop)
50	Avalon, Santa Catalina Island	S	9.7	Mod.-Steep	-	-	100	S, L, S/A, E	Avalon Tour (loop)

1,2 See footnotes on page 12

10

MASTER TRIP MATRIX

TRIP NO.	GENERAL LOCATION	LEVEL OF DIFFICULTY			ROUTE QUALITY			TRIP CHARACT.[2]	COMMENTS
		L.O.D.[1]	MILES	ELEV.	BIKE TRAIL (%)	BIKE LANE (%)	OTHER (%)		
51	Dominguez Hills	E	3.5	Flat	-	-	100	S, L	California State, Dominguez Hills campus
52	Agoura Hills, Thousand Oaks	M	8.7	Mod.	-	80	20	S	Agoura Hills Loop
53	Westlake Village, Thousand Oaks	E	9.2	Mod.	10	90	-	S, N, L	Westlake Lake Loop
54	Thousand Oaks, North Ranch	M	10.9	Mod.	-	60	40	S	North Ranch Loop
55	Chatsworth, Granada Hills	M	28.4	Mod.	-	30	70	S, M	Chatsworth-Northridge-Granada Hills Loop
56	Chatsworth-Simi Valley	S (1-w) S-VS (r/t)	4.1 (1-w)	Steep	-	-	100	S, L	Santa Susana Pass
57	Porter Ranch	E	3.8	Mod.	80	-	20	S, N	Limekiln Canyon Trail (loop) (some unpaved trail)
58	Northridge	E	3.0	Flat	40	-	60	S, L, S/A	California State Northridge campus (loop)
59	Woodland Hills, Tarzana	M	22.5	Mod.	5	5	90	S, S/A	Woodland Hills-Tarzana Loop
60	Pacoima, San Fernando	E (E)	4.5 (4.1)	Flat (Mod.)	-	-	100	S, N, L	Hansen Dam ride (bottomlands ride)
61	San Fernando	E	2.2	Flat	100	-	-	S, N	El Cariso Park (loop)
62	Glendale, La Crescenta	M (1-w) M (r/t)	9.6 (1-w)	Mod.	-	-	100	S, L	Verdugo Mountains Foothills
63	La Crescenta, Tuna Canyon, Burbank	M-S	23.9	Mod.-Steep	-	20	80	S, L, E, M	Verdugo Mountains Loop

1,2 See footnotes on page 12

MASTER TRIP MATRIX

TRIP NO.	GENERAL LOCATION	LEVEL OF DIFFICULTY			ROUTE QUALITY			TRIP CHARACT.[2]	COMMENTS
		L.O.D.[1]	MILES	ELEV.	BIKE TRAIL (%)	BIKE LANE (%)	OTHER (%)		
64	Duarte	E	5.0	Flat	30	-	70	S, N	Duarte Bikeway (loop)
65	San Dimas	M-S	8.9 (r/t)	Mod.-Steep	-	-	100	S, N, L	San Dimas Canyon Road
66	Claremont	E	4.7 (r/t)	Mod.	100	-	-	S, N, L	Thompson Creek Trail
67	Bouquet Canyon, Saugus, Santa Clarita	S (M-S)	20.3 (12.8)	Mod.-Steep	30	20	50	S, N, L, S/A, E	Canyon Country Tour (loop) (Whites/Plum Cyn. bypass)
68	Valencia	E	7.8	Flat	-	10	90	S, L, S/A	Valencia Loop
69	Santa Clarita, Green Valley / Green & Leona Valleys	VS / S-VS	40.8 / 22.8	Steep-Sheer / Stp.-Shr.	-	20 / -	80 / 100	S, N, L, E, M / S, N, E	San Francisquito and Bouquet Canyons (loop) / Rift Zone Loop
70	Castaic, Lake Hughes, Sandberg	VS	68.7	Steep-Sheer	-	10	90	S, N, L, E, M	Lake Hughes, Pine Canyon & Old Ridge Rte. Rds. (loop)
70A	Castaic-Lake Hughes	S-VS (1-w) VS (r/t)	23.5 (1-w)	Steep-Sheer	-	-	100	S, N, L, E, M	Lake Hughes Road
70B	Lake Hughes-Sandberg	S (1-w) S (r/t)	17.2 (1-w)	Mod.-Steep	-	-	100	S, N, E, M	Pine Canyon Road
70C	Sandberg-Castaic	S (1-w) VS (r/t)	28.0 (1-w)	Mod.-Steep	70	-	30	S, N, L, E, M	Old Ridge Route Road (non-maintained section)
71	Pearblossom, Hesperia	M (1-w) M-S (r/t)	27.5 (1-w)	Flat	100	-	-	S, N, L, M	California Aqueduct

[1] L.O.D. - Overall trip level of difficulty: **VS**-very strenuous; **S**-strenuous; **M**-Moderate; **E**-easy; **1-w**-one way; **r/t**-round trip or up and back

[2] TRIP CHARACTERISTICS - General trip features and highlights: **S**-scenic; **N**-nature trail; **L**-landmark(s); **S/A**-sight-seeing attractions; **E**-elevation workout; **M**-mileage workout

TRIP DESCRIPTION/TERMINOLOGY

The trip descriptors in the "Master Trip Matrices" are described below in further detail. Several of these same descriptors are also used in the individual trip writeups.

GENERAL LOCATION: The general location of the bike trail is provided in terms of a city, landmark or general area description, as applicable. The "Master Trip Map" may be useful in conjunction with this general locator.

LEVEL OF DIFFICULTY: The rides are rated on an overall basis with consideration for elevation gain, trip distance and condition of the bike route.

A *very strenuous* trip can be of any length, has very steep grades and is generally designed for bikers in excellent physical condition. Trips are well enough described such that the biker might plan to ride the easier part of a stressing trip and link up with other easier trips.

A *strenuous* trip has some steep grades and/or relatively long mileage (on the order of 50 miles total). The trip is of sufficiently long duration to require trip planning and strong consideration of weather, water, food and bike spare parts. Some portions of the trip may be on surfaces in poor condition or on shared roadway.

A *moderate* trip may have mild grades and moderate mileage, on the order of I5-30 miles. The trip is typically of several hours duration and is generally on well-maintained bike route.

An *easy* trip is on the order of I0 miles or less, is relatively flat and is generally on well maintained bike trails or bike paths.

TRIP MILEAGE: Trip mileage is generally computed for the one-way trip length for *up and back* trips and full-trip length for *loop* trips. *Up and back* is specifically used for trips that share a common route in both outgoing and return directions. *Loop* specifically means that the outgoing and return trip segments are on predominantly different routes. *Round trip* is used without distinction as to whether the trip is an *up and back* or *loop* trip. In the trip writeups, the mileage from the starting point or "trailhead" is noted in parentheses to the nearest tenth mile, for example, (6.3).

Obviously, the one-way trips listed can be exercised with a planned car shuttle, ridden as an *up and back* trip, or biked in connection with another bicycle trip listed in this book. Connections with other trips are noted in the trip text or in a separate subsection for that trip titled, "Connecting Trips."

TRIP ELEVATION GAIN: The overall trip elevation gain is described in a qualitative fashion. *Flat* indicates that there are no grades of any consequence. Steepness of upgrades is loosely defined as follows: 1) *light* indicates limited slope and very little elevation gain; 2) *moderate* means more significant slope requiring use of low gears and may be tens of feet of upgrade; 3) *steep* indicates workout-type grades that require low gears and high physical exertion; 4) *sheer* indicates gut-buster grades that require extreme physical exertion (and a strong will to live!).

The frequency of upgrades is divided into the following categories: 1) *single* for flat rides with a single significant upgrade; 2) *periodic* for flat rides where uphill segments are widely spaced; 3) *frequent* where narrowly spaced upgrades are encountered (e.g., rolling hills).

Elevation contour maps are provided for trips with significant elevation change. A reference 5% (*steep*) grade is shown on all such maps.

BIKE ROUTE QUALITY: The trip is summarized with respect to route quality in the "Master Trip Matrices" and a more detailed description is given in the individual trip writeups. The following route terminology (which is similar to that used by CALTRANS) is used:
  • *Class I* - off-roadway bike paths or bike trails
  • *Class II* - on-roadway, separated (striped) bike lanes
  • *Class III* - on-roadway, signed (but not separated) bike lanes
  If the route is on-roadway and not signed (i.e., not marked as a bike route), it is arbitrarily referred to as *Class X*. All routes are paved unless otherwise noted.

TRIP CHARACTERISTICS: The overall highlights of the bike trip are provided in the "Master Trip Matrices" to assist in general trip selection. The trip may be scenic (*S*), with sweeping vistas, exciting overlooks or generally provide views of natural or man-made attractions such as cities. Alternatively, the trip may be a nature trail (*N*) or a path through areas which have an abundance of trees, flowers and other flora. The nature trips or portions thereof are generally on Class I bike routes. The trip may highlight historical or well-known landmarks (*L*) or may have one or more sightseeing attractions (*S/A*). An example of the former is the Whittier Narrows Dam on the San Gabriel River (Trip #22C) while the latter might be the Los Angeles Zoo in Griffith Park (Trip #33). Finally, some trips are potentially good workout trips in that there is significant elevation change (*E*) or lengthy mileage (*M*) if the entire trip is taken. Some trips may provide a mix of these characteristics and are so noted.

Several descriptors are unique to the individual trip writeups. Those descriptors are defined below.

TRAILHEAD: The general location of the start of the bike path is provided for a single starting point. Driving directions to that trailhead and/or directions for parking are included where there is a possibility of confusion. Always check to ensure that parking is consistent with current laws.

Note that for most trails, there are multiple points of entry beyond the primary point listed. For some of the trips in this book (particularly the river routes), alternate bicycle entry points are noted on maps by arrows (✦) along the bike route. Alternate trailheads may be found using information obtained from other bikers, or from state or local publications for more popular routes.

WATER: In the "Trailhead" description, general statements are provided about water needs. In the "Trip Description," available water along the route is noted where water is scarce. Particular emphasis is placed on public facilities for water and use of restrooms. Stores, shopping centers and gas stations are sometimes noted, although the availability of water or other facilities in these instances is subject to the policies of those establishments.

CONNECTING TRIPS: Where bike trips can be linked, they are so noted. *Continuation* trips are those where there is direct linkage at the beginning or end of the trip being described. *Connection* trips are either not directly linked (i.e., a Class X connector is required) or the linkage occurs at the interior of the trip being described. A brief "connector" route description is provided.

BIKE TRIP MAPS: Each ride in the book has an accompanying detailed bike map. A summary of symbols and features used in those maps is provided below.

— — — —	Bike trail in trip description (unless otherwise noted).		
• • • • • •	Alternate bike route (unless otherwise noted).		
L.A. RIVER ~~~~~	River or creek when it is a point of interest.	MAIN ST	Roadway
VENICE	Nearby City	Park	Landmark #5
W	Public Water Source	P Parking	→ Entry Point to Trail
•—•	Locked Gate/ Limited Entry	Railroad Crossing or Overcrossing	School (as a trip point of interest)
†	Mission	✕ Gravel Pit	5% Reference 5% grade

MAP SYMBOLS AND FEATURES

14

GENERAL BIKING CONSIDERATIONS

These are a collection of the thoughts that we've had in the hundreds of miles of biking that we have done:

SAFETY: Use common sense when you are biking. Common sense when combined with courtesy should cover most of the safety-related issues. The four safety "biggies" are: 1) understand bike riding laws; 2) keep your bicycle in safe operating order; 3) wear personal safety equipment as required (helmet is a must, bright or reflective clothes, sunglasses); 4) ride defensively--always assume that moving and parked car inhabitants are not aware that you are there.

Common courtesy is to offer assistance to bikers stopped because of breakdowns. Point out ruts, obstructions, and glass to bikers behind you.

TRIP PLANNING/PREPARATION: We are absolute believers in advance planning. You minimize nasty surprises and have the joy of two trips for one (the anticipated trip and the physical trip itself). Familiarize yourself with the trip ahead of time -- start by reading recent tour guides and talking to people who have been there before. For long-distance and/or more remote adventures, we do not recommend going alone.

Plan bicycle trips that are within your (or your group's) physical and technical abilities. Start with less-demanding trips and work your way up the difficulty ladder. Work on physical fitness and technical skills between trips to maintain or improve your abilities. Take rides with professional leaders and/or learn the necessary skills with an accomplished veteran in that activity area. As part of the training, learn first-aid techniques and use of the kit as appropriate for your activity.

The discussion which follows is applicable to both high-difficulty and/or extended-mileage day trips and multi-day tours: Look over the topographic maps and get a feel for the key areas of elevation change and locate the key road junctions. Where relevant, check that the roads/river trails are open and available for public travel by making advance inquiries. Identify contingency routes if there is any doubt as to your ability to follow the nominal plan or if adverse weather or road conditions could require trip alteration.

Once you have identified your outdoor adventure, assess your gear needs for the trip. Work with your group to define individual responsibilities for group gear items. Ensure that you know how to use each piece of activity gear before departure. Maintain your gear, particularly that most critical to safety, and perform a pre-trip check that gear is in design-operable condition.

EQUIPMENT: This subject is covered in great depth in B-D Enterprises' most recent publication, *Outdoor Recreation Checklists*. That reference covers gear needs for about every major outdoor activity, including on-road and mountain biking for both daytime and multi-day trips. Refer to the last page of this book for more information.

The discussion which follows focuses on day trips: The minimum biking equipment includes a water bottle or two, tire pump, tool kit (typically tire irons, wrench(s), screwdriver), patch kit, and (sorry to say) bike lock. For longer day trips add a spare tube and bike repair manual. We recommend a bike light even if there are no plans for night biking.

Necessary cyclist apparel includes a helmet, sunglasses, and clothes which will fit pessimistic weather conditions (particularly for longer trips). On all-day, cool or wet winter outings, we carry a layered set of clothes (this includes long pants, undershirt, long-sleeve shirt, sweater, and a two-piece rain suit). Padded cycling pants and biking gloves are a must for long trips. Modern day, warm-when-wet clothes are light and extremely functional. For cool and dry days, we may drop the rain suit for a windbreaker (look for a windbreaker that folds up into a fanny pack). For other conditions, our outfits are normally shorts, undershirt, long-sleeve shirt and windbreaker. Laugh if you must, but wait until you find yourself biking home at night, in mid-winter, along a beach with a healthy sea breeze after you spent the day biking in the warm sun (an example of poor trip planning, we admit).

Bring a first-aid kit. For urban tours, our packaged, baggie-sealed kit has the following: sunscreen (15 SPF or greater), lip salve, aspirin and band aids. For trips where help may not be so readily available, we add gauze (roll), ace bandage (roll) and butterfly clips, small scissors, moleskin, needle and an antiseptic such as hydrogen peroxide or iodine. Think about insect repellent if you think conditions may warrant.

If you are going to get your money out of this book, **get an automobile bike rack**! The cost of bike racks is cheap compared to most bikes. Besides, it just doesn't make sense to bike fifty miles to take the planned twenty-mile bike trip.

GENERAL INFORMATION: A collection of seemingly random, unconnected, and useless comments are provided which we actually think are "gems of wisdom" based on hard experience:

• Develop and follow a checkist for a pre-trip bike examination (tires, brakes, cables, etc.) and equipment (water, food, clothing, tools, spare parts, etc.). It's embarrassing to start a trip and realize that you've forgotten your bicycle! (Strongly consider purchasing the B-D Enterprises *Outdoor Recreation Checklists* reference book.)

• Check the weather (including smog conditions in urban areas) before going on an extended trip. Select trips and plan clothing accordingly.

• Plan the trip timing to ensure that there is a "pad" of daylight. Night biking just isn't as fun when it wasn't in the original plans. Night biking without the proper equipment is dangerous!

• Trip timing should include allowance for finding parking, trailheads, or connector routes. You never can fully trust authors of bike books!

• Trip conditions and routing are subject to change as a result of weather damage, building and highway construction, bikepath rerouting, etc. Especially for long trips, research these key elements before departing.

• Plan for afternoon headwinds when heading toward the beach (particularly west-facing beaches). "Pain" is what you feel when the last several miles of your fifty miler is spent bucking the sea breeze.

• Stay out of riverbeds, even concrete ones, unless it is marked part of the route. It may be a very long way to the next exit and it may also rain.

• Some marked river and creek trails flood out during heavy rains, particularly at river crossings and underpasses. More than likely, these areas will be closed off in inclement weather. Don't take these trips after heavy rains unless you are willing to plan on many route detours.

• Portions of the river trails are isolated and an increasing incidence of theft and assaults have been reported. Bike in daylight, with a partner.

• Take water, no matter how short the trip. Bring enough to provide for the contingency that "guaranteed" water spots may be dry. Having water available provides a feeling of security. Being thirsty creates a bad attitude.

• The best time of day for most trips on busy thoroughfares is before the rush-hour morning traffic. Morning is also best for rides on narrow country roads. With few exceptions, the best time of the week is the weekend, particularly Sunday.

• The best season for some trips depends on the person. If you want camaraderie, ride the more popular routes in the summer. If your pleasure is free-wheeling and wide-open spaces, save these routes for other seasons.

• Bring snacks for longer trips. Snacks provide needed energy and attitude improvement when the going gets tough. Having snacks available also allows more flexibility in selecting a "dining out" stop.

• Walk your bike through heavy glass-strewn areas. Lift your bike onto and off of curbs. Trips are more fun when you can ride your bike!

• Bring a map for trips that are not on well-marked bike routes. Once off the prescribed route, it is amazingly easy to lose the sense of direction.

• Maintain a steady pace when taking a long bike ride. For pleasure trips, the pace is too fast if you cannot carry on conversation while biking.

THE COAST

Long Beach Shoreline Park

TRIPS #1A-#1C - SOUTH BAY BIKE TRAIL

It is appropriate that the book should start with the most popular bike route in Los Angeles County. The moderate-to-strenuous level South Bay Bike Trail (44-miles round trip) travels the beach front from Torrance State Beach to Will Rogers State Beach. This trail is a segment of the Pacific Coast Bicentennial Bike Route.

Trip #1A starts at Torrance State Beach, explores King Harbor, Hermosa and Manhattan Beaches and ends at the Manhattan Beach Pier. Trip #1B leaves that pier and continues north through Manhattan and Dockweiler Beaches, Playa Del Rey and the Del Rey Lagoon, terminating at Marina Del Rey. Trip #1C cruises the periphery of Marina Del Rey, visits Venice Beach and the Venice Pavilion, passes the Santa Monica pier and ends at Will Rogers State Beach.

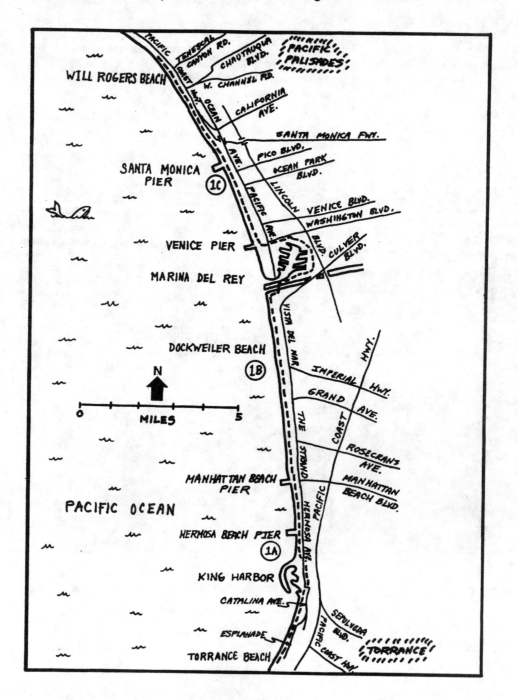

TRIP #1A - SOUTH BAY BIKE TRAIL:
REDONDO BEACH TO MANHATTAN BEACH

GENERAL LOCATION: Redondo Beach - Manhattan Beach

LEVEL OF DIFFICULTY: Up and back - easy
Distance - 5.4 miles (one way)
Elevation gain - essentially flat

HIGHLIGHTS: The southern segment of the Class I South Bay Bike Trail cruises Torrance, Redondo and Hermosa Beaches. This segment includes the Redondo Beach Pier and the King Harbor area where there is plenty of sightseeing, as well as shopping spots and eateries. The path also visits Hermosa Beach Pier and passes near several small parks. The views south to the Palos Verdes (P.V.) Cliffs and north along the L.A. County beaches are spectacular. Water is plentiful and several bike parking racks are placed strategically along the route.

TRAILHEAD: From Pacific Coast Highway in Torrance/South Redondo Beach, turn south toward the ocean at Palos Verdes Blvd. Continue about 1/2 mile and turn right at Calle Miramar. In a few hundred feet, veer left on Via Riviera and continue 0.1 mile to the terminus at Paseo De La Playa. Find free parking on this street, but subject to local parking regulations.
Bring a light water supply; this segment is well stocked with water and restrooms.

TRIP DESCRIPTION: **Redondo Beach.** Near Via Riviera and Paseo De La Playa, follow the asphalt path down the small bluff to the South Bay Bike Trail origin on the beach. There is a great view of the P. V. Cliffs south and Santa Monica and intervening beaches north Bike north past the walkers, skaters, bathers, model airplane flyers, metal detector searchers and other bikers along one of several lovely beaches on this segment. In about one mile, the trail passes a 1/2-mile stretch of condominiums built up along the beach path.

Redondo Beach Village Area

At condomania's end is a small grassy rest area which is part of Veteran's Park (1.8). Just beyond is Monstad Pier and a host of restaurants and shops. There is a walking entry (i.e., no biking) into this area which leads left to the pier and straight ahead into a parking structure. Our route leads into the structure where bikers can remount and ride through, exiting the garage at Fisherman's Wharf. This scenic structure was partially destroyed by high seas in the Winter of 1987 and a disastrous fire in the Spring of the following year. There is shopping, sightseeing and munching for the easily side-tracked.

The path continues alongside Redondo Beach Village, Basin No. 3 with its fishing boat moorings, and then the Redondo Beach Marina (2.1). In 0.2 mile at Beryl St., the route crosses Harbor Dr. and continues north on a Class II path. There is a diversion trip west on Beryl St. (which becomes

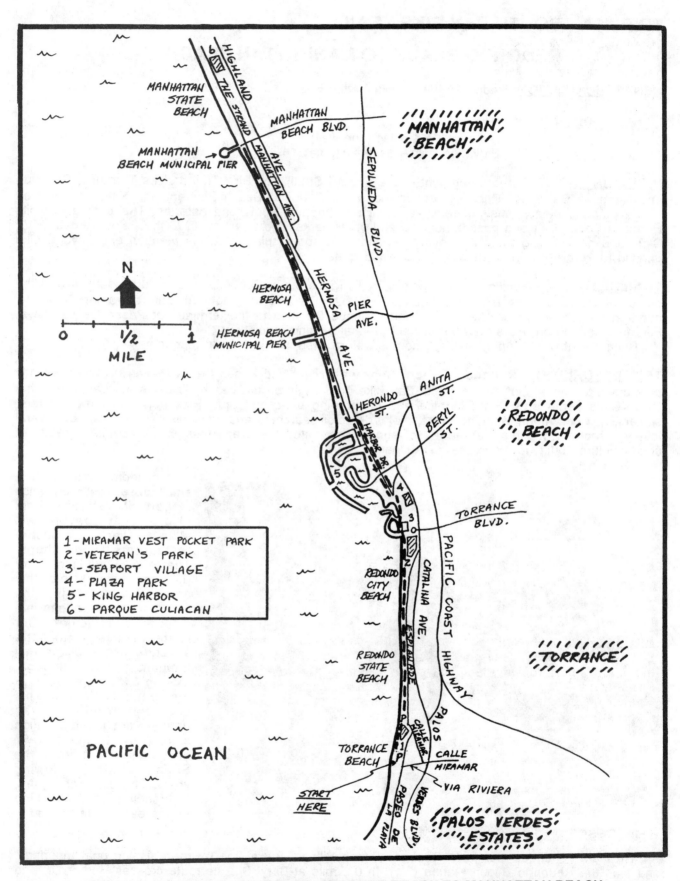

TRIP #1A - SOUTH BAY BIKE TRAIL: REDONDO BEACH TO MANHATTAN BEACH

Portofino Wy.) that leads to inner King Harbor and a swimming lagoon. However, we continue north past a series of beachfront restaurants/watering holes which includes the Cheesecake Factory. Continue past Marina Wy. and the steam powerplant to Herondo St. (2.9).

   Hermosa Beach. Cross Herondo St. and follow the bikepath to the Hermosa Beach Strand. This is a shared pedestrian/biker path alongside the local residences. For the next mile, the city has a 10-mph speed limit, and flashing lights during busy periods which require cyclists to walk their bikes. The bikeway passes more great beach, volleyball courts, and one-after-another residences until it reaches the Hermosa Beach Municipal Pier and the Tim Kelly Memorial (3.7). Just beyond are a series of rental shops (surfboards, bikes) and several beachfront eateries. A favorite is La Playita, just off the path, which dishes up some mean Mexican and Gringo dishes.

   The path returns to residential beachfront and continues 0.9 mile before jogging away from the beach. The trail temporarily ends at 35th St. at a small series of steps where bikes must be carried a short distance. An option is to turn right three blocks earlier, at Longfellow Ave., then left at The Strand and follow the marked bike route.

   Manhattan Beach. The route continues on Class I bikeway along Manhattan State Beach passing more beach and volleyball country. Though still crowded together, the beachfront homes in this area are more stately and architecturally varied. There is a fine view back to the Palos Verdes Peninsula from this area. Continue 0.6 mile from 35th St. to reach the Manhattan Beach Municipal Pier (5.4). There is some interesting sightseeing at the pier and some local rest stops just up the hill on Manhattan Beach Blvd. Take a break before starting the return trip.

CONNECTING TRIPS: 1) Continuation with the South Bay Bike Trail to Marina Del Rey (Trip #1B) - continue north from the Manhattan Beach Pier; 2) connection with the bike routes along Palos Verdes Dr. North (Trip #6A) and Palos Verdes Dr. West (Trip #6B) - from the trip origin, return to Palos Verdes Blvd. and turn right (south), continuing another 0.8 mile to the three-way junction in Malaga Cove.

TRIP #1B - SOUTH BAY BIKE TRAIL:

MANHATTAN BEACH TO MARINA DEL REY

GENERAL LOCATION: Manhattan Beach, El Segundo, Playa Del Rey, Marina Del Rey

LEVEL OF DIFFICULTY: Up and back - easy
                          Distance - 7.3 miles (one way)
                          Elevation gain - essentially flat

HIGHLIGHTS: The middle segment of the Class I South Bay Bike Trail, this route tours Manhattan and Dockweiler Beaches. The segment starts from the Manhattan Municipal Pier, includes a pass below the L.A. Airport runway, and visits the Del Rey Lagoon of Playa Del Rey, Ballona Creek and Fisherman's Village in Marina Del Rey. There are excellent views into Santa Monica Bay, the Santa Monica Mountains and a great boat-watching vista along the Marina Del Rey entrance channel. Water is available at strategic spots along the way.

TRAILHEAD: From Sepulveda Blvd. in Manhattan Beach, turn west at Manhattan Beach Blvd. and continue about a mile. Find parking, subject to local parking laws, on Highland Ave., Manhattan Ave. or The Strand, most likely south of Manhattan Beach Blvd. From the San Diego Fwy., exit west on Manhattan Beach Blvd. and proceed about 2-1/2 miles to the parking area discussed above.

   Bring a light water supply. There are scattered sources along the way.

TRIP DESCRIPTION: Manhattan Beach. From the Manhattan Beach Pier at the foot of Manhattan Beach Blvd., follow the curved, marked bikepath to the right as it separates from the pedestrian walkway. There is a view across Santa Monica Bay in this area. Continue north past the tournament volleyball courts, playgrounds and the expensive residences above the pedestrian walkway. A 1/2-mile

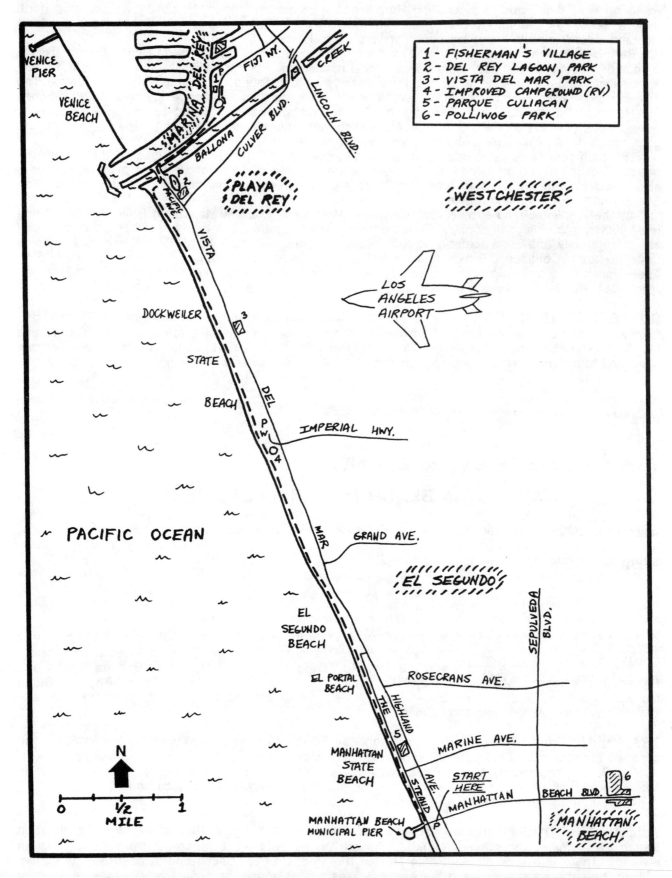

TRIP #1B - SOUTH BAY BIKE TRAIL: MANHATTAN BEACH TO MARINA DEL REY

from the pier is a great view of the city of Santa Monica. The houses come in all shapes, styles and sizes up to the point where the path reaches the foot of Rosecrans Ave. at "Volleyball City" (1.2).

El Segundo. The path cruises El Porto Beach, then swings west and passes alongside the fenced-off power generating station (1.6). There is a narrow, exposed bike strip for the next 0.3 mile. There are large rocks on the seaward side and the signs warn of sand on the path, testifying that this strip can be very exciting and possible dangerous in rough weather. Next is a small breakwater and probably the most secluded section of beach along the bikepath (2.0). In 0.2 mile is the Grand Ave. automobile entry to the beach and 0.4 mile further is the northern end of the fenced-in plant (2.6).

Levee Between Ballona Creek and the Exit Channel

The beach widens and the bikepath twists and winds, then climbs to some bluffs which are one of the favorite local hang-glider training spots (3.0). Next is the Imperial Blvd. beach entry and a water stop in the middle of the only dry stretch on the trip. In another 0.4 mile is a small rise and a nice view down the beach to Santa Monica (3.6). For the next 0.3 mile, the path winds under the busy L.A. Airport flight path. Stop and watch the air traffic from an unusual vantage point.

Playa Del Rey. The route passes an automobile access road (4.0) and a large playground area with several sculptures (4.5). With the small bluffs to the landward side, the path reaches a pleasant palm-tree lined rest and watering area near the residential edge of Playa Del Rey (5.2). In 0.4 mile the bike route passes residences built near the bikepath. The bikeway transitions from beach to strand and passes near Del Rey Lagoon Park and the Del Rey Lagoon. The trail then swings north along Ballona Creek (6.2) and continues to a small bridge across the creek in 0.1 mile. There are views of the creek and of the exit channel and marina for the next 1/2 mile.

Marina Del Rey. Once across the bridge, the bikepath follows a levee between Ballona Creek and the exit channel. Because of the winds, this is a "bear" of a bike segment when heading west in the late afternoon! There are unique views of the Westwood and Century City skyscrapers from the levee (northeast direction), as well as a peek into the Ballona Wetlands to the south.

The trail reaches a junction point with the Ballona Creek Bikeway just beyond the end of a single apartment complex (7.0). Turn left at the junction, passing through a fence and biking 0.1 mile to the Fiji Wy. cul-de-sac. In 0.2 mile north on Fiji Wy. is the Fisherman's Village (7.3). This is a fine place to stop and take a munchie break or to do some sightseeing before returning.

CONNECTING TRIPS: 1) Continuation with the South Bay Bike Trail to Redondo Beach (Trip #1A) - at the trip origin, head south; 2) continuation with the South Bay Bike Trail to Santa Monica (Trip #1C) - at the trip terminus, continue north; 3) connection with the Ballona Creek Bikeway (Trip #4) - at the junction discussed above at (7.0), take the right-hand junction along Ballona Creek.

TRIP #1C - SOUTH BAY BIKE TRAIL:

MARINA DEL REY TO PACIFIC PALISADES

GENERAL LOCATION: Marina Del Rey, Venice, Santa Monica, Pacific Palisades

LEVEL OF DIFFICULTY: Up and back - easy
                                Distance - 9.3 miles (one way)
                                Elevation gain - essentially flat

HIGHLIGHTS: The northern segment of the Class I South Bay Bike Trail starts from scenic Marina Del Rey and visits exceptional Venice Municipal, Santa Monica State and Will Rogers State Beaches. This segment includes Venice Pier, Venice Pavilion, the Venice Beach Carnival and Santa Monica Pier. The tour through Marina Del Rey includes scenic views of the marina and pleasure boats of all types, a passage through Venice Pavilion includes a visit to individualism at its finest, or the other side of Mars, depending on your outlook. Be prepared for unusual flea markets, a guitar playing swami on skates, mimes, sidewalk preachers, and other surprises.

TRAILHEAD: Follow the Marina Fwy. to its terminus and continue west to Lincoln Blvd. Turn left (south) on Lincoln Blvd. and continue about 1/2 mile to Fiji Wy. Take Fiji Wy. to the parking area at Fisherman's Village or use the overflow parking lot between the village and Lincoln Blvd.
    Bring a light water supply. There are plentiful sources along the route.

TRIP DESCRIPTION: **Marina Del Rey.** Pedal north past Fisherman's Village with its shops and restaurants and pass a yacht dealership. In 0.5 mile, just before reaching Admiralty Wy., follow the signed path left into the boat storage and repair area. The route parallels Admiralty Wy. and passes Mindinao Wy. (0.8); to the left, a short spur path leads to Burton Chase Park where there is an elevated platform for harbor viewing. Our route crosses Bali Wy. (1.0) and passes behind the Marina Library, then turns sharply right and follows the library parking lot to Admiralty Wy.

Muscle Beach Gym

Cross the street and follow the bike route along Admiralty Park. There is an interesting Class X spur trip along Admiralty Wy. and south on Via Marina, however, our route continues along the park past the Marina Towers and Duck Pond (1.7). This pond is one of the last remnants of the Ballona Wetlands in this area and does have a fair number of friendly inhabitants. The route crosses Washington St. and follows that street toward the ocean on a Class II bikepath. The path crosses a small Venice Canal (2.6) and in 0.1 mile passes a couple of outdoor bistros.

    Venice. At the foot of Washington St. is the Venice Pier (2.7). Just before entering onto the pier, follow the signs right (north) to the Class I bikeway along the beach. There are residences along the beach and a small strip of grass for resting. In 0.5 mile the path weaves past the Venice Beach

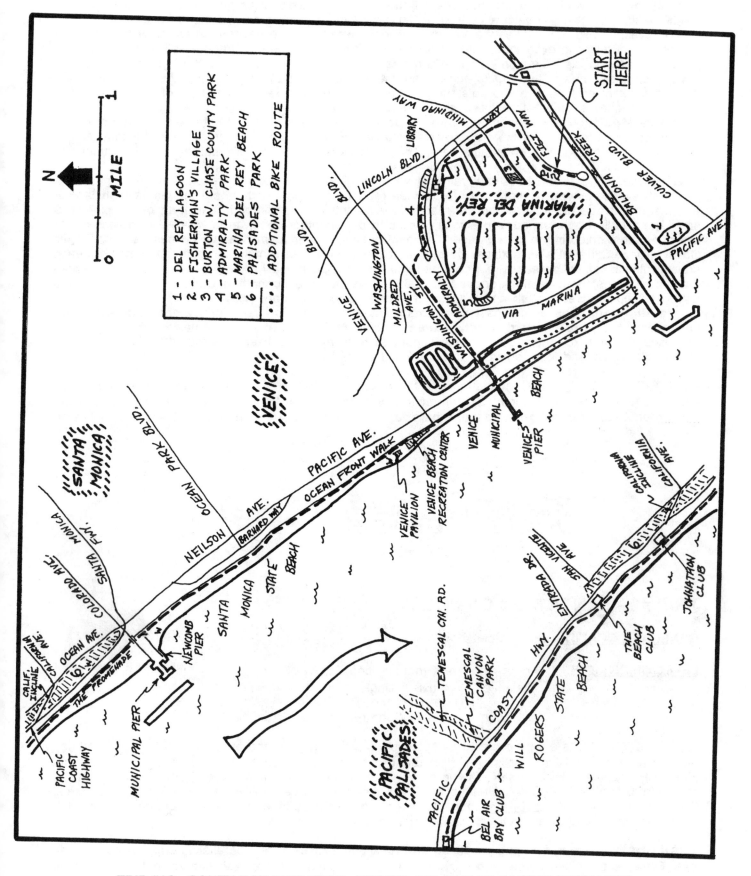

TRIP #1C - SOUTH BAY BIKE TRAIL: MARINA DEL REY TO PACIFIC PALISADES

Recreation Center which has a paddleboard and other courts, as well as gymnastics and weight lifting areas. Included within is Venice's version of Muscle Beach with alike-named indoor/outdoor gym.

The twisting bikeway passes the Venice Pavilion where there are several structures with some very interesting murals and even more interesting people (3.5). In addition to the sidewalk entertainers and preachers, this is also the home of the Kamikaze skater! In 0.1 mile is a palm-tree lined area and several outdoor cafes at the sand's edge, then 1/4 mile of flea markets and mobile salesrooms in the form of hawkers on foot. In a short distance, the path crosses a more traditional set of store fronts (4.1-4.3), then cruises a series of enclosed picnic shelters.

Santa Monica. The path bends toward the ocean -- there is an option to stay on the path or cruise a large parking area in what is now Santa Monica Beach (4.7). There is a great view of Santa Monica Bay and the Santa Monica Mountains here. The route passes a large volleyball area and continues to a series of beachfront commercial stores (5.4).

Next there is a biker/pedestrian trail split with the bikeway nearer the beach. The route passes a gymnastics and general workout area (5.6), then reaches and passes beneath the Santa Monica Pier (5.8). The pier boardwalk itself can be reached by turning off the bikepath just north of the pier on a small boardwalk. However, our route continues north past another beach area with the palisades of the city of Santa Monica in the background. The path crosses under a walkway which passes over Pacific Coast Hwy. (PCH) (6.1), then cruises by a group of isolated homes/rentals. In another 1/2 mile of beach cruising, the bikepath passes a restroom just south of the California Incline on PCH (6.6) and reaches the northernmost path section (opened in 1989). Bike past the Johnathan Club below the palisades until reaching the Beach Club and Will Rogers State Beach boundary (7.5).

Pacific Palisades. Pedal past the Entrada Dr. entry, cross on a bridge over a small wash and cruise past the area lifeguard headquarters. Continue alongside a narrower beach before reaching Temescal Canyon Rd. and the end of the separated bikeway (8.9). Bikers are routed to the parking lot. In 0.4 mile, this grand tour comes to an abrupt halt at the Bel Air Bay Club.

CONNECTING TRIPS: 1) Continuation with the South Bay Bike Trail to Manhattan Beach (Trip #1B) - bike south from the trip origin; 2) connection with the Santa Monica Loop (Trip #2) - from the Johnathan Club area, follow an asphalt path to PCH. Pedal up steep and busy California Incline to Ocean Blvd.

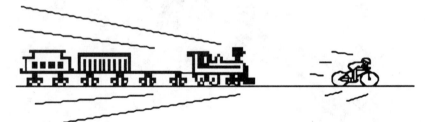

TRIP #2 - SANTA MONICA LOOP

GENERAL LOCATION: Santa Monica

LEVEL OF DIFFICULTY: Loop - moderate (double loop)
Distance - 6.4 miles (single loop)
- 11.9 miles (double loop)
Elevation gain - single short steep grade (double loop)

HIGHLIGHTS: This is a very pleasant and scenic trip which takes in the pretty residential neighborhood along San Vicente Blvd., Palisades Park on the bluffs about Santa Monica State Beach, Santa Monica Pier and the beach itself. This is one of the premier trips within the "big city." The trip can be divided into two loops, the 6.4-miles up and back along San Vicente Blvd. and the 5.5-mile Palisades Park-Santa Monica State Beach loop. Take one or both loops and take advantage of the well-designed Class I and Class II bike trails that exist for almost the entire trip.

TRAILHEAD: There is free public parking on San Vicente Blvd. or any paralleling street above Ocean Ave. Observe the signs before parking to ensure concurrence with the law. Another option is to "feed the meter" at Palisades Park where there is a five-hour limit. Take the Santa Monica Fwy. exit at Fourth

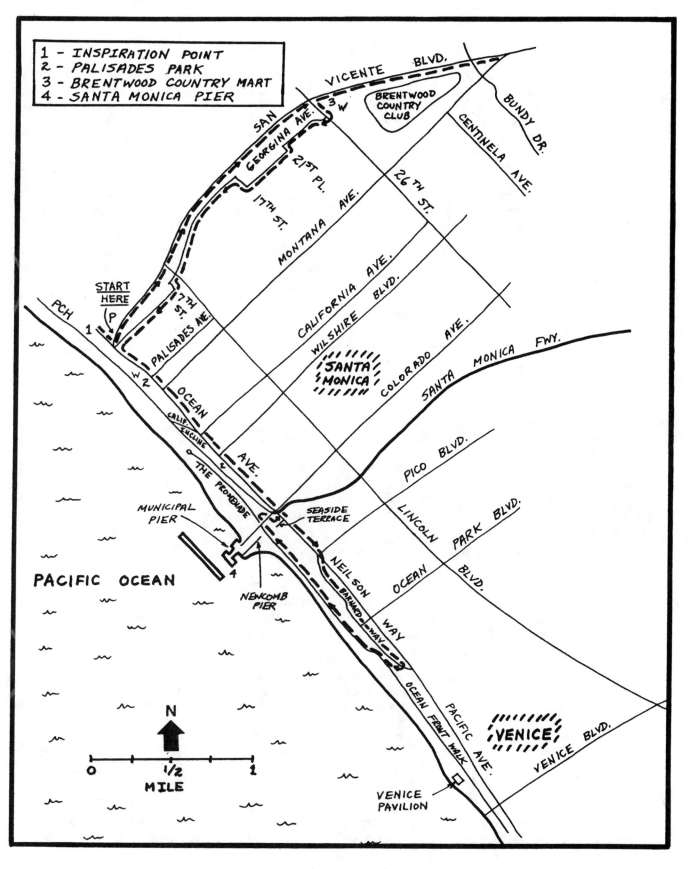

1 - INSPIRATION POINT
2 - PALISADES PARK
3 - BRENTWOOD COUNTRY MART
4 - SANTA MONICA PIER

TRIP #2 - SANTA MONICA LOOP

St., drive north about 1-1/4 miles to San Vicente Blvd. and turn left (toward the beach). Continue about 1/4 mile and park on San Vicente Blvd. just about Ocean Blvd.

Bring a light water supply. There are commercial shops in the Brentwood Country Mart complex and public facilities at Palisades Park and on Santa Monica Pier.

TRIP DESCRIPTION: **San Vicente Blvd. Loop.** Start northeast along the tree-lined, divided San Vicente Blvd. The entire route is a well-marked Class II bikeway. The broad grassy center strip is normally filled with joggers. Continue through this beautiful, elegant and well-kept residential area and pass the Brentwood Country Mart (a great place to stop for exotic snacks or interesting meals (2.0). A short distance later, the route travels alongside the exclusive Brentwood Country Club (2.7) and continues past Bundy Dr. to its terminus at Montana Ave. (3.2).

Turn around and return to 26th St. (4.4). Bikers can return via San Vicente Blvd. from this junction or take one of the many lovely residential alternate paralleling routes to the left (southeast). The entire area is lightly traveled with good roads. The recommended alternate is to take Georgina Ave. (one block from San Vicente on 26th) and follow its zig-zag route back to Ocean Blvd. (6.4). The upper portion of Georgina Ave. is excellent Class X which turns into Class III near 17th St.

Palisades Park with Santa Monica Pier Backdrop

Palisades Park-Beach Loop: Ocean Avenue. Turn right (northwest) on Ocean Ave., proceed up one block and take in the view from Inspiration Point. Turn around and head southeast on Ocean Ave. along lovely palm-lined Palisades Park. There are many scenic views along the 1-1/2-mile park, particularly impressive because the park is high on the bluffs overlooking Santa Monica Bay. Bikers should walk their bikes into the park at some point and look "over the edge" from the restraining wall. One of the most beautiful sections of the park is 0.3 mile from the start at Palisades Ave. (6.8).

At 0.9 mile from Inspiration Point (7.4), the route passes the California Ave./California Incline turn-off to the beach. Our tour follows Ocean Ave. past Santa Monica Blvd. (7.7) and Colorado Blvd. and the auto entrance to Newcomb Pier (8.0). Palisades Park ends here. The route continues under the Santa Monica Fwy. to Pico Blvd. (8.4). At Pico Blvd. it turns to the right and diagonally onto Bernard Wy.

Palisades Park-Beach Loop: The Promenade. Barnard Wy. descends to the beach and parallels the South Bay Bike Trail (Trip #1C). Just at the curve where Bernard Wy. turns towards Neilson Wy. and ends (9.2), turn toward the beach and link up with the South Bay Bike Trail. Pedal northward along the strand and pass under the Santa Monica Pier.

To visit the pier, turn right on the road which skirts the parking lot, then walk up the concrete steps which lead to the pier. After visiting the pier, return via the steps. Turn right (south) along Appian Wy. and continue two blocks to Seaside Terrace (10.4). A short testy climb up Seaside Terrace returns cyclists to Ocean Ave. Continue across Ocean Ave. to the northbound Class II bike route and return to the parking area at San Vicente Ave. (11.9).

Another option when leaving the pier is to continue north on the South Bay Bike Trail to the Johnathan Club, follow the asphalt path to Pacific Coast Hwy. (PCH), cross it, and bike up California Ave./California Incline to Ocean Blvd. There are exposed stretches along both PCH and California Incline which make this a less preferred route.

28

CONNECTING TRIPS: 1) Connection with the South Bay Bike Trail (Trip #1C) - as described in the trip text above; 2) connection with the Westwood Tour (Trip #3) - from the San Vicente Blvd./Montana Ave. intersection, follow Montana Ave. 1/2 mile southwest to Centinela Ave. Turn right (southeast) and continue about 1/2 mile to the trailhead at Texas Ave.

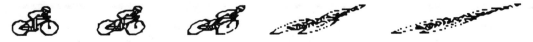

TRIP #3 - WESTWOOD TOUR

GENERAL LOCATION: Westwood

LEVEL OF DIFFICULTY: Loop Option 1 or 2 - moderate
Distance - 6.7 miles (Option 1); 7.5 miles (Option 2)
Elevation gain - periodic moderate grades

HIGHLIGHTS: This trip through Westwood and surrounding areas visits some pleasant residential territory and skirts the edge of Westwood Village and the U.C.L.A. campus. The best part of the tour might be a free-wheeling ride through the U.C.L.A. campus and surrounding residential areas, which is left as an exercise for the student. Although this is a trip through exceptionally scenic surroundings, there are many roadway intersections, much traffic, and an abundance of borderline Class III bike routes. A portion of the route is on a busy Class X roadway.

TRAILHEAD: The trip starts in the Sawtelle area of the City of Los Angeles at the beginning of the bike trail at Centinela Ave. and Texas Ave. There are Class III bikepaths throughout the area. This starting point was selected because it leads directly into the Westwood area.

Exit the San Diego Fwy. at Santa Monica Blvd., turn west and proceed about 1-1/4 miles to Centinela Ave. Turn right (north) and travel I/4 mile to Texas Ave. Park in the residential area nearby; observe the parking signs, and do not block driveways.

The Bruin Bear on the U.C.L.A. Campus

TRIP DESCRIPTION:
Trip Origin to U.C.L.A. Head northwest on the Class III bike route past Bundy Ave. (0.3) and turn right (south) at Westgate Ave. at University High School (0.6). Head downhill and continue another 0.2 mile to Ohio Ave. Turn left on Ohio Ave. and continue on a moderate upgrade through pleasant residential areas. At Sawtelle Ave. (I.4) the route turns into a Class II bikepath. In another 0.1 mile, the route passes under the San Diego Fwy., then continues to Sepulveda Blvd. (I.7).

Cross to the east side of Sepulveda Blvd. In about 100-200 yards, turn right at a walkway/bikeway entry and follow the signed Class I bikeway into Westwood Park. This well-shaded park has water,

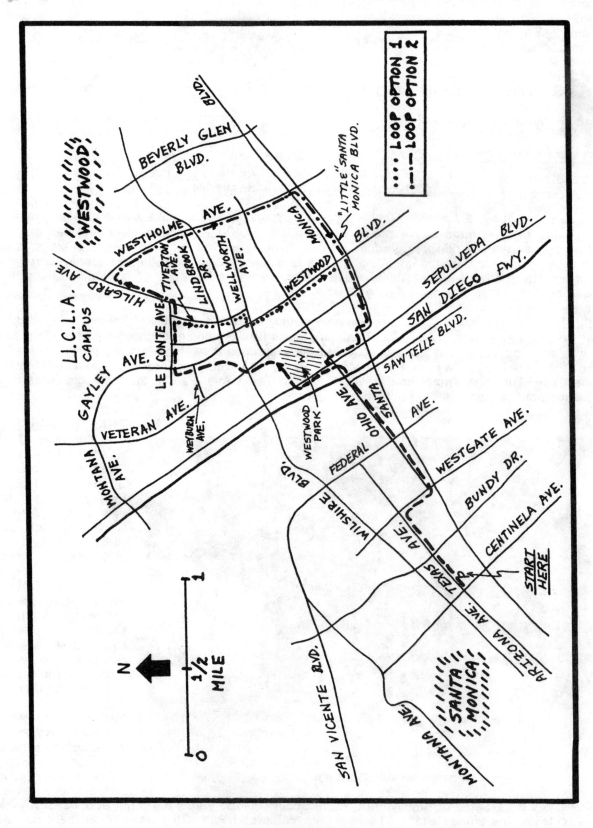

TRIP #3 - WESTWOOD TOUR

restrooms, tennis and basketball courts, as well as grassy playground areas. Follow the path on the west side of Veteran Ave. (2.0) and continue north to Wilshire Blvd. (2.4).

Cross to the northeast corner of the intersection and continue on the U.C.L.A. bike route through the parking area. The path parallels Gayley Ave. and fuses with a small road behind the buildings along Gayley Ave. This is the exotic "backside" of Westwood Village!

Turn right at Weyburn Ave. and in 100-200 feet, turn left onto Class II Gayley Ave. (2.6). Continue on a mild grade to Le Conte Ave. (2.8). One option is to continue up Gayley Ave. and explore Fraternity Row and the pleasant (but hilly) residential areas. However for this reference tour, turn right on Le Conte Ave. and continue 0.1 mile on a Class X roadway to Westwood Blvd. A left turn here (north) would take cyclists into the U.C.L.A. campus and many riding areas. However, the described trip continues on to Tiverton Ave. (3.1) and a choice of two continuation options.

Loop Option 1 - Westwood Blvd. If your desire is to see a part of the city of Westwood, this is your tour. Continue downhill on the Class III bike route on Tiverton Ave. past an automobile roadblock and follow the zig-zag path across Lindbrook Ave. (3.3). The street is now named Glendon Ave. Cross Wilshire Blvd. onto a short Class II stretch and continue another 0.1 mile to Wellworth Ave. Turn right (west) and continue a short distance to make a left turn onto Westwood Blvd. (3.5). Take this Class III route across Santa Monica Blvd. to "little" Santa Monica Blvd. just beyond the intersection (this less traveled Class X roadway parallels the main boulevard). Turn right (west) on "little" Santa Monica Blvd. and continue another 0.5 mile to Sepulveda Blvd. (4.7). Turn right (north) on Sepulveda Blvd. and continue 0.2 mile to Ohio Ave. From this intersection, retrace the original route back to Texas Ave. and Centinela Ave (6.7).

Loop Option 2 - Westholme Ave. This option provides a Class X route along Sorority Row and a pleasant Class III ride through some lovely outlying residential areas. Continue on Le Conte past Tiverton Ave. and turn left in another 0.1 mile at Hilgard Ave. (3.2). This route heads up a testy grade along Sorority Row, then flattens out and meets Westholme Ave. (3.6).

Turn right (south) and bike downhill along a pleasant tree-lined residential street which continues across Wilshire Blvd. (4.3) and meets Santa Monica Blvd. in another 0.5 mile. Cross Santa Monica Blvd. and turn right just after the intersection onto "little" Santa Monica Blvd. Pedal another 0.5 mile on the Class X route to Westwood Blvd. and continue on the route as described for "Loop Option 1" above. The total trip length is 7.5 miles.

CONNECTING TRIPS: Connection with the Santa Monica Loop (Trip #2) - continue 1/2 mile northwest on Centinela Ave. and turn right (northeast) on Montana Ave. Follow Montana Ave. l/2 mile to its intersection with San Vicente Ave.

TRIP #4 - BALLONA CREEK BIKEWAY

GENERAL LOCATION: Marina Del Rey, Culver City

LEVEL OF DIFFICULTY: One way - easy; up and back - moderate
Distance - 6.6 miles (one way)
Elevation gain - essentially flat

HIGHLIGHTS: This is one of many 100 percent Class I river and creek trails. The route starts from Marina Del Rey along a segment of the South Bay Bike Trail (Trip #1B) and continues northeast along Ballona Creek to its termination at National Blvd. and nearby Kronenthal Park. The route is lightly used, generally by folks who are adding extra miles to the South Bay Bike Trail and who enjoy the rapid-fire ups and downs at the street underpasses (or who are lost!). There is little scenery along the route and there are long stretches of wall-to-wall cement landscape. Perhaps the highlights of the route may be the side trips to three very pleasant parks, including Culver City Park with its excellent scenic vista.

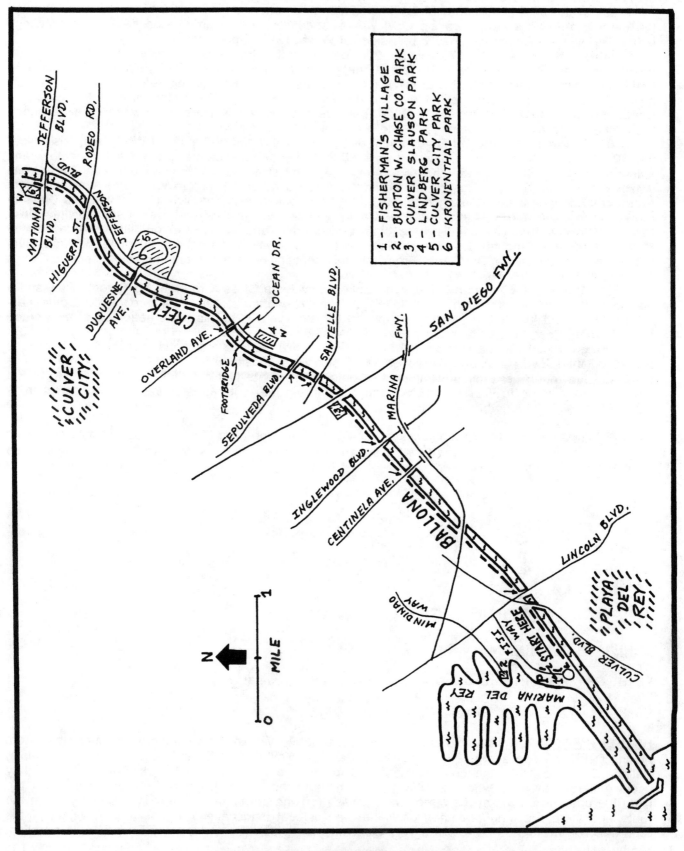

TRIP #4 - BALLONA CREEK BIKEWAY

TRAILHEAD: Follow the Marina Fwy. to its terminus and continue west to Lincoln Blvd. Turn left (south) on Lincoln Blvd. and continue about l/2 mile to Fiji Way. Take Fiji Way to the parking area at Fisherman's Village or use the overflow parking lot between the village and Lincoln Blvd. Kronenthal Park is tricky to reach by car. To start this trip from Kronenthal Park, turn southeast from Washington Blvd. onto McManus Ave. and continue to the parking lot near that street's end.

Bring a filled water bottle. Water is available with a short diversion to Lindberg Park or at the Kronenthal Park terminus. Be wary and also bring a bike partner, as there have been reports of harassment and assault on some isolated creek stretches.

TRIP DESCRIPTION: **Ballona Creek and Trip Diversions.** Head south to the turnaround loop at the end of Fiji Way (0.3). Cross the street and travel alongside the condominiums, passing through a gate at Ballona Creek (0.4). Take a hard left and head north along the cemented Ballona Creek Channel. The route passes under Culver Blvd. (1.2), Lincoln Blvd. (1.3), and at (1.7) passes a small channel split. There are more ups and downs at the Marina Expressway (1.8), Centinela Ave. (2.5), and Inglewood Blvd. (2.8).

After passing another small channel split, the route passes alongside pleasant little Culver/Slauson Park (3.3). Beyond this point are the roller coaster rides below the San Diego Fwy. (3.4), Sawtelle Blvd. (3.6), Sepulveda Blvd. (3.8), and Overland Ave. (4.4). An option is to cross Ballona Creek using the small footbridge at the Culver City Junior/Senior High School, just before Overland Ave. After crossing the creek, turn right (south) and cruise one block to shady Lindberg Park for water and a rest break.

However, the reference route continues along Ballona Creek and passes under Duquesne Ave. 0.9 mile further up the path. Another highly recommended option is to take Duquesne Ave. east across Jefferson Blvd. and proceed uphill to Culver City Park about 1.0 mile from the creek exit point. At the top of the route, stop and enjoy one of the most spectacular, unobstructed views of the greater Los Angeles Basin available in the South Bay area. Note that this "diversion" has some steep uphill along an unshaded route and adds two miles to the overall trip.

Kronenthal Park. Again, the reference route continues northward to Higuera St. (6.1) and ends at National Blvd. (6.5), where a chain partially blocks the path. Follow the paved switchback up to the opening in the fence which leads directly into Kronenthal Park. There are water, restrooms, playing fields and picnic facilities in this pleasant, grassy, shaded park. If the gate to the park is locked, ride west a short distance on National Blvd. to a short stairway entry (a short bike carry is required to enter from this direction).

CONNECTING TRIPS: Connection with the South Bay Bike Trail (Trip #1) - return to the gate at (0.4) in the trip description; continuing on the route back toward Fisherman's Village leads to the northern segment of the South Bay Bike Trail (Trip #1C); following Ballona Creek to the beach leads to the middle segment (Trip #1B).

TRIP #5 - OLD SEPULVEDA HILL CLIMB

GENERAL LOCATION: Westwood, Encino

LEVEL OF DIFFICULTY: One way - strenuous; up and back - strenuous to very strenuous
Distance - 7.3 miles (one way)
Elevation gain - long, steep grades

HIGHLIGHTS: This week-end or non-rush-hour trip follows the old Sepulveda Blvd. route from the L.A. basin to the San Fernando Valley via Sepulveda Pass. The hill climb to the pass is a gut-buster on what varies between a Class II and Class X bikeway, depending on road width. In a few places, there is essentially no marked bike lane. There are excellent views into both valleys, although the uphill is tough enough to force bikers into a head-down, tail-up posture, and some of the downhill will demand

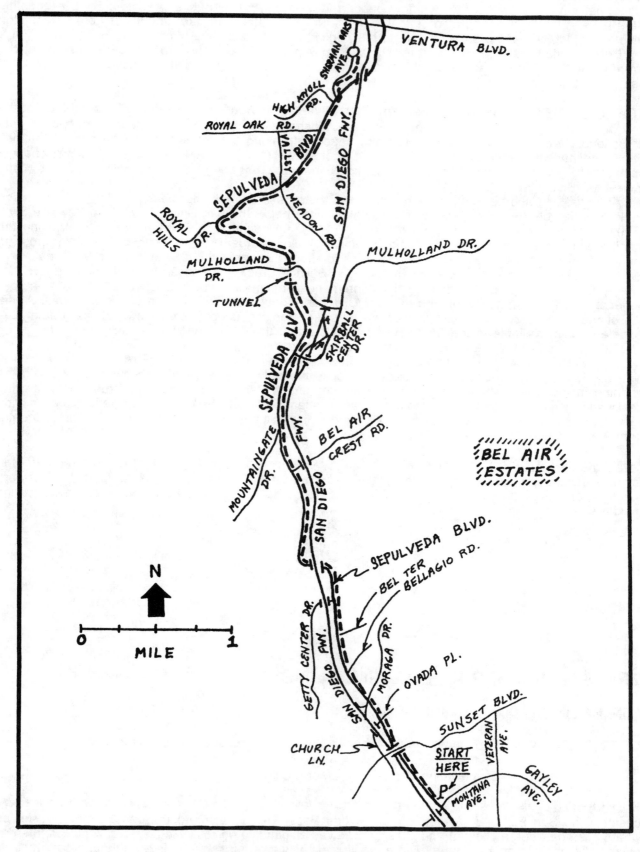

TRIP #5 - OLD SEPULVEDA HILL CLIMB

full attention. This trip is basically a workout! Don't take the downhill over the other side of the pass until you have thought it over carefully; the return uphill is equally rugged.

TRAILHEAD: From the San Diego Fwy., take the Montana Ave. exit in the Bel-Air/Westwood area. Park along Sepulveda Blvd. near Montana Ave. just east of the San Diego Fwy. Parking duration is restricted during weekdays.
Bring plenty of water. This is a hot, tiring, exposed trip with no water stops.

TRIP DESCRIPTION: **The Upgrade.** The route starts along a residence-lined section of Sepulveda Blvd. and heads north, passing under Sunset Blvd. (0.4), then crossing Ovada Pl./Church Ln. (0.6), and Moraga Dr. (0.7). There is a beautiful, live floral display in the center section of that divided street, the last of such lush beauty for a long while. There is also a gas station at the intersection. The route heads steadily uphill and views into the scrub-lined canyon open up almost immediately. At (1.5) there is a steep uphill for about 1/4 mile, followed by the Getty Center Dr. intersection (1.9). The magnificent building complex at the top of that road is the Getty Museum. In 0.2 mile, the route crosses under the San Diego Fwy. and continues parallel to that thoroughfare on its west side.

For about the next mile, the route continues up a grade interspersed with limited flats. There are some sections of this part of the route where the bike lane all but disappears. Beyond about (3.2) the path heads steeply uphill; this is a good chance to stop and admire the view back into the L.A. basin (that's what we call "research stops"). The rugged upgrade continues past Mountaingate Dr. (3.5), Skirball Center Dr. (4.2) and finally levels off at the tunnel which passes under Mulholland Dr. (4.8).

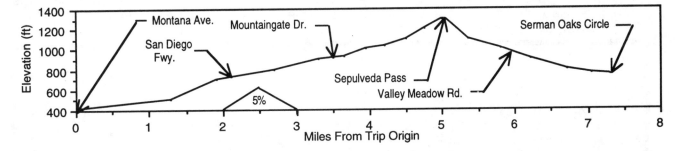

The Downgrade. At the tunnel exit is a really fine view of the San Fernando Valley. (This exit is also a possible trip turnaround point.) Just beyond this exit, the road begins to twist and wind through a steep downgrade and continues almost all the way into the valley. On the way down, this residentially-surrounded route passes numerous streets including Royal Hills Dr. (5.3), Valley Meadow Rd. (6.0), Royal Oak Rd. (6.3), High Knoll Rd. (6.7), and Sherman Oaks Ave. (6.9). Turn left at Sherman Oaks Ave. and take a break at the traffic circle about 1/2 mile further down the road (7.3).

CONNECTING TRIPS: 1) Connection with the Westwood Tour (Trip #3) - at the trip origin, follow Montana Ave. east to Gayley Ave.; 2) connection with the Mulholland Dr. route (Trip #37) - exit at Skirball Center Dr. and pass over the freeway to the east side. Continue north to the Mulholland Dr. bridge back across the freeway (west segment) or continue north beyond the bridge (east segment).

Biking   Worldwide

TRIPS #6A-#6D - PALOS VERDES PENINSULA LOOP

The strenuous to very strenuous Palos Verdes Loop Trip (23.2 miles, periodic steep grades) is broken up into individual Palos Verdes (P.V.) segments. The general area map is provided below. Also shown is a strenuous to very strenuous Hawthorne Blvd. option as well as a strenuous option that replaces the P.V. Dr. East segment with Western Ave. Most of the routes are Class X with the exception of a major segment of P.V. Dr. North and some portions of P.V. Dr. West:

• Trip #6A explores a beautiful residential stretch through rolling hills which starts near the P.V. Reservoir and ends at pleasant Malaga Cove Plaza.

• Trip #6B follows the western Peninsula shoreline above the bluffs, starting at Malaga Cove Plaza and ending at scenic San Vicente County Park.

• Trip #6C leaves San Vicente County Park, traverses the bluffs above the southern beaches, wiggles its way through the Portuguese Bend landslide area, and terminates near the P.V. Dr. East junction.

• Trip #6D starts at the junction of P.V. Dr. East, winds its way up a steep set of switchbacks and traverses the scenic peninsula "high country," letting out at the P.V. Reservoir.

• The Hawthorne Blvd. segment is more difficult than P.V. Dr. East, with the steepest grade encountered just below Dupre Dr. The route is provided for variety; use of this segment also provides the option for a shorter Peninsula trip (11 miles). This option features potential rest stops at Golden Cove Shopping Center, Rancho Palos Verdes Park and Peninsula Center (south to north).

• The Western Ave. route provides the option to circumvent the steep, winding P.V. Dr. East trip segment. The total route mileage is increased slightly to 26 miles. The route is through rolling hills on a busy thoroughfare. Potential rest stops are the 25th. Ave. Shopping Center, Peck Park, and the Park Western Plaza (shopping center) on Park Western Dr.

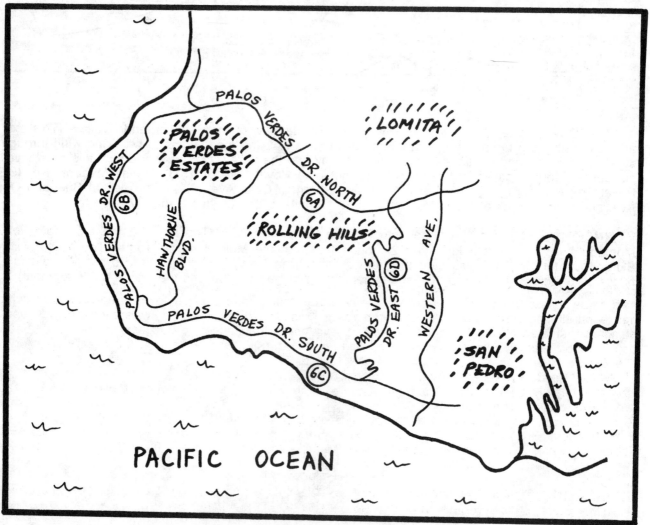

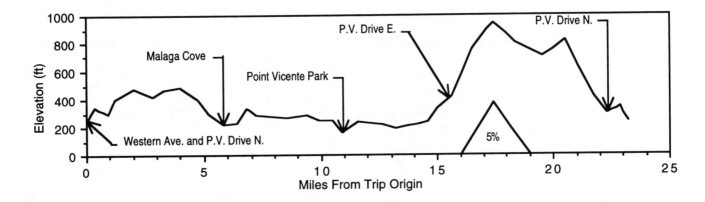

TRIP #6A - PALOS VERDES PENINSULA: P.V. DRIVE NORTH

GENERAL LOCATION: Rolling Hills Estates, Rolling Hills, Palos Verdes

LEVEL OF DIFFICULTY: One way - moderate; up and back - moderate to strenuous
Distance - 5.8 miles (one way)
Elevation gain - frequent moderate grades

HIGHLIGHTS: This is a pleasant but hard-working trip through the rolling hills along the tree-lined northern segment of Palos Verdes (P.V.) Dr. The trip starts at Western Ave., passes the P.V. Reservoir, continues on rolling hills through several rural, wooded peninsula communities, and ends on a long downhill run to Malaga Cove Plaza. More than two-thirds of the trip is on a Class I bikeway (with a faster, paralleling Class II alternate available) and the remainder is on a wide Class X roadway with plenty of room for bikers.

TRAILHEAD: Free parking is available along P.V. Dr. North, west of Western Ave. Read the parking signs carefully for current laws. Other options: 1) ask permission to park in one of the real estate office parking lots at the P.V. Dr. East intersection; 2) start the trip from Harbor Regional Park (see Trip #13), although this additional segment adds significant elevation to the trip; or 3) do the trip in reverse and use the parking in Malaga Cove Plaza or on nearby streets.
   Bring a moderate water supply. There is water along the way at the Rolling Hills Road Plaza and the Malaga Cove Plaza.

TRIP DESCRIPTION: **Rolling Hills.** The two-way Class I bike trail is on the north side of P.V. Dr. North. When riding the trail, keep an eye open for cars pulling out from the small side streets. (Another option is to ride the Class II path on the roadway which is a higher-speed route.) The path immediately starts up a moderate grade and reaches a small shopping plaza at the summit (0.3). After another 0.6 mile of mostly downhill, the route crosses P.V. Dr. East and passes the Dapplegray Equestrian Park. For the next three miles, the path roller-coasters over small rolling hills along a lovely tree-lined path which has a paralleling horse path. At (2.0) the route crosses Rolling Hills Rd. where bikers may use a pleasant rest area which has benches and an available water faucet. In succession, the up-and-down path then crosses Crenshaw Blvd. (2.8), Hawthorne Blvd. (3.3), and the end of the Class I path at Via Campesina (4.0).
   Palos Verdes Estates. The biking in this area is Class X, but has plenty of room for bikers. The street is heavily tree-lined with a lovely center strip which is frequented by walkers, joggers, and horseback riders. The route begins a moderate downgrade of about one mile, and then a sharp downgrade (5.0). At (5.2), the route reaches a three-point intersection of P.V. Dr. North, P.V. Blvd, and P.V. Dr. West. Bikers should stay to the left and take P.V. Dr. West into the Malaga Cove Plaza (5.8). There is a water fountain in the grassy square in the plaza - a great place for a break. The plaza also has a small market and delightful outdoor cafe.

CONNECTING TRIPS: 1) Continuation with the bike route along P.V. Dr. West (Trip #6B) - bike west from the plaza; 2) connection with the South Bay Bike Trail (Trip #1) - return to the three-point intersection just above Malaga Cove Plaza and turn left (north) onto P.V. Blvd. Turn left toward the

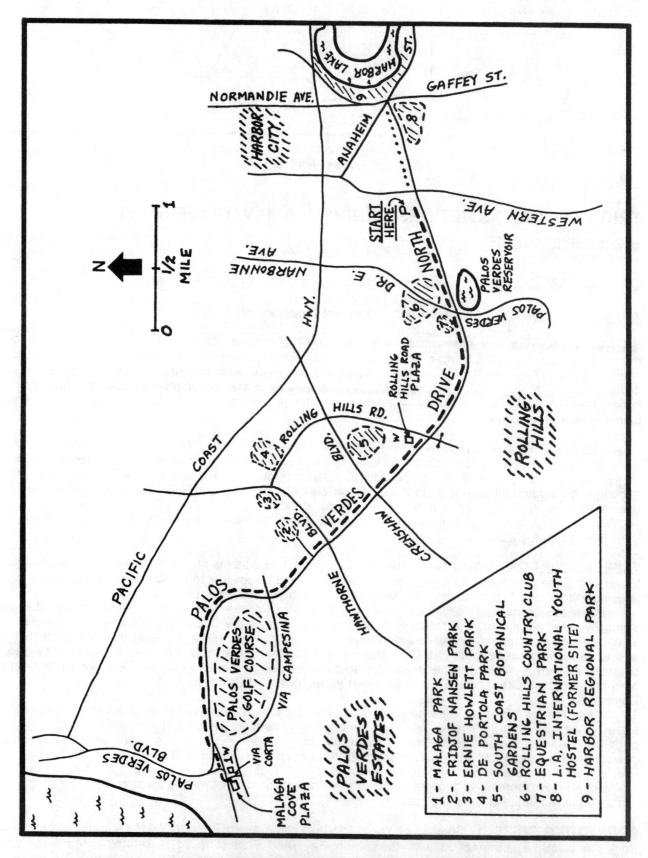

TRIP #6A - PALOS VERDES PENINSULA: PALOS VERDES DRIVE NORTH

beach on Calle Miramar, veer left on Via Riviera, and continue about 0.1 mile to the beach parking lot; 3) connection with the Harbor Regional Park bike ride (Trip #13) - continue this trip east on P.V. Dr. North across Western Ave. to Anaheim St. and take the bikepath under the highway.

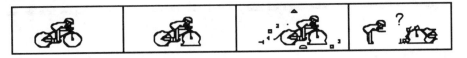

TRIP #6B - PALOS VERDES PENINSULA: P.V. DRIVE WEST

GENERAL LOCATION: Palos Verdes Estates, Rancho Palos Verdes

LEVEL OF DIFFICULTY: One way - moderate; up and back - moderate
Distance - 5.1 miles (one way)
Elevation gain - periodic moderate grades

HIGHLIGHTS: This highly scenic route leaves Malaga Cove Plaza and follows a moderately hilly route along Palos Verdes (P.V.) Dr. West, ending at Point Vicente County Park. Along the way, the route passes a spectacular scenic overlook of the local coastline and Santa Monica Bay. Part of the trip is along a pleasant divided highway in Palos Verdes Estates. There is also a nice side trip which explores the Lunada Bay area. Point Vicente Park sports a lighthouse, small museum, and serves as a whale watch center.

Most of the trip is on a Class X bike route (i.e., on open roadway). The initial 1/2 mile is narrow, but the road widens beyond.

TRAILHEAD: There is free parking in the Malaga Cove Plaza on Sunday or on nearby streets on other days of the week. From the South Bay area, take P.V. Blvd. south and stay to the right after passing the intersection with P.V. Dr. North. This road fuses into P.V. Dr. West. Turn left in a couple of hundred yards into the plaza. Another option is to do the trip in reverse. Park at the periphery of the Golden Cove Shopping Center on Hawthorne Blvd. or at Point Vicente Park. To reach this area, continue 4.7 miles and 5.1 miles, respectively, from Malaga Cove Plaza on P.V. Dr. West.

Bring a moderate water supply. There are public water fountains at the trip origin and terminus.

TRIP DESCRIPTION: **Malaga Cove - Lunada Bay.** The route leaves Malaga Cove Plaza and proceeds about 1.0 mile on a steady upgrade to a spectacular overlook of Malaga Cove, Santa Monica Bay, and the beaches up to and beyond Santa Monica. A little further is a turnoff to the right at Paseo Del Mar (1.1). This leads to a nice side trip into the charming residential area around Lunada Bay. The reference trip remains on P.V. Dr. West along a separated roadway with a foot and horse path in the center section of the road. Continue on a relatively flat roadway, passing a small shopping center at Yarmouth Rd. (2.7). There are scattered views out to the ocean until the view completely opens up at about (3.5).

Golden Cove - Point Vicente. Shortly afterward, the route passes the Golden Cove Shopping Center at Hawthorne Blvd. (4.7) which has a homey little delicatessen hidden within. In another 0.4 miles of moderate downhill, the route intersects a small sharp turnoff towards the ocean. Take this signed roadway a short distance to the parking/rest area at Point Vicente County Park (5.1). There are water and restrooms here. Stop and enjoy an excellent ocean view, museum, and the Point Vicente Lighthouse. This is also a great picnic spot.

CONNECTING TRIPS: 1) Continuation of the P.V. Dr. North trip (Trip #6A) - ride east from Malaga Cove Plaza; 2) continuation of the P.V. Dr. South trip (Trip #6C) - ride east from the Point Vicente Park; 3) connection with the Hawthorne Blvd. (strenuous) alternate route over the Palos Verdes Hills ridge (Trip #6D) - turn north at Hawthorne Blvd.

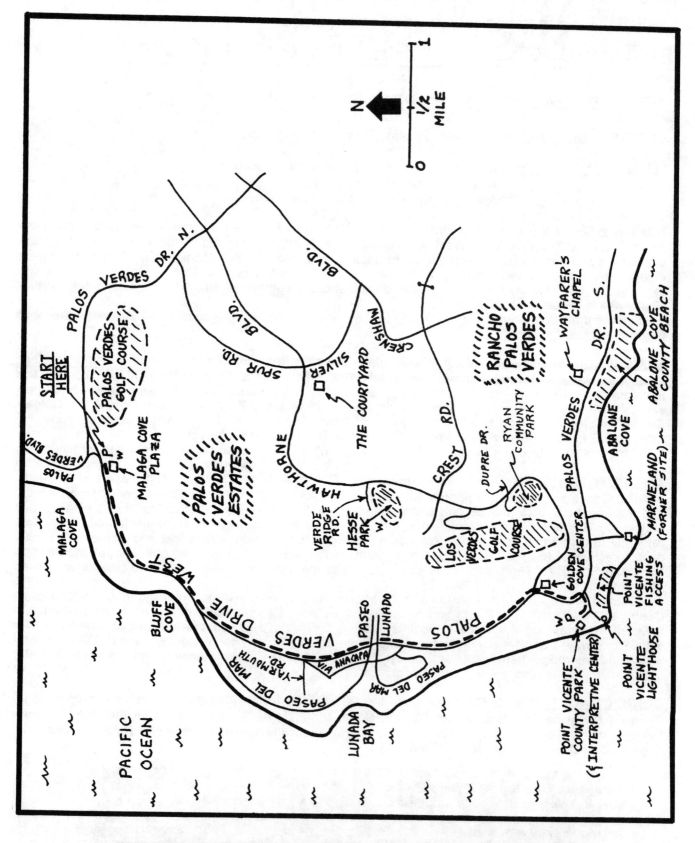

TRIP #6B - PALOS VERDES PENINSULA: PALOS VERDES DRIVE WEST

TRIP #6C - PALOS VERDES PENINSULA: P.V. DRIVE SOUTH

GENERAL LOCATION: Rancho Palos Verdes

LEVEL OF DIFFICULTY: One way - moderate; up and back - moderate
Distance - 5.7 miles (one way)
Elevation gain - periodic moderate grades

HIGHLIGHTS: This highly scenic route leaves the Point Vicente County Park, travels along rolling hills past the old Marineland turnoff, passes alongside the lovely Wayfarer's Chapel, and winds its way along the bumpy road through Portuguese Bend. The route continues up a long scenic grade, passes the junction with Palos Verdes (P.V.) Dr. East and continues to 25th St. overlooking Palos Verdes Shoreline Park. There are numerous grand views of the coastline, Pacific Ocean, and Catalina Island along the way.
    This is not a trip for children or for inexperienced or nervous bikers. Though a very excellent trip, it is mostly on Class X roadway with a very narrow, hilly, and bumpy stretch through the Portuguese Bend slide area. There are portions of the 0.5-1.0 mile Portuguese Bend slide area where automobiles and bikers literally share the roadway. (Note that the road was improved significantly in the late 1980s, although it still has it's uplifted patches.)

TRAILHEAD: There is parking at Point Vicente County Park, as described in Trip #6B. Another option is to park along 25th St. in San Pedro, roughly 0.5 mile east of the P.V. Dr. East intersection and do the trip in reverse. Read the parking signs to ensure compliance with the latest laws. To reach the 25th St. parking area, take Western Ave. south to within about 1/2 mile of the ocean and turn right (west) on 25th St. Continue about 3/4 mile to reach the parking area.
    Bring a moderate water supply. There are water and restrooms at Point Vicente County Park. The next facilities are available on a "beg and borrow" basis in the shopping area near 25th St. and Western Ave., about 3/4 mile from parking on 25th St.

Point Vicente County Park

TRIP DESCRIPTION: **Point Vicente - Old Marineland.** From the Point Vicente County Park parking area, turn right onto P.V. Dr. South and begin the journey through the rolling hills. In 0.8 mile, the route passes the old Marineland turnoff. (Thanks to some very unpopular corporate manipulations, Marineland is now ancient history.) There are views of the ocean and Catalina Island along this stretch and the scenery gets even better later on. Another mile down the road is Frank Lloyd Wright's stunning glass church, the Wayfarer's Chapel.

    Portuguese Bend. In 1/2 mile (2.3), the road enters the Portuguese Bend landslide area. The road is bumpy, and very narrow, with little or no shoulder. The ride is also very hilly and requires the biker's complete attention between avoiding the largest bumps and the accompanying automobiles. Stop or slow down and enjoy the lovely views into Portuguese Bend and the surrounding hills, as well as of the cliffs and beaches on the opposite side of the road. A short bicycle tour of the residential portion of

41

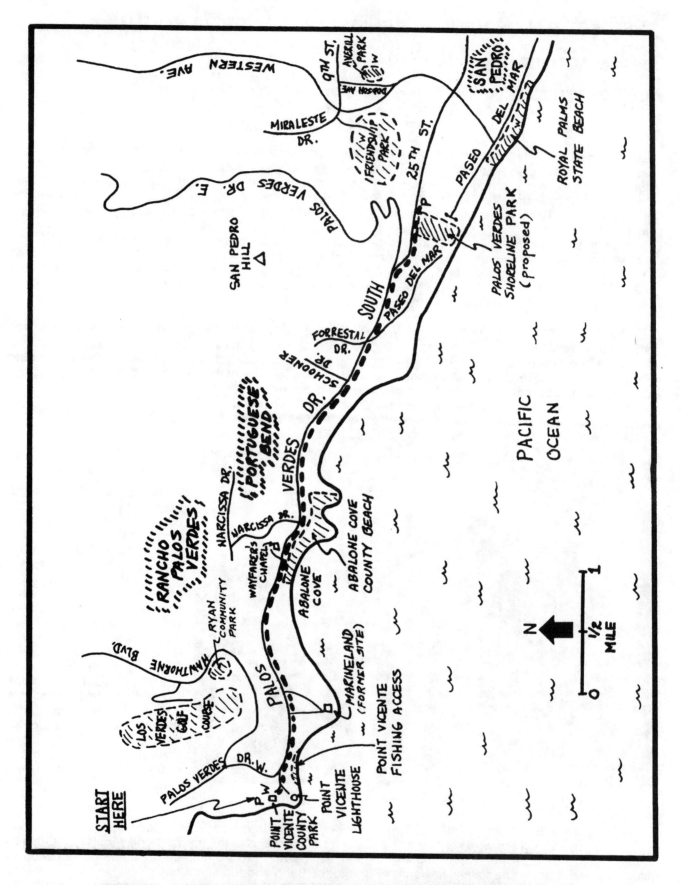

TRIP #6C - PALOS VERDES PENINSULA: PALOS VERDES DRIVE SOUTH

Portuguese Bend is, in itself, a real experience. The route is on Narcissa Dr.

P.V. Drive South - 25th Street. Once out of the slide area, the route returns to an improved and roomy Class X roadway and at (3.7) begins a gradual steady ascent. There are more sweeping vistas that take in the coastline and Catalina. Near the top of the grade is the intersection with P.V. Dr. East (4.7), the most strenuous of the four P.V. Dr. routes. There is a glorious unbroken ocean view in this area. Bike on P.V. Dr. South until it becomes 25th St. and the route transitions to Class II (5.2). A continuation on the bikepath leads past (above) undeveloped Shoreline Park (5.7) and the turnaround point. A option is to continue on 25th St. through residential areas to Western Ave. (6.4).

<u>CONTINUING TRIPS</u>: 1) Continuation of the P.V. Dr. West ride (Trip #6B) and P.V. Dr. East ride (Trip #6D) - from the trip origin or terminus, respectively, continue on the P.V. Drive loop; 2) connection with the San Pedro Beaches Tour (Trip #7) - continue east on 25th St. about one mile past the P.V. Dr. North intersection. Turn right (south) on Anchovy Ave. and free-wheel downhill about 0.5 mile to Paseo Del Mar.

TRIP #6D - PALOS VERDES PENINSULA: P.V. DRIVE EAST

GENERAL LOCATION: Rancho Palos Verdes, Miraleste, Rolling Hills Estates

LEVEL OF DIFFICULTY: One way - strenuous; up and back - strenuous to very strenuous
Distance - 6.6 miles (one way)
Elevation gain - periodic steep grades

HIGHLIGHTS: This segment of the Palos Verdes (P.V.) Drive loop is a gut-buster! The uphill ride to the crest of the roadway is steep and the downhill is winding and fast. Yet for those in shape to bike this segment, it offers the finest views of the Los Angeles Harbor and the surrounding basin that can be found. On the early leg of the trip, there are clear Catalina Island views and near the terminus, there are excellent views into the city of Los Angeles and of the surrounding mountains. The route is highly scenic in itself, passing through some of the most beautiful residential areas in the county.

TRAILHEAD: Park on 25th St. in San Pedro roughly 1/2 mile east of the intersection of P.V. Dr. South and P.V. Dr. East (see description in Trip #6C). Another option is to park along P.V. Dr. North (as described in Trip #6A) and do the trip in reverse.
There are no public facilities along this route. Bring a filled water bottle on hot days.
The entire route is Class X. Sections of the roadway are narrow and, when combined with the high-speed downhill stretches, are dangerous. It should be noted that in spite of these conditions, this roadway is well used by experienced bikers.

TRIP DESCRIPTION: **The Switchbacks.** From the parking area on 25th St., continue west 0.5 mile and make a sharp right turn up P.V. Dr. East. The road starts steeply upward immediately and proceeds through a series of three challenging switchbacks to the crest near Marymount College. In this stretch, the biker pumps through an elevation gain of 600 feet in 1.8 miles, roughly a 11% average grade! There are great views of Catalina Island, San Pedro South Shores, and old Marineland along this stretch of the roadway (and an excuse for a rest break along one of the turnouts).
The Second Crest. The route continues through roughly a mile of moderate downhill and then becomes a fast, winding, free-wheeling descent leading to the intersection with Miraleste Dr. (3.9). There are fantastic views of the harbor area in this stretch of the route. Near this intersection, there is a gas station and small strategically-placed delicatessen. The road winds uphill again through some extremely pleasant, wooded residential areas, and crests at Rockinghorse Rd. (4.9).

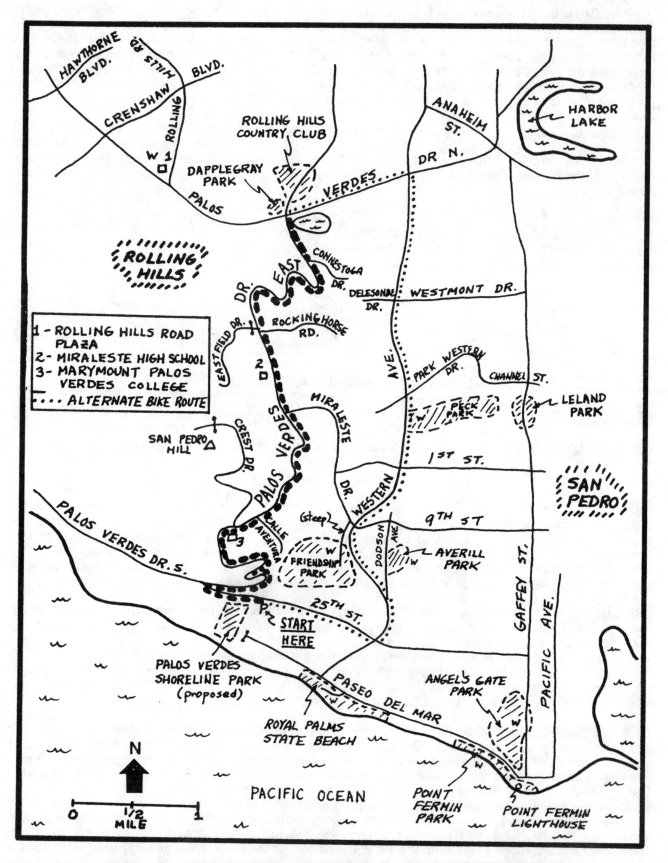

LEGEND:

1 - ROLLING HILLS ROAD PLAZA
2 - MIRALESTE HIGH SCHOOL
3 - MARYMOUNT PALOS VERDES COLLEGE
••• - ALTERNATE BIKE ROUTE

TRIP #6D - PALOS VERDES PENINSULA: PALOS VERDES DRIVE EAST

Palos Verdes Drive East Switchbacks Above 25th Street

The Mad Downhill. Now begins a narrow, winding downhill section. Hug the shoulder and watch for automobiles. This dangerous route segment lasts for about 1-1/2 miles. At Connestoga Dr. (6.1), the route diverts over to a Class II bikepath (a little late!) and continues on the downgrade past the Palos Verdes Reservoir to P.V. Dr. North (6.6). Note that just above Connestoga Dr. is a premier view across the L.A. basin into the City of Los Angeles and into both the San Gabriel and San Bernardino Mountains. Cross P.V. Dr. North and turn right (east) or onto Class I bikeway to your parked shuttle vehicle. Otherwise stand by for a rugged return trip.

CONNECTING TRIPS: 1) Continuation of the P.V. Dr. North pedal (Trip #6A) and the P.V. Dr. South tour (Trip #6C) - from the trip terminus or the trip origin, respectively, continue on the P.V. Drive loop; 2) connection with the San Pedro Beaches Tour (Trip #7) - see directions from the Trip #6C description; 3) connection with the Harbor Regional Park ride (Trip #13) - see directions from the Trip #6A writeup.

TRIP #7 - SAN PEDRO BEACHES TOUR

GENERAL LOCATION: San Pedro

LEVEL OF DIFFICULTY: One way - easy to moderate; up and back - moderate
Distance - 6.2 miles (one way)
Elevation gain - periodic moderate grades;
two short steep grades

HIGHLIGHTS: This trip starts from the 22nd St. Landing at the terminus of Trip #8. Bikers visit the Cabrillo Marina, Cabrillo Beach, Point Fermin Park, Angel's Gate Park, and Royal Palms State Beach. This is one of the most scenic trips in the county, particularly the views of the rugged bluffs and coastline along Paseo Del Mar. This trip is primarily Class I or Class II, with a small stretch of Class X roadway on the lightly-traveled stretch of Paseo Del Mar west of Western Ave. There is a slightly different route provided for the return leg of this trip.

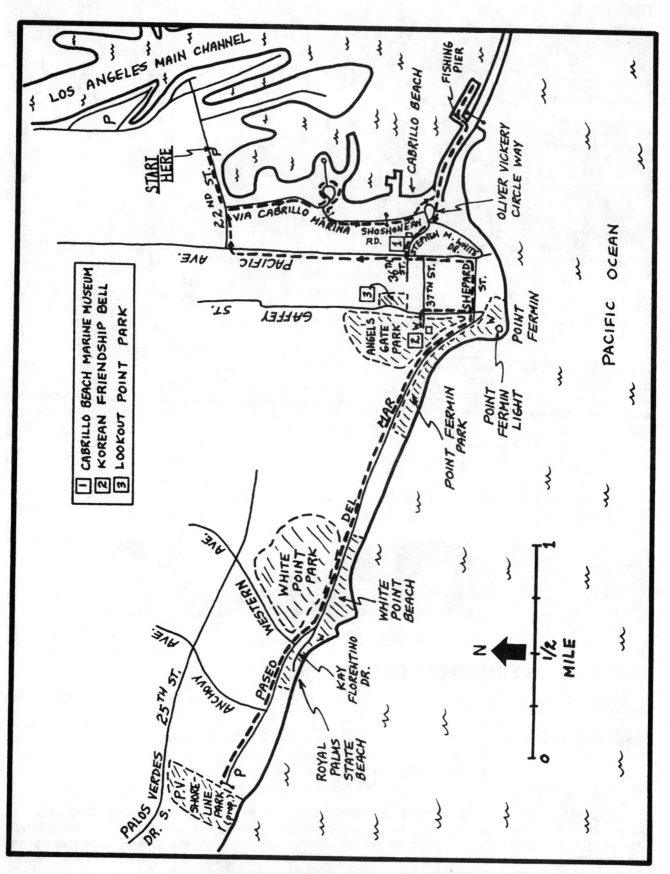

TRIP #7 - SAN PEDRO BEACHES TOUR

<u>TRAILHEAD</u>: Free parking is available along 22nd St. or along the periphery of the Cabrillo Marina parking lot. To reach 22nd St., travel south on Pacific Ave. and follow the numbered streets (numbers increase in the southbound direction). Turn left (east) and find a parking spot within the next mile or so along 22nd St.; check parking signs to ensure compliance with current laws. Another option is to park along the west section of Paseo Del Mar and do the trip in reverse.

There are water and restroom facilities at each of the beaches and parks mentioned, except for Angel's Gate Park, which has only a water fountain.

<u>TRIP DESCRIPTION</u>: **Cabrillo Marina and Cabrillo Beach.** About 1/4 mile east of Pacific Ave. on 22nd St., turn south onto Via Cabrillo Marina. Travel about 0.2 mile and turn into a large parking loop with water and private restrooms. From this area, there is a view of the Cabrillo Marina/hotel complex and a view across the bay to the Cabrillo Beach area. Return to the main road and check out the benches up on the bluff--there is a steep bikeway/walkway up to that overlook for the adventurous.

Continue down Via Cabrillo Marina a few hundred feet, veer right, and use the walkway around the roadway gate which separates the marina from Cabrillo Beach. The roadway name becomes Shoshonean Rd. Bike around a second gate, pass a boat launch area a few hundred yards further, and enter the bikepath along the beach at (0.4) mile. In the background is the Cabrillo Beach Marina Museum. In another 0.3 mile, follow the path and roadway out towards the Cabrillo Beach jetty. Along this jetty, there are nice views of Cabrillo Beach to the left and the open ocean and Catalina Island to the right. In 0.3 mile, there is a large fence with an ever-reopened hole in it. Through these portals pass the "crazies" who (illegally) fish directly on top of the breakwater. Don't follow - just look!

Bicentennial Korean Friendship Bell

The path jogs to the left and enters Cabrillo Pier. Continue another 0.2 mile to the end of the pier. (This may mean walking your bike if the pier is heavily crowded with fisherman.) There is a fine view of the ships in the harbor and the opening in the harbor breakwater known as Angel's Gate.

There are also water and restrooms on the pier. Return back to the end of the jetty, turn left, and take Oliver Vickery Circle Way through the Cabrillo Beach entrance (1.8). Turn right on Stephen M. White Dr. and in 0.1 mile of testy upgrade, turn left (south) onto Class II Pacific Ave.

Point Fermin. Continue another 0.1 mile on a testy upgrade to the top of the hill and then 0.2 mile to the end of Pacific Ave. at scenic Point Fermin parking area and overlook. There is a fine Catalina Island view from here and frequently a nice view of one of the entering or departing ships. Follow Shepard St. west on the Class II bikepath and, in another 0.5 mile (2.6), turn left on Gaffey St. to Point Fermin Park. There are park benches and barbecue areas. Ride through this lovely treed park which sits on a bluff overlooking the Pacific Ocean; one of the best routes is along the walled periphery of the park. If time permits, stop over at Walker's Burgers across from the park - this is one of the favorite biker stops (chopper bikers, that is). Return to Gaffey St. and head north across Shepard St.

Angel's Gate Park. Pedal on Gaffey St. and head up a very steep hill; chances are, unless you're in very excellent shape, this will be an opportunity to walk your bike about 0.1 mile to 37th St. Turn left (west) into Angel's Gate Park and enjoy a spectacular unobstructed view of the south-facing coastline. You can walk your bike up to the temple on the knoll to look over the Bicentennial Korean Friendship Bell. Just north of the bell is the Fort MacArthur Military Museum. Exit the park and take in the fine view (down 37th St.) of Angel's Gate. For the hearty souls, one of the best L.A. harbor views is just a little further up Gaffey St. at small Lookout Point Park. The park has pay-for-view telescopes. Return downhill to the intersection of Gaffey St. and Shepard St. and turn right (3.4) on Shepard St.

Paseo Del Mar and Royal Palms State Park. Cycle on Shepard St. on the Class II bikeway; in a short distance, the street becomes Paseo Del Mar (PDM). There are spectacular views of the bluffs and cliffs, the general southern coastline, and out to sea for the next 0.3 mile. At (3.9) there is a grassy rest area with a restroom and water on the ocean side of PDM. This is a pleasant tree-lined section of road. In another 0.6 mile, there is another impressive view/overlook of the general coastline.

At (5.0) is a small park and restroom followed by the Kay Florentine Dr. turn-off, both to the seaside of PDM. The road leads about 0.2 mile very steeply downhill to Royal Palms State Beach. It is work walking your bike both down and back uphill just to see this area close up. There is a small beach area to the right (west) and some excellent tide pools and natural reefs to the left. (Don't go out into this area near high tide!) Return to Paseo Del Mar and enjoy another fine coastline view about 0.2 mile down the road. At Western Ave. the bikepath ends. Continue another 0.6 mile along PDM through a quiet and pretty residential section to a locked gate (6.2) near Anchovy Ave.

A convenient alternate method of return is to continue back on PDM/Shepard St. to Pacific Ave., turn left (north) and take this Class II route back to 22nd St. This is a mild return leg which passes along the west (entry) side of the lower reservation of Fort MacArthur Military Reservation.

CONNECTING TRIPS: 1) Connection with Palos Verdes Dr. South ride (Trip #6C) - near the trip terminus turn north on Anchovy Ave. and bike up a very steep grade for 0.5 mile to 25th St., turn left and continue to Palos Verdes Dr. South; 2) continuation with the L.A. Harbor: Main Channel tour (Trip #8) - from the starting point, head east on 22nd St. (toward the harbor).

TRIPS #8-#12 - LOS ANGELES AND LONG BEACH HARBORS

The five trips, #8, #9, #10, #11, and #12, are connecting tours which explore the L.A. and Long Beach Harbors. Note that trips #9 through #11, in particular, require that you develop the skills to bike safely across railroad tracks. The general area map for these excursions is provided below:

• Trip #8 explores the scenic Main Channel of L.A. Harbor and includes several sightseeing attractions, such as Ports O'Call Village.
• Trip #9 visits the East and West Basins of the L.A. Harbor, which have both loading docks and yacht basins.
• Trip #10 tours the Long Beach Harbor, Cerritos, and Back Channels. This is the "working man's" look at some of the most remote parts of the harbor area.
• Trip #11 explores the Southeast Basin of the Long Beach Harbor. The route has several scenic highlights including the Queen Mary and Mary's Gate Village.
• Trip #12 visits Terminal Island, which includes visits to the aromatic Fish Harbor and the dry docks near Reservation Point.

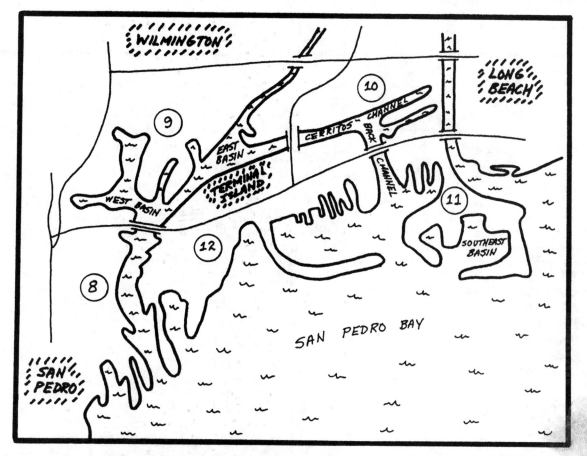

TRIP #8 - LOS ANGELES HARBOR: MAIN CHANNEL

GENERAL LOCATION: San Pedro

LEVEL OF DIFFICULTY: Up and back - easy
Distance - 6.2 miles (one way)
Elevation gain - essentially flat

HIGHLIGHTS: This harbor trip is on the west side of the main channel of the Los Angeles Harbor. The route passes the L.A. World Cruise Center, the large passenger ship terminal visited by such ships as the Queen Mary II, the Elation and the "Love Boat." In addition, the trip includes the L.A. Maritime Museum, Ports O 'Call Village, and 22nd St. Landing. There are several particularly scenic spots on the tour, including the point at the end of Admiral Higbee Way. This is probably the best view point along the L.A. Harbor Main Channel.

Most of the trip is on Class X roadway. However, much of the ride is through parking lots, along wide sidewalks, or in areas where motor vehicle traffic is very light. This is an "any-day-of-the-week" trip; however, the best time to travel along Signal St. and Miner St. in the dock area is probably the weekend, when traffic is lightest.

TRAILHEAD: Free parking is available at the Los Angeles "Park and Ride" on Channel St. directly below the Harbor Fwy. in San Pedro. From the Harbor Fwy. southbound, take the Channel St. off-ramp to Gaffey St. Turn right and in one block turn right on Channel St., then left into the parking area. From central San Pedro, take Gaffey St. north to Channel St. as above. From Pacific Ave. northbound, take a left at Channel St. and turn right into the parking area. Another free parking option is at the periphery of Ports O'Call Village. In the latter case, the full round trip can be exercised with a modified itinerary.

Bring water for the first part of the trip, although there are water and restrooms at Ports O'Call in the middle section. There are several restaurants to stop at should hunger or thirst strike along the way.

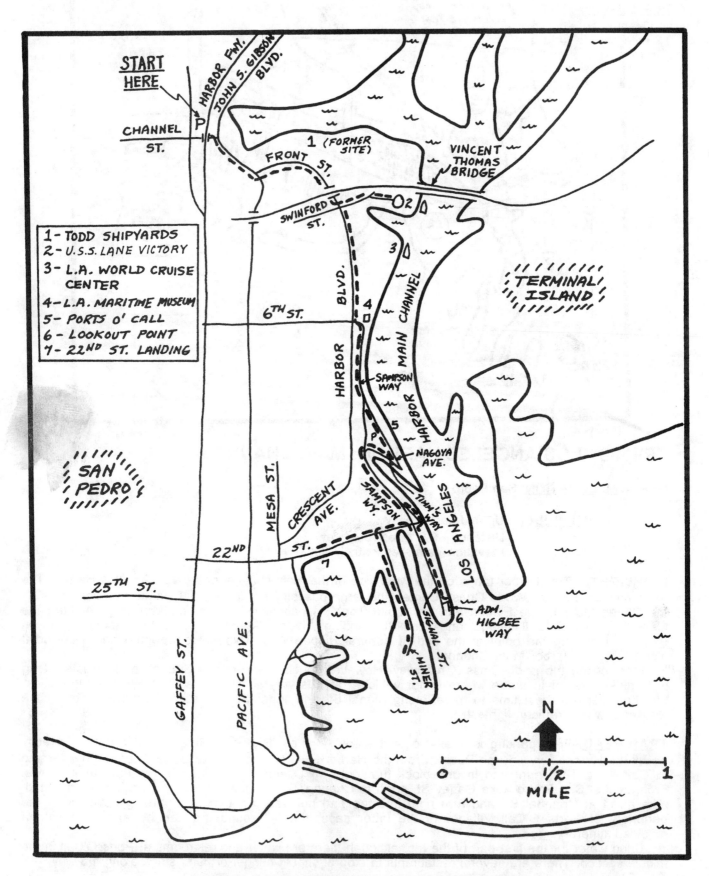

START HERE

HARBOR FWY.
JOHN S. GIBSON BLVD.
CHANNEL ST.
P
FRONT ST.
1 (FORMER SITE)
VINCENT THOMAS BRIDGE
SWINFORD ST.
O 2

1 - TODD SHIPYARDS
2 - U.S.S. LANE VICTORY
3 - L.A. WORLD CRUISE CENTER
4 - L.A. MARITIME MUSEUM
5 - PORTS O' CALL
6 - LOOKOUT POINT
7 - 22ND ST. LANDING

3
TERMINAL ISLAND
6TH ST.
HARBOR BLVD.
4
MAIN CHANNEL
SAMPSON WAY
SAN PEDRO
MESA ST.
CRESCENT AVE.
5
NAGOYA AVE.
SAMPSON WY.
TUNA ST. WAY
LOS ANGELES HARBOR
22ND ST.
7
25TH ST.
6
ADM. HIGBEE WAY
SIGNAL ST.
MINER ST.
GAFFEY ST.
PACIFIC AVE.

N

0   1/2   1
MILE

TRIP #8 - LOS ANGELES HARBOR: MAIN CHANNEL

TRIP DESCRIPTION: Upper Main Channel. Exit the "Park and Ride" to the left (east toward the harbor) on Channel St. and in about 100 feet turn right on Pacific Ave. At (0.2) turn left on Front St. and pedal 0.2 mile past the old Todd Shipyard. At one time it was home to drydocks and a myriad of cranes and ship repair equipment. This street fuses into Harbor Blvd. and in 0.8 mile reaches Swinford St.

Turn left and cruise on Swinford St. into a small parking area with a close-up view of the U.S. World Cruise Center (to the right) and, most likely, a large cruise ship. Continue east and cycle through the pay parking gate (don't pay) and pass by the U.S.S. Lane Victory, a refurbished World War II merchant ship and scenic attraction. (This operational vessel relaced the Spirit of Los Angeles and the venerable S.S. Princess Louise -- where we were married!).

Continue to the Banquet Pavilion, Catalina Island boat terminal and helicopter pads and enjoy a neck-breaking view of the Vincent Thomas Bridge from its underside. Return to Harbor Blvd. (1.0) and turn left onto the sidewalk along the street. Bike beside the harbor cranes and cargo containers for 0.9 mile and turn left at Sixth St.

Main Channel from Admiral Higbee Way

L.A. Maritime Museum and Ports O' Call Village. Just beyond the turnoff is the L.A. Maritime Museum with a fine display of nautical artifacts, historical L.A. maritime goodies, and a great scale model of the Titanic. Turn right on Sampson Way and continue to the middle of the Ports O'Call Village parking lot (2.4). Stop and take a walking tour of this interesting village. Shop, have a bite to eat, or for "hard-core" bikers, forget the rest break and continue along Nagoya Ave.

In 0.1 mile at a locked gate, make a sharp right turn and return along Timm's Wy. This is a great area to check out the local fishing fleet close-up. Bike 0.1 mile, passing a little outdoor cafe and make a hard left, returning to Sampson Way. Continue south on Sampson Way, staying on the marked scenic route. At (3.0) there is an interesting view across the channel into a Navy drydock. Shortly, the road turns to the right (west) and passes the landmark Canetti's Seafood Grotto (great fish dishes); the street name is now 22nd St.

The "Piers" and Twenty-Second Street Landing. In a few hundred feet, turn left on Signal St. Cruise down the road until it jogs to left and becomes Admiral Higbee Wy. At (3.6) the road ends at the tiny park-like area at the end of the landfill pier. There is a great view across the main channel into Reservation Point and to outer L.A. Harbor, and this is a pleasant place to stop for a breather.

Return to 22nd St. (4.2), make a left turn, and continue for about 0.1 mile. Turn left at Miner St. and head down another landfill pier. There is nearly continuous marina and a string of pleasure boats to the right. At (4.7) the route passes a yacht and marine supply store. At (5.1) at a parking lot near the pier's end, check out the San Pedro Boat Works or gaze in awe at the mammoth coal conveyer on the east side. Return to 22nd St., turn left, and pedal to the 22nd St. Landing for a close-up look at the local fishing fleet (6.2). This is a great place to buy fresh fish before heading back to the car and home.

CONNECTING TRIPS: 1) Connection with the bike route to San Pedro Beaches Tour (Trip #7) - continue west on 22nd St. 0.7 mile past the 22nd St. Landing and turn left on Via Cabrillo Marina to the Cabrillo Marina; 2) connection with the bike route to L.A. Harbor/East and West Basins (Trip #9) - after returning almost to the "Park and Ride" area on Pacific Ave., continue past Channel St. on Pacific Ave. as it transitions into John S. Gibson Blvd.

TRIP #9 - LOS ANGELES HARBOR: EAST AND WEST BASINS

GENERAL LOCATION: San Pedro, Wilmington, L.A. Harbor

LEVEL OF DIFFICULTY: One way - easy; up and back - easy to moderate
   Distance - 9.6 miles (one way)
   Elevation gain - essentially flat

HIGHLIGHTS: At its best, this is a free-form bike trip with no set route. However, a reference route is provided which allows a chance to visit the Los Angeles Harbor first hand and close up. This is one of three trips (also see Trips #10 and #11) that tour the harbor area west of the Los Angeles River. Most of the suggested route is Class X, but generally on small streets with limited traffic on weekends. The tour passes near several freighter loading docks, the classic old Matson Terminal, and terminates at the East Basin Yacht Center (anchorage).

TRAILHEAD: Free public automobile parking is available at the Los Angeles "Park and Ride" located on Channel St. directly below the Harbor Fwy. in San Pedro. From the Harbor Fwy. southbound, take the Channel St. off-ramp to Gaffey St. Turn right and in one block turn right again on Channel St., then left into the parking area. From central San Pedro, take Gaffey St. north to Channel St. as above. From Pacific Ave. northbound, take a left at Channel St. and turn right into the parking area.
   Bring a full water supply. There are gas stations near the trailhead and cafes at the end of the trip, but no water stops in the middle segment.

TRIP DESCRIPTION: West Basin. Exit the "Park and Ride" area and turn left toward the harbor on Channel St. Turn left at the road's end (a few hundred feet) onto John S. Gibson Dr. (note that the street is named Pacific Ave. to the right). Ride onto the Class I bikepath along the harbor. At about one mile, there are excellent views, from behind the restraining fence, of ships unloading containerized cargo. At Figueroa St. (1.3), the road name becomes Harry Bridges Blvd. and the marked bike route ends.
   Pedal another 0.6 mile and make a right turn on Neptune Ave. The road passes an electrical generating plant and reaches Water St. Turn left, then right in a short distance at Fries Ave. (2.5). The first turn to the right is Pier "A" St. where bikers parallel the railroad tracks and head directly toward the massive Vincent Thomas Bridge. Pier "A" Pl. is effectively at roads' end where there is a closer look at the bridge, as well as views of the L.A. World Cruise Center (3.3).
   Return on Pier "A" St. and turn right on Fries Ave. Turn right again on La Paloma Ave. at (4.4) and take the "loop" tour of Mormon Island (La Paloma to Falcon St. to San Clemente Ave. and back to Fries Ave.). San Clemente Ave. runs right alongside some busy berths and provides ship viewing up close, while Falcon St. leads through a liquid bulk terminal.
   Turn right from Fries Ave. onto Water St. (5.4), and bike across Avalon Blvd., where the road name is now Nissan Wy. True to form, there is an auto storage area near road's end, together with a restricted entry gate leading to a fire station. Return to Avalon Blvd. (6.1), turn right and veer to the right again at Broad Ave., biking to Bridges Blvd. (6.5).
   Turn right and follow the road as it bends Northeast and becomes Alameda St. In this bleak territory to the right are wide expanses of auto storage and the upper East Basin boat docks. The route turns right again on Anaheim St. (7.6). Bike on this poor quality, well-traveled road and make a right turn (south) on Henry Ford Ave. in 0.1 mile.
   East Basin. Follow Henry Ford Ave. and pass over a small marina via a bridge. Stay on this road (do not turn onto the bridge route to the left as bikers are not permitted) and pedal down to the end at the "retired" Henry Ford Bridge (8.7). Turn right and bike on Anchorage Rd. along the Cerritos Channel -- pick your own "dream" yacht or stop and watch some hard work being done on others.
   Continue past Shore Rd. (at the Holiday Harbor sign) (9.1), and take in the additional boat works and boats. Bike to a large free parking lot near the East Basin Yacht Center and turn toward the right on Peninsula Rd. Here is an outstanding view of the container ship terminals and scrap iron

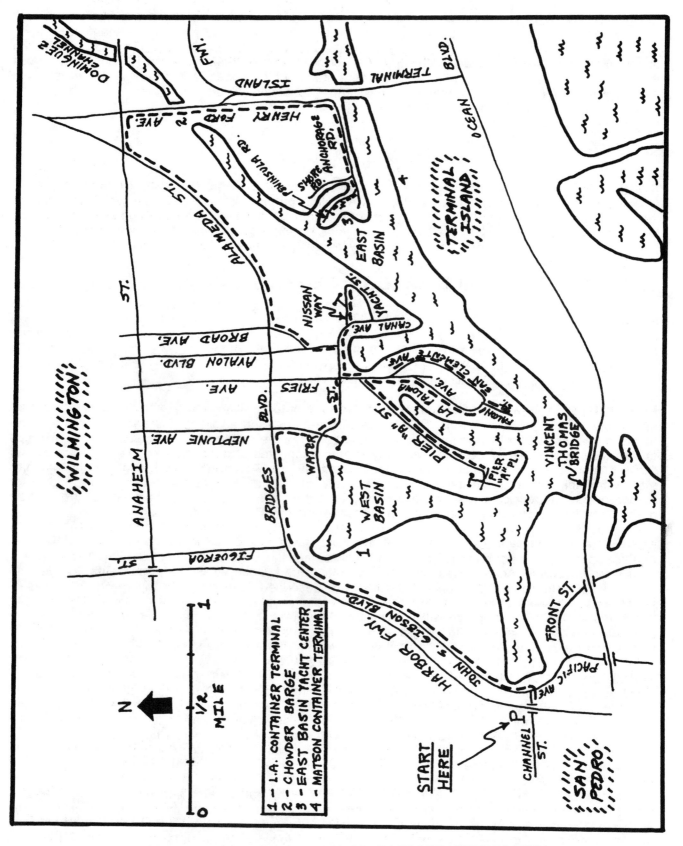

TRIP #9 - LOS ANGELES HARBOR: EAST AND WEST BASINS

"mountains" across the channel. At (9.6) the route ends at a locked gate (walking access only) at the edge of another part of the marina. This is a good spot to take a break at one of the local cafes.

CONNECTING TRIPS: 1) Continuation with the bike route to Long Beach Harbor: Cerritos and Back Channels (Trip #10) - at the trip terminus, return to Henry Ford Ave. and continue to Anaheim St., then turn right; 2) connection with the bike route along the L.A. Harbor: Main Channel (Trip #8) - at the trip origin, leave the "Park and Ride," turn right on Pacific Ave. (street name John S. Gibson Ave. across the intersection); 3) connection with the bike route at Harbor Regional Park (Trip #13) - turn left from John S. Gibson Ave. onto the Figueroa St. bikepath (1.3), continue north on Figueroa St. and take the "L" St. tunnel below the Harbor Fwy. Continue on "L" St. to the park.

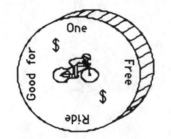

TRIP #10 - LONG BEACH HARBOR: CERRITOS AND BACK CHANNELS

GENERAL LOCATION: Long Beach Harbor, Long Beach

LEVEL OF DIFFICULTY: One way - moderate; up and back - moderate
Distance - 13.1 miles (one way)
Elevation gain - essentially flat

HIGHLIGHTS: There are a multitude of ways to bike the harbor. This sample route provides a "working-man's tour" of Long Beach Harbor. This is one of three trips (see also Trips #9 and #11) that tour the harbor area west of the Los Angeles River. It can serve as the middle link between the other two trips for the truly hearty (nearly 30 miles one way for the suggested routes). Most of the reference tour is Class X, but generally on small streets with limited traffic on weekends. This link of the three harbor trips is probably the least exciting in terms of scenery and landmarks, but has the true harbor flavor for harbor lovers. The tour passes near several freighter docks and provides a spectacular view from below of the Gerald Desmond Bridge and ends at the tourist-friendly Sports Fishing Landing.

TRAILHEAD: Free parking is available at the East Basin Yacht Center at the terminus of Trip #9. Another option is to start from the large parking area near the Long Beach Pilot Station (Trip #11) and do this trip in reverse. Another less attractive option is to park along 9th St. between Santa Fe Ave. and Pico Ave. in Wilmington. The parking locations are described as part of the trip route. In all cases, read the parking signs for latest parking rules.

Bikers should come prepared with a couple of filled water bottles or plan to "beg or borrow" at the commercial establishments along the way. There are cafes at both start and end points, as well as a eateries on Henry Ford Ave. and 9th St. along the way in the middle segment.

TRIP DESCRIPTION: **Cerritos Channel Area.** Start at the East Basin Yacht Center along Anchorage Road and turn left at the road terminus onto Henry Ford Ave. At (1.7) turn right on Anaheim St. and continue on a bridge over the Dominquez Channel (2.0). The route passes under the Terminal Island Fwy. (2.8) and in another 0.1 mile, there is an option to get off Anaheim St. at Paul Jones Ave. and continue on Pier "B" St. For bikers willing to stay with a relatively unattractive but classic harbor route, continue on Anaheim St. to 9th St. (3.1). Veer right (southeast). The route soon passes a grill and pub on the right. At (3.9), the street ends and leaves the run-down industrial area. The intersecting street is Pico Ave. to the left and Pier "B" St. to the right.

Turn right and head into biker's territory with its light traffic. Just beyond, the tour passes a mountain of large tires suited for construction machinery. At (4.8) the route meets Paul Jones Ave. and at (5.3) the road splits, with our route following Pier "B" St. to the right. Bike to the end of the road across from Hanjin Container Terminal (6.9) and turn left on Pier "A" Wy., completing a small loop by

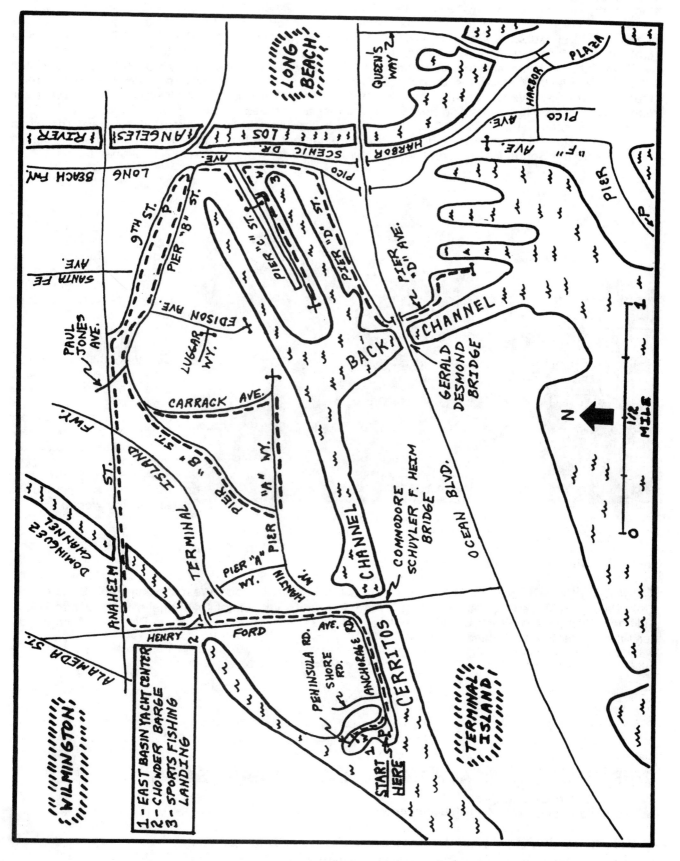

TRIP #10 - LONG BEACH HARBOR: CERRITOS AND BACK CHANNELS

55

turning left again on Carrack Ave. There is a superb over-the-shoulder view of the Gerald Desmond Bridge here. Return about 0.4 mile and turn right on Pier "B" St..

In 0.5 mile (7.9), turn right on Edison Ave. Cruise about 0.4 mile for another great view of the channel, as well as a mammoth gypsum storage dome, then return to Pier "B" St. Turn right and at (8.9) return to Pico Ave.

Turn right, and almost immediately, pass the freeway ramps, bike beneath an overpass, and then turn right at Pier "C" St. At the gate, make a U-turn onto the one-way street going in the opposite direction, then jog over to a small paralleling road which reverses your direction again. This small road leads to a parking area sitting next to several massive cranes.

Return almost to Pico Ave. (10.1) and turn right into the Queen's Wharf parking area. The wharf has a coffee shop, the venerable Queen's Wharf Restaurant and well-stocked fresh fish market. Behind the market is the Sports Fishing Landing, the starting point for many "part-time" fisherman's trips.

Cerritos Channel Container Terminal

Back Channel Area. Cycle 0.3 mile on Pico Ave. and turn right on Pier "D" St. Continue about 0.6 mile to the gate at the fire boat station (11.3) and turn left on Pier "D" Ave. This route travels directly under the middle of the Gerald Desmond Bridge and along the Back Channel; the spectacular view of the bridge is a guaranteed "neck breaker." At (11.5) the road swings left before reaching a locked gate and continues about 0.1 mile to another closed gate. Barring the ship traffic, this seems like the end of the world!

Return the same way and turn left at Pico Ave. (12.8). All that remains is to backtrack 0.3 mile to the Sports Fishing Landing.

CONNECTING TRIPS: 1) Continuation of the L.A. Harbor: East and West Basins (Trip #9) - from the East Basin Yacht Center, return to Henry Ford Ave., turn left, pedal to Anaheim St. and turn left; 2) linkage with the Long Beach Harbor: Southeast Basin (Trip #11) - bike south on Pico Ave. from the trip terminus at the Sports Fishing Landing.

TRIP #11 - LONG BEACH HARBOR: SOUTHEAST BASIN

GENERAL LOCATION: Long Beach Harbor, Long Beach

LEVEL OF DIFFICULTY: One way - easy; up and back - easy to moderate
                Distance - 8.4 miles (one way)
                Elevation gain - essentially flat

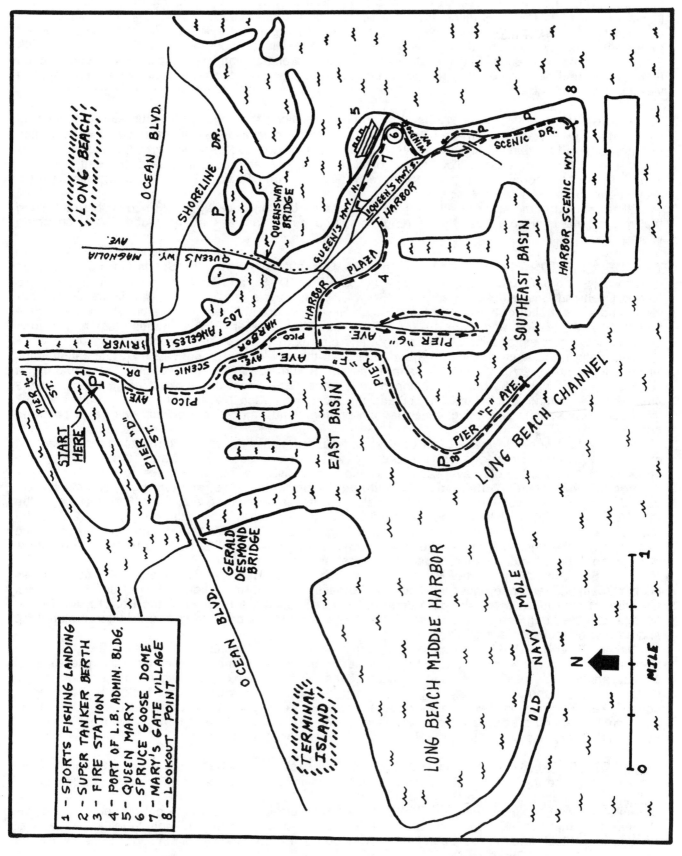

TRIP #11 - LONG BEACH HARBOR: SOUTHEAST BASIN

BICYCLE RIDES: LOS ANGELES COUNTY

HIGHLIGHTS: This free-form trip has no set route; however, the reference route provides a chance to see the harbor area at its best. Of the three trips visiting the L.A. Harbor/Long Beach Harbor areas (Trips #9 and #10), this is definitely the most scenic and landmark-filled.

This trip can serve as the end link of Trips #9 and #10 (over 30 miles one way for the suggested route) or can be taken alone. Most of the suggested route is Class X, but generally on small streets with limited traffic on weekends. The trip starts in a super-tanker berthing area, includes the Long Beach Pilot Station and harbor views, visits the Queen Mary and ends at the end of Harbor Scenic Dr. with views of San Pedro Bay.

TRAILHEAD: Free parking is available at several places along the suggested route, allowing bikers to choose their own starting point and free-form route. Parking is available in the Port of Long Beach Administration Bldg. parking lots (Sunday only), in either of two large scenic parking areas off of Pier "F" Ave. near the Long Beach Pilot Station, or at the equally scenic parking area at the end of Harbor Scenic Dr. Another option is to park at Shoreline Park in Long Beach (Trip #14) and cross Queen's Way bridge to the Southeast Basin.

Bikers should come stocked with a filled water bottle or plan once again to "beg or borrow" along the way. There is a cafe near the starting point and public facilities at the Queen Mary shopping village area.

TRIP DESCRIPTION: **Pico Ave. and Pier "F" Ave.** Our route starts from the Sports Fishing Landing as described in Trip #10. Bike south on Pico Ave. past Pier "D" St. and Broadway, then duck under the Gerald Desmond Bridge ramps. Pass Pier "F" St. (0.6) and cycle onto a bridge with interesting harbor views and a great shot of the City of Long Beach Skyline. A downhill leads to Harbor Plaza and a right turn (1.3). A short climb and a veer to the left places bikers on Pier "F" Ave. heading south. The road passes a large coal storage facility, bends right and cruises by a house-size mound of sea salt.

Turn right into a large parking area and check out the now-closed Long Beach Naval Station ships which still houses a few U.S. Navy ships in its harbor. Returning to Pier "F" Ave. bike to the end into a large parking lot with a harbor fire station on one edge (2.5). From this lookout point, check out the busy channel leading to the outer harbor and the old Long Beach Naval Station Mole. With any luck the Boeing consortium sea-going space launch platform and launch control ship will be in port and berthed there.

Pier "F" Ave. bends to the left just beyond and passes alongside several terminals before reaching a closed gate near piers' end (3.1) There are views of the outer breakwater, the Queen's Gate breakwater entrance, the old naval station site and a long-distance look at San Pedro Hill.

Port of Long Beach Administration Building. Return to Pico Ave. and turn right. The street, now named Pier "G" Ave., continues to a locked gate near two large storage elevators (5.4). Return on the Pier "G" Ave. northbound loop (one-way traffic) and turn right at Harbor Plaza (6.2). In 0.2 mile the road angles to the right. A left turn at the next junction leads to Queen's Way Bridge, but the reference route stays to the right and passes the Port of Long Beach Administration Building (6.4). Stop and take a close look at the historical murals painted on the face of this building.

H. M. S. Queen Mary. Harbor Plaza bears left and ends at Harbor Scenic Dr. (6.8). Turn left, cross Harbor Scenic Dr. and ride under the freeway overpass. Turn right on Queen's Hwy. North and revel in the glory of the Queen Mary, the dome that previously housed the Hughes Flying Boat Exhibit Center (Spruce Goose), and Mary's Gate Village. The village is a nice place for a rest and replenishment stop and has sturdy racks for locking bikes.

Harbor Scenic Drive. Pedal back on Queen's Way N. and Windsor Wy. until the latter fuses with Harbor Scenic Dr. (7.5). Stay right and duck beneath an overpass, then bike along a 0.6-mile string of public parking sites beside the road's eastern edge. There are excellent views of the Long Beach Outer Harbor, Long Beach city skyline, cruising yachts, and with a little luck, maybe even a supertanker. The ride on the roadway ends at a private entry gate (8.4). Continue back north to the open public parking area and have a few laughs with the individuals and families who are fishing at lands' end. There is a simply unique view of the outer harbor from this area.

CONNECTING TRIPS: 1) Continuation with the Long Beach Harbor: Cerritos and Back Channels route (Trip #10) - at the trip origin at the Sports Fishing Landing, continue north on Pico Ave.; 2) connection with the Long Beach Shoreline Park tour (Trip #14) - at (4.5) on Harbor Plaza, turn left (northeast) on Queen's Way and continue over Queen's Way Bridge. (There is a Class I path on the south side of the bridge.) Exit right at the "Convention Center/Shoreline Area" turnoff and right again at Pine Ave. Parking is available around the Shoreline Park lagoons, in the Shoreline Marina Village parking lot or on the side streets of Shoreline Dr.

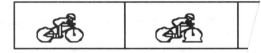

TRIP #12 - TERMINAL ISLAND TOUR

GENERAL LOCATION: Terminal Island

LEVEL OF DIFFICULTY: Loop - easy
Distance - 6.0 miles (lo
Elevation gain - essen

HIGHLIGHTS: This is a touring trip around an i
for that matter).The tour offers some great vista
the home of the long-departed tuna fleet at
ships. This is one of those trips for bikers whu
just flat out like to explore out-of-the way territory. The
with very little traffic on weekends.

TRAILHEAD: On weekends, free parking is readily available throughout the islanu. ,
the streets are overrun with truck and auto traffic.) This journey starts from Ferry St. acros̄ ..
Federal Building where there is parking in the shade of a few eucalyptus trees. From San Pedro, cross
the Vincent Thomas Bridge and exit to the right just beyond the toll gate ("free" direction). Follow the
road through a hairpin turn and continue to the road's end at Ferry St. Cross Ferry St. and find parking.

From the Long Beach area, cross the Gerald Desmond Bridge and continue on Ocean Blvd. which
eventually changes its name to Seaside Ave. Just before passing under the Vincent Thomas Bridge,
turn left on Ferry St. and proceed under the bridge to parking across from the Federal Building. From
Wilmington, take the Terminal Island Fwy. across the Commodore Shuyler F. Heim Bridge to the road's
terminus at Ocean Ave. Turn right and continue on Ocean Blvd./Seaside Ave. as just described.

The single walking access to the island is over the Gerald Desmond Bridge. The views from the
bridge are breath-taking! However the access is steep, on a small raised walkway (it is nearly
impossible to walk a bike on the walkway), and right next to fast-moving traffic. Truck your bike over on
a car bike rack unless you enjoy cheap thrills!

Bring water, munchies, and make a pit-stop before you start. There are no gas stations and only
two small cafes and a mini-market on the island.

TRIP DESCRIPTION: Earle St. Head north on Ferry St. and pass under the Vincent Thomas Bridge. At
Seaside Ave. turn left and pedal back under the bridge. From this area, there is an excellent view
across the channel to the L.A. World Cruise Center, the U.S.S. Lane Victory and a "neck breaker" view
from below the Vincent Thomas Bridge. The street name changes to Earle St. and continues another
1.1 miles past massive coal conveyers as well as large lots of cargo containers and new cars. At the
end of Earle St., jog right and work toward harborside at a tugboat docking area.

Fish Harbor. Backtrack along the same route and turn left (west) on Cannery St. (2.1). In a short
distance, turn left and follow Barracuda St. south to a terminus at a pet food processing plant. Turn
right on Sardine St. and left at road's end onto Ways St.. A short spur leads to street's end at Fish
Harbor. At this pleasant point (pleasant view, unpleasant odor) is a view down the docks which berthed
a massive tuna fleet 20-25 years ago.

Return along Ways St. and turn left on Cannery St. The area here almost has the appearance and
desolation to remind one of a long-deserted razed town (at least on weekends). Turn left (south) on
Tuna St. (3.3) and pass the local mini-mart. The street terminates at Wharf St. at a classic Fish Harbor
viewpoint. Turn right and continue to South Seaside Ave. (3.6).

Drydocks/Federal Prison. The tour reaches a nice viewpoint in 0.2 mile that provides a view of
outer Fish Harbor as well as the ships at anchor in outer Los Angeles Harbor. The road veers right and
passes a small rustic cafe (3.9). In a short distance are two massive drydocks; if the drydocks are
occupied, the close-up, bow-on look at these mammoth ships is nothing but impressive! The path
terminates at the Federal Prison at the visitors parking area (4.1). (Don't venture in and take notes, as
we found out when a guard in the tower above used a bullhorn to ask that we leave!).

Terminal Way Return Route. Retrace the original route and continue on S. Seaside Ave. past
Wharf St. S. Seaside Ave. bends right (east) and fuses into Terminal Way (4.7). In 0.2 mile, the bike

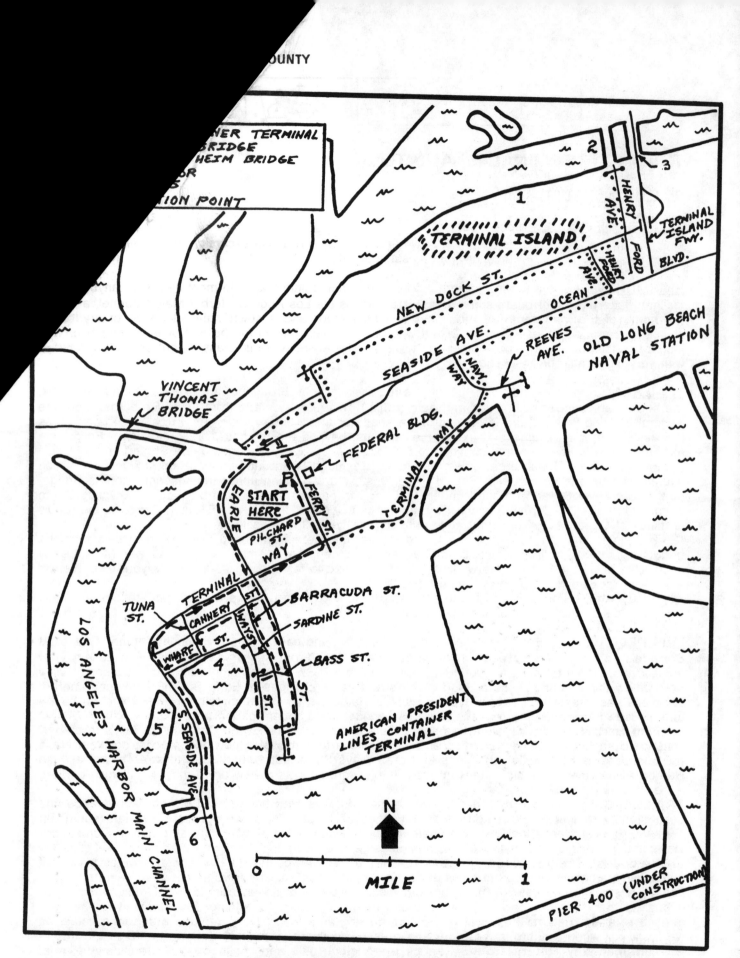

TRIP #12 - TERMINAL ISLAND TOUR

route meets Earle St.; here a biker can take a well deserved food and drink break at "salty" Joe Biff's Bar and Grill and shoot some pool, too. Continue on Terminal Way to Ferry St. and turn left (north). The route passes Pilchard St. (5.8) and returns to the Federal Building at 6.0 miles from the trip start.

Trip Excursion. At Ferry St. and Terminal Wy. (at 5.3 miles in the description above),cycle east on the latter street. The road veers right and enters an elevated area with a nifty vista of the Long Beach city skyline. The route passes a multi-domed sanitation facility and a gigantic container storage area, then cruises the periphery of a massive coal/petroleum coke facility. The road becomes Reeves Ave. and ends at Seaside Ave. in another 0.1 mile.

Bike on busy Seaside Ave./Ocean Blvd. and turn left at Henry Ford Ave. A right turn at the next intersection (New Dock St. to the left) leads to a close-up look of the long-retired Henry Ford Drawbridge at the end of Henry Ford Ave. (7.7). Return to New Dock St. and cycle 1.5 miles past a series of shipping terminals and into a massive truck/container/railroad car staging and storage area.

Backtrack to Henry Ford Ave. and Ocean Blvd. (11.0). Turn right and bike with the heavy traffic, following Seaside Ave. to the right at the Vincent Thomas Bridge entry junction (12.2). Pedal another 0.5 mile to Ferry St., turn left and pass under the bridge. Continue a short distance to the trip origin (12.8).

CONNECTING TRIPS: (Review the warnings in the "Trailhead" section before attempting the Gerald Desmond Bridge connector.) 1) Connection with the Long Beach Shoreline Park route (Trip #14) - continue over the Gerald Desmond Bridge and the bridge over the Los Angeles River. Turn right on Shoreline Dr. and turn right again at Golden Shore Blvd.; 2) connection with the southern segment of the Lario Trail (Trip #32B) - continue as above except turn right into the first public parking area on Shoreline Dr.

TRIP #13 - HARBOR REGIONAL PARK

GENERAL LOCATION: Harbor City

LEVEL OF DIFFICULTY: Loop - easy
Distance - 4.5 miles (loop); 5.5 miles (with campus excursion)
Elevation gain - essentially flat

HIGHLIGHTS: This is a short trip that explores Harbor Regional Park. More specifically, it visits Harbor Lake and its highly accessible west side, as well as its less visited east side. The trip provides a good look at the lake and the marshy wildlife preserve that surrounds it. In addition, there is a side excursion through the L.A. Harbor College campus. The segment along the lake is Class I. The route along Pacific Coast Highway (PCH) and Figueroa Pl. is on Class X roadway; however, there is plenty of room for bikers. The route through the ride mixes travel on roads with light traffic and combination bikeways/walkways.

TRAILHEAD: Free parking is available at the park. From the Harbor Fwy., exit at Anaheim St. and head west about one mile. Turn right into the park at the Harbor Regional Park sign. From Anaheim St., Palos Verdes Dr. North or Gaffey St. (these streets intersect near the park), take Vermont St. north at the intersection. In about 0.3 mile turn right into the park at the park sign. Note that there is a separate bike/walk access to the park. Just east of Gaffey St. at the intersection is a path which travels under Anaheim St. and enters at an undeveloped area near the southwest end of the park.

Bring a light water supply. There are water and restroom facilities at the park and city college.

TRIP DESCRIPTION: **The Overlook.** The bikepath follows the edge of the lake with spokes radiating out from this path to the individual parking areas. From the southernmost parking lot, head toward the Anaheim St. entrance and take a paved turnoff to the small roofed overlook above the south edge of the lake (0.1). There is a water fountain at this dandy spot.

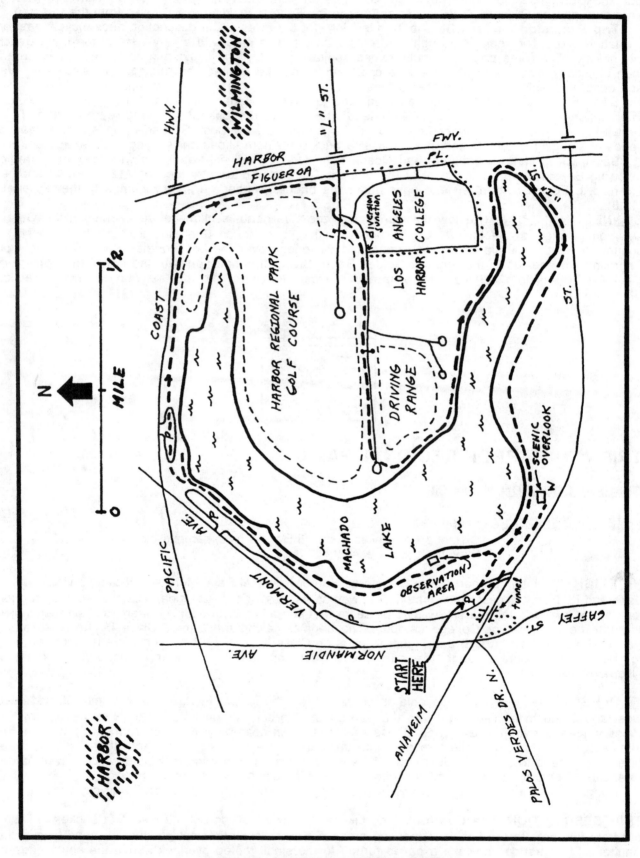

TRIP #13 - HARBOR REGIONAL PARK

Harbor Lake, West and North Sides. Head back to the parking lot and then follow the path which leads to the main bike trail/walkway along the lake. At (0.3) cruise by an observation area with a couple of sheds and a porta-pottie and at (0.5) pass a point which juts out into the lake; this is "duck city" with every type of duck you can imagine. There are usually plenty of fisherman along the lake in harmony with the ducks. At (0.6) pass a second lake finger and restroom just beyond. Continue around to the north end of the lake to the end of the trail (1.1). Head towards the northern parking lot and follow it parallel to PCH about 0.1 mile. At the end of the parking lot, join PCH and ride along the Harbor Lake drainage (1.3). At (1.8) turn right (south) on Figueroa Pl. and continue 0.4 mile to "L" St. Next is a right on "L" St. onto the L.A. Harbor College Campus.

Harbor College Campus and East Side. Ride 0.2 mile on "L" St. until it jogs to the left along a fence. The Class I path zigs left in a short distance. A diversion trip through the campus (described later) is straight ahead, while the reference route follows the road right (south) to an auto blockade near the head of the driving range. The Class II path heads south to the lake proper and then bends southeast (2.7).

The South Side Return. The path skirts the lake, passing alongside the campus' outer reaches before reaching its easternmost point (3.5). What remains is a one-mile traverse next to the undeveloped south side of the lake. This segment includes a pass directly below the scenic overlook and a return to the start point (4.5).

Westside Lakeshore in Harbor regional Park

Additional Campus Excursion. At the diversion junction mentioned above, cycle south next to the athletic fields. Cycle along the parking area and enjoy the view into the southeast corner of the preserve. The roadway continues along the marsh, and in about 0.3 mile, returns to Figueroa Pl. A left turn onto that street leads back to "L" St. and the college entrance, then back to the diversion junction. The diversion route is about one mile. Note that a bikers can make an interesting route completely off the roads by just wandering throughout the campus.

CONNECTING TRIPS: 1) Connection with the northern section of Palos Verdes Peninsula Loop (Trip #6A) - take the bike underpass to Gaffey St. Continue along the south side of Palos Verdes Dr. North for 0.8 mile. At Western Ave. cross the street to the west side; 2) connection with the L.A. Harbor: East and West Basins tour (Trip #9) - take "L" St. under the Harbor Fwy. an in 0.1 mile turn right (south) on Figueroa St. Bike about one mile to link up with Trip #9 on Bridges Blvd.

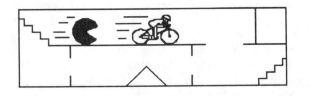

TRIP #14 - LONG BEACH SHORELINE PARK

GENERAL LOCATION: Long Beach

LEVEL OF DIFFICULTY: Loop - easy
Distance - 7.6 miles; 9.0 miles with excursion trip
Elevation gain - essentially flat

HIGHLIGHTS: This is one of the prime candidates for an easy-going family trip. Almost the entire trip is on an excellent, well-marked Class I bike route and resides within the Shoreline Park/Long Beach Marina area away from heavy traffic. The scenery is great and there are plenty of recreation spots along the way, including playgrounds, barbecue and picnic facilities, and fishing platforms. The trip is of modest length but provides a wide variety of interesting biking territory, including activity-filled Rainbow Harbor, the Long Beach Aquarium, views of water skiers in Queensway Bay, the Catalina Island cruise ships at Queensbay Landing, the yacht-filled downtown Long Beach Marina, and terrific views of the Queen Mary. Bike traffic is light and the bike lanes are large; however, the Shoreline Park and Marina Green Park areas have heavy competing foot traffic on pleasant days, particularly weekends.

An option exists to add a small segment to the trip. This involves crossing Shoreline Dr. and traveling the bikepath along the Hyatt Regency/Rainbow Lagoon Park and into the Long Beach Convention Center area.

TRAILHEAD: From Ocean Blvd. in Long Beach, turn south (toward the harbor) on Pine Ave. and continue to its terminus at S. Pine Ave. Circle. There is limited, time-restricted parking here. From the Long Beach Fwy., head south and take the *Downtown Long Beach* exit. Use the turnoff to *Convention Center/Catalina Island* and drive along Shoreline Dr. past the *Golden Shore* exit. Turn right on S. Pine Ave. Circle, which is the southward extension of Pine Ave.

There is also pay parking at the parking structure north of the aquarium, as well as the area east of Shoreline Village. (The easternmost parking lot is free.) For busy days, pay parking is available between Ocean Blvd. and Shoreline Dr. An option is to park for free along the north-south streets above Ocean Blvd., then bike to the trailhead. Check parking signs carefully if the latter option is used.

There are plenty of water and public restroom facilities along the route. Shoreline Village offers many options to "eat, drink and be merry."

TRIP DESCRIPTION: **Rainbow Harbor and L.A. River Channel.** From the parking area, bike to the harbor edge and take the walking/bikepath west (towards Queensway Bridge). Near the west end of the harbor, veer left and pass alongside the Long Beach Aquarium of the Pacific. Pass the Pierpoint Landing (with bait/tackle/snacks/drink shop) and continue on this path to the L.A. River Channel. Take a hard right turn (north), staying along the channel. Note the steps leading to the south side of the Queensway Bridge just before passing underneath (0.4). There is a Class I path on the bridge's south lane. Follow the path around the entire Queensway Landing rim and admire both the small lighthouse and Catalina cruisers (1.1).

Return from the rim to the main bikepath, turn right and backtrack about 100 yards. Bike up the east ramp of the Catalina Landing Building to the second-story walking plaza. Leave the building via the west ramp and pass in front of the CSU Chancellor's Offices, then turn left (south) along the Golden Shore Reserve and bike to its terminus (1.5). Backtrack and turn left (west), following the path as it makes a sharp turn to the left and travels alongside a recreation vehicle parking area. In 0.1 mile is the L.A. River and the marked entry to the Lario Trail (1.9). This is a great spot to watch water skiers and jet skiers.

Return to the Queensway Landing. Just before passing under the Queensway Bridge, note the steps to the left; this is a route up to the bridge's southbound lanes. Pedal along the river to a three-way junction (2.6). A hard left leads to Aquarium Wy. This trip continues back to the Pierpoint Landing area and hugs the river, heading to an excellent vantage point at the entrance to Rainbow Harbor (2.9). Along the way are alternate paths that criss-cross the grassy knolls to the left. There are benches, playgrounds, restrooms and vista points scattered among the knolls. Next, follow the path as it curves and reverses direction, now following along the Rainbow Harbor edge. The harbor and Long Beach city views are gorgeous! The loop is completed near the Pierpoint Landing area (3.1).

Long Beach Marina. Return to the original parking area and turn east along the harbor's edge. Follow the walking path/bikepath for about 0.1 mile. The bikeway crosses under a concrete walkway

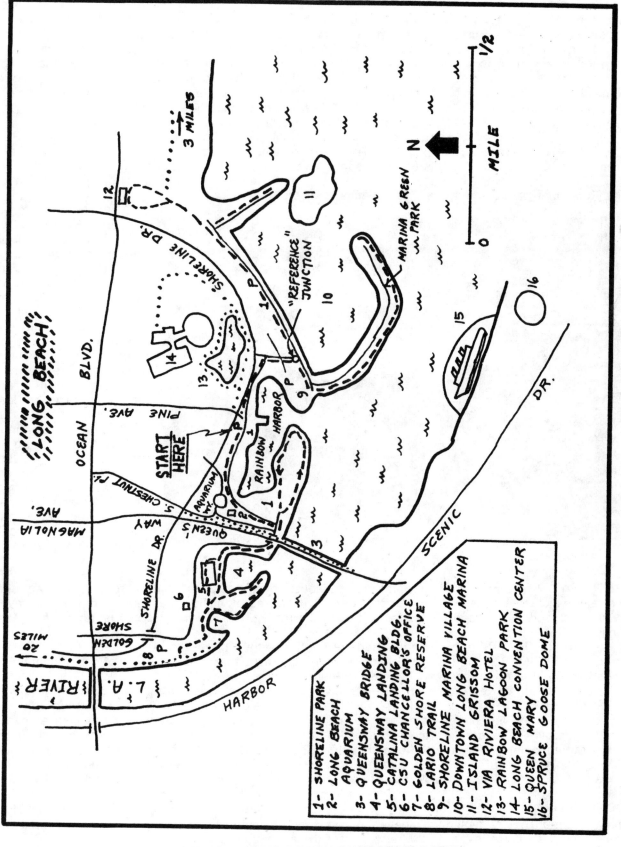

1- SHORELINE PARK
2- LONG BEACH AQUARIUM
3- QUEENSWAY BRIDGE
4- QUEENSWAY LANDING
5- CATALINA LANDING BLDG.
6- CSU CHANCELLOR'S OFFICE
7- GOLDEN SHORE RESERVE
8- LARIO TRAIL
9- SHORELINE MARINA VILLAGE
10- DOWNTOWN LONG BEACH MARINA
11- ISLAND GRISSOM
12- VIA RIVIERA HOTEL
13- RAINBOW LAGOON PARK
14- LONG BEACH CONVENTION CENTER
15- QUEEN MARY
16- SPRUCE GOOSE DOME

TRIP #14 - LONG BEACH SHORELINE PARK

65

(3.4). Stop and climb the overhead walkway which provides a views of the harbor, channel, marina and the convention center area.

Turn right (east), paralleling Shoreline Dr., and bike to Shoreline Village Dr., the entry road to Shoreline Village. Turn right and soon cross the access to the village pay parking area. The southbound route then crosses a street which is along the marina edge. There is a flower-bedecked vehicle turning circle here. The bike route will explore both directions at this reference junction (3.8).

First take a right turn (west) at the junction and bike along the Shoreline Village perimeter about 0.1 mile to the road's end. To the right is Parker's Light House. Turn left onto the outermost bike trail along the jetty. Ride along the jetty and enjoy the vista of the pleasure craft and large commercial ships in the harbor, a spectacular view of the Queen Mary across the channel, and a good look at the yachts in the marina. Stop and watch from one of several observation/fishing platforms.

Ride to the end of the jetty at the Downtown Marina Office Building (Department of Parks, Recreation and Marine Activities) (4.5). There are benches, playgrounds, restrooms and view areas scattered among the knolls. This is a fine spot to watch the marine craft slipping by Island Grissom on their way to or from the marina. Follow the same path back to the reference junction noted above, since the inner path along the jetty is off limits to bikers (5.3).

View from Catalina Landing Building

Pass this reference junction and pedal east along the path through the parking area to the excellent city beach (5.8). At a nearby junction is a small southbound asphalt road along a chain-link fence. Bypass this route and swing north, passing a restroom, then a snack shop/equipment rental shop. There is a Class I path which junctions east in this area, continuing three miles along the beach to Belmont Shore. However the reference bikepath turns north at this point and terminates in the parking lot just beneath the historic Via Riviera Hotel (6.0).

Return 0.2 mile and turn south onto the previously bypassed small asphalt road. This road follows the jetty which forms the east end of the marina. It passes alongside the edge of one of the favorite local beach spots. The road terminates at one of the more popular fishing spots just across from Island Grissom (6.6).

Return to the reference junction and turn left (west). Follow the route back to the Pine St. intersection (7.5). Turn left and continue another 0.1 mile to the parking lot at the trip origin. An option at the Pine St. intersection is to take the short side trip below.

Long Beach Convention Center. Pedal north across Pine Ave. and take the bikepath to the right alongside the Hyatt Regency Hotel. Soon the path travels along a lagoon. Take a short trip around the lagoon and enjoy the birds, water fountains and the serene surroundings (do not bike across the footbridges over the lagoon as they were not designed for bicycle travel). At (0.5) return to the lagoon loop starting point and bike on the path along Shoreline Dr. until it terminates at the Long Beach Convention Center (0.7). Options here are to cruise the convention center area and then the quaint Seaside Ave. area (Class X roadway) or to return directly to the parking area at the Rainbow Harbor.

CONNECTING TRIPS: 1) Continuation with the Los Angeles River/Lario Trail (Trip #20B) - bike to the marked Lario Trail as described above; 2) connection with the Long Beach Harbor: Southeast Basin route (Trip #11) - bike to the northwest corner of the aquarium parking structure (at Shoreline Dr. across from S. Chestnut Pl.) Stay to the left and enter the separated Class I path on the Queensway Bridge; 3) connection with the Belmont Shore/Naples Tour (Trip #15) - turn east at the junction at (5.8) in the trip writeup.

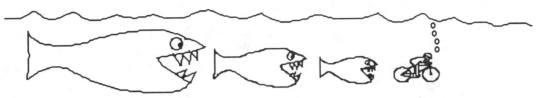

TRIP #15 - BELMONT SHORE/NAPLES TOUR

GENERAL LOCATION: Long Beach

LEVEL OF DIFFICULTY: Loop - easy
Distance - 10.9 miles, 12.9 miles with Marine Stadium Park extension
Elevation gain - essentially flat

HIGHLIGHTS: This is a very pleasant trip, particularly for sightseeing, which concentrates on the beach community setting. The trip starts at the Belmont Pier, transverses a jetty to the Alamitos Bay entrance, passes onto Naples Island and ends at Long Beach Marine Stadium. An alternate and more direct return route along the Alamitos Bay shore is also provided. The highlight of the trip is the Naples tour.

A reference route is provided, although bikers might plan for a more thorough exploration of this island community, particularly around the Rivo Alto and Naples Canals. The route is a mix of Class I along the jetty, Class I and Class X throughout the Naples area, and a mix of Class II and Class X along the Marine Stadium. The only heavy traffic area is along 2nd St. leading into Naples.

TRAILHEAD: Free parking is available along Ocean Blvd. or pay parking near the Belmont Pier. Other options are to alter the trip itinerary and start at other free parking locations along the route (for instance, at the end of the jetty or along Appian Wy in Naples).

From Long Beach proper, take Ocean Blvd. southeast into Belmont Shore. Continue to the right on Ocean Blvd. at the Livingstone Dr. junction and park along the street or in the pay parking area on the beach side of Ocean Blvd. From Pacific Coast Highway (PCH), turn west onto 2nd St. (Westminster Ave. to the east) and drive 1.2 miles across two bridges. Just after the second bridge, turn left on Bay Shore Ave. and continue to its terminus with Ocean Blvd. Turn right and park along Ocean Blvd., or ride one mile further and park at Belmont Pier.

Bring a light water supply. Water and restrooms are available at the pier. There is plenty of water along the way and several opportunities for other "pit stops."

TRIP DESCRIPTION: Belmont Shore. Pedal southeast on Ocean Blvd. and pass Bay Shore Ave. (0.7). Continue about 0.1 mile and turn right (toward the ocean) on 55th Pl. At the end of this pleasant little street is Seaside Walk. Follow this walkway/bikeway and enjoy the beach folk as well as the great views of outer Long Beach Harbor and the ocean. (Maximum speed limit on all walkways is 15 mph and 5 mph when pedestrians are present.)

Ride to the path's end at 69th Pl. (1.7) then follow Ocean Blvd. 0.1 mile further to the end of the jetty. At this point there is parking, a life guard building, and a nice view of the channel and Seaport Village across the channel.

For the return trip, turn right (toward the bay) at 69th Pl. and pedal along Bay Shore Walk to Bay Shore Ave. (2.5). Turn north (right) and cruise along one of the nicer, better sheltered and more populated beaches in the territory. Ride about 0.6 mile further and turn right (west) on 2nd St. Continue on this busy and rather narrow street over the bridge into beautiful Naples.

Naples. This small community consists of three islands, one large island, one small island which is nearly surrounded by the large island, and a second small island which nearly "seals off" the small central island. At the next intersection, turn right at The Toledo and pedal about 0.3 mile (3.4) to another smaller bridge. Cross onto the small central island, pass a small market and bike to the lovely spray water fountain (and drinking fountain) in the pleasant outdoor central plaza (3.6).

Take a spin around the traffic circle and find The Colonnade; follow this little street to its terminus at the grassy mini-park along the bay and turn left (east). Follow the walkway/bikeway around the island and cross the following streets (bridge exits) in succession: Neopolitan Ln. East, The Toledo (east),

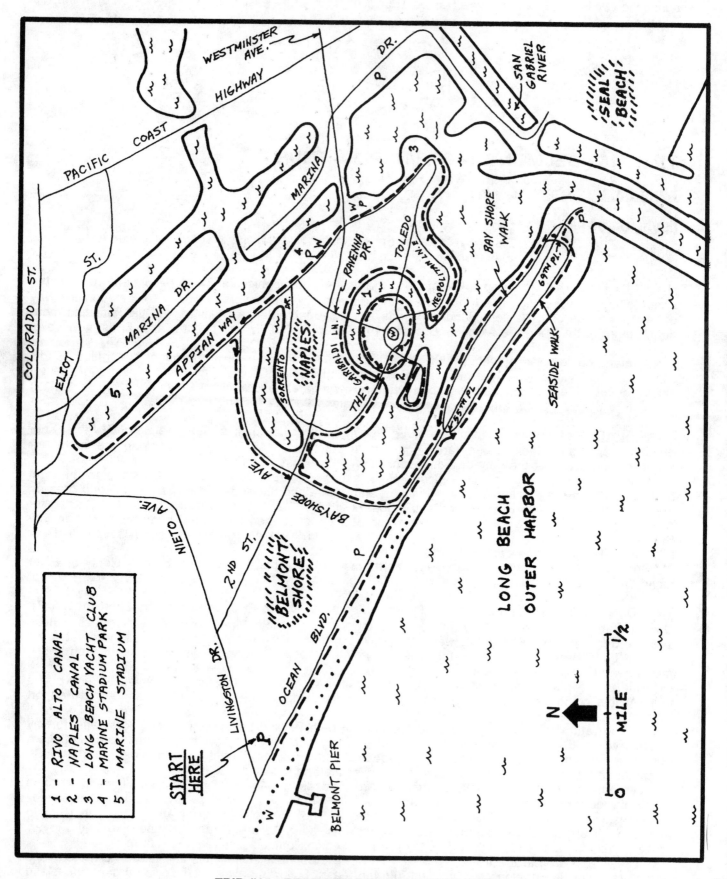

TRIP #15 - BELMONT SHORE/NAPLES TOUR

Ravenna Dr., The Toledo (west), and Neopolitan Ln. West (4.9). (Note that the route zig-zags and appears to end at every street crossing, but continues on the opposite side of the street.) Cross over the bridge at the latter junction and take the small walkway/bikeway (Corso De Napoli) around the smallest of the three islands. Return across the Neopolitan Ln. West bridge (5.4) and backtrack across the central island bridge, returning to the main island.

Turn right immediately at Garibaldi Ln. and follow a small walkway/bikeway along the Rivo Alto Canal. Bike along the small path and admire the tightly packed little community of gardens and varied architecture's along the canal. There are small sailboats, power boats, kayaks and canoes in this 0.8 mile stretch of canal. The street crossings in order are at Ravenna Dr., The Toledo (east), and Neopolitan Ln. West.

Rivo Alto Canal in Naples

The path takes a sharp change of direction at (6.4) and leaves the canal for a 0.7-mile open stretch along Alamitos Bay. At (6.9) the route passes a cozy little overlook park and at (7.1) ends near the Long Beach Yacht Club. This spot is at the southern terminus of Appian Wy. and is one of the better spots to watch the water traffic in Alamitos Bay. Bike 0.1 mile north on Appian Wy. past the yacht basin (parking, water fountain, private restrooms), pass under the 2nd St. bridge and reach Marine Stadium Park at (7.3).

Marine Stadium Park. Marine Stadium Park has parking, a grassy lawn for resting, water and restrooms, a great beach, and a fine place to watch the sailboaters and windsurfers. Pedal north along Appian Wy. (Class II bikepath), pass over the small bridge and turn right about 100 yards before Nieto Ave. At (8.3) is the entrance to the Marine Stadium parking lot (free to bikers). The stadium is a great place to watch boat races and individual power boats performing time trials.

One option at this point is to head north to Nieto Ave., turn right on Eliot St., and bike down Marina Dr. on the other side of the stadium. This route terminates at a launch ramp/view point at the Pete Archer Rowing Center and adds 2.2 miles to the total trip mileage.

Return Route. This route returns directly to Appian Wy. from Marine Stadium. Return south about 0.7 mile and turn right just before the bridge at Bay Shore Ave. (9.0). Cruise 0.9 mile across 2nd St. to Ocean Blvd. and turn right. About 1.0 mile up the road is the Belmont Pier -- a total trip length of 10.9 miles.

CONNECTING TRIPS: Continuation with Long Beach Shoreline Park (Trip #14) - at the trip origin, bike toward the ocean to the Class I beachfront path and turn right (northwest); 2) connection with the trailheads for San Gabriel River Trail and Coyote Creek (Trips #20A, #24, respectively) - from Marine Stadium Park, take Appian Way south of the 2nd St. bridge, turn onto the marked "on-ramp" to 2nd St., and turn right at the next traffic signal at Marina Dr. Take Marina Dr. to the parking area along the San Gabriel River (see Trip #20A instructions for further specifics).

TRIP #16 - EL DORADO PARK

GENERAL LOCATION: Long Beach

LEVEL OF DIFFICULTY: Loop - easy
Distance - 4.3 miles (eastside peripheral loop)
Elevation gain - essentially flat

HIGHLIGHTS: This is near the top of the list as a great family bike route and general outing. The entire route resides within East El Dorado Regional Park. There is something for everybody. The Class I bikepaths and routes along the park roadways are relatively uncrowded and in great condition. Cyclists can roam just the park boundaries in the two basic picnic areas (Area II north of Spring St. and Area III north of Wardlow Rd.) and travel 4.3 miles. The route is free form and bikers can travel the interior park paths as well, putting in whatever mileage is suitable. There are four small lakes to cruise around, lovely stands of trees, and a variety of beautiful birds, including ducks and geese in the lakes.

   In addition to the biking paths, there is an archery range, model boat pier, model glider area, paddle boats, youth camping area, and plenty of nice picnic sites with barbecue facilities. There is a Nature Center in Area I across Spring St. (near the Area II entrance) with an excellent nature hike (for a small fee). Finally, one can leave the El Dorado East Regional Park and head across the San Gabriel River to the west portion of the park. This is a non-fee area with a tennis center and baseball diamond just south of Spring St., and an additional picnic area with a small lake south of Wardlow Rd. The entry to both areas is via Studebaker Rd.

TRAILHEAD: From the San Diego Fwy., turn north on Palo Verde Ave. and drive 0.9 mile to Spring St. Turn right (east) and continue about 0.8 mile to free parking along Spring St. just west of the bridge over the San Gabriel River. Other options are to continue over the bridge and park in the Nature Center parking area (turn south at the park entrance) or continue up Spring St., make a U-turn, and return to the Area II park entrance to the north (right). Both the latter options are pay parking.

El Dorado Park Area II

From the San Gabriel Fwy., turn west on Willow St. (Katella Ave. to the east), continue about one mile to Studebaker Rd. and turn right (north). Continue about 0.3 mile to Spring St. and turn right (east). Follow the parking instructions above. For direct entry at Area II (pay parking) from the southbound San Gabriel Fwy., take the Spring St. exit and turn right into the park entrance.

There is plenty of water and many restroom facilities in this park. Bring some good food to barbecue and enjoy great munchies after a "tough" bike ride.

TRIP DESCRIPTION: From the free parking area on Spring St., ride over the bridge and turn right (south) at the Nature Center entrance (0.3). Make another sharp right and continue parallel to Spring St. (but now in the opposite direction) along the Nature Center roadway. Continue 0.2 mile to the fence along the San Gabriel River bike route. Rather than passing through that fence entry, follow the roadway as it turns to the right (north) and passes under Spring St. The road enters Park Area II.

70

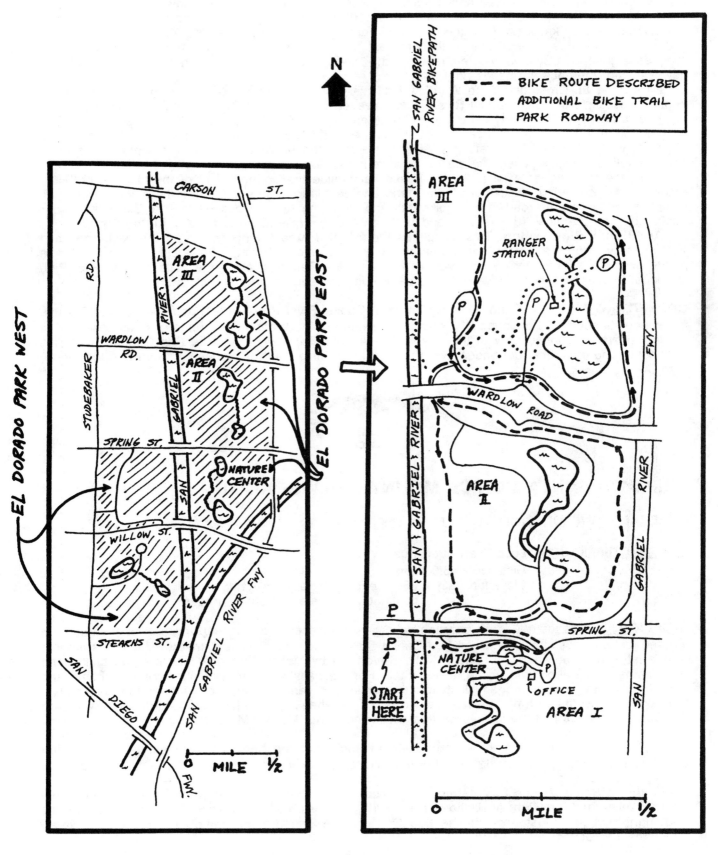

TRIP #16 - EL DORADO REGIONAL PARK

Park Area II. Turn to the right at (0.5) and travel along the bikepath paralleling Spring St. At (0.7) the trail passes the archery area and 0.1 mile later, crosses the park entry roadway and a little outlet stream from the lake to the north. The path turns north a short distance later and passes along several tree-covered grassy knolls. At (1.4) the now west-heading path crosses over the feeder stream between Areas II and III; this is near one of the prettiest picnic areas on the lake. At (1.8) the path again reaches a junction. By heading left (south), the Area II loop (2.3 miles total) can be completed; however, the reference trip heads right.

Park Area III. Cross under the Wardlow Rd. overpass and continue over to Area III. To the left is another access to the San Gabriel River Trail; however, this route proceeds to the right and continues along a roadway which nearly skirts the entire Area III. In 0.5 mile from the Area III entry, the road passes one of the nicer picnic areas near the south end of the lake at the outlet stream. This is a great place for water fowl and bird watching. At 0.6 mile from the Area III entry (2.4), the road turns north and in another 0.1 mile passes the paddle boat rental area.

Next, the road bends west (2.9) and passes alongside the northern end of the lake. At (3.2) the roadway passes a firing range (outside the park) and begins to head south along the model glider bluff. Continue south on both roadway and bikepath and close the Area III outside loop at 2.0 miles. Cross back under the Wardlow Rd. overpass and cycle another 0.5 mile south to the Area II trip origin.

Additional Sightseeing. This completes the 2.3-mile Area II loop and the 2.0-Area III loop and allows plenty of time to investigate the inner bikeways. Particular points of interest in Area III are the bridge over the isthmus, the lovely wooded area near the Ranger Station, the Billie Boswell Bike Path Memorial marker and the little walkway/bikepath along the edge of the lake below the bridge.

<u>CONNECTING TRIPS</u>: 1) Connection with the San Gabriel River Bike Trail (Trips #20A and #20B) - use access points south of the Spring St. underpass or north of the Wardlow Rd. underpass as described in the trip above; 2) connection with the Coyote Creek Trail (Trip #24) - take the San Gabriel River Bike Trail south and cross the foot bridge over the river at 0.6 mile south of Spring St., then turn left (north) onto Coyote Creek.

TRIP #17 - SANTA MONICA MOUNTAINS WORKOUT

<u>GENERAL LOCATION</u>: Santa Monica Mountains

<u>LEVEL OF DIFFICULTY</u>:   Loop - very strenuous
                            Distance - 43.8 miles
                            Elevation gain - 2500 feet total elevation gain;
                                            continuous moderate-to-sheer grades

<u>HIGHLIGHTS</u>: This journey is an absolute scenic masterpiece! The tour starts with a long warm-up in the see-forever coastal hills between Leo Carillo State Beach and Malibu Canyon Rd. Next is a climb on the latter road between the canyon walls carved out by Malibu Creek. A turn west on Mulholland Hwy. leads to a steep climb above Malibu State Park, a passby of Straus Ranch/Lake Enchanto and The Rock Store, a very rugged climb to the Seminole Overlook and a crest near the Decker Rd. intersection. The final 10-mile Mulholland leg is a free-wheeling downhill with long-distance vistas to the Channel Islands and the valleys nestled within the Santa Monica Mountains.

<u>TRAILHEAD</u>: The trailhead has been selected such that the final trip segment is an extended downhill. There are options to start the trip from points closer to Santa Monica, for instance, Malibu or Zuma County Beach.

From the Santa Monica Fwy. terminus at Pacific Coast Highway (Hwy. 1) in Santa Monica, drive west 28 miles and turn right at Mulholland Hwy. (If you pass Yerba Buena Rd., you've gone too far.) Turn right in a short distance into the Leo Carillo State Beach picnic/camping area (shade, water, restrooms, barbecues).

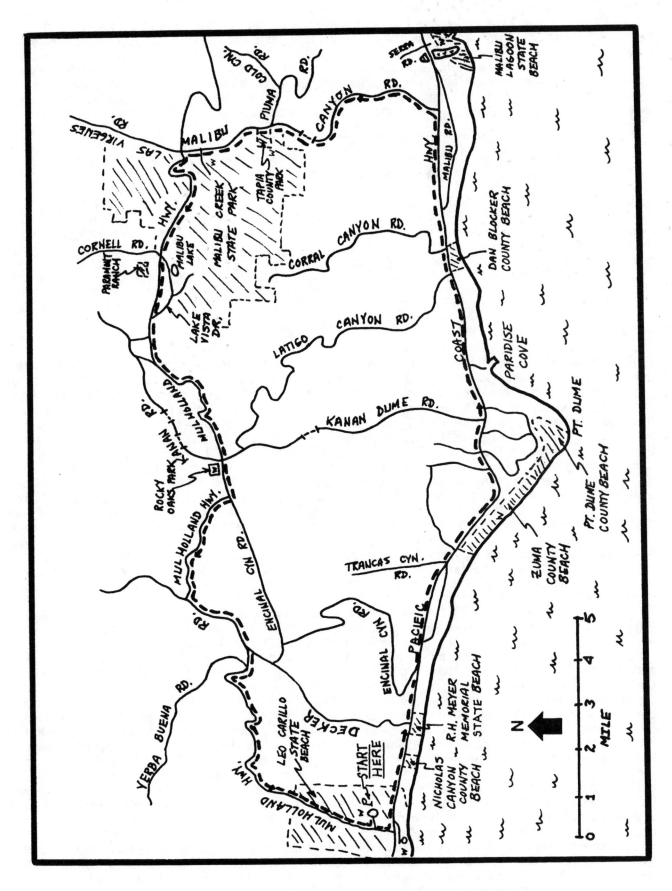

TRIP #17 - SANTA MONICA MOUNTAINS WORKOUT

From the Ventura Fwy. in the San Fernando Valley, exit south at Westlake Blvd. Continue on what becomes Decker Rd. (Hwy. 23) to the coast. Turn right (west) and continue 2-l/2 miles to Mulholland Hwy.

For folks going the entire loop, bring at least two filled water bottles. In the mountains, we found water at Tapia County Park, Malibu Creek State Park (requires a short diversion), the Rock Store just beyond the Peter Straus Ranch, and at Rocky Oaks Park just beyond Kanan Rd. on Mulholland Hwy. Perform a thorough bicycle maintenance check, including brakes, before starting this mountain tour.

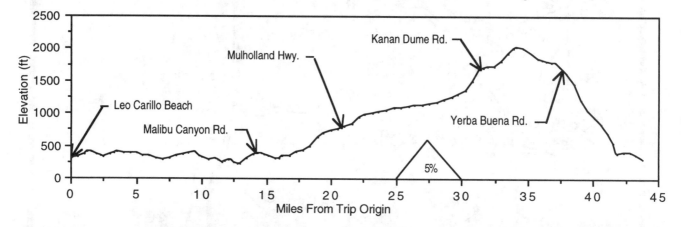

TRIP DESCRIPTION: **Pacific Coast Highway (Leo Carillo State Beach to Malibu Canyon Rd.).** The trip starts on the Pacific Coast Bicentennial Bike Route. (Note that a more detailed discussion of this segment is found in Trip #18B) Most of this segment and that on Malibu Canyon Rd. is on a highway with a striped shoulder. The Malibu Canyon Rd. stripe disappears in some areas so caution is required. Bike east on Pacific Coast Hwy. (PCH) and follow a half-mile steep upgrade which levels and passes Nicholas Canyon County Beach (1.2). Ride a roller-coaster downgrade-upgrade, passing Decker Rd. at the low point. Pass La Piedre State Beach, Encinal Canyon Rd., El Matador State Beach (3.4) and follow another roller coaster to a flat near Trancas Canyon Rd. (gas station) (5.4).

Continue past the entrance to Zuma County Beach (water, restrooms) (7.0) and follow a long workout upgrade past the Corral Beach turnoff. This grade crests near Heathercliff Rd. (gas station) (7.8). Just beyond, the road heads back downhill past Kanan Dume Rd. (8.1) and stairsteps its way down to Paradise Cove Rd. (9.0). Next is a stairstep upgrade which leads to a flat near Geoffrey's Restaurant (9.9).

Follow the continued steep roller-coaster route past Latigo Canyon Rd. (11.1) and then pedal on the flat to Corral Canyon Rd. (gas station) (11.7). Just beyond is a long, steep upgrade; at the crest is an excellent coastal view back to the north (12.8). Continue past John Tyler Dr. and bike uphill to a crest at Malibu Canyon Rd. (13.9).

Malibu Canyon Rd. Turn left and follow a mild upgrade past the elegant, well-manicured Pepperdine University Campus. Bike on a flat past Seaver Dr.; there is a fine long-distance view west and south, as well as a nice look down into the Malibu Lagoon. Start a steeper upgrade and pass Harbor Vista Dr. (14.8); the coastal view is even more spectacular here. Follow the winding roadway and, in another mile, bike a steady, moderate-to-steep upgrade with the Santa Monica Mountains peaks dead ahead.

In 2.6 miles from PCH, the roadway is clearly within the canyon. There is a turnout with a great canyon overlook in this area plus a peek back to the ocean (16.8). (Note: pull completely to the edge of the turnouts or take the chance of becoming a large automobile hood ornament!) Follow the winding downhill which hugs the mountainside; the deep canyon and surrounding mountain views in this area are nothing short of spectacular! At the canyon bottom is Malibu Creek. The road continues winding through the canyon between the towering peaks, then follows a workout upgrade. This grade becomes steep just before cresting near yet another turnout (Don used these turnouts for "research breaks"). Just beyond is the Malibu Canyon Rd. tunnel (18.0). The roadway roller-coasters northward in this area alongside the paralleling canyon. There is a nifty open area canyon view to the north and east at about a mile north of the tunnel.

The grade lessens as the route passes Piuma Rd. (19.1) and Tapia County Park (camping, shade, water). The road follows another roller-coaster section of more open canyon and reaches a little valley just beyond (20.5). In 0.3 mile and 6.9 miles from PCH is an entry to Malibu Creek State Park and just beyond is Mulholland Hwy.

Mulholland Highway: Malibu Canyon Rd. to Cornell Rd. The remainder of the tour is on Mulholland Hwy. The little two-lane country road heads uphill almost immediately, becoming progressively steeper and eventually transitioning into a series of switchbacks. (Don calls this "Pukeout Hill," a carryover from his long-distant first try at this tour.) There is an exceptional view from the summit down into Malibu Creek and Malibu Creek State Park (22.7). Next the road traverses a small valley on a moderate uphill and proceeds to Cornell Rd. (north)/Lake Vista Dr. (south) (24.3).

Cornell Rd. to Kanan Rd. The first mile is through rolling hills with a nice view across the paralleling canyon to the left (south). The roadway passes the west end of Lake Vista Dr. (25.5), crosses a small meadow, and reaches Peter Straus Ranch/Lake Enchanto (possible water, restrooms) and Troutdale Dr. (26.5). Next the road stairsteps upward past Sierra Creek Rd. and in a half mile reaches The Rock Store (water, refreshments, motorcyclist haven) (27.4).

The road continues on mild rolling terrain for a short distance before heading up a murderous two-mile upgrade which crests near the Seminole Canyon Overlook. The panoramic view of the canyon and surrounding mountains is great! While parked along the roadway on his initial fateful trip, Don commented to the biker in the accompanying photo that it must be a tough ride. His slow smile and accompanying response as he pedaled uphill was, "It's all part of the plan." A half mile on flatter terrain puts cyclists at Kanan Dume Rd. (Kanan Rd. northbound) (31.0).

Seminole Canyon Overlook

Kanan Rd. to Yerba Buena Rd. Continue on Mulholland Hwy. past Rocky Oaks Park (water, shade, restrooms) and follow a workout upgrade in an open and exposed hilly area. The road becomes progressively steeper, passes Encinal Canyon Rd. (32.0), and reaches a summit after about a total one-mile workout. There are periodic peeks at the Pacific Ocean and some of the Channel Islands on the upgrade, plus nice views into a valley to the northwest from this summit area.

The road rides the crest with continuous views into the canyons and valleys before reaching Decker Rd. (34.6). The route proceeds left (south) on an extreme winding roadway (5-10 mile-per-hour curves), then enters a light residential valley. In two miles from this intersection, turn sharply right off Hwy. 23 (Decker Rd.) onto the Mulholland Hwy. continuation. Bike a short distance to Yerba Buena Rd. (37.3).

Yerba Buena Rd. to PCH. The earlier hard work pays off on the predominantly downhill final segment. The winding downhill provides an overlook of the GTE Satellite Tracking Station and in a mile reaches the valley where the station is sited. In two miles from the Yerba Buena Rd. junction, Mulholland Hwy. follows a steep, winding downgrade. The canyon outlet to the coast comes into view in the far distance. After about two miles of exciting downgrade, the road winds through a sparsely populated valley (41.7), passes Camp Bloomfield, and in 0.2 mile, enters the upper reaches of Leo Carillo State Beach (as noted by the roadsign). There is a l/2-mile upgrade which graduates from moderate to very steep and reaches a crest with a refreshing ocean view (43.7). In another 0.2 mile, the route reaches the park and the end of a grueling, but satisfying trip.

CONNECTING TRIPS: You've got to be kidding! 1) Continuation with the PCH ride (Trip #18B) - near the trip origin, turn either east or west on PCH.

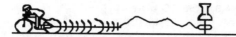

TRIPS #18A-#18C - PACIFIC COAST HIGHWAY

The entire tour described follows the Pacific Coast Bicentennial Bike Route. The main part of the trip hugs the coastline, following Pacific Coast Highway (PCH) from Santa Monica to an outlet near Point Mugu. The remaining 4.9 miles follows Navalair Rd. inland, turns west on Hueneme Rd., and follows that road to Bubbling Springs Linear Park. The total 44.7 mile trip, which is mapped below, is a strenuous one-way shot, and a strenuous to very strenuous up and back trip. With a short extension into Port Hueneme/Oxnard, the round trip could be turned easily into a "Century" ride.

Trip #18A is relatively flat, but on congested roadway with limited bike room over long stretches. There are, however, some fine coastal views on the route, plus the bonus of tours through Santa Monica, Topanga Beach, and Malibu. Trip #18B is on roadway with a wide, striped shoulder (Class II bikeway but unmarked) and is the most naturally scenic; it is also one mean roller-coaster ride! This tour visits Malibu, Pt. Dume, and Leo Carillo Beach. Trip #18C, the easiest segment of the tour, is on the same quality roadway as Trip #18B. On this trip portion, cyclists visit Sycamore Cove, Pt. Mugu, the agricultural Ventura County countryside and Port Hueneme.

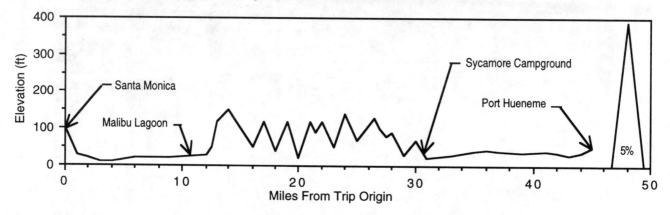

TRIP #18A - PCH: SANTA MONICA TO MALIBU LAGOON

GENERAL LOCATION: Santa Monica, Topanga State Beach, Malibu

LEVEL OF DIFFICULTY: One way - moderate; up and back - moderate
Distance - 10.5 miles (one way)
Elevation gain - periodic moderate grades

HIGHLIGHTS: An excellent scenic stretch of Pacific Coast Hwy. (PCH), this well-trafficked portion of the Pacific Coast Bicentennial Bike Route is short on bike room, but long on outstanding views, landmarks and sight-seeing attractions. Don't bike this one if you are nervous about sharing roadways with high-speed traffic. The relatively flat roadway starts at cozy Palisades Park and, as part of its itinerary, passes near such points of interest as the original J. Paul Getty Museum, Will Rogers State Beach, Topanga State Beach, Big Rock, Las Flores Beach, and Malibu Lagoon State Beach. There are also numerous exploratory adventures that can be taken off this 10.5 mile Class X tour.

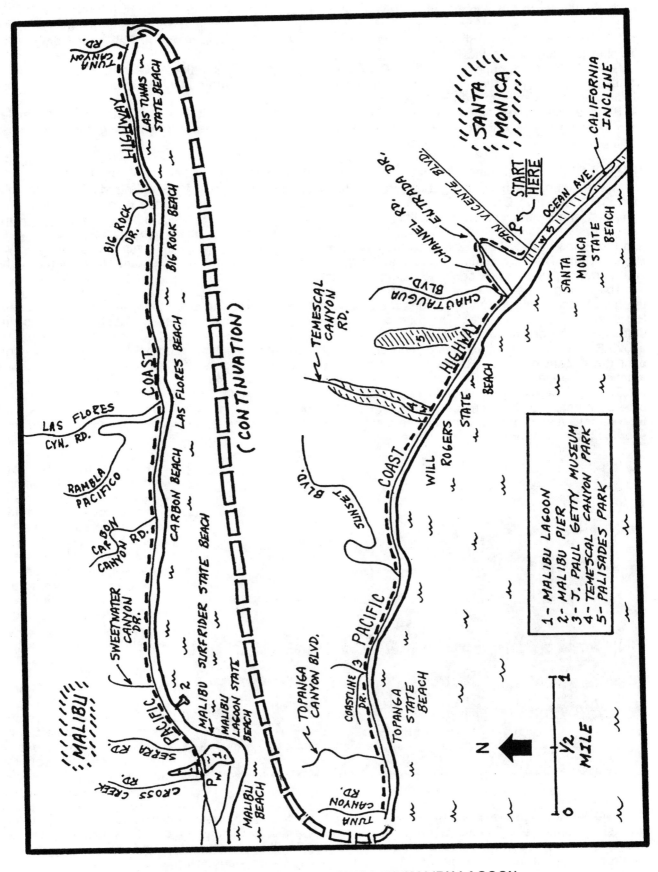

TRIP #18A - PCH: SANTA MONICA TO MALIBU LAGOON

TRAILHEAD: From the Santa Monica Fwy., exit at 4th St. (the last turnoff before the freeway fuses into PCH). Drive I-I/4 miles to San Vicente Blvd. and turn left, following this street to its terminus at Ocean Ave. Park on San Vicente Blvd. near Ocean Ave. Do not use the pay parking at Palisades Park unless you plan to return within the five-hour meter limit.

From PCH southbound, turn left at Chautauqua Blvd., then immediately veer right onto Channel Rd. Drive 0.3 mile to its terminus, turn right and proceed across Entrada Dr. to Ocean Ave. Follow this winding uphill 0.3 mile to San Vicente Blvd.

Bring a filled water bottle. There are a couple of public water sources and scattered commercial sources along the way. Bring a second bottle if you want to squirt water at non-yielding car drivers (just kidding!).

TRIP DESCRIPTION: **Santa Monica to Topanga State Beach.** Bike northwest on Ocean Ave. and follow the steep 0.3 mile downgrade, then continue around the hairpin turn to Entrada Dr. Cross this road and turn left at Channel Rd., freewheeling another 0.3 mile to Chautauqua Blvd. After a left, turn right in a short distance and follow beach-hugging PCH below the bluffs of northern Palisades Park (entry from Chautauqua Blvd. at Corona Del Mar). There are views of the jagged coastline to the west and the Palos Verdes Peninsula back to the southeast. The winding highway continues to hug the Will Rogers State Beach coastline. Bikers are forced to ride on varying width shoulder alongside high-speed traffic; this situation continues all the way into Malibu.

The road passes Temescal Canyon Rd. (l.9) (Temescal Canyon Park with its shade and water is to the north), enters the Pacific Palisades area, passes along a mile-long slide zone, then reaches Sunset Blvd. and a gas station (2.8). The road continues to hug the coast and passes Coastline Rd. and the entrance to the original J. Paul Getty Museum (3.8). (The new museum has been relocated to the hills above Brentwood.) Bike through an area with a high density of residences in the nearby palisades and past the oceanside Chart House Restaurant (an old favorite of ours). In a short distance, the road reaches Topanga Canyon Rd. and Topanga Canyon State Beach (4.6).

Topanga Canyon State Beach to Malibu Lagoon State Beach. This coastal tour passes another slide area near Big Rock, crosses Big Rock Rd. (6.0), and reaches the waterfront Moonshadows Bar and Restaurant. Just beyond is Las Flores Canyon Rd. (6.7) and the entry into a light commercial area sporting a mix of sports shops, boutiques and eateries.

Malibu Lagoon

Bike past Rambla Pacifico and a gas station (7.7), then visit a lovely and mixed hillside/ seaside residential area just before reaching Carbon Canyon Rd. (8.5). The hillsides still contain scattered burned-out structures from the disastrous fires of the early nineties. Next is a high-density residential area with frequent stop signs. Inviting "pork-out" stops in this area are the Nantucket Light Restaurant (9.6), Malibu Beach Bar and Grill, and La Salsa Tacos El Carbon Restaurant (complete with a giant sombreroed Mexican caricature on the roof).

Continue through the well-trafficked section of town with limited bike shoulder past the Malibu Inn. In a short distance is Malibu Surfrider State Beach and the Malibu Lagoon Museum. Bike on the bridge over the ocean-side tide pools and land-side Malibu Lagoon. Stop and enjoy the cozy and picturesque lagoon before proceeding to Serra Rd. and Malibu Lagoon State Beach.

CONNECTING TRIPS: 2) Continuation with the Santa Monica Loop (Trip #2) - at the origin, bike northeast on San Vicente Blvd.; 2) continuation of the PCH: Malibu Lagoon to Sycamore Grove tour (Trip #18B) - at the trip terminus, continue west on PCH.; 3) connection with the South Bay Bike Trail (Trip #1C) - bike southeast on Ocean Ave. past Colorado Ave. to Seaside Terrace; turn right and follow the beach entry route.

TRIP #18B - PCH: MALIBU LAGOON TO SYCAMORE COVE

GENERAL LOCATION: Malibu, Leo Carillo Beach, Pt. Dume, Sycamore Cove

LEVEL OF DIFFICULTY: One way - moderate to strenuous; up and back - strenuous
Distance - 20.1 miles (one way)
Elevation gain - continuous moderate-to-steep grades

HIGHLIGHTS: This is the roller-coaster portion of the Pacific Coast Hwy. (PCH) route, rich in hills and also in breathtaking coastal scenery. The tour leaves Malibu Lagoon State Beach and visits Malibu, Point Dume, Zuma County Beach, Leo Carillo State Beach, ending at the Sycamore Cove Campground. The hills are many and varied in challenge, with the entire workout trip being on a wide, striped bike shoulder. A round-trip tour provides what appears to the eye to be two distinctly different trips.

Why did God made hills? More knowledgeable bikers than us explain: "so that bikers can stand up and pump, thereby awaking their backsides."

TRAILHEAD: From Santa Monica, drive on PCH about 12 miles from the Santa Monica Fwy. terminus. At Serra Rd., find pay parking at Malibu Lagoon State Beach or park for free on PCH itself per local parking laws.

Bring a filled water bottle. Add a second bottle on hot days if you prefer to minimize the number of stops. There are several scattered, but reliable, water stops on this challenging trip.

TRIP DESCRIPTION: **Malibu Lagoon to Paradise Cove.** Exit Malibu Lagoon State Beach and bike past Cross Creek Rd. and the Malibu Country Mart. The road moves away from the coast and continues through less-developed countryside with several beautiful structures built upon the hillside to the north. This refreshing scenery continues past Webb Way and a gas station (0.4), where the road divides and bikers are treated to a very nice and wide biking shoulder. This excellent bikeway continues nearly all the way to Port Hueneme.

Shortly after is a steep upgrade and the beginning of a series of rolling hills for about the next l5 miles. At the top of the grade to the north is lovely Pepperdine University campus and Malibu Canyon Rd. (1.2). The roller coaster route continues and sporadic views open up in about a mile. In another half mile is a particularly steep grade, followed by a nice downhill that returns bikers to near sea level at Dan Blocker State Beach (3.1). The road is next to a long line of steep palisades in this area.

After enjoying the beach scenery, "suck it in" and begin the long and relatively steep upgrade, passing Latigo Canyon Rd. (4.7) and reaching the crest in another 0.3 mile. The road moves inland

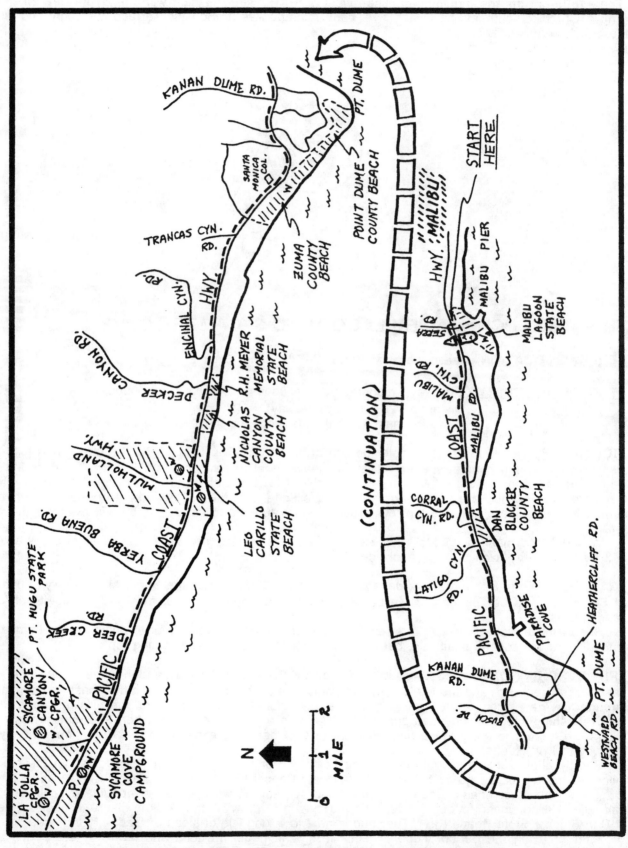

TRIP #18B - PCH: MALIBU LAGOON TO SYCAMORE COVE

and roller coasters through more hills, passes posh Geoffry's Restaurant (5.5), and follows a downgrade to the Paradise Cove area.

Paradise Cove to Trancas Beach. In another I-I/2 miles of stair-step uphill is the first of three southern road accesses to the Point Dume area and just after this is Kanan Dume Rd. (7.6). Note that there are some very scenic coastal coves off these roads which can be reached with a modest hike. However, for the steady pedaler, continue on this hilly road to Heathercliff Rd. (gas station) and enjoy the scenic ocean views which open up in this area. Freewheel downhill past the Corral Beach turnoff (gas station) and return to sea level at Zuma County Beach (water and restrooms) (8.6).

The bike tour generally hugs the coastline from this point until reaching the Pt. Mugu area. The ocean views are constant and spectacular and the ocean breeze is refreshing any time of year. Pedal alongside scenic Zuma County Beach, then pass Trancas Creek and the local marina, which is the home of the Malibu Yacht Club. In a short distance is Trancas Canyon Rd. and the Trancas Beach turnoff (gas station) (9.7).

Trancas Beach to Leo Carillo State Beach. Follow a long overdue flat stretch before returning to the series of rolling hills. There are scattered residences in the area and more great coastal views. Follow the workout upgrade past the El Matador State Beach turnoff (11.7) and continue to Encinal Canyon Rd. In 0.2 mile is the La Piedra State Beach turnoff and a high-density pocket of expensive beach homes.

Follow the refreshing downhill past Decker Canyon Rd. and stare straight ahead at yet another challenging upgrade. Pedal past the Malibu Ride and Country Club, the Nicholas Canyon Country Beach turnoff (13.9), and follow a half-mile runout which returns cyclists to sea level and Leo Carillo State Beach; there are water and restrooms at this beach.

Leo Carillo State Beach to Sycamore Cove Campground. The bikeway follows the steep uphill and passes Mulholland Hwy. (15.1). At the end of the beach boundary, the route crosses the Los Angeles County/Ventura County Line. Bike on the long upgrade and enjoy the views directly ahead into the Santa Monica Mountains. The road returns quickly to sea level, passes a surfing area, and reaches Yerba Buena Rd. (16.8). Mercifully, the worst (or best?) is over as the path enters a section of lightly rolling hills.

PCH continues through the hills with steep palisades just to the inland side. There are excellent views in both directions along the coastline in this area. The route passes the coastal access at Deer Creek Rd. (18.4), continues through the gentle hills and reaches the westernmost edge of the extensive Pt. Mugu State Park. In about one-quarter mile is the entry to the Sycamore Canyon Campground and, just beyond, is the access to Sycamore Cove Campground (20.1). There is water and a restroom here, a fine beach, and a ranger station. It is also a scenic rest point before returning east or continuing to Port Hueneme.

CONNECTING TRIPS: 1) Continuation with the PCH: Santa Monica to Malibu Lagoon ride (Trip #18A) - at the trip origin, bike east; 2) continuation with the PCH: Sycamore Cove to Port Hueneme tour (Trip #18C) - from the trip terminus, continue west; 3) connection with the Santa Monica Mountains Workout (Trip #17) - at Malibu Canyon Rd., turn north (inland).

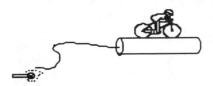

TRIP #18C - PCH: SYCAMORE COVE TO PORT HUENEME

GENERAL LOCATION: Sycamore Cove, Point Mugu, Port Hueneme

LEVEL OF DIFFICULTY: One way - moderate; up and back - moderate
Distance - 13.7 miles (one way)
Elevation gain - periodic moderate grades

HIGHLIGHTS: The northern segment of this tour along Pacific Coast Hwy. (PCH) starts at Sycamore Cove Campground and cruises the scenic coast with a visit to "picture postcard" Point Mugu. The route passes along the Pacific Missile Test Center, then tours the open farmland of eastern Port Hueneme before reaching the Bubbling Springs Linear Park terminus. The tour passes through varied

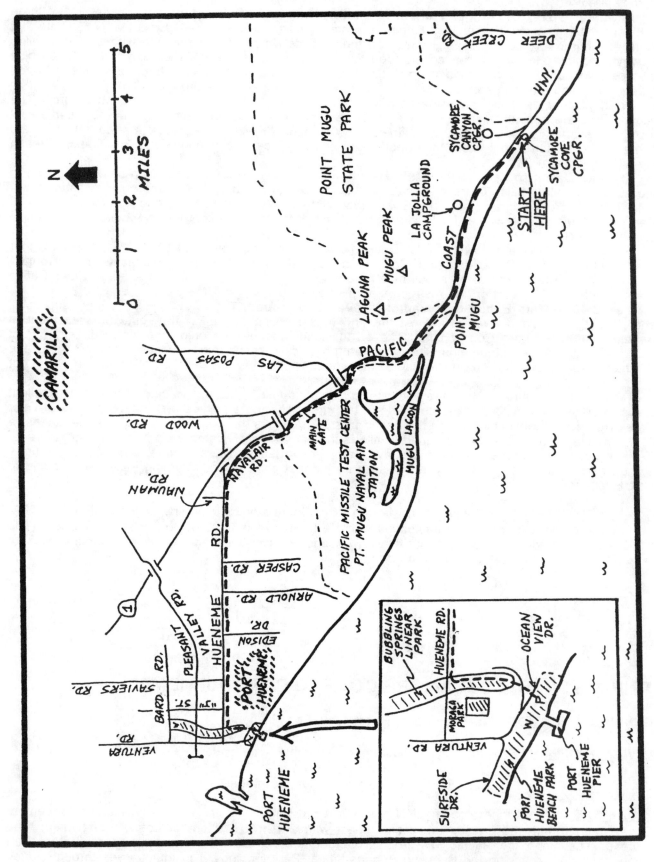

TRIP #18C - PCH: SYCAMORE COVE TO PORT HUENEME

scenic areas on a mix of roadway classes; the highlight area is certainly the scenic coastal portion from Sycamore Cove Campground to Pt. Mugu. The route is primarily Class II or on a marked roadway with a very wide shoulder.

TRAILHEAD: From Santa Monica, drive on PCH about 32 miles from the Santa Monica Fwy. terminus. About a mile beyond the Los Angeles County/Ventura County Line, turn into the Sycamore Cove Campground.

Bring a filled water bottle. For the up and back trip on a hot day, think about a couple of bottles. There are few water sources between the trip start and end points.

TRIP DESCRIPTION: **Sycamore Cove Campground to Point Mugu.** Exit the campground and follow the flat which gives way to a modest steady upgrade. PCH passes a massive natural sand dune built up alongside the cliffs - an impressive sight! Next is a passby of the La Jolla Canyon Campground and a seemingly unending line of recreational vehicles, as well as rock-strewn La Jolla Canyon Beach (1.5).

Beach at Point Mugu

Just beyond, the route meanders along the land-side cliffs about 20 feet above the ocean and passes several scenic locations. The road climbs a grade and returns to the beach near Point Mugu (3.1). The road has been blasted through the rock in this area; once up to and through the resultant portals, there are fine views in both directions. To the west are the first views into the Oxnard/Port Hueneme area and back to the east is the rugged coastline. Take advantage of the scenic turnouts near Point Mugu.

Point Mugu to Hueneme Road. Pass a rifle range, saltwater marshes of Mugu Lagoon, and bike under the "watchful eye" of the tower-bedecked Mugu Peak (5.1). Cross over Calleguas Creek and continue to the Las Posas Rd. off-ramp (7.0). Exit at this street since PCH becomes an automobile-only road just beyond, cross over PCH, and follow Navalair Rd. alongside the Pacific Missile Test Center/Point Mugu Naval Air Station. Follow the fenced-in road past the main entrance gate, the missile model display (7.5), and Wood Rd. In another mile is Hueneme Rd.

Port Hueneme. Turn left and take a country bike ride through a predominantly agricultural area. The Port Hueneme/Oxnard skyline is directly ahead. This is a Class X road with a wide bike shoulder and limited traffic. Pass Edison Dr. (11.9), Saviers Rd. (12.4) and bike through what becomes a mixed residential/light commercial area. Continue about 3/4 mile, passing "J" St. and turn left into pleasant Bubbling Springs Linear Park.

This is a fine place to end the trip as there are water, shade, grass and restrooms at the park. Another option is to continue biking south another mile along the manicured canal to Port Hueneme Beach Park.

CONNECTING TRIPS: 1) Continuation with the PCH route (Trip #18B) - at the trip origin at Sycamore Grove Campground, bike south.

RIVER TRAILS

San Gabriel River in the Seal Beach Area

TRIPS #19, #20A, #20B - UPPER RIO HONDO AND LARIO TRAILS

The Upper Rio Hondo Trail (Trip #19) and Lario Trail (Trips #20A and #20B) can be ridden as a complete 28 mile one-way trip. This is a moderate one-way workout and a strenuous round trip. The overall map is provided below. The entire route is a Class I bike trail. In the distant past, there were four street intersections where the biker would have to leave the bike trail in high water. They were in the southern (third) segment of the trip. The upgraded bike undercrossings eliminated any need to leave the bikeway under any river conditions.

The Upper Rio Hondo Trail explores the segment from its current "origin" at the Peck Road Water Conservation Park (reservoir) through a short stretch of some river bottom land, and ends in the Whittier Narrows Recreation Area (Whittier Narrows Dam, Nature Center and Legg Lake). Trip #20A (Upper Lario Trail) starts near the Whittier Narrows Dam and follows the lower Rio Hondo River just past its conjunction with the Los Angeles River and ending at Hollydale Park. The lower segment of the Lario Trail (Trip #20B) starts at Hollydale Park and finds its way into Long Beach Harbor and San Pedro Bay.

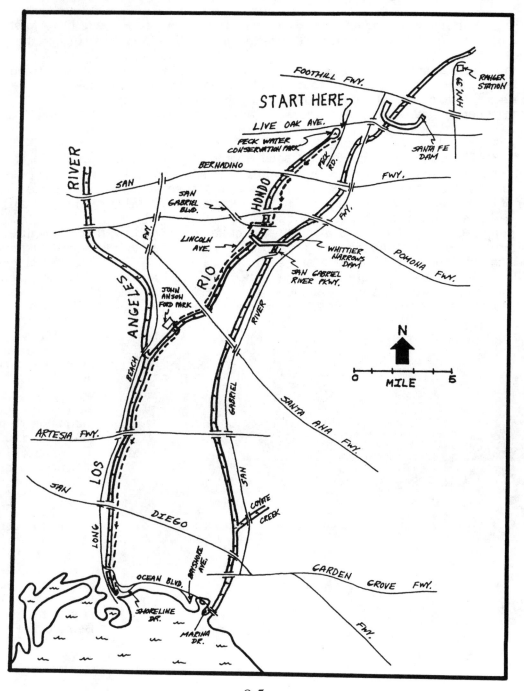

TRIP #19 - UPPER RIO HONDO TRAIL

GENERAL LOCATION: El Monte-Whittier Narrows

LEVEL OF DIFFICULTY: One way - easy; up and back - moderate
Distance - 8.2 miles (one way)
Elevation gain - short, steep grade at Whittier Narrows Dam

HIGHLIGHTS: This uppermost section of this river trail follows the Rio Hondo River from its origin to its confluence with the Los Angeles River and ultimately to Long Beach Harbor. This lightly used segment travels from the pleasant Peck Road Water Conservation Park (reservoir) through the Whittier Narrows Recreation Area to the top of the Whittier Narrows Dam. There is fishing in the park at the trip origin. The lower section of the trip is exceptionally pretty, traveling along natural, forested riverbeds. The entire route is Class I and also qualifies as a nice, fast workout trip.

TRAILHEAD: From the San Gabriel River Fwy., exit at Lower Azusa Rd. and drive west 1.2 miles to Peck Rd. Turn right (north) and proceed 0.6 mile to Rio Hondo Pkwy. Turn left into the parking area alongside the reservoir.
From the San Bernardino Fwy., exit north on Peck Rd., travel 2.3 miles to Rio Hondo Pkwy. and turn left. From the Foothill Fwy., exit south to Myrtle Ave. Drive 2.3 miles on Myrtle Ave., which becomes Peck Rd., and turn right at Rio Hondo Pkwy. into the parking lot.
Bring a moderate water supply. There is water at two strategically placed parks near the middle of the trip.

TRIP DESCRIPTION: **Upper River.** Near the southern end of the parking area, follow a short direct trail through an opening in the fence and proceed on a Class I bike trail on the east side of the lake. In 0.4 mile, the route passes the lake spillway where there is a raised diversion trail across the backside (lakeside) of the spillway. Our route stays on the main trail on the east side of the lake. Just beyond the spillway, the Upper Rio Hondo Trail actually begins.
The upper segment of the trip is along the concrete Rio Hondo riverbed through a commercial area. Other then counting the shopping carts in the riverbed, the greatest excitement is the undercrossings at Santa Anita Ave. (0.9) and Lower Azusa Rd. (1.2). Soon there is a small rest area next to the El Monte Airport where bikers can watch the small aircraft takeoff and land (1.4). The stretch along the airport continues for about 3/4 mile, followed by passage under a railroad trestle (2.2), then alongside a raised railway structure and under Valley Blvd. (2.5).

Peck Road Water Conservation Park

Next is Pioneer Park which stretches for another 0.3 mile along the bikeway. The park has water, restrooms, picnic areas, baseball diamonds, tennis courts and playground areas. The architecturally-striking El Monte Busway Station and RTD Park and Ride are just east of the park. The path eventually passes under a raised concrete railroad overpass (2.7), a special bus-lane overpass (2.8) and passes beside quaint little Fletcher Park before reaching the San Bernardino Fwy. (3.0).

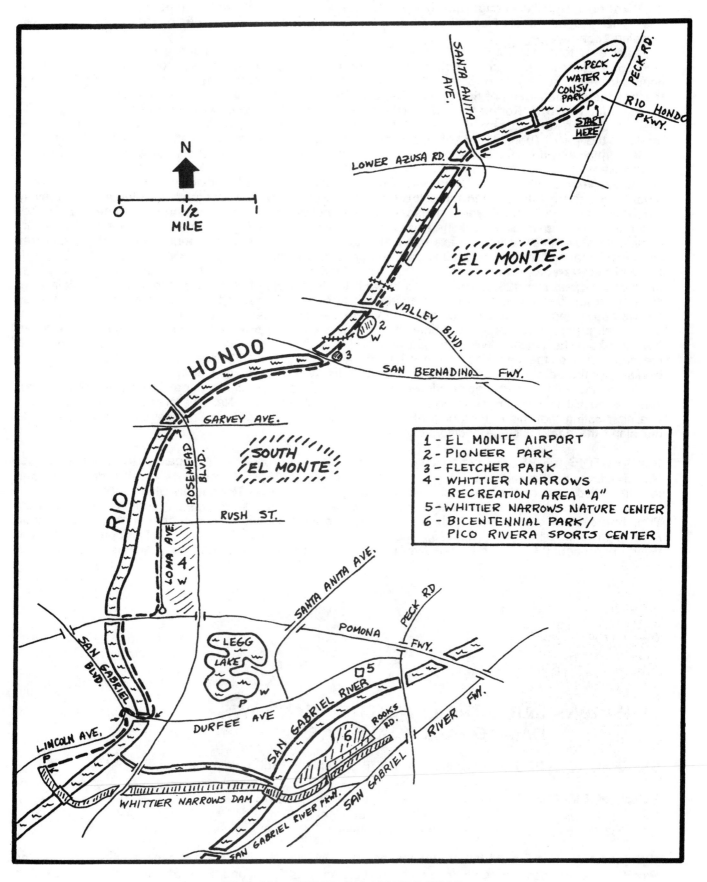

TRIP #19 - UPPER RIO HONDO TRAIL

Bike the next mile through an area with residences to the left and commercial areas across the river. The bikepath meets Rosemead Blvd. (4.1), Garvey Ave (4.2) and later passes a "cablecar" river crossing apparatus (4.7)

After over four miles of concrete, there is a sudden transition to a natural riverbed just beyond this point (5.0). Near the juncture is a short spur to the right that provides an overlook of the river transition point. However, our trip follows the main trail and heads south and away from the river. In 0.2 mile it reaches the northeast end of the Whittier Narrows Recreation Area "A" at Loma Ave. and Rush St.

Whittier Narrows Recreation Area. Recreation Area "A" is about 1/2 mile north-south and 1/4 mile east-west. There are numerous spur routes on bikepaths and on the slow, lightly-traveled automobile roads in the park. There are restrooms, water, shade, picnic areas, recreational fields, playgrounds, model airplane flying area and model car racing area. Our trip follows the west edge of the park on Loma Ave.

At the very south end of Loma Ave. (5.8), pass through the opening in the fence. Pedal west, parallel to and on the same level as the Pomona Fwy. In 0.6 mile, the path cuts under the freeway and rejoins the Rio Hondo River. This is natural river bottom with lush trees and other greenery. Further down-river, the undergrowth thickens and blocks the river from view (6.7). In 1/2 mile or so of this lovely stretch, the river gives way to an exit trail which takes cyclists up to San Gabriel Blvd. (7.3). A spur trail just before that exit leads to a wading and rest area below the San Gabriel Blvd. bridge.

Whittier Narrows Dam. To the east on San Gabriel Blvd. is Legg Lake and the Four Corners Trail Intersection (see Trip #26). Our trip heads west on San Gabriel Blvd. over the river to Lincoln Ave. (7.6). Turn left and make another immediate left turn onto an asphalt road blocked to cars. The trail follows above and at some distance from the west bank of the Rio Hondo. This section has scrub brush, an oil well pump or two and low eroded hills to the west. The trail pulls away from the river at about 0.2 mile from the Lincoln Ave. entrance and comes within close view of that street. Just beyond are the first views of the backside of the Whittier Narrows Dam. In 0.2 mile, follow a steep trail up the backside of the dam and summit the west levee of the Whittier Narrows Dam (8.2).

Stop and enjoy the sweeping views from the dam's crest, including the San Gabriel Mountains, surrounding hills, local communities and the lush bottomland of the Narrows area back up river. There is a sign noting that this is the origin of the Lario Trail (see Trip #20A). Bike beyond the sign and ride out along the dam for some additional scenery.

CONNECTING TRIPS: 1) Continuation with the Lario Trail (Trip #20A) - pedal south from the Whittier Narrows Dam at the end of the trip; 2) connection with the San Gabriel River Trail (Trips #22C and #22D) - head east on San Gabriel Blvd. as above. Once across Rosemead Blvd., follow the Class I bikepath to the right into the Whittier Narrows Wildlife Refuge. Cruise on this path past the Four Corners Trail Intersection to the San Gabriel River.; 3) connection with the Whittier Narrows Recreation Area/Legg Lake Bike Trail (Trip #26) - head east on San Gabriel Blvd. from the bridge over the Rio Hondo and pedal 0.9 mile on Durfee Ave. (same street, new name) to the Legg Lake parking lot;

TRIP #20A - LARIO TRAIL: WHITTIER NARROWS DAM TO HOLLYDALE PARK

GENERAL LOCATION: Montebello, Downey, Bell Gardens, Hollydale

LEVEL OF DIFFICULTY: One way - easy; up and back - moderate
Distance - 9.0 miles (one way)
Elevation gain - essentially flat

HIGHLIGHTS: This Class I trip starts from atop the Whittier Narrows Dam, travels southward along the Rio Hondo River past its confluence with the Los Angeles River and ends at pleasant, little Hollydale Park. The river is not the attraction, but rather the running streams and holding basins beside the river

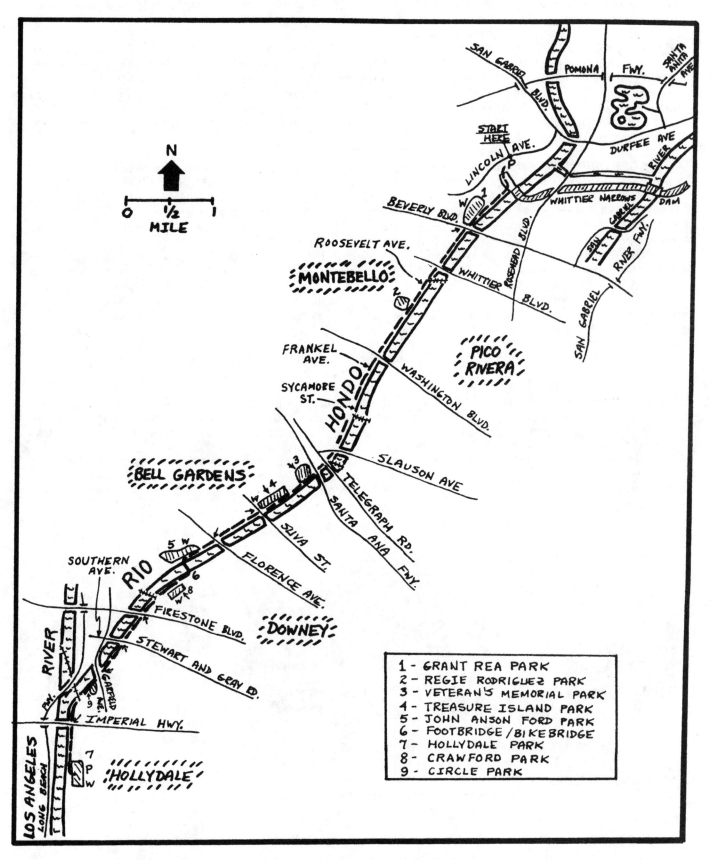

TRIP #20A - LARIO TRAIL: WHITTIER NARROWS DAM TO HOLLYDALE PARK

and the interesting trail diversions that interweave this particular territory. This is an interesting trip right after a heavy winter rain! There are several parks worth visiting. Finally, this is a limited-use stretch; it is a good route for bikers looking for a speedy, unobstructed workout.

<u>TRAILHEAD</u>: From the Pomona Fwy., exit south at San Gabriel Blvd., drive 0.8 mile to Lincoln Ave. and turn right (south). Proceed 0.8 mile to the parking area at the dam west levee/view site. From the San Gabriel River Fwy., exit west on Beverly Blvd. and cruise 1.2 miles to Rosemead Blvd. Turn right (north) and drive 1.5 miles to San Gabriel Blvd. Turn left and continue 0.3 mile to Lincoln Ave. Turn left again and proceed 0.8 mile to the parking area at the dam viewing site.

The route is exposed, with almost no shade other than underpasses and parks. Bring a moderate water supply and refill at the parks.

<u>TRIP DESCRIPTION</u>: **Whittier Narrows Dam.** Leave the parking area, lift your bike over the low barrier and proceed up and across the Whittier Narrows Dam's west levee. At 0.4 miles bike the paved downhill route which exits the south face. The path winds downhill and rejoins the Rio Hondo River's west levee beyond the spillway (1.0). The riverbed is solid concrete. More interesting scenery mainly is to the right (west) where there are ravines, equestrian trails and running streams. (Note: If the route gets confusing over the next several miles, stick to the path nearest the river.)

Grant Rea Park. In 0.4 mile beyond the spillway, there is a footbridge over the equestrian trails which leads to Grant Rea Park. This small park has recreation fields, tree cover, a small barnyard zoo (with common farm animals and then some) and pony-cart rides. Pedal past the bridge and see the red barn and barnyard animals. Further south is a footbridge over a ravine (and a diversion route) which leads to Beverly Blvd. (1.7); the area beyond the ravine is marshy with a crush of greenery.

The Middle Section. Further down the reference river path, the bikeway passes Whittier Blvd. (2.2), a railroad trestle (2.4) and a stagnant marshy area. Just beyond are barnyard and horse stalls in a treed rural setting. Pass another footbridge, this one heading to Roosevelt Ave. and Regie Rodriguez Park (2.8). In 0.8 mile, cross under Washington Blvd. and pass a series of water holding basins interspersed with equestrian trails. (Bikers can exit the river route by biking 1/4 mile south of Washington Blvd. on the wide paralleling path nearest the bluffs, then following the short, steep diversion trail that leads up to Bluff Rd./Frankel Ave.) Later the bike route leaves the river and races downhill through a tunnel under a railroad bridge before returning to the levee (4.3). Before reaching the tunnel, note the trail exit up the side of the bluffs; this steep path ends at Sycamore St.

Further south, the trail crosses Slauson Ave. (4.6) and then follows another diversion off the levee through a railroad tunnel underpass (5.1). Shortly afterward, the path crosses under Telegraph Rd. and the Santa Ana Fwy. Immediately afterward, the bikepath leaves the levee and crosses a little bridge over the marshes, soon returning to the levee (5.3).

River Crossing at John Anson Ford Park

In 0.1 mile pass a footbridge which leads to Veteran's Memorial Park. Then the river route passes alongside the long and narrow Treasure Island Park (5.8). Access to the park (shade, water, picnic facilities) is from the south.

John Anson Ford Park and the River Crossing. The route passes Suva St. (5.9) and Florence Ave. (6.2) before reaching John Anson Ford Park (6.4). This park is an excellent rest stop or alternate turnaround point. There is plenty of shade, restrooms, picnic facilities, a small lake and even a swimming pool!

Just south of the park is a small wood pedestrian bridge that takes the Lario Trail across the river to the east levee; it is important not to miss this crossing as the west levee path deadends 3/4 mile down the path.

Rio Hondo River to the L. A. River Confluence. On the east levee, the route passes the Rio Hondo Country Club/Golf Course and little Crawford Park (6.5) which has restrooms, water and a playground. The next two miles are through areas surrounded by commercial/industrial facilities with little to offer in the way of scenery. For example, the outdoor "Bandini Planter Mix" factory near Imperial Hwy. is one of the trip "highlights" in this segment! The route passes Firestone Blvd. (6.8), a trans-river cable car (7.1), Southern Ave. (7.2), Garfield Ave. (7.6), tiny Circle Park, a railroad trestle underpass (7.9) and reaches the confluence of the Rio Hondo and L. A. Rivers (8.2). Just south of the junction is Imperial Hwy. (8.4).

Hollydale Park. A 1/4 mile beyond Imperial Hwy. is the north edge of Hollydale Park. This park is a mixture of people-playground and horse-playground. To the north are playgrounds and equestrian show areas which give way to tennis courts and recreation fields to the south (9.0). There is sparse tree cover here, as well as water, providing a chance to rest up for the return trip.

CONNECTING TRIPS: 1) Continuation of the Upper Rio Hondo Bike Trail (Trip #19) - bike the trip north from Whittier Narrows; 2) continuation of the Lario Trail (Trip #20B) - cruise south from Hollydale Park; 3) connection with the L.A. River Trail (Trip #21) - cross the L.A. River at Imperial Hwy. Just beyond the bridge on the north side of the street, follow the bike trail sign onto the west levee.

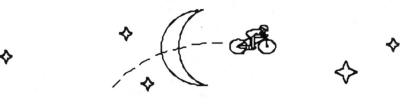

TRIP #20B - LARIO TRAIL: HOLLYDALE PARK
TO LONG BEACH HARBOR

GENERAL LOCATION: South Gate, Paramount, North Long Beach, Long Beach

LEVEL OF DIFFICULTY: One way - easy; up and back - moderate
Distance - 10.9 miles (one way)
Elevation gain - essentially flat

HIGHLIGHTS: This Class I trip starts near the midpoint of the Lario Trail at Hollydale Park and proceeds to the trail's end in Long Beach Harbor. It passes several parks on the way south and provides some excellent views near the lower segment which includes the Long Beach city skyline, Long Beach Harbor, Dominguez Hills, and a long-distance view of San Pedro Hill. In times long past, there were four intersections where the biker was forced to leave the levee (Rosecrans Ave., Compton Blvd., Alondra Blvd., and Del Amo Blvd.) and either bike into the river or cross busy road intersections. Bike undercrossings rebuilt in the early 90s eliminated any need to leave the Class I path under any conditions.

TRAILHEAD: From the Long Beach Fwy., exit east on Imperial Hwy. and continue 0.5 mile to Garfield Place (Ruchti Rd. to the north). Turn right and drive 0.6 mile to Monroe Ave. Turn right (west) and continue to the parking lot at Hollydale Park.

Bring a moderate water supply or fill up at the parks in the upper part of this tour. There is no near-trail water supply for the last seven miles before reaching the harbor.

TRIP DESCRIPTION: North Segment. At the south end of the park is an asphalt entry path up to the Lario Trail. Once up on the L. A. River east levee, head south past a horse pasture (0.3) and an old blocked off railroad bridge (0.7). Continue through a commercial/industrial area with a "lovely" view of the Long Beach Fwy. across the river and a concrete riverbed. Next are the awesome multi-level interweaving structures which make up the Long Beach Fwy./Century Fwy. Interchange (1.1).

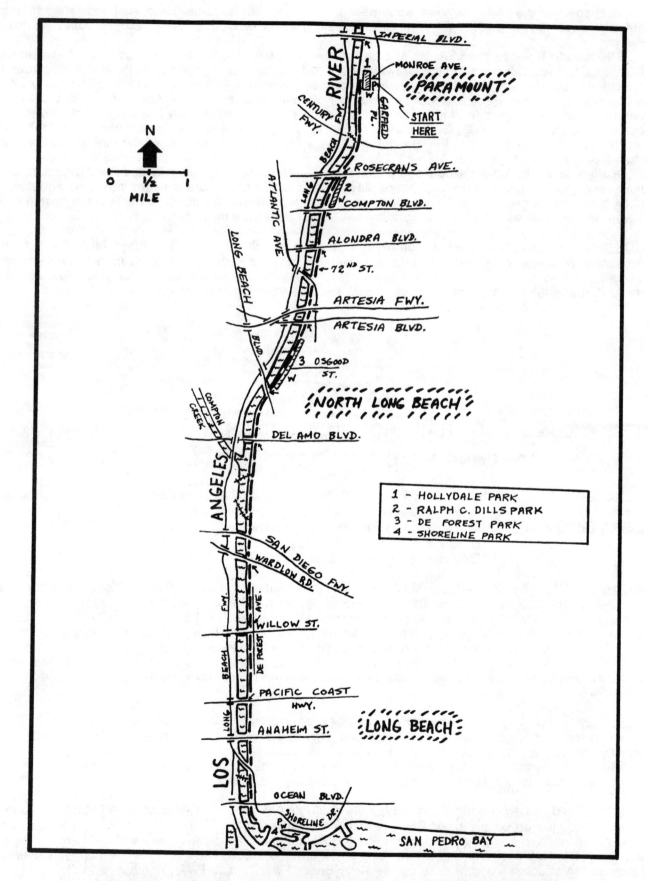

TRIP #20B - LARIO TRAIL: HOLLYDALE PARK TO LONG BEACH HARBOR

The Middle Segment. Pass Rosecrans Ave. and proceed to a long, thin park that has various athletic courts, playgrounds, play areas and water (near the south end) (1.4). This is "world famous" Ralph C. Dills Park which runs between Rosecrans Ave. and Compton Blvd. (1.9). Just beyond is the compact Par-3 Compton Golf Course and, in 0.5 mile, Alondra Blvd.

Cruise by horse stables and a training area (2.7), cross Atlantic Ave. (2.9), and visit another equestrian area. In succession, the bikeway transits below the Artesia Fwy. (3.2), Artesia Blvd. (3.4), passes a "trailer city" and meets up with the ultimate thin strip of park, De Forest Park (3.7). This is another nice rest spot with water (the last readily-accessible water until Long Beach). Water and restrooms are at the south end of the park.

Beyond the park, the path parallels a marsh for the next 2-1/2 miles; stop and look for awhile, as there are some interesting plants and other wildlife. Shortly afterward, the bikepath crosses Long Beach Blvd. (4.6); there is a nice view of Dominguez Hills to the right (west). Pass Del Amo Blvd., the last of the former "river dippers" (5.5). In 0.3 mile is the river confluence with Compton Creek. Proceed under a railroad crossing (6.0), pass the Virginia Country Club and continue beside a lovely residential area in the hills to the east (6.4). Pedal by the San Diego Fwy. (6.9) and Wardlow Rd. (7.2) where the trip reenters residential surroundings. There is a passenger cable car over the river (7.4) and another group of horse corrals coupled with a training area (7.8).

Southern Segment and the "Real" Los Angeles River. Finally comes the trip juncture where the river bottom transitions from "C-for concrete to N-for natural (thank goodness!). The most scenic part of the trip follows. There is year-round water and wildlife not too far from the transition point. The route passes under Willow Ave. (8.4) and PCH. (9.1). There are views of the harbor area and the Gerald Desmond Bridge. Within another 0.6 mile at Anaheim St., the waterway transitions into a deep channel that reminds one of a "real" river.

At Seventh St., there is an excellent view of the Long Beach city skyline and Long Beach Harbor (10.1). In 0.6 mile, the bikepath reaches Ocean Blvd. There are ski-boaters, water-skiers and jet skiers everywhere. Shortly the Lario Trail reaches a gated area with a sign marking the trail's end (10.9). (See Trip #11 for more information about this area.) At this point is a nice look at the Queensway Bridge and the Long Beach Harbor area

CONNECTING TRIPS: 1) Continuation with the Long Beach Shoreline Park tour (Trip #14) - continue south through the parking lot at the Lario Trail terminus and steer toward Queensway Landing (Catalina Boat Terminal); 2) continuation with the upper Lario Trail segment (Trip #20A) - pedal north from the trip origin at Hollydale Park; 3) connection with the Long Beach Harbor: Southeast Basin ride (Queen Mary, Harbor Scenic Dr.) (Trip #11) - bike to the northwest corner of the Aquarium of the Pacific parking structure (at Shoreline Dr. across from S. Chestnut Pl.) Stay to the left and enter the separated Class I path on the Queensway Bridge, cross Queensway Bay and follow the road signs .

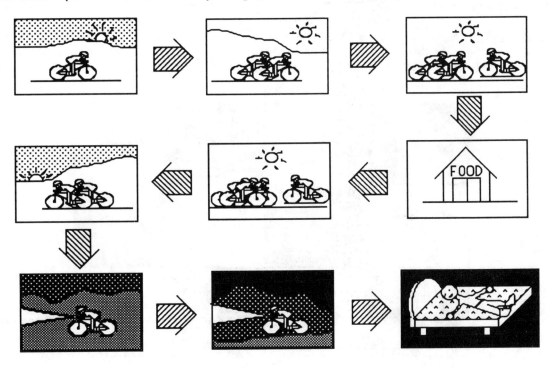

TRIP #21 - LOS ANGELES RIVER TRAIL

GENERAL LOCATION: Southgate, Cudahy, Bell

LEVEL OF DIFFICULTY: Up and back - easy
Distance - 5.6 miles (one way)
Elevation gain - essentially flat

HIGHLIGHTS: This is a short Class I trip along the Los Angeles River starting just south of its confluence with the Rio Hondo. There is little scenery and broken glass at spots along the bikeway. This may be an excellent trip someday if the route is ever maintained and it is extended northward. Concerned groups like the Los Angeles County Bicycle Coalition (LACBC) are lobbying the city to extend the route southward from the current segment near Griffith Park (see Trip #33). Hopefully, in the farther term, the roughly 15-mile gap between segments will be completed, resulting in a Glendale-to-the-ocean bike trail. However, for now, it is a segment for bikers who want to "see it all" or who want to build up an appreciation for other bike routes.

TRAILHEAD: From the Long Beach Fwy., exit west on Imperial Hwy. Turn left (south) at Duncan Ave. and find parking subject to the local laws. Another option is to park across the river at Hollydale Park. To get there exit east on Imperial Blvd., turn right on Garfield Ave., and drive about 3/4 mile to Monroe Ave. Turn right toward the river and drive to road's end.
    Bring a biking partner and a light water supply. No direct access public supply was found.

TRIP DESCRIPTION: Bike to Imperial Hwy., cross it and pedal right (east) on the north sidewalk over the Long Beach Fwy. Carefully cross the freeway entrance ramp. Turn left (north) at the bike trail sign that appears just before reaching the bridge over the L.A. River (0.3) and bike down to the west levee.
    Soon the route passes a viewing point of the river confluence, heads under the Long Beach Fwy. (0.6) and then under a railroad crossing. In further succession, pass Firestone Blvd. (1.7), a second railroad crossing, Clara St. (2.7) and Florence Ave. (3.2). Further north the trail ducks under Gage Ave. (3.8), passes under a railroad trestle, crosses Slauson Ave., and veers northwest before reaching Atlantic Ave. and the trip terminus (5.6).
    In the first 3-1/2 mile river stretch, there is a continuous line of industrial plants, commercial businesses and mini-junk yards. The one breath of fresh air is just south of Clara St. at Cudahy Neighborhood Park. The environs improve little on the north segment, although the nearby railroad tracks provide some variety.

CONNECTING TRIPS: Connection with the Lario Trail (Trip #20) - at the trip origin, pedal across the Imperial Hwy. bridge over the L.A. River (stay on the north sidewalk). Follow the trail sign down to the east levee and bike either north to the Whittier Narrows Dam (Trip #20A) or south to Long Beach (Trip #20B).

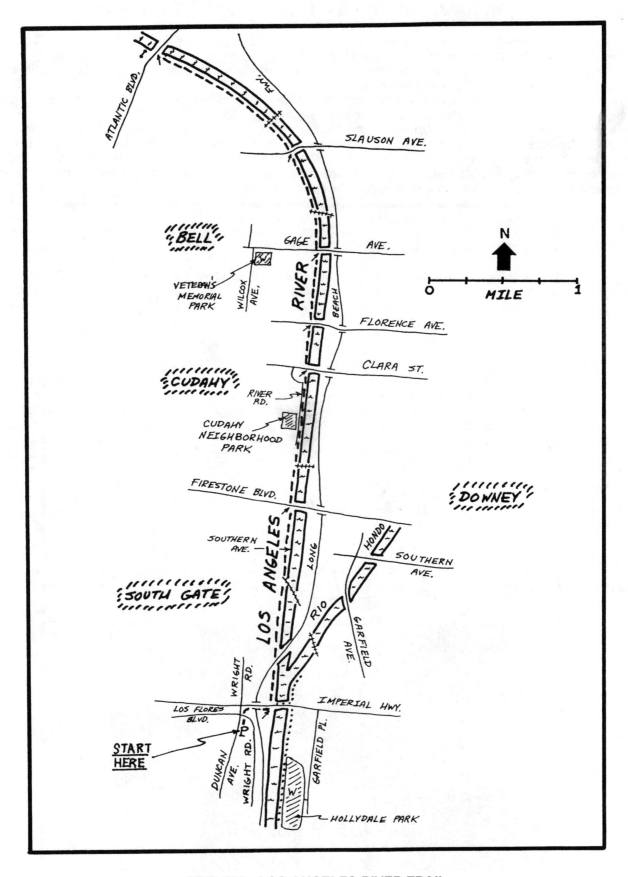

TRIP #21 - LOS ANGELES RIVER TRAIL

TRIPS #22A-#22E - SAN GABRIEL RIVER TRAIL

The San Gabriel River Trail is probably the premier single river trail in this book. The route captures Southern California from the sea through the inland valley to the mountains, all in one continuous 39-mile shot. Taken in the winter after a cold storm, this trip is one of the best in every sense. The general area map is provided below.

The first segment (#22A) explores the river outlet near Seal Beach, a wildlife area to the north and ends at super El Dorado Park. The connection segment (#22B) visits no less than five parks and finishes at Wilderness Park in Downey. The next northerly segment (#22C) leaves Wilderness Park, travels alongside some fine San Gabriel river bottom and ends at one of the tour highpoints, the Whittier Narrows Recreation Area. Trip #22D starts at that fabulous recreation area and ends at another, the Santa Fe Dam Recreation Area. The most northerly segment (#22E) leaves from that dam and ends in the foothills at the entrance to San Gabriel Canyon.

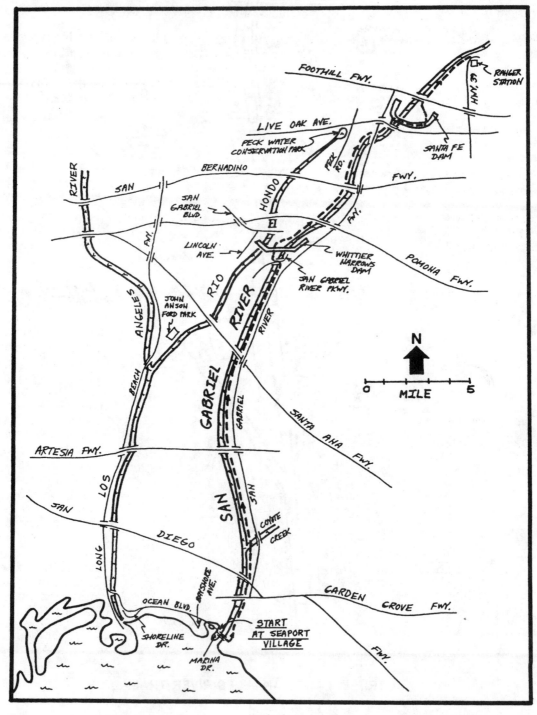

TRIP #22A - SAN GABRIEL RIVER: SEAL BEACH TO EL DORADO PARK

GENERAL LOCATION: Seal Beach - Long Beach

LEVEL OF DIFFICULTY: Up and back - easy
Distance - distance - 5.6 miles (one way)
Elevation gain - essentially flat

HIGHLIGHTS: This is the starting segment of one of the most varied and interesting trips in this book. This is a completely Class I bike route that starts at the scenic lower section of the Gabriel River Trail near the Long Beach Marina and winds up at El Dorado Park. The early part of the trip provides a look at "recreation city" with water, boats, water skiers and jet skiers. The trip transitions into a nature area rich in wildlife and ends in a park that is so inviting that it could serve as a separate family excursion.

TRAILHEAD: Free public parking is available at the Long Beach Marina along Marina Dr. in Naples or along First St. in Seal Beach. From Pacific Coast Highway (PCH) in Seal Beach, turn west on Marina Dr. (2-3 blocks from Main Street in Seal Beach) and drive roughly 1/2 mile to First St. In 1/4 mile, cross the San Gabriel River and continue a short distance into the marina near Seaport Village for parking. The trailhead is at Marina Dr. at the east end (Seal Beach side) of the bridge over the San Gabriel River.

Only a light water supply is needed for this short trip. There are public water sources at the trip origin and terminus.

TRIP DESCRIPTION: **The Scenic Lower River Segment.** The first part of the trip provides views of boaters, water skiers and an interestingly-developed shoreline. The natural river basin passes PCH (0.4), the Westminster Ave. access, and the Haynes Steam Plant (electricity generation). At (2.2), a small alternate Class I bikepath leads off to the east along a 1.2-mile shaded route to Seal Beach Blvd. In this stretch of the river, up to the concrete portion (3.5), one has views of the large bird population that includes pelicans, egrets and the ever-present seagulls. The trip passes under the Garden Grove Fwy. (2.3); just beyond is an exit which takes cyclists to College Park Dr. and Edison Park. Next is the San Diego Fwy. undercrossing (3.5). In this part of the bikepath are many "freeway orchards" -- those freeway-locked areas under the power poles filled with containerized plants.

Bridge North of San Gabriel River/Coyote Creek Confluence

The River Crossing and El Dorado Park. In 0.4 mile, cross a signed bikeway/walkway bridge across the river. Do not miss the bridge unless you've decided to change plans and see Coyote Creek (Trip #24). Once over the bridge, there are views across the river to the El Dorado Golf Course and El Dorado Park West. At 0.7 mile from the bridge crossing, reach Willow St. and skirt the edge of the Nature Study Area which is the south end of El Dorado Park East (5.0). Shortly afterward, the bikepath reaches Spring St. and the entry to Areas I and II of the park (5.6).

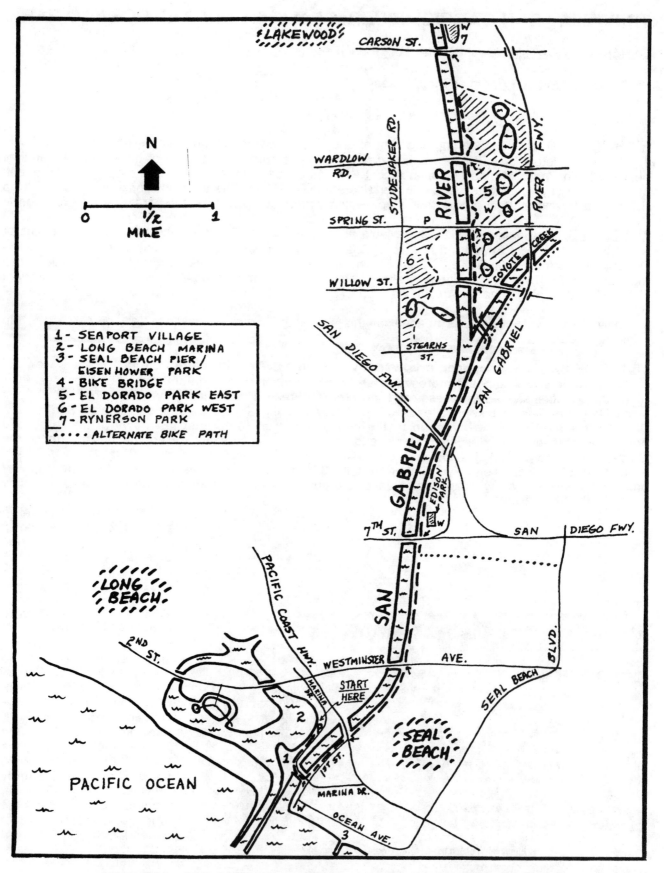

TRIP #22A - SAN GABRIEL RIVER: SEAL BEACH TO ELDORADO PARK

There are a myriad of bikepath options within the park. This portion of the trip is worth a good exploration effort in itself (see Trip #16).

CONNECTING TRIPS: 1) Continuation with the San Gabriel River Trail (Trip #22B) - bike north beyond El Dorado Park toward Wilderness Park; 2) connection with the Belmont Shore/Naples Tour (Trip #15) - from the origin, bike north on Marina Dr. to Second St. Turn left (west) and pedal over the bridge to Naples Island; 3) connection with the El Dorado Park tour (Trip #16) - cruise through the park at the trip terminus; 4) connection with the Coyote Creek Trail (Trip #24) - at the eastern end of the bike bridge across the San Gabriel River, stay on the eastern river bank.

TRIP #22B - SAN GABRIEL RIVER: EL DORADO PARK TO WILDERNESS PARK

GENERAL LOCATION: Long Beach, Lakewood, Cerritos, Norwalk, Downey

LEVEL OF DIFFICULTY: One way - easy; up and back - moderate
Distance - 9.7 miles (one way)
Elevation gain - essentially flat

HIGHLIGHTS: This segment of the Class I San Gabriel River Trail has direct access to five major parks. In particular, this trip should not be completed without a tour of El Dorado Park. Rynerson Park provides a pleasant diversion from the river route and Wilderness Park is a fine rest stop with a small pond/lagoon to dip the toes into before returning to the trip origin. There are horse corrals and equestrian trails beside the bike route in some sections. This is a good workout section as the bike and foot traffic is relatively light.

TRAILHEAD: From the San Diego Fwy., turn north on Palo Verde Ave. and drive 0.9 mile to Spring St. Turn right (east) and continue about 0.8 mile to free parking along Spring St., just west of the bridge over the San Gabriel River. Other options are to head over the bridge and park in the Nature Center parking area (turn south at the park entrance), or to drive up Spring St., make a U-turn and return to the Area II park entrance to the north (right). The latter two options are pay parking.

From the San Gabriel Fwy., turn west on Willow St. (Katella Ave. in Orange County), continue about one mile to Studebaker Rd. and turn right (north). Drive 0.3 mile to Spring St. and turn right. Follow the parking instructions above. For direct entry at Area II (pay parking) from the southbound freeway, exit at Spring St. and turn right at the park entrance.

Bring a light water supply. There is plenty of water and many restroom facilities at the parks along the way. El Dorado Park is a particular delight! Bring some food for the barbecue and enjoy munchies at the park after a tough" bike ride.

TRIP DESCRIPTION: **El Dorado Park**. From the parking area on Spring St., ride over the bridge and turn right (south) at the Nature Center entrance. Make another sharp right and pedal parallel to Spring St. (but in the opposite direction) along the Nature Center roadway. Continue 0.2 mile to the fence along the San Gabriel River Bike Route. Rather than passing through the fence entry, follow the roadway as it turns to the right and passes under Spring St. The road enters Park Area II.

Stay to the left rather than bike into El Dorado Park. Pass through the fence and head right (north) along the San Gabriel River Trail (0.6). The first part of the trip parallels Park Area II. The path leaves the river again and follows the roadway under Wardlow Rd. (1.1). Again, stay to the left and pass through a fence which returns to the river trail (the other option is to bike through Park Area III and rejoin the trail 1/2 mile later). The path stays beside a stand of trees and passes the end of Park Area III (1.6) near the weapons firing range.

Rynerson Park. Pass a pedestrian bridge, cross over to De Mille Junior High School and then pass Carson St. (2.0). For the next 0.7 mile, cruise alongside fun River Park. which boasts tree cover, horse stalls and corrals, horse trails, a little footbridge leading to a connecting alternate bike trail (which

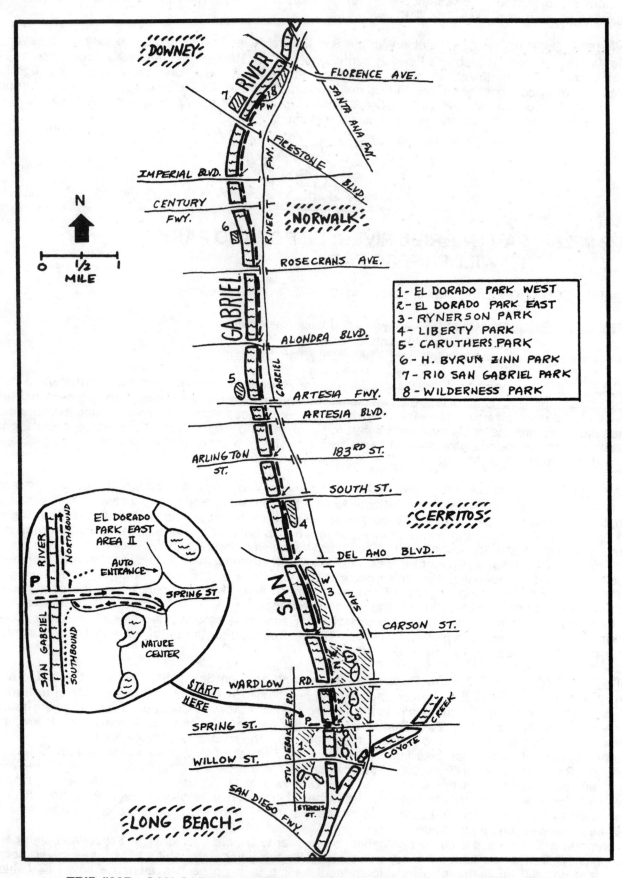

1- EL DORADO PARK WEST
2- EL DORADO PARK EAST
3- RYNERSON PARK
4- LIBERTY PARK
5- CARUTHERS PARK
6- H. BYRUN ZINN PARK
7- RIO SAN GABRIEL PARK
8- WILDERNESS PARK

TRIP #22B - SAN GABRIEL RIVER: ELDORADO PARK TO WILDERNESS PARK

reconnects near Del Amo Blvd.), baseball diamonds and water (near the baseball fields). The shady park area ends near Del Amo Blvd. (3.0).

Bikepath Viewed from Rynerson Park

The Middle Trip Section. For the next half mile, the trip highlight is the clever (and in some cases not so clever) graffiti on the concrete river walls. In 0.8 mile, reach little Liberty Park which is effectively a grassy rest area. Just beyond the park is South St. (3.8), followed by a passage below l83rd St. through a narrow tunnel (4.5). (Reduce speed and keep an eye "peeled" for oncoming bikers.) The route then passes more horse stalls.

The path dips down into the riverbed to cross under Artesia Blvd. (4.9). If you miss the marked route, you can walk (crouch) under the roadway. There is a short section where bikes must be walked across a railroad crossing, followed by passage under the Artesia Fwy. (5.3). The first of many river spillways is near this junction.

The trail passes the Cerritos Ironwood Golf Course; nearby is the pedestrian bridge across the river that leads to Caruthers Park (5.6). This reference path stays on the east levee. Enter a several-mile long pleasant residential stretch beyond Alondra Blvd. where horses are in many of the backyards (we even spotted a llama). Pass Rosecrans Ave. (7.0), another walk bridge over the river and a newer bridge that is part of the Century Fwy. (7.8). In 0.3 mile, the path reaches Imperial Hwy. and later dips down nearer the river, passing below a railroad trestle (8.7).

Wilderness Park. At (9.0), the bike trail passes Firestone Blvd., then reaches the transition to a natural river bottom after 11 solid miles of concrete. Rio San Gabriel Park is across the river and a small spillway graces the river bottom. There is some excellent river bottomland north of this area (see Trips #22C and #22D). In about 0.7 mile the tour reaches a refreshing terminus at Wilderness Park. This is a 1/2-mile strip of park that offers water, restrooms, shade trees, sports and recreation areas, playgrounds, a small pond and a lovely decorative water fountain.

CONNECTING TRIPS: 1) Continuation with the San Gabriel River Trail south to Seal Beach (Trip #22A) from the trip origin, or north to the Whittier Narrows (Trip #22C) from the trip terminus; 2) continuation with the El Dorado Park tour (Trip #16) at the trip origin.

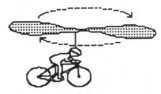

TRIP #22C - SAN GABRIEL RIVER: WILDERNESS PARK TO LEGG LAKE

GENERAL LOCATION: Downey, Santa Fe Springs, Whittier, Pico Rivera

LEVEL OF DIFFICULTY: One way - easy; up and back - moderate
Distance - 7.7 miles (one way)
Elevation gain - essentially flat (single steep grade at Whittier Narrows Dam)

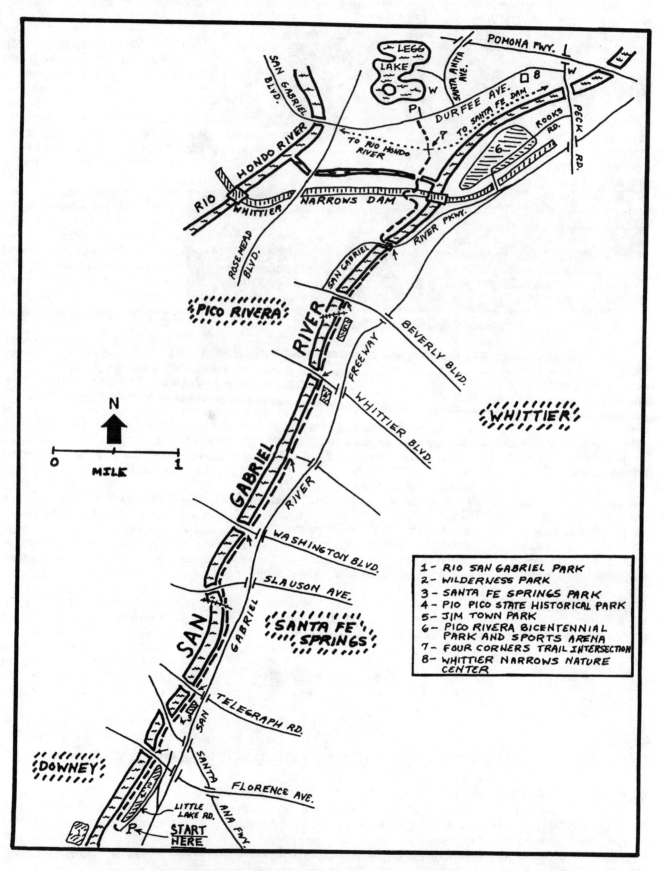

1- RIO SAN GABRIEL PARK
2- WILDERNESS PARK
3- SANTA FE SPRINGS PARK
4- PIO PICO STATE HISTORICAL PARK
5- JIM TOWN PARK
6- PICO RIVERA BICENTENNIAL PARK AND SPORTS ARENA
7- FOUR CORNERS TRAIL INTERSECTION
8- WHITTIER NARROWS NATURE CENTER

TRIP #22C - SAN GABRIEL RIVER: WILDERNESS PARK TO LEGG LAKE

HIGHLIGHTS: This is a pleasant segment of the San Gabriel River Trail that starts at Wilderness Park, visits Santa Fe Springs Park and ends at the trip highlight in the Whittier Narrows Recreation Area. A short diversion at Whittier Blvd. leads to Pio Pico State Historical Park. The Whittier Narrows area sports a ride on the dam levee, a visit to a wildlife refuge area, and a trip at the end to relaxing Legg Lake. This is one of the few river segments that is predominantly natural river bottom and there are some lush areas that beckon for rest stops. This is 99% Class I trail (two street crossings) with light bike traffic south of the Whittier Narrows Dam.

TRAILHEAD: From the San Gabriel River Fwy., exit west on Florence Ave. A short distance west of the freeway, turn left (south) on Little Lake Rd. This road also leads back onto the southbound freeway; therefore, in a few hundred feet, turn right onto Little Lake Rd. proper. Continue on this roadway to the free parking area at Wilderness Park. From the Santa Ana Fwy., exit west on Florence Ave. Pass under the San Gabriel Fwy. and follow the directions above.

Bring a moderate water supply. There is no enroute water supply between Santa Fe Springs Park and the Whittier Narrows Recreation Area. (Water sources near the recreation area are at Legg Lake and the Nature Center).

TRIP DESCRIPTION: **Wilderness Park to Santa Fe Springs Park.** From the south end of the parking lot, skirt the south edge of Wilderness Park and follow the path to the river entry. Turn right (north) and bike past Florence Ave. (0.2) and the first of many spillways 0.2 mile further. There are scattered trees and a great deal of brush along the path and the riverbed is built up into holding basins. At (0.7) reach Santa Fe Springs Park where there are play areas, shade, recreation fields and restrooms. Fill up with water here if you are running low.

The Railroad Route and Pio Pico Historical Park. About 0.4 mile from the park, cross Telegraph Rd. At (1.4) the bikeway passes the highest (about six feet) spillway on this segment of the river. In this area is a stand of eucalyptus trees and a collection of horse stalls tucked between the river and the San Gabriel Fwy. At (2.1) pass under a railroad trestle. Soon after, another railroad track comes in from the east and parallels the bike route for several miles. There is a high likelihood of having a train for company on this stretch.

Four Corners Trail Intersection (Susan Cohen Photo)

Soon the route passes under another railroad trestle which, in turn, lies below the highly-elevated Slauson Ave. overpass (2.3). The riverbed and greenery in the riverbed continue, while there is brush and railroad tracks to the right. At (3.0) is Washington Blvd. and the beginning of a long exposed stretch of bikeway. In about 0.6 mile is the biker/pedestrian entry at Dunlap Crossing Rd. At (4.7) the path meets Whittier Blvd.; it is a 0.2-mile diversion to the right (east) to visit Pio Pico Historical Park and the Pio Pico Museum.

Our route transits a short tunnel under Whittier Blvd. and passes alongside dense brush on the right. At (5.3) the path heads under another railroad trestle; the paralleling railroad tracks fuse and the merged track leaves the river heading east. In 0.2 mile is Beverly Blvd. Further north is a spillway with a large enough collecting basin to support a flock of young water frolickers. There is a view into Rose Hills to the east.

Whittier Narrows Dam. The trip reaches a junction where the trail changes from asphalt to dirt at San Gabriel River Pkwy. (6.1). The dam is viewable at this point. Continue ahead if you have a wide tire bike and a desire to see Pico Rivera Bicentennial Park and Sports Area. Our reference route follows the parkway and crosses the river to the west side. Pedal north and observe the lush tree-filled river bottom. Pass the Pico Rivera Golf Course (6.7) and make a hard left at the dam base. From this point is a short, steep path to the top of the dam (6.9). Stop and take in some of the excellent sights viewable here.

Whittier Narrows Recreation Area. (See Trip #26 map for additional detail). Cruise down the meandering concrete bikeway on the backside of the dam, cross a water run-off channel and reach the marked Four Corners Trail Intersection (7.2).

Bike straight ahead and pedal about 0.3 mile to a junction near another water channel. Turn left, crossing over the channel and bike a couple hundred yards through the lush bottomland to Durfee Ave. and pass through the gate Turn right (east) and cruise a few hundred feet to the Legg Lake parking area entry within the Whittier Narrows Recreation Area (7.7).

CONNECTING TRIPS: 1) Continuation with the San Gabriel River Trail south to El Dorado Park (Trip #22B) - from the trip origin, bike south; 2) continuation with the San Gabriel River Trail north to Santa Fe Dam (Trip #22D) - from the Four Corners Trail Intersection, turn right (east) at the junction; 3) connection/continuation with the Whittier Narrows/Legg Lake Trail (Trip #26) - from Legg Lake, return to the Four Corners Trail Intersection and turn right (west).

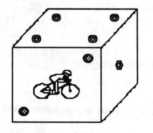

TRIP #22D - SAN GABRIEL RIVER: LEGG LAKE TO SANTA FE DAM

GENERAL LOCATION: Whittier Narrows, El Monte, Baldwin Park, Irwindale

LEVEL OF DIFFICULTY: One way - easy; up and back - moderate
Distance - 11.4 miles (one way)
Elevation gain - essentially flat (single steep grade at Santa Fe Dam)

HIGHLIGHTS: This is one of our favorite segments of the river trips. The San Gabriel River in the Whittier Narrows region is river stomping at its best; there are trees, thickets, clear running water and readily visible wildlife in all. The Whittier Narrows Recreation Area offers a wildlife sanctuary, Legg Lake, vista points from the top of the dam and a diversion trip to the Pico Rivera Bicentennial Park and Sports Area. The Santa Fe Dam Recreation Area offers an expansive, pleasant picnic and recreation area at the edge of the lake, as well as superb lookout points from the top of the dam. Set aside a few hours and fully explore these territories. The best time to take this trip is within several days of a cold winter storm when the snow level in the nearby mountains is low. The route is nearly 100% Class I (one street crossing).

There are also some excellent trip excursions in the Santa Fe Dam area. They range from on-road explorations to the west of the San Gabriel River Fwy. and on the west levee to some dirt bike meandering in the flood control basin behind the dam.

TRAILHEAD: From the Pomona Fwy., exit at Rosemead Blvd. south, travel about 0.8 mile to San Gabriel Blvd./Durfee Blvd. and turn left. Drive on Durfee Ave. 0.6 mile and turn left into the pay parking area at Legg Lake. Find a tree under which to park your car. Bring four quarters for the parking area fee.

Bring a moderate water supply. There are rest and water stops directly on the route and at the Santa Fe Recreation Area terminus.

TRIP DESCRIPTION: **Whittier Narrows Recreation Area.** (See the Trip #26 map for additional detail.) Leave the parking area and cross Durfee Ave. a few hundred feet west of the parking area. Pass

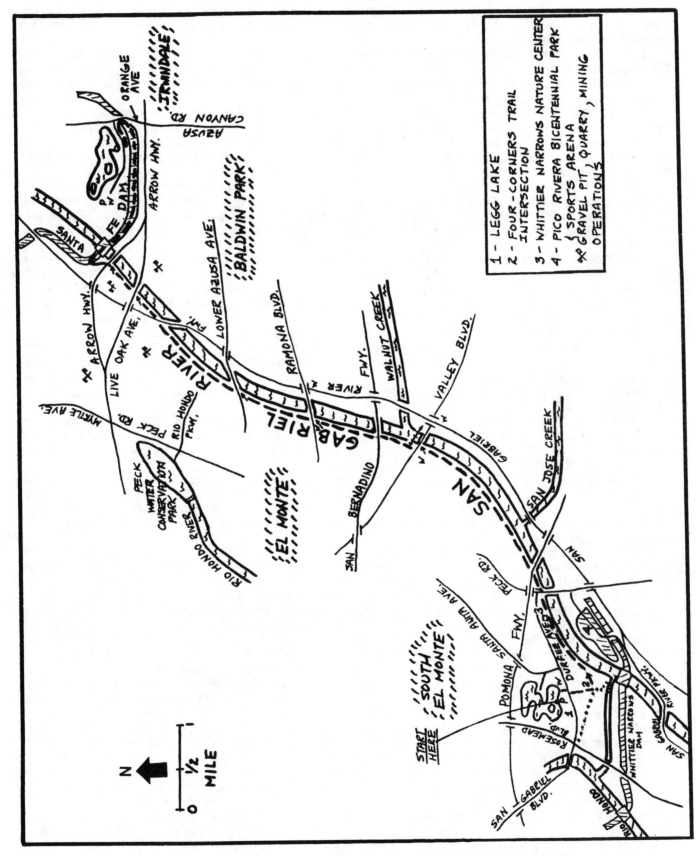

Legend:
1 - LEGG LAKE
2 - FOUR-CORNERS TRAIL INTERSECTION
3 - WHITTIER NARROWS NATURE CENTER
4 - PICO RIVERA BICENTENNIAL PARK
※ SPORTS ARENA
⚒ GRAVEL PIT, QUARRY, MINING OPERATIONS

TRIP #22D - SAN GABRIEL RIVER: LEGG LAKE TO SANTA FE DAM

through the signed gate and pedal down a small asphalt road through an area surrounded by bushes, plants, trees and brush. In a short distance is a junction just beyond a small water channel. The path left leads toward (but bypasses) the Whittier Narrows Nature Center. However, our route proceeds to the right and meets the Four Corners Trail Intersection in 0.3 miles (0.5). There is a nice view into the backside of the Whittier Narrows Dam from this area.

Turn left (east) and follow the path as it turns northward and rejoins the San Gabriel River (0.7). There are permanent horse trails to the left (west) and also "find-your-way" paths in the lush river bed; both are well used by horse riders, the latter accompanying our path for the next couple of miles. This area has excellent views of Rose Hills to the east.

The Unofficial Recreation Area/San Jose Creek Confluence. Pass the first of many spillways that stair-step their way up the river (1.4). Small children slide down the rounded portion of the spillway into a holding basin below and even a swimming dog might be seen. In 0.4 mile is Peck Rd. and a second spillway with a large pool backed up behind it. (There are gas stations and restaurants not too far from the river at this exit.)

The trail passes under the Pomona Fwy. (2.0) and reaches the third spillway, which usually has some fishermen and a few swimmers using the upstream water pool. In 0.3 mile is the confluence with San Jose Creek and one of the most well-used of the unofficial recreation spots on the river. There are inner-tube riders, swimmers, fishermen, horses with riders crossing the river and even some off-road bicycling.

The Middle Segment. At (2.7) is a small rodeo ring where bikers have a free chance to watch the trainers work with horses or, with luck, to watch a mini-rodeo. Just beyond is one of the highest spillways on the river (about ten feet) with a holding basin stretched across the river on the downstream side. The route continues alongside residential areas, passes Mountain View High Athletic Field (3.9) and reaches Valley Blvd. (4.1). There is a small bike rest stop here with a simple pipe water fountain. On a clear day, there is a striking view into the San Gabriel Mountains from this point.

The bikepath travels under a railroad bridge and later meets the Walnut Creek junction (4.3). From this point north, the water level drops significantly and the river bed is much less interesting. At this junction, to the left (west) of the trail, is a corral that holds Brahma bulls and a buffalo. Continuing onward, the bikeway passes the San Bernardino Fwy. (4.7) and then meets another biker rest area at Ramona Blvd. (5.6).

The Gravel Pits. At (6.5), the route passes the first of several large gravel dredging operations (to the right). In 0.2 mile, the trip passes Lower Azusa Rd. There is a large, open, water-filled gravel pit to the left (west) (5.9), followed by a "granddaddy" gravel pit across the river to the right (6.4). Also there are several highly visible above-ground mining operations.

Santa Fe Dam. At (7.5), the path crosses under the San Gabriel River Fwy. and points cyclists directly into the Santa Fe Dam face. The route passes a power station (7.0), Live Oak Ave., and appears to dead-end at Arrow Hwy. (8.8). Cross that street and follow the signed path left and bike to the base of the dam. Pass through the walker/biker entry opening in the fence and pump a short, steep grade to the top of the dam (9.2).

From the top of the dam in winter are views into the San Gabriel Mountains that are awe-inspiring! along with views into the San Jose Hills to the southeast and Puente Hills to the south. The cities of the foothills are spread out all the way to the western horizon.

There is a paved trail left (northwest) that ends just below the west levee terminus. (See the last of the "Santa Fe Dam Excursions" below.) However, our route goes right and continues another 1.9 miles along the top of the dam providing other fine views, including those down into the Santa Fe Recreational Area. The dam trail descends and ends at the bike trail access gate. The route then proceeds 0.2 mile further to the auto access road into the recreation area (Orange Ave. which is named Azusa Canyon Rd. south of Arrow Hwy.). The mileage at this point is (11.4).

Santa Fe Dam Recreation Area. The recreation area behind the dam is a charmer. To get there, make a hard left onto the automobile roadway access just downhill of the auto pay gate. There are bikepaths and a low-speed-limit, lightly-traveled paved road that can be linked into a couple of miles more biking. The entire park is built alongside a lake and comes equipped with water and restrooms, picnic areas, swimming area with a sand beach, playgrounds, fire pits, shaded pagodas (group area at the western end of the lake), boat rental and a snack bar.

There are also bicycle roadways beyond the west end of the lake. In periods of low water, fat-tire bikes can be ridden through this maze of dirt trails to the westside dam levee access. (See the last of the "Santa Fe Dam Excursions" below.)

Santa Fe Dam Excursions. At the west base of the dam, just before beginning to climb to the top, there is a trail heading north and west to a tunnel under the San Gabriel River Fwy. On the west side of the freeway is a "T" junction; The south fork transitions to dirt in 0.5 mile and follows the Buena Vista Channel west almost to Buena Vista St. -- a fence prevents access to that street. The north fork climbs a small levee in 0.8 mile to San Gabriel Fwy. level, then drops down to the Santa Fe Dam Flying Area (model airplanes). Climbing to the opposite levee leads to a ride extension of 0.5-mile, paralleling Duarte Rd., to the levee's terminus. At the terminus, the packed-dirt road leading west towards Duarte Rd. is blocked by the City of Duarte Maintenance Yard, while the eastern path leads into the dirt areas of the main flood control basin. The path south parallels the freeway and loops back to the incoming route in 0.5 mile. The north fork route totals three miles round trip.

Atop Santa Fe Dam with Recreation Area Below

Another choice, once on top of the Santa Fe Dam, is to bike northwest and explore the one-mile west levee, which parallels the San Gabriel River Fwy. The outlet is a downhill into the main flood control basin behind the dam. There are dirt paths winding over the entire basin, including routes leading across to the lakeside recreation area or under the San Gabriel River Fwy. and Foothill Fwy. (Do not attempt to bike in this area during rainy periods!)

CONNECTING TRIPS: 1) Continuation with the southbound San Gabriel River Trail to Wilderness Park (Trip #22C) - from the Four Corners Trail Intersection, head south and over the Whittier Narrows Dam; 2) continuation with the northbound San Gabriel River Trail to the San Gabriel River Canyon (Trip #22E) - at the recreation area auto access, bike north (nearly straight ahead). Follow the trail signs.

TRIP #22E - SAN GABRIEL RIVER: SANTA FE DAM TO SAN GABRIEL CANYON

GENERAL LOCATION: Irwindale, Azusa

LEVEL OF DIFFICULTY: One way - easy; up and back - moderate
Distance - 7.5 miles (one way)
Elevation gain - essentially flat (single steep grade at Santa Fe Dam)

HIGHLIGHTS: This 100% Class I trip starts downstream of the Santa Fe Dam, then climbs onto and follows the dam levee. The route cruises from the dam upstream to the end of the San Gabriel River Trail at the L.A. National Forest Information Center in San Gabriel Canyon. Along the way, the path traverses the Santa Fe Dam Nature Area which has a natural river-bottom cactus garden. There are spectacular close-up views of the foothills and surrounding mountains. These views are absolutely great after a cold winter storm. The stretch north of the dam is little used and makes a good work-out trip.

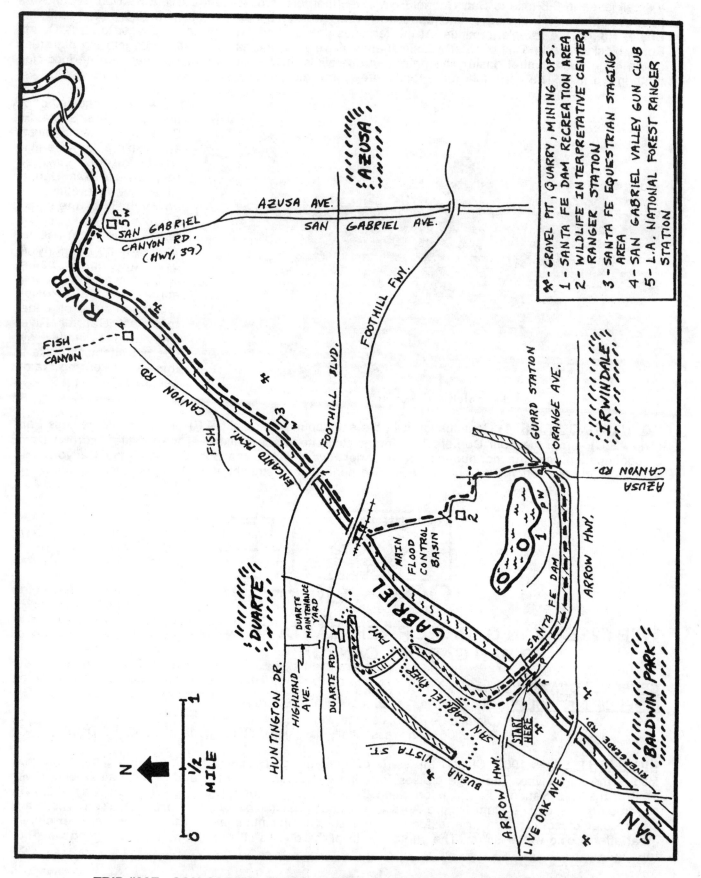

TRIP #22E - SAN GABRIEL RIVER: SANTA FE DAM TO SAN GABRIEL CANYON

TRAILHEAD: From the San Gabriel River Fwy., exit east on Live Oak Ave. and continue 0.9 mile to the junction with Arrow Hwy., making a U-turn onto Arrow Hwy. Drive in the reverse direction about 0.8 mile to free parking near the dam outlet.

An option is to use pay parking in the Santa Fe Dam Recreation Area. This is particularly useful if you wish to avoid riding up onto the dam and want to start from the recreation area. Exit on Live Oak Ave. (east) as above, but continue one mile past the junction of Live Oak and Arrow Hwy. Turn left (north) at the Recreation Park entrance at Orange Ave. (named Azusa Canyon Rd. to the south).

TRIP DESCRIPTION: Santa Fe Dam. From the free parking area on Arrow Hwy., pedal to the bike entry through the fence (to the west of the spillway near the dam base). Follow the bike trail signs and pump the steep roadway to the top of the dam (0.2). At the top is a great 360-degree view. Most prominent are the San Gabriel Mountains to the north and the San Jose Hills and Puente Hills to the southeast and south, respectively. The view into the mountains is a real "heart grabber" when the snow level is down to low elevations and the sky is clear.

There is a paved trail left (northwest) that ends just below the west levee terminus. (See the last of the "Santa Fe Dam Excursions" below.) However, our route goes right and continues another 1.9 miles along the top of the dam providing other fine views, including those down into the Santa Fe Recreational Area. The dam trail descends and ends at the bike trail access gate. The route then proceeds 0.2 mile further to the auto access road into the recreation area (Orange Ave. which is named Azusa Canyon Rd. south of Arrow Hwy.). The mileage at this point is (11.4).

There is a paved trail left (northwest) that ends just below the west levee terminus. (See Trip #22D under "Santa Fe Dam Excursions".) However, our route goes right and travels 1.9 miles on the dam levee, providing additional interesting views, including a look down into the Santa Fe Dam Recreation Area. The dam trail ends at a bike access gate and proceeds 0.2 mile to the pay gate/auto access road into the recreation area (2.3).

Head downhill and turn sharply left below the pay gate to visit the developed park (southern) section of the Santa Fe Dam Recreation Area (see Trip #22D). Our route follows the signed bike route and keeps straight ahead.

Northern Santa Fe Dam Recreation Area. Follow the road to the dead-end at a little walled park-like area (2.8). Turn left and continue tracking the well-marked road 0.2 mile until it turns right (north) again. In 0.2 mile reach the Wildlife Interpretive Center which has both picnic and tent camping areas near the roadway intersection (3.2). Turn left again and pedal a few hundred feet to the ranger station. There are two bike route options at this point, plus marked walking/nature trails which tour the wildlife area. All routes head west and shortly meet an old north-south asphalt road. Follow the bike trail marker and turn right (north) on that old road.

The roadway passes through an interesting ecological area which is surrounded by a wide variety of cactus. At (3.8) reach the top of a small rise; from here is a nice view which includes a good look at the surrounding bottomland, the backside of the Santa Fe Dam and a view north to the Foothill Fwy. In 0.4 mile, the path returns to the San Gabriel River and passes under the Foothill Fwy. just beyond (4.3).

The Gravel Pits. At (4.8) pass a trans-river passenger cable car. In 0.1 mile is Huntington Dr./Foothill Blvd. Next is the Santa Fe Equestrian Staging Area which has restrooms and water (5.2). There is a large above-ground gravel mining/processing works in the background. The river bed is boulder- and brush- filled with a low spillway breaking the continuity of the scene every half-mile or more.

At (5.5), the path goes by an old closed-off railroad bridge. There is a residential area across the river with the homes continuing up into the nearby foothills. There are more gravel operations along the roadway to the right (east) with one sand and gravel operation lying right next to the trail (6.1). The route also passes a large water-filled gravel pit (6.5).

San Gabriel Canyon Entrance. The trail heads into a progressively more well-defined canyon environment. At (6.8), the route passes Fish Canyon in the hills to the left (west). There is an exquisite series of waterfalls (wintertime) several miles back into the canyon called Fish Falls. (Sorry, this is hiking country only.) At this point on the bike trail, there is also a firing range, the San Gabriel Valley Gun Club. The hills echo the sounds, providing a "Gunfight at the OK Corral" aura.

Just beyond, the trail dead-ends at a fence (7.5). A small trail to the right leads to Hwy. 39 and the L.A. National Forest Ranger Station. There is water and parking here if you want to start from this direction or to use this as a pickup or turnaround point.

CONNECTING TRIPS: 1) Continuation with the San Gabriel River Trail south to Whittier Narrows (Trip #22D) - cross Arrow Hwy. and bike east a few hundred feet (in front of the spillway); 2) continuation with a very strenuous Class X "gut-buster" up San Gabriel Canyon Rd. - we <u>observed</u> a few hearty bikers working their way up the several miles of continuous steep grade; 3) connection with the Duarte Bikeway (Trip #64) - exit at Huntington Dr./Foothill Blvd. and bike west 1/4 mile to Las Lomas Rd.

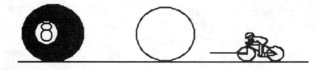

TRIP #23 - SAN GABRIEL, RIO HONDO, L.A. RIVER LOOP
- - "THE BIG BANANA"

GENERAL LOCATION: Long Beach-San Gabriel Canyon-Peck Water Conservation Park-Long Beach

LEVEL OF DIFFICULTY: Loop - very strenuous
Distance - 83.5 miles
Elevation gain - essentially flat (three short, steep dam climbs)

HIGHLIGHTS: This trip starts from the Pacific Ocean, visits the foothills of the San Gabriel Mountains, and returns to the ocean in one big loop. The route tours the San Gabriel, Rio Hondo and Los Angeles Rivers. Along the way are some of the finest parks and recreation areas in Southern California, e.g., El Dorado Park, Whittier Narrows and Santa Fe Dam Recreation Areas and John Anson Ford Park.

Portions of the route are little known to most Angelenos (and Orange "Countians"), such as the San Gabriel Canyon segment and the Upper Rio Hondo segment, including the Peck Water Conservation Park (reservoir). Taken soon after a cool, wet winter storm, this may be the most scenic and inspiring trip in our book!

TRAILHEAD: Refer to the parking instructions for Trip #14.

Bring 2-3 filled water bottles or load up at the trailhead. There are many water stops along the way, but having plenty lessens the number of required stops. Start this trip in the early morning to lessen the effect of headwinds coming off the ocean and to minimize sun exposure

TRIP DESCRIPTION: The trip description will detail only the new or confusing portions of the loop. The tour starts at Shoreline Park (Trip #14), travels to Marina Dr. in Seal Beach (Trip #15), proceeds north up the San Gabriel River (Trip #22), transitions west to Peck Water Conservation Park and returns to Long Beach via the Rio Hondo and Los Angeles Rivers (Trips #19 and #20, respectively).

Long Beach to Seal Beach. (Refer to Trip #14.) Exit the Shoreline Village parking area and follow the parking access road that parallels Shoreline Dr. Bike past the overhead walkway along the perimeter of Shoreline Village and turn left at the street's end (0.3). Pedal through the easternmost village parking area on roadway which parallels Shoreline Dr. At the end of the parking lot, follow the bikepath north toward the Villa Riviera Hotel (0.8).

At the first bikepath junction just beyond, turn right and follow the Class I oceanfront path 3.0 miles to its end at Bay Shore Dr. Follow Bay Shore Dr. 0.3 mile and turn right on 2nd St. (see Trip #15 map) (4.1). Cross the two Naples Island bridges and, just past the second bridge, turn right on Marina Dr. (5.2). Follow Marina Dr. around the marina periphery and, near the Seaport Village entry, turn left (6.3). Just across the bridge (southeast side) is the bike entry to the San Gabriel River (see Trip #22A) (6.4).

San Gabriel River. Pedal 3.9 miles to the "Y" river channel junction. Cross the bike-pedestrian bridge across the river (see Trip #22A). Bike along the east levee of the San Gabriel River and make two short passages along the edge of El Dorado Park (13.0). The next major decision point is about 14 miles down the road where the path crosses to the west side of the river at the San Gabriel River Pkwy. (see Trips #22B, #22C) (27.1).

The path leads to the top of the dam, then downhill to the Four Corners Trail Intersection (28.2). Turn right (east) and follow the river on the west levee to the river outlet at the Santa Fe Dam (36.5). Cross Arrow Hwy., turn left (west), then follow the trail up to and across the dam top. The outlet trail passes the automobile entry fee station, heads downhill and continues straight ahead (north) (see Trip #22D) (39.1).

The junction to the left enters the Santa Fe Dam Recreation Area. Follow the bike trail signs and rejoin the river on the east levee (41.0). Bike 3.3 miles to the trails' end at the entry to San Gabriel

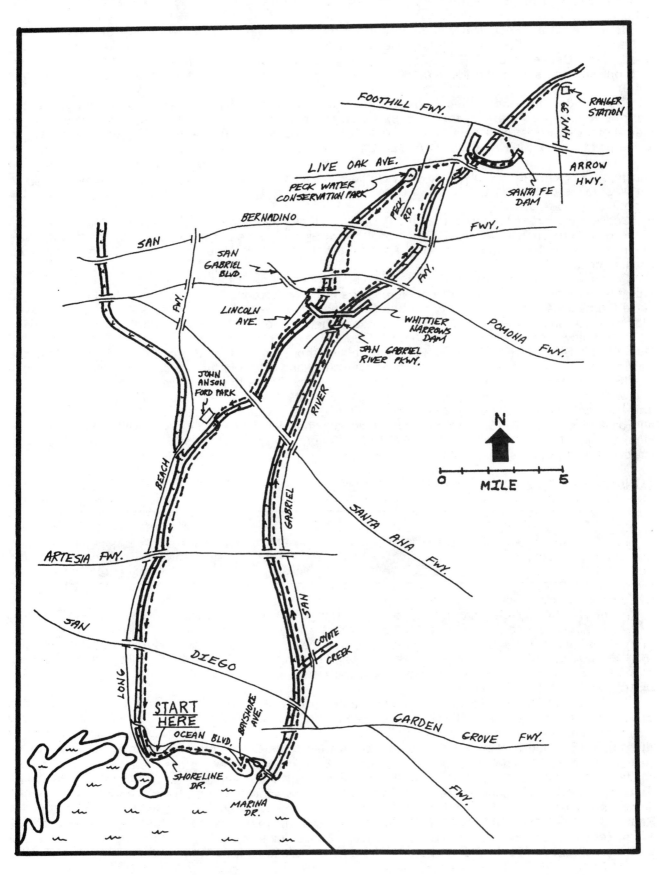

TRIP #23 - SAN GABRIEL, RIO HONDO & L.A. RIVERS -- "THE BIG BANANA"

Canyon (see Trip #22E). Reverse the route and return to the base of Santa Fe Dam at Arrow Hwy. (51.8).

Santa Fe Dam - Peck Water Conservation Park. Bike west on Arrow Hwy./Live Oak Ave. 1.9 miles to Peck Rd. Turn left (south), ride 0.8 mile on Peck Rd. and turn right at Rio Hondo Pkwy. into Peck Road Water Conservation Park (54.5). Pedal to the south end of the parking lot and follow the small path on the west side of the reservoir. At the spillway is a sign noting the start of the formal bike trail (54.9).

Rio Hondo and Los Angeles River. Follow the Upper Rio Hondo bikeway 5.2 miles to Whittier Narrows Recreation Area A" (see Trip #19). Pedal to the very south end of the recreation area and find the trail that is almost right next to and parallels the Pomona Fwy. Follow the route under the freeway to the point where it leaves the river at San Gabriel Blvd. (61.8).

Ride west on the bridge over the river and bike 0.3 mile to Lincoln Ave. and turn left and left immediately again into the bike trail entry. Follow the path 0.6 mile to a point at the western edge of the west levee of the Whittier Narrows Dam (next to Lincoln Ave.). This is the official beginning of the Lario Trail (Trip #20) (62.7).

Cruise east across the top of the dam 0.4 mile and take the path down the south side (spillway side) of the dam (see Trips #20A and #20B). Pedal 5.4 miles on the west levee of the Rio Hondo and cross the river on a bike bridge near John Anson Ford Park (68.2). The route reaches the L.A. River confluence at (70.9).

Continue on the east levee of the L.A. River into Long Beach to the end of the Lario Trail (82.6). With the recently-constructed bike undercrossings in this segment of the trip, bikers no longer have to leave the river path in high water conditions (as used to be the case at Rosecrans Ave., Compton Ave., Alondra Blvd. and Del Amo Blvd.). Just past the signed end of the Lario Trail, ride through the parking lot and follow the shoreline around the Queensway (Catalina Cruise) Landing and under the Queensway Bridge. Hug the L.A. River shoreline, then turn left at Pierpoint Landing. Follow the walking/biking trail on the north side of Rainbow Harbor and return to the starting point (83.5).

"Small Banana" Trip Option. A 50-mile version of this trip is to park at De Forest Ave. just north of Willow St. (see Trip #20B map) and proceed over Signal Hill to the San Gabriel River. Follow the river trail north to the Whittier Narrows Dam to the Four Corners Trail Intersection. Take the left (west) trail and bike to Durfee Ave./San Gabriel Blvd. Turn left, then left again (south) at Lincoln Ave. (Trip #26 map) and join the Lario Trail along the Rio Hondo River. Cruise the Rio Hondo and L.A. Rivers back to the starting point (Trips #19, #20A and #20B).

<u>CONNECTING TRIPS</u>: See individual trip writeups.

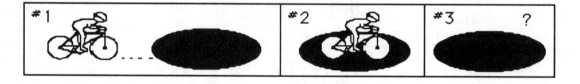

TRIP #24 - COYOTE CREEK TRAIL

<u>GENERAL LOCATION</u>: Long Beach, Seal Beach, Cerritos, Santa Fe Springs

<u>LEVEL OF DIFFICULTY</u>: One way - easy; up and back - moderate
Distance - 14.0 miles (one way)
Elevation gain - essentially flat

<u>HIGHLIGHTS</u>: Another of the river trails, this is a 99.44% pure Class I route. It starts at the scenic lower section of the San Gabriel River outlet near the Long Beach Marina and proceeds to the Coyote Creek junction. The Coyote Creek path is well maintained, but lightly used. The 10.1-mile Coyote Creek section is not highly scenic, unless one enjoys "window shopping" into backyards of the adjoining homes and apartments. It is a fine workout bikeway, however. The trip passes alongside Cerritos Regional County Park, which is a convenient and pleasant rest point near the center of the Coyote Creek segment. Beyond the Artesia Fwy. is the 2.5-mile (most recent) extension through commercial area to a terminus at Foster Rd. A short ride from here leads to shaded Frontier Park.

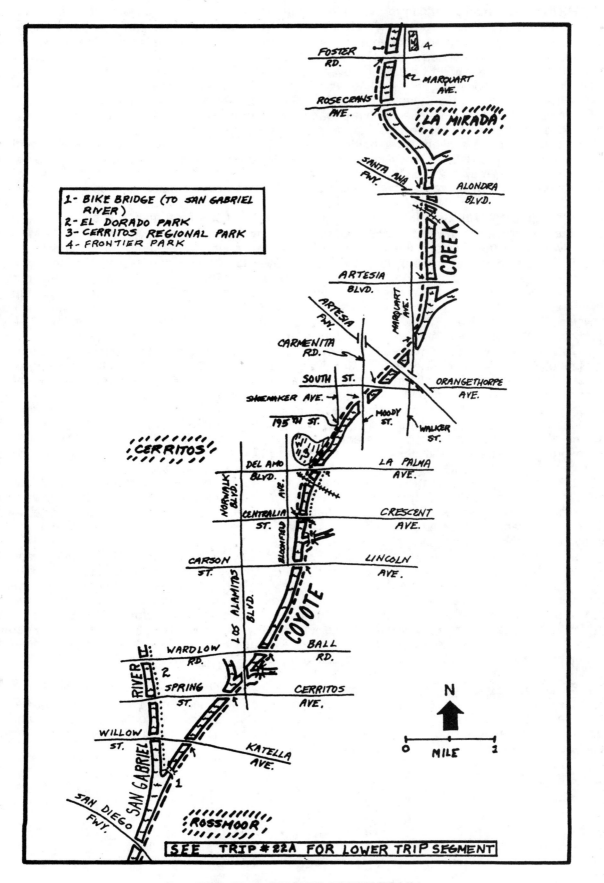

1- BIKE BRIDGE (TO SAN GABRIEL RIVER)
2- EL DORADO PARK
3- CERRITOS REGIONAL PARK
4- FRONTIER PARK

FOSTER RD.

MARQUART AVE.

ROSECRANS AVE.

LA MIRADA

SANTA ANA FWY.

ALONDRA BLVD.

CREEK

ARTESIA BLVD.

ARTESIA FWY.

MARQUART AVE.

CARMENITA RD.

SOUTH ST.

ORANGETHORPE AVE.

SHOEMAKER AVE.

195TH ST.

MOODY ST.

WALKER ST.

CERRITOS

DEL AMO BLVD.

LA PALMA AVE.

NORWALK BLVD.

BLOOMFIELD AVE.

CENTRALIA ST.

CRESCENT AVE.

CARSON ST.

LINCOLN AVE.

LOS ALAMITOS BLVD.

COYOTE

WARDLOW RD.

BALL RD.

RIVER

SPRING ST.

CERRITOS AVE.

WILLOW ST.

KATELLA AVE.

SAN GABRIEL

SAN DIEGO FWY.

ROSSMOOR

N

0   MILE   1

SEE TRIP #22A FOR LOWER TRIP SEGMENT

TRIP #24 - COYOTE CREEK TRAIL

113

TRAILHEAD: Free public parking is available on Marina Dr. in Long Beach or along First St. in Seal Beach. From Pacific Coast Highway (PCH) in Seal Beach, turn west on Marina Dr. (2-3 blocks from Main Street in Seal Beach) and continue roughly 0.5 mile to First St. In another 1/4 mile, cross the San Gabriel River and continue a short distance along the marina for parking. The trailhead is located at Marina Dr. at the east end of the bridge over the San Gabriel River (across from Seaport Village).

An alternate start point is Edison Park, which starts cyclists much nearer to the Coyote Creek/San Gabriel River junction. From Studebaker Rd. in South Long Beach, turn east on E. 9th St. and right (south) immediately after. Continue on that unnamed road to its end at College Park Dr., cross the San Gabriel River, and turn left just beyond into the park. Carefully observe posted parking signs.

Bikers should have a filled water bottle since the trip is waterless up to Cerritos Regional Park. Riders starting at Seal Beach can cycle south about 0.3 mile from the trailhead to use restrooms at the beach. The side trip may also serve as a very pleasant scenic diversion. After the ride, Seaport Village at the marina edge may serve as a nice dining spot, watering hole, or place to shop.

TRIP DESCRIPTION: **The Scenic Lower Segment.** (See Trip #22A for a map of this segment.) The first part of the trip provides views of boaters, water skiers, and an interestingly-developed shoreline. The natural river basin then passes the PCH access, the Westminster Ave. entry (1.2), and the Haynes Steam Plant (electricity generation). At (2.2), a small diversion Class I path leads off to the east along a 1.2-mile shaded route to Seal Beach Blvd. In this stretch of the river, up to the concrete portion at about (3.5), one has views of a large bird population that includes pelicans, egrets, and the ever-present seagulls. The path goes under the Garden Grove Fwy. (2.3), passes Edison Park, then ducks below the San Diego Fwy. (3.5). In this portion of the path are many "freeway orchards" -- those freeway-locked areas under the power poles which are used for growing containerized plants.

Coyote Creek. At (3.9), a marked bridge over the river takes bikers to the connecting portion of the San Gabriel River Bike Trail (Trip #22A). However, at this junction, our route continues along the east side (stay to the right) of the channel and passes the Katella Ave. entry, the San Gabriel River Fwy., and the Cerritos Ave. access (5.2). Nearby, the channel junctions to the north (no easy access at this junction was found), although our reference route stays along the east side of the channel. Two additional small channel junctions to the east are encountered at (5.6) and (7.3). However, both junctions are closed off by locked gates and the main Coyote Creek path crosses those junctions via small overpasses. The Los Alamitos access is at about (5.6). Pass Ball Rd., a small walking-only bridge across the creek at (6.3), Lincoln Ave., and bike to Crescent Ave./Centrailia St.

Exit the bikeway and cross to the west bank. Continue 1/2 mile to La Palma Ave./Del Amo Blvd. and pass alongside Cerritos County Regional Park. There is water within sight of the bikeway plus a park complete with restrooms, recreational fields, and a limited amount of shade. Pedal along a residential area and pass under Moody St./Carmenita Rd., then South St./Orangethorpe Ave. (Note the fast food establishments and gas stations to the west.) (9.2).

In a short distance, bike under the Artesia Fwy. and pass alongside residential developments (with scattered shade trees), then cycle past Walker St./Marquart Ave. The path veers left (due north) along the La Canada Verde Creek fork (the main Coyote Creek fork branches northeast) and continues another 0.4 mile to Artesia Blvd. The channel dips under the Santa Ana Fwy. and Alondra Blvd. on a recently opened 2.5-mile path extension through a strictly commercial zone. The bikeway passes alongside the Santa Fe Springs Drive-in Theater (12.3), then beelines 1.7 miles to its end at Foster Rd.

A short ride east on Foster Rd. leads to Marquart Ave. and Frontier Park. The park has shade (a rare commodity on the ride), water, restrooms, a children's play area and barbecue facilities.

CONNECTING TRIPS: 1) Continuation/connection to lower and middle portions of the San Gabriel River tour (Trips #22A and #22B) - take major access streets west and cross the San Gabriel River Fwy., noting that distance between Coyote Creek and the San Gabriel River increases the further north one goes on Coyote Creek; 2) connectors to the lower portion of this trip along the San Gabriel River are described in Trip #22A.

TRIP #25 - WEST FORK, SAN GABRIEL RIVER

GENERAL LOCATION: Angeles National Forest

LEVEL OF DIFFICULTY: **Glen Camp Loop**: Up and back - moderate
Distance - 13.4 miles (up and back)
Elevation gain - 450 feet

Cogswell Reservoir Loop: Up and back - strenuous
Distance - 15.0 miles (up and back)
Elevation gain - 800 feet (sheer grade up to reservoir)

HIGHLIGHTS: This is one of the most natural scenic rides in our book. This trip follows the meandering West Fork of the San Gabriel River from Hwy. 39 to Cogswell Reservoir. The route is through a forested canyon along a well-maintained service road and is Class I since it is closed to public traffic. The views of the surrounding canyon, connecting streams and the abundant floral and wildlife are wonderful. There are plenty of good fishing and swimming holes along the way.

After light rains, there are spectacular small waterfalls over the surrounding bluffs which fall near the trail; conversely, this trail is dangerous immediately after heavy rains. There are two trip options, one to the mostly flat trip to Glen Trail Camp, the other a trip extension up the sheer grade to Cogswell Reservoir.

TRAILHEAD: Exit the Foothill Fwy. at Azusa Ave. (Hwy. 39) and head north 8-1/2 miles to the road junction at the north end of the San Gabriel Reservoir. Stay to the left and drive up Hwy. 39 about 1-1/2 miles. Cross the bridge over the river. To the left (west) is a public parking area.

There are public facilities here, so fill up with water (two water bottles if you plan to "dawdle"). Since there are sometimes bacterial problems with the river water in the local mountains, it must be filtered, chemically treated or boiled prior to ingestion.

TRIP DESCRIPTION: **Trail Entry to Bear Creek.** Recross the bridge to meet West Fork Rd. and lift your bike over the entrance guard (motorized bikes and public cars are not allowed). Begin with a moderate

115

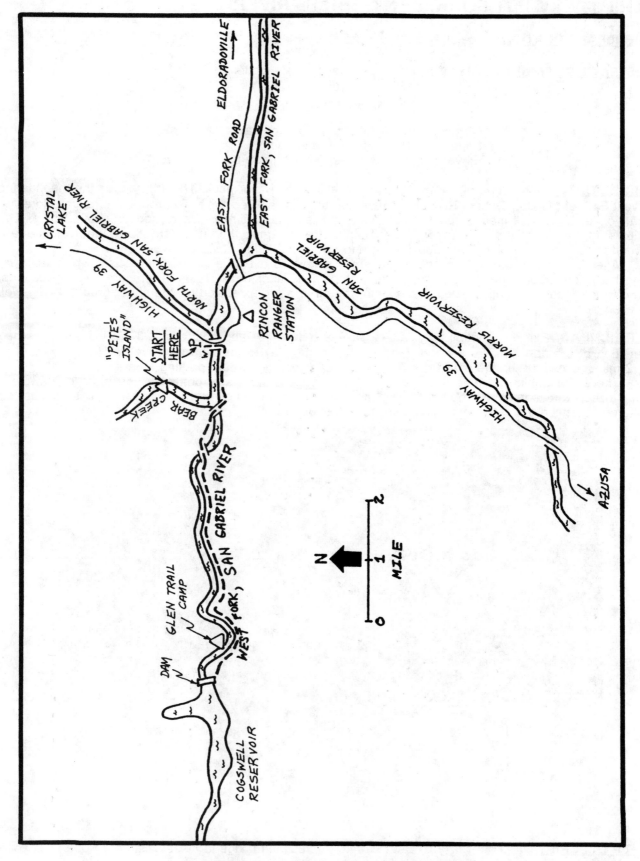

TRIP #25 - WEST FORK, SAN GABRIEL RIVER

uphill along an open section of the river. In a short distance are several small water runoffs cross the road. (These little dribbles pass a lot of water after a heavy rain!) Pass a small waterfall which is across the river (0.5), then cross a small bridge over the San Gabriel River at the inviting junction with Bear Creek (0.9). (A short hike up Bear Creek leads to some very scenic territory, as well as a "private" camping spot that we call "Pete's Island.") From this bikepath junction, most of the journey is beside a lush tree-lined river with sporadic tree cover and a canyon wall to filter the sun.

At (1.5) recross the river and enter the West Fork Wild Trout Area (no bait, no barbs on hooks and fish must be thrown back). In one mile (2.6) pass alongside a steep bluff through a large open area. Another steep bluff is passed in one more mile (3.5), with two small waterfalls flowing over the bluffs. The most westward waterfall cascades down a series of stair steps before dropping within feet of the trail. Just beyond is an area where the road is periodically washed out for a few hundred feet; a look up the fractured cliff hints that during heavy rains, the water is funneled down the cliff side at a frightening rate!

Glen Trail Camp. In 1/2 mile, the route enters an area where high canyon walls enclose the trail for about 1/2 mile. Just beyond is a small creek which spills across the road and a solitary, private residence(4.5). Follow the meandering river and cross a small bridge over an unnamed creek (5.7). In 1/2 mile is Glen Trail Camp, a pleasant rest stop. It has a shaded section near the river and an open field across the trail with picnic tables, fire stoves, and plenty of spots to pitch tents (permits required).

Cogswell Reservoir. Returning to the parking area from this point results in a 13.4 mile round-trip. An option is to bike 0.4 mile to the bottom of a steep road which leads up to Cogswell Reservoir (6.6). This road remains as steep as it looks at this point, rising roughly 350 feet in the remaining 0.7 mile up to the spillway. This is steep for walking, and exhaustive for biking for all except those bikers in excellent condition.

On the way up, pass a heliport and a private residential area (quiet please, as a courtesy). Once at the spillway, the way left leads steeply up West Fork, Red Box Rd. There is a 360-degree vista from the area just past the junction with views back down into the river canyon and the reservoir. The trail crosses the dam and ends at the opposite side (7.5) -- for all but those with mountain bikes. A return to the trailhead from here results in a round-trip distance of l5 miles.

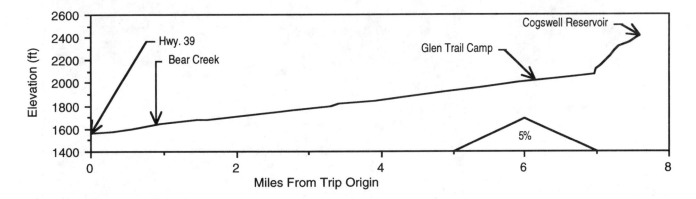

CONNECTING TRIPS: Recreational mountain bikers should try the riverbed recreation area just 1/2 mile south of this trip origin. For the truly serious mountain biker, continue from the Cogswell Dam up the West Fork, Redbox Rd. Another serious option is to head back into the East Fork, San Gabriel River, from the Eldoradoville Ranger Station. For the latter option, check first with the Rangers regarding river conditions.

INLAND

Rose Bowl In Pasadena

TRIP #26 - WHITTIER NARROWS/LEGG LAKE TRAIL

GENERAL LOCATION: Montebello, Pico Rivera (Whittier Narrows Recreation Area)

LEVEL OF DIFFICULTY: Round trip - easy
Distance - 11.2 miles (round trip)
Elevation gain - essentially flat

HIGHLIGHTS: This fiendishly clever route allows exploration of nearly the entire Whittier Narrows Recreational Area on Class I bikeways. It includes a tour around Legg Lake, a visit to the bottomland behind Whittier Narrows Dam, a cruise along the Rio Hondo River and a "secret passage" under the Pomona Fwy. to the northern recreation and picnic area. This is a family special that involves crossing only one street and one intersection. Other options are to ride up the east levee of the Whittier Narrows Dam and connect up with the San Gabriel River.

TRAILHEAD: From the Pomona Fwy., exit at Rosemead Blvd. south, travel 0.8 mile to San Gabriel Blvd./Durfee Blvd. and turn left. Drive on Durfee Ave. 0.6 mile and turn left into the Legg Lake pay parking area. Bring four quarters for parking.
    The route has plenty of water, so bring a light supply. Food stands are open on weekends at Legg Lake. Bring some bug spray for gnats if you plant to picnic near the lake in the summer.

TRIP DESCRIPTION: **Legg Lake.** The entire lake trip is on well-compacted dirt. It is easy to ride with any type of bike, but some care is needed in a couple of fine gravel and wet areas. Leave the parking lot and head north toward the lake. Veer right for the counterclockwise tour. Pass a roofed picnic area, a little spillway into the lake visit a giant sandy play area with a ten-foot high cement octopus (0.2).

West Shore of Legg Lake (Susan Cohen Photo)

Shortly the route passes a food stand and boat rental area. There are numerous ducks and geese in the area. Further on is a "rocket" playground and some lovely shaded picnic sites situated at the lake edge (0.4). Just beyond is a trail junction. Diverting to the left leads to a bridge crossing between the northernmost lake and the main lake. Our trip heads right and passes around the north lake through the green, natural, tree-covered surroundings. On this southbound segment the path meets the other end of the junction route between the lakes at (1.6). This area is one of the fishermen's favorites.

    In 0.1 mile pass a spillway near the western end of the lake, one of the few areas of the lake where motor traffic is visible. Shortly we passed a group of ducks sleeping on the grass six feet away from a busy fisherman. The route turns eastward later and roughly parallels Durfee Ave. (2.1). The final stretch continues to wind along the lake edge and returns to the trip origin in another half mile (2.6).
    Dam Bottomland/Wildlife Sanctuary. Leave the parking area and cross Durfee Ave. a few hundred feet to the west. Pass through a signed gate and pedal on a small asphalt road through an area surrounded by bushes, plants, trees and brush.

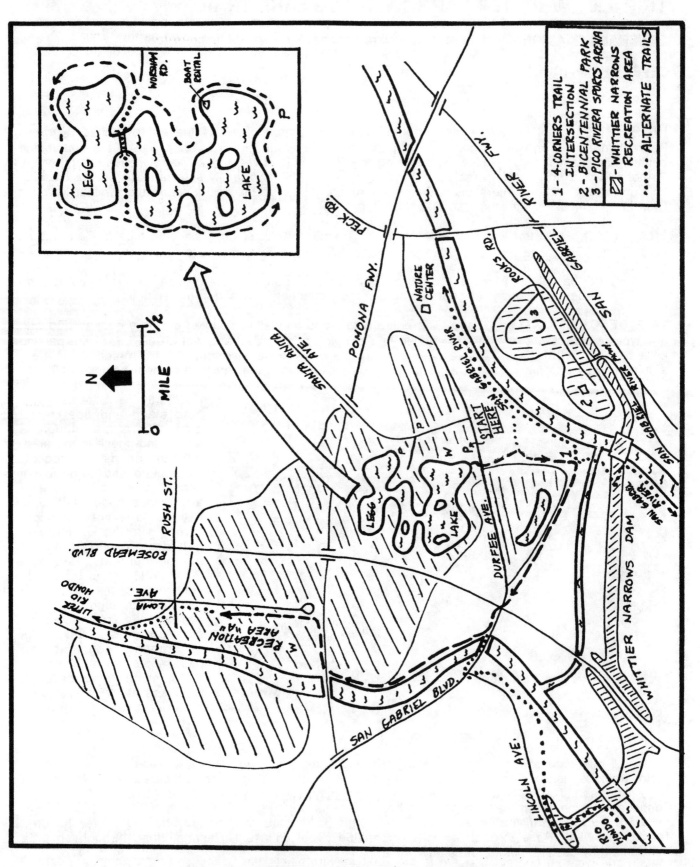

TRIP #26 - WHITTIER NARROWS/LEGG LAKE TRAIL

There are many nature exhibits and animals in this area. In a couple of hundred yards, the route reaches a "T" junction just beyond a small water channel. The asphalt trail left heads east towards (but skirts) the Whittier Narrows Nature Center. Our reference route goes to the right and continues about 0.3 mile through lush greenery to the "Center of the Universe," commonly known as the "Four Corners Trail Intersection." This is a pleasant, open area with a nice view of the backside of the Whittier Narrows Dam.

At that intersection, the route to the left (east) meets the San Gabriel River and heads north, while the route dead ahead (south) heads towards the dam and leads to the south San Gabriel River segment. Our route turns right (west) and roughly parallels the dam, passing alongside some very interesting vine-covered trees. In a 1/2 mile is a view back into Rose Hills (3.7). The trail crosses a small footbridge over a wash and reaches Durfee Ave. in 0.1 mile. The trip remains Class I and continues 0.2 mile to the intersection of Rosemead Blvd. and Durfee Ave./San Gabriel Blvd.

Upper Rio Hondo Trail Segment. Cross the intersection to the north side and bike on Class I San Gabriel Blvd. until reaching the bike entry to the Rio Hondo River (just before the bridge and on the east levee) (4.1). Ride along a pleasant, natural tree- and brush-lined stretch of the river. The growth is so dense that the river view does not open up for a 1/4 mile or so. Pass under the Pomona Fwy. (5.0), then parallel that freeway at road level for 0.6 mile before reaching the northern recreation area entrance.

Whittier Narrows Recreation Area "A." The bike entrance to the park is at its south end. Cyclists can cruise both the bikeways and slow-moving, lightly-traveled roads within the recreation area. The park dimensions are roughly 1/2 mile north-south and 1/4 mile east-west, providing plenty of room to roam. The park is moderately treed and has restrooms and water, picnic areas, recreation fields, model airplane flying and model car racing areas. This recreation area, combined with Legg Lake, is certainly on par with the recreation/biking areas as El Dorado Regional Park in L.A. County (Trip #16) and Mile Square or Irvine Regional Parks in Orange County.

CONNECTING TRIPS: 1) Continuation with the Upper Rio Hondo Bike Trail (Trip #19) - bike north on the west park edge on Loma Ave. for the north-heading segment (the south-heading segment of Trip #19 is part of this trip); 2) connection with the San Gabriel River Bike Trail (Trips #22C and 22D) - from the Four Corners Trail Intersection, pedal east to reach the north-heading segment or south toward the dam to meet with the south-heading segment.

TRIP #27 - HACIENDA HEIGHTS LOOP

GENERAL LOCATION: Hacienda Heights

LEVEL OF DIFFICULTY: Loop trip - moderate
                              Distance - 5.6 miles
                              Elevation gain - periodic moderate grades

HIGHLIGHTS: This loop trip around the eastern end of Hacienda Heights combines a Class II tour along Colima Ave. and a Class III tour through local residential areas. There are some views into the San Gabriel Mountains on the route's western segment on Stimson Ave. Additional trip highlights are Stimson County Park and the Puente Hills Mall. The route is well-laid out and well marked and does contain one workout upgrade leading to the southwestern point near Colima Ave. and Stimson Ave.

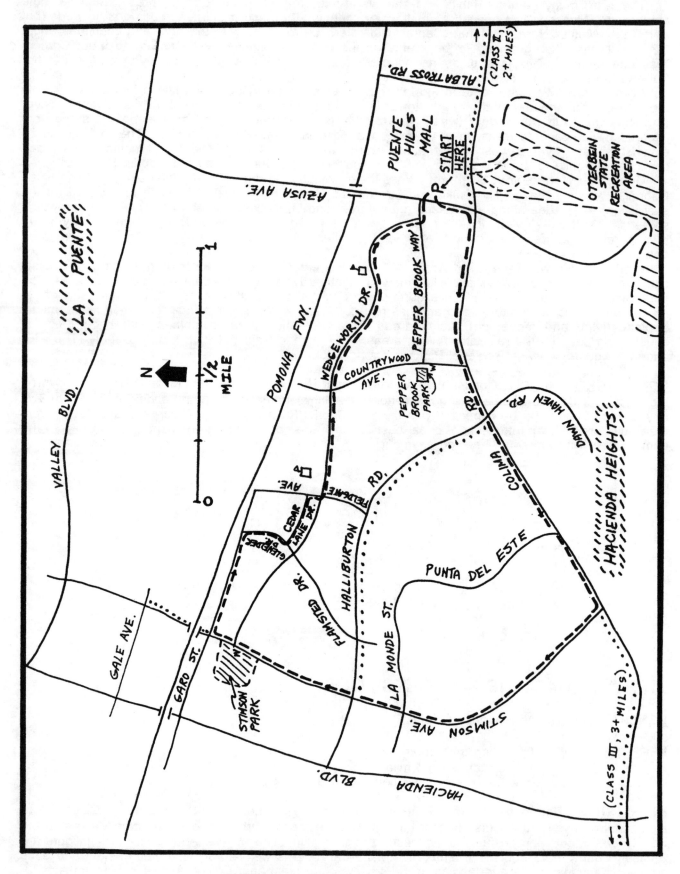

TRIP #27 - HACIENDA HEIGHTS LOOP

TRAILHEAD: Exit the Pomona Fwy. south at Azusa Ave. and turn left into the Puente Hills Mall. The Park and Ride area is near Pepper Brook Wy. at Azusa Ave.

Bring a light water supply. The Puente Hills Mall is a nice place for snacks after your tour. Stimson County Park also has water, along with the public schools on the route if you're willing to search for it (non-school periods).

TRIP DESCRIPTION: **Colima Road and the Trip Crest.** Exit the parking area and head south on Azusa Ave. 0.1 mile to Colima Rd. A left turn here leads to Otterbein State Recreation Area, where there is some fun hill hiking and possible off-road bicycling (balloon-tire bikes). Our route turns right and cruises down a Class II bikeway next to some heavy car traffic. There are hills to the left (south) with a light mix of commercial and residential development. The route starts uphill (0.4) passing Countrywood Rd. (0.6) and Dawn Haven Rd./Halliburton Rd. (0.8). The upgrade continues and steepens into a workout grade just before reaching the crest near Punta Del Este (1.4). This is the highest elevation point of the trip.

Stimson Ave. and Stimson Park. The path heads back downhill and flattens out near Stimson Ave. (1.8). Turn right and pedal downhill on a Class II bikepath with some views into the San Gabriel Mountains. There is a long-running downgrade with hillsides to the left and residential areas at road level to the right. The downhill runout continues past La Monde St. (2.6) and flattens out in the vicinity of Stimson Park (3.2). There are restrooms, water, recreation areas, and some shaded, grassy rest spots in this pleasant park.

The Residential Circuit. In 0.2 mile and before reaching the Pomona Fwy., turn right at Garo St. Note that the marked bikepath also continues down Stimson Ave. This segment of bikeway is Class III in light traffic, residential areas. The route turns right (south) at Glenelder Ave. (3.8) and left at Cedarlane Dr. in front of a school. Bike down this street and turn right at Fieldgate Ave. (4.2).

Shortly after, turn left on Wedgeworth Dr. and pass in front of Wilson High School. There are some nice views into the local hills to the north in this area. The route continues through residential areas past another school and crosses a small creek just beyond (5.1). In 0.3 mile turn left on Pepper Brook Wy., cross Azusa Ave. and return to the loop starting point (5.6).

CONNECTING TRIPS: There are numerous local spurs off the described route. Connection with the Diamond Bar Tour (Trip #42) - from Azusa Ave. and Colima Rd., proceed east 3-1/2 miles on the latter road to Brea Canyon Cutoff; and 2) connection with the San Jose Hills ride (Trip #43) - from Azusa Ave. and Colima Rd., cycle east 2-1/2 miles on the latter road to Nogales St., turn left (north) and bike another mile to Valley Blvd.

TRIP #28 - SAN MARINO TOUR

GENERAL LOCATION: San Marino

LEVEL OF DIFFICULTY: Loop - moderate (hill loop)
Distance - 6.8 miles (hill loop)
Elevation gain - periodic moderate grades

HIGHLIGHTS: This stately San Marino tour is not a bikepath or bike route. It is entirely Class X, but is too good not to include. Most of the route is through residential neighborhoods on lightly traveled, mainly wide roadways. There are some hills in the first 1-1/2 miles, but the biking is primarily flat or downhill beyond that point. The tour highlights stately mansions and well-groomed, upscale neighborhoods. Our route passes by the Huntington Library and Botanical Gardens and provides a selected number of view points into the hills and San Gabriel Mountains.

TRAILHEAD: From the Foothill Fwy., exit south on Sierra Madre Blvd. Drive 2-1/2 miles and turn right (west) on Huntington Dr. Continue about 1/2 mile and turn right at St. Albans Rd. Drive 1/2 mile further

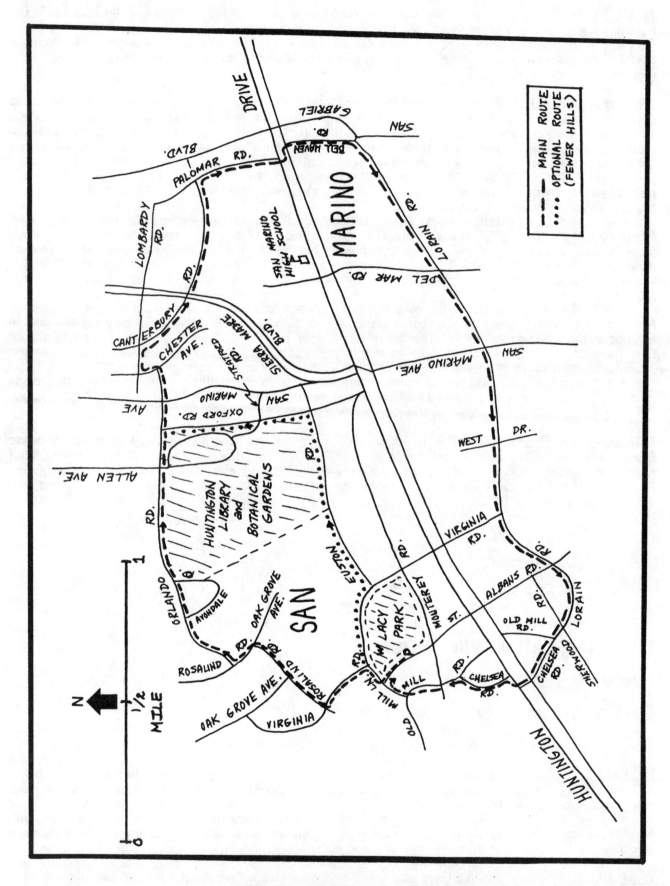

TRIP #28 - SAN MARINO TOUR

and park on the street near the Lacy Park entrance; be very careful to observe the local parking laws. Note that the park is not open on weekends.

From the San Bernardino Fwy., exit north at Atlantic Blvd. Continue 2-1/2 miles to Huntington Blvd., turn right (east) and drive 3/4 mile to St. Albans Rd. Turn left (north) and continue as described above.

From the Pasadena Fwy., exit south at Fair Oaks Ave. and drive a mile to Monterey Rd. Turn left (east) and drive about 1-1/2 miles to St. Albans Rd. Turn left and continue several hundred yards to parking just outside Lacy Park.

Bring at least one filled water bottle. We didn't find any public water supply other than at Lacy Park. Also bring a roadmap as a backup since this is not a marked bicycle path and it is easy to miss the described route.

TRIP DESCRIPTION: The Hills. The trip leaves Lacy Park and heads north on St. Albans Rd. In a short distance, turn right on Mill Ln. and bike uphill to Virginia Rd. (0.2). There is an option to turn right here and take the less hilly optional route along Euston Rd. and Oxford Rd. The prettier and more challenging route is to turn left and pedal uphill to Rosalind Rd. (0.4).

Turn right on Rosalind Rd. and bike through a rural setting where most residential grounds seem like mini-parks. The road winds downhill, junctions with one segment of Oak Grove Ave., turns a hard left and proceeds on another upgrade (0.7).

San Marino Along Old Mill Road

The route flattens out, then turns right on Orlando Rd. and proceeds uphill again (0.9). A refreshing downhill segment follows with a nice view into the San Gabriel Mountains. The bikepath continues through well-groomed residential areas, heads up another short upgrade (the last workout for a long time) and passes the Avondale Rd. loop (1.0-1.1). Cruise along the periphery of the Huntington Botanical Gardens, which shelters several magnificent set-back private residences.

Huntington Library and the Botanical Gardens. The route proceeds past the Allen Ave. entry to the Huntington Library Gallery and Botanical Gardens (1.7). Biking is not allowed within the grounds; note also that the grounds are open only on afternoons, Tuesday through Sunday, with limited public access on Sunday. If you wish to see the Huntington Library, call first for special instructions.

Northeast San Marino. The level route crosses Oxford Rd. (1.9), San Marino Ave. (2.0) and dead ends at Chester Ave. (2.2). Turn left at Chester Ave. then right at Lombardy Rd. and cruise downhill to Canterbury Rd. (2.3). Follow this street across busy Sierra Madre Blvd. and bike through a less shaded and less spectacular residential area to Palomar Rd. (3.1).

"The Southside." Proceed downhill to Huntington Dr. passing the beautiful Saint Felicities and Perpetua Church (3.4). After crossing Huntington Dr., the route zig-zags a short distance to the left (east) to Bell Haven Rd. and proceeds downhill about 0.3 mile. South of Huntington Dr. is the "other side of the tracks," where the mansions and oversized lots reduce to merely well-groomed, expensive residences. Turn right on Lorain Rd. (3.8) and bike on flat terrain through more residential areas past busy Del Mar Ave. (4.3), San Marino Ave. (4.7), Virginia Rd. (5.2), and St. Albans Rd. (5.5). In 0.2 mile (just beyond Sherwood Rd.), veer left (not a hard left) and bike up a light upgrade on Chelsea Rd.

The Estates. Cross Huntington Dr. (6.0) and follow a short jig-jog to the right (north) to stay on Chelsea Rd. Stop and admire some of the lovely estates. The road veers right and dead ends at Old Mill Rd. (6.4). Turn left and bike up a mild grade to Mill Ln. The historic El Molino Viejo (The Olde Mill) is just up the hill on Old Mill Rd. However, our route turns right on Mill Ln. and continues 0.1 mile to St. Albans Rd. Turn right and return to the trip starting point (6.8).

CONNECTING TRIPS: An option to visit the San Gabriel Mission and Grapevine Park about two miles south of the West Dr./Loraine Rd. intersection. About 0.4 mile west of San Marino Blvd. on Lorain Rd., turn left (south) on West Dr. West Dr. becomes Mission Dr. and leads directly into the mission. Connection with the Pasadena Phase I Biking System (Trip #31 map) - at Canterbury Rd. and Sierra Madre Blvd., bike north on the latter street 3/4 mile to Del Mar Blvd.

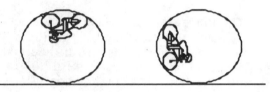

TRIP #29 - ARROYO SECO BIKE TRAIL

GENERAL LOCATION: Montecito Heights

LEVEL OF DIFFICULTY: Loop - easy
Distance - 7.5 miles (includes excursion trips)
Elevation gain - 0.1 mile steep upgrade on trip excursion (walk bikes)

HIGHLIGHTS: This bike trip combines an enjoyable ride along the Arroyo Seco and into two parks with excursion trips to several points of interest. The bikeway visits two separate sections of pleasant, shaded Arroyo Seco Park and touches the periphery of massive, hilly, and pretty Ernest E. Debs County Regional Park.

Excursions include visits to Heritage Square (restored Victorian mansions), the Lummis Home and Casa de Adobe (historical sites), and the Southwest Museum. Most of the route is on a marked bikeway (Class I or Class III), with some Class X on mostly lightly traveled roads. A large section of the Arroyo Seco path is flooded during winter storms.

Plan trip timing to be at Heritage Square in the afternoon if you can. Hours and dates of operation vary and should be checked ahead of time.

TRAILHEAD: Exit the Pasadena Fwy. east on Ave. 43. Drive two blocks and turn left (north) at Homer St. Drive to the end of Homer St. and park within the Montecito Heights Recreation Center parking lot.

Bring a light water supply. Water is available at the parks and some of the excursion sites.

TRIP DESCRIPTION: **Arroyo Seco Outward Bound.** Exit the parking lot at the west end and follow the tree-shaded path along the Arroyo Seco. Watch for broken glass near any sections that are around park picnic areas. In 0.3 mile is a junction (referred to as "reference" junction later in the text) with the right-hand path heading up to Ave. 52 within the park. Pedal to the left and down into the Arroyo Seco riverbed. The route leaves the freeway sounds here and drops into a quiet riverbed that is sheltered by trees for much of the trip. In 0.4 mile is the Ave. 52 overcrossing. In this area is a collection of varied types of graffiti that may classify as artwork and some nifty views into the local hills.

The route passes Via Marisol (1.1), Ave. 60 (1.4), and the Ave. 60 on-ramp (1.5), with views of the distant foothills. In 0.1 mile, the path ducks under a railroad trestle, then the Arroyo Dr. off-ramp and Ave. 64/Marmion Wy. overpass (1.9). In 0.2 mile, the bikepath climbs out of the river to Arroyo Seco Park where there is a shaded cul-de-sac, the Arroyo Horse Stables, and a nice picnic area with water to the right about 0.2 mile further down the street (Arroyo Dr.).

Arroyo Seco Return Route. Returning from the picnic area, the route backtracks along the Arroyo Seco to the Ave. 60 overpass (3.2). Just before reaching the overpass, take the trail out of the riverbed; follow the path under the roadway to the southernmost segment of Arroyo Seco Park.

There is a bikeway/walkway that leads back up to Ave. 60; however, our route tours the pleasant shaded park past picnic areas, tennis courts and restrooms. Bike through the park and turn right at Via

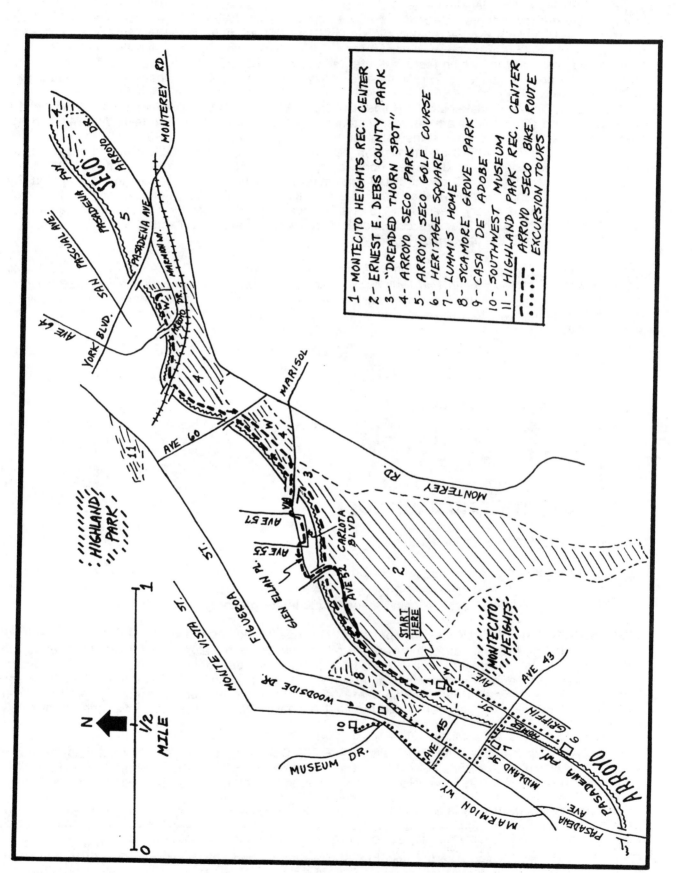

TRIP #29 - ARROYO SECO BIKE TRAIL

127

Marisol (3.6). Do not explore the grassy area across that street, even by walking bikes, as there are thorns on the ground that are guaranteed tire and tube wreckers. (We know from experience!)

Cross the Pasadena Fwy. and follow the signed Class III bike route as follows: Left on Ave. 57 (3.7), right on Carlota Blvd. (3.8), right on Ave. 55 (4.0), left on Glen Ellen Pl. (4.1) and left on Ave. 52 (4.3). Bike on this Class III road which recrosses the freeway and becomes Griffin Ave. In 0.7 mile, the route meets the "reference" junction. Turn right and follow the Class I bikepath back to the starting point (5.2).

Excursion Tours. Pedal south on Homer St. Cross Ave. 43 and bike 0.2 mile to the street's end at Heritage Square (5.6). There are several Victorian mansions here. Return north to Ave. 43, turn left (west) and bike 0.1 mile to the historic cobblestone Lummis Home, "El Alisal" (5.9).

Pedal 0.1 mile on Ave. 43 and turn right (northeast) on Figueroa St. Follow that street about 0.2 mile just past Woodside Dr. to Casa de Adobe, a replica of an 1850's California hacienda (6.2).

Cruise 0.1 mile to Ave. 45 and turn right (northwest), continuing a short distance to Marmion Wy. (6.4). Turn right again and follow that street 0.2 mile to Museum Dr. Turn left and angle right almost immediately, following a very steep uphill (probably a walking stretch) to the Southwest Museum (6.6). This museum contains an extensive collection of Southwestern Indian artifacts.

Return 0.9 mile to the park area (7.5).

CONNECTING TRIPS: 1) Connection with the Highland Park Loop (Trip #30) - at the Southwest Museum turnoff, bike north on Marmion Wy.; 2) connection with the Kenneth Newell Bikeway (Trip #31) - from the trip terminus, head northeast on Arroyo Dr., which becomes Marmion Wy. Pedal 0.2 mile on Pasadena Ave. to Arroyo Dr., turn left (north) and cruise 1-1/4 miles to the northernmost section of Arroyo Seco Park.

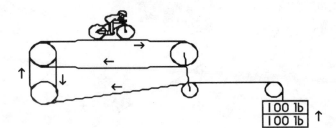

TRIP #30 - HIGHLAND PARK LOOP

GENERAL LOCATION: Highland Park

LEVEL OF DIFFICULTY: Loop - easy
Distance - 7.6 miles
Elevation gain - periodic moderate grades

HIGHLIGHTS: This mainly Class III loop tours the edge of Montecito Heights, traverses a series of rolling hills through the first half of the trek and returns via the parks along the Arroyo Seco. There are numerous side trips, including visits to Heritage Square, Casa de Adobe and the Southwest Museum (see Trip #29). Primarily in a residential zone, most of this trip is on lightly used roads. The areas on either side of the Pasadena Fwy. are an interesting contrast, the western side having light tree cover and a high density residential area, while the east is heavily treed, some residential and full of lovely parks.

TRAILHEAD: Exit the Pasadena Fwy. east on Ave. 43. Drive two blocks and turn left (north) at Homer St. Continue to the end of Homer St. and park in the Montecito Heights Recreation Center parking lot.
Bring a light water supply. Water is available at the parks and at several gas stations on the route.

TRIP DESCRIPTION: **Western Segment.** Exit the Montecito Heights Recreation Center area and bike south on Homer St. Turn right on Ave. 43 (biking south leads to Heritage Square) and pedal over the Pasadena Fwy. 0.3 mile to Figueroa St. (stay on Figueroa St. to visit Casa de Adobe and Sycamore Grove Park). Turn right and bike 0.1 mile to Ave. 45, turn left and right again on Class III Marmion Wy. Follow the mild upgrade past Museum Dr. (0.7) (turn left here to visit the Southwest Museum). Turn left at Shanley Ave., then right at Malta St. Cruise to Ave. 50 and turn left (1.4).

128

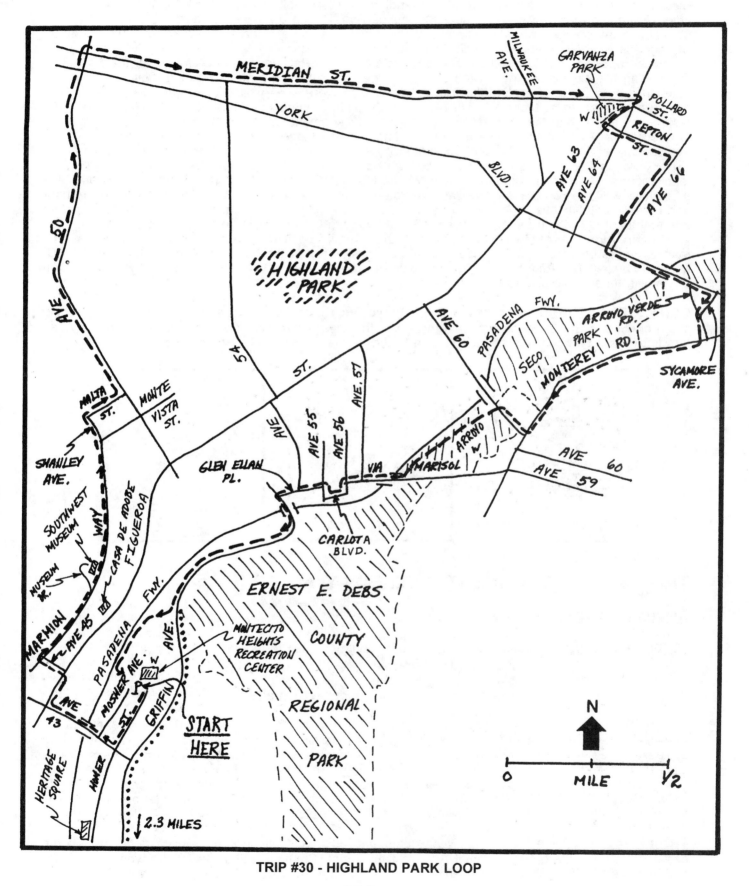

TRIP #30 - HIGHLAND PARK LOOP

Pedal on this Class III road through the residential community situated in rolling hills, cross York Blvd. and turn right one street beyond at Meridian St. (2.4). Follow the 0.8-mile upgrade through this quiet residential area which crests near Milwaukee Ave. Cruise 0.7 mile and turn sharply right at Ave. 63, skirting the covered water reservoir and passing shady, green Garvanza Park. Turn left at Repton St., right on Ave. 66, then bike to York Blvd. (4.4).

Eastern Segment. Turn left (southeast), cycle past San Pascual Ave and cross over the Pasadena Fwy. using the signed walkway. Stop on the bridge and admire the riders training their horses in the equestrian area below. Turn left and bike up shady Sycamore Ave., which fuses with Arroyo Verde Rd., and turn right again at Monterey Rd. (4.9). Pedal uphill through the well-treed area with large rustic residences just above the northern Arroyo Seco Park segment. After a 0.3-mile climb, coast downhill to a level near Ave. 60. Turn right and pedal almost to the bridge over the Arroyo Seco (5.6).

Cross Ave. 60 and pass through the motorized vehicle barrier on a walk/bike ramp. Follow the Class I path through the lovely southern segment of cozy Arroyo Seco Park, which has restrooms, shade, tennis courts and many inviting rest spots. At Via Marisol (6.1) cross over the Pasadena Fwy. and bike on several well marked Class III zig-zags, recrossing the freeway at Ave. 52 (6.7). The road veers right and becomes Griffin Ave. Bike 0.7 mile along Griffin Ave. and turn right at the marked Class I junction trail that leads down into the Arroyo Seco. Pedal this path 0.2 mile back to the parking area (7.6).

Griffin Ave. Spur. There is an option at the 7.4-mile point to remain on Griffin Ave. Follow this road 2.3 miles on Class II road to it's terminus at Mission Rd. at the backside of the L.A. County/U.S.C. Medical Center. This segment has some moderate grades and a winding road primarily in residential areas with reasonable bike room.

CONNECTING TRIPS: 1) Connection with Arroyo Seco Bike Trail (Trip #29) - at the trip origin, bike south on Homer St.; 2) connection with the Kenneth Newell Bikeway (Trip #31) - at San Pascual Ave., turn left (north) and continue about one mile to the northern segment of Arroyo Seco Park.

TRIP #31 - KENNETH NEWELL BIKEWAY

GENERAL LOCATION: Pasadena

LEVEL OF DIFFICULTY: One way- easy (north to south); moderate (south to north);
up and back - moderate
Distance - 6.8 miles (one way)
Elevation gain - periodic moderate upgrades

HIGHLIGHTS: One of the premier inland trips, this popular, well-marked bikeway explores an interesting north-south slice of Pasadena with picturesque old homes near the starting point. It follows a pleasant tree-shaded residential area along the Arroyo Seco, passes the Rose Bowl, visits Devil's Gate Reservoir and Oak Grove County Park, and ends at Jet Propulsion Laboratories (JPL).

Most of the route is on roomy, lightly-traveled Class III bikeways with one workout upgrade (south to north) that places this trip at the "moderate" difficulty rating upper limit. An additional option is to link this route with the Phase I inner-city bikeway system.

TRAILHEAD: From the Pasadena Fwy. southbound, exit west on York Blvd. (Pasadena Ave. to the east). Drive 0.2 mile to San Pascual Ave. and turn right. Continue about 3/4 mile beyond Comet St. and just short of the Arroyo Seco overcrossing. Park in the Arroyo Seco Park lot. From the northbound

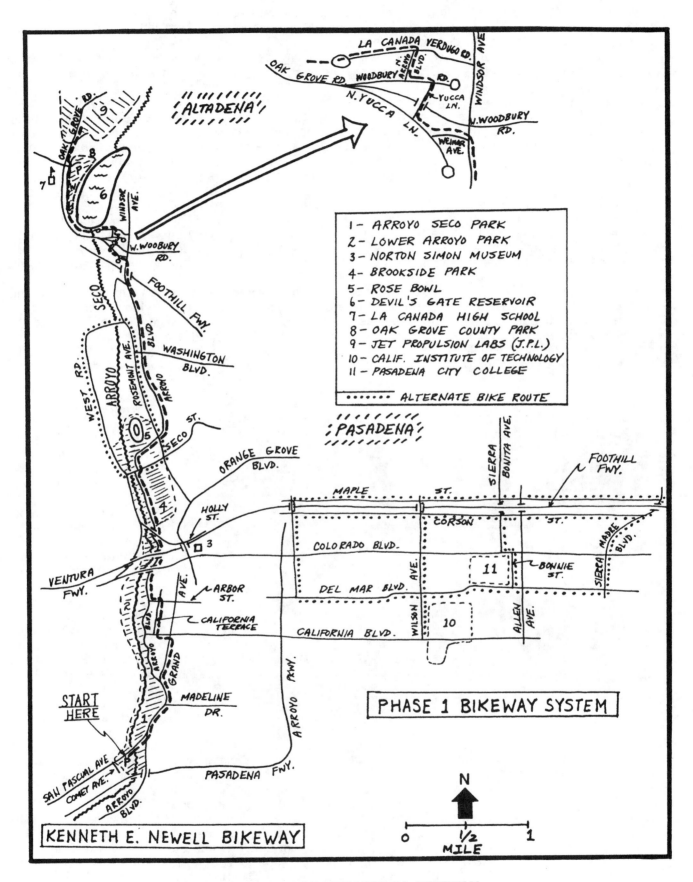

1 - ARROYO SECO PARK
2 - LOWER ARROYO PARK
3 - NORTON SIMON MUSEUM
4 - BROOKSIDE PARK
5 - ROSE BOWL
6 - DEVIL'S GATE RESERVOIR
7 - LA CANADA HIGH SCHOOL
8 - OAK GROVE COUNTY PARK
9 - JET PROPULSION LABS (J.P.L.)
10 - CALIF. INSTITUTE OF TECHNOLOGY
11 - PASADENA CITY COLLEGE

•••••• ALTERNATE BIKE ROUTE

PHASE 1 BIKEWAY SYSTEM

KENNETH E. NEWELL BIKEWAY

TRIP #31 - KENNETH NEWELL BIKEWAY

direction, exit at Marmion Wy., turn left and follow that street over the freeway. Stay on a road now named Ave. 64 to York Blvd. Turn right and drive to San Pascual Ave. Turn left (north) and continue to the Arroyo Seco Park lot as described above.

Bring a moderate water supply. There are strategically located public water sources at Brookside Park near the Rose Bowl and Oak Grove County Park near trip's end, as well as at both start and finish.

TRIP DESCRIPTION: **Classic Residential Pasadena.** Exit the parking area and turn right (north). Soon the Class III path crosses in succession the Arroyo Seco, Stoney Dr. near a recreation field and the San Pascual Stables. The rural area path climbs a short, steep uphill which crests at the San Pascual Ave. terminus at Arroyo Blvd. (0.2). Turn left (north) and pedal past a collection of lovely fenced estates with their turn-of-the-century homes. The bike route here is in a tree-shaded, rural, serene setting. Cruise past Madeline Dr. (0.5) and junction to the right at Grand Ave. (0.7). The path is well-marked at this, as well as all upcoming junctions.

Cycle a moderate upgrade for 0.3 mile which becomes rather steep the next 0.1 mile. Turn left at California Blvd. (1.2) and right in another 0.1 mile at California Terrace. Bike the slow, steady uphill in the shaded, classic residential area to Arbor St. (1.6). Turn left and, very shortly, turn right back onto Arroyo Blvd. The path is now alongside the Arroyo Seco and offers a look down into Lower Arroyo Park. Just beyond, the route passes historical La Casita Del Arroyo, a replica of an early Southern California hacienda (1.8).

Brookside Park. In 0.2 mile, pass under the majestic Colorado Blvd. bridge. Up the hill from this area is a view of the classic Federal Building. Nearby, but out of view, is the Norton Simon Museum of Art. In another 0.1 mile, pass under the massive Ventura Fwy. bridge with a "window" view to the mountains achieved by sighting through the bridge supports northward and down the canyon. The route heads steeply downhill for 0.2 mile, flattens out, and passes under Holly St. (2.3). The flat roadway continues past the southern portion of Brookside Park, which has a nice picnic area and water (2.5).

Ventura Freeway Overpass

Rose Bowl. In 0.3 mile cross Seco St., jog to the right, and head north beside the east side of the Rose Bowl. This area has recreation fields and restrooms (3.0). Cross Rosemont Ave. and bike on a workout upgrade through tree-lined residential areas past Westgate St. and Everts St. (3.7). The upgrade eases and proceeds 0.2 mile to a great turnout/vista area overlooking the Brookside Golf Course and offers a look at the local hills. Then cross Washington Blvd. to a crest at La Cresta (4.5).

The "Maze." Cross over the Foothill Fwy. and turn left at N. Weimar Ave., just before W. Woodbury Rd. (4.9). Follow a well-marked route on N. Yucca Ln. to Yucca Ln. and turn right again. Pass over W. Woodbury Rd. Turn left on Woodbury Rd. near a cul-de-sac, right on N. Arroyo Blvd. and left on La Canada Verdugo Rd. (5.2). Cruise downhill to the road's end at a cul-de-sac (5.4).

Devil's Gate Reservoir and Oak Grove County Park. Follow the Class I path across Devil's Gate Reservoir (5.7) and bike downhill above the reservoir area. There are excellent views into the San Gabriel Mountains here. Cruise past a little shady park with benches into the main area of Oak Grove County Park. Continue 0.3 mile along the park periphery past a junction to the right (west) which leads to the lower picnic area. At (6.3), the route meets Oak Grove Dr. Turn right and bike 0.5 mile to JPL (6.8).

CONNECTING TRIPS: 1) Connection with the Arroyo Seco Bike Trail (Trip #29) - from the junction of San Pascual Ave. and Arroyo Dr., pedal 1-1/4 miles south on Arroyo Blvd./Pasadena Ave. and turn left at Marmion Wy. Turn right in 0.2 mile at Arroyo Verde and proceed to the Arroyo Seco; 2) connection with the Highland Park Loop (Trip #30) - at the trip origin, bike one mile south to York Blvd.; 3) connection with the Pasadena inner-city bikeway shown on the eastern portion of the trip map - bike east at California Blvd. or Colorado Blvd.

TRIP #32 - ARCADIA LOOP

GENERAL LOCATION: Arcadia

LEVEL OF DIFFICULTY: Four loop trips - moderate to strenuous; Highland Oaks segment of
Rancho Oaks Loop is strenuous
Distance - 29.4 miles (not including the 3.0-mile strenuous
Rancho Oaks segment)
Elevation gain - periodic moderate grades (Rancho Oaks Loop);
single extended, steep upgrade (Highland Oaks segment)

HIGHLIGHTS: The delightful Arcadia bikeway system consists of four well-laid-out, well-marked loops. Most of the route is Class III on lightly used roads with plenty of bike room. The system is mainly flat, except for the northern portions of the Rancho Oaks Loop, particularly the steep upper segment of Highland Oaks Dr. Bikers can follow individual marked loops or free-lance among them. Rancho Oaks Loop is the longest and most varied with such points of interest as the L.A. Arboretum, Santa Anita Race Track, Arcadia Park, Wilderness Park and elegant residential neighborhoods in the foothills.

TRAILHEAD: From the Foothill Fwy., exit south at Michillinda Ave. Follow Colorado St. to Michillinda Ave., turn right (south) and drive one mile to Huntington Dr. Turn left and continue 0.4 mile to Golden West Ave. Turn left and find parking in this residential area subject to local parking laws. From the San Bernardino Fwy., exit north on Rosemead Blvd. and drive about four miles to Huntington Dr. Turn right and continue 3/4 mile to Golden West Ave. Turn left and park as stated above.

Bring plenty of water unless you are willing to search or beg and borrow along the way. There may be water at some of the parks that we did not visit.

TRIP DESCRIPTION: Individual loops should be biked in the direction shown since the bikepath signs are only posted in one direction. Bring a map on this trip as a backup whether following the signed routes or "free-lancing." Below are highlight descriptions of each loop.

Hugo Reid Loop. The shortest of the four loops, the counterclockwise 3.0-mile route cruises a pleasant, quiet, well-manicured residential area bordered by Baldwin Lake and the L.A. Arboretum on the east. This area is neatly tucked away, isolated from the busy roads to the north, west and south. Peacocks wander this territory at will. This loop has some light upgrades and views into the San Gabriel Mountains, particularly from Altuna Rd. looking back.

Lucky Baldwin Loop. This counterclockwise 6.8-mile loop enfolds a major portion of the Hugo Reid Loop. From the parking area, cross Huntington Dr. to a modest residential area, pass Tripolis Park (0.3) and meander as far south as Camino Real. The route goes north at El Monte Ave. (2.1) on a Class II route and turns left (west) at Duarte Ave., returning to Class III biking. The path zig-zags north and west, passes Holy Angels Church and crosses Huntington Dr. near the exquisite Rose Garden (2.9).

The bike route passes directly south of the Santa Anita Raceway with its great mountain backdrop. The path cruises past Santa Anita Fashion Park (shopping center) (3.4), crosses Baldwin Ave. and heads north on Old Ranch Rd. (3.8). Just beyond this junction, the bike path shares a common route with the Hugo Reid Loop, returning to the starting point (6.8).

Rancho Oaks Loop. The longest of the loops, this counter-clockwise 9.9-mile favorite is described starting at Hugo Reid Dr. and Baldwin Ave. The parking previously described is near this starting point or bikers can park at Santa Anita Fashion Park. Start south on Baldwin Ave. and turn left on Huntington

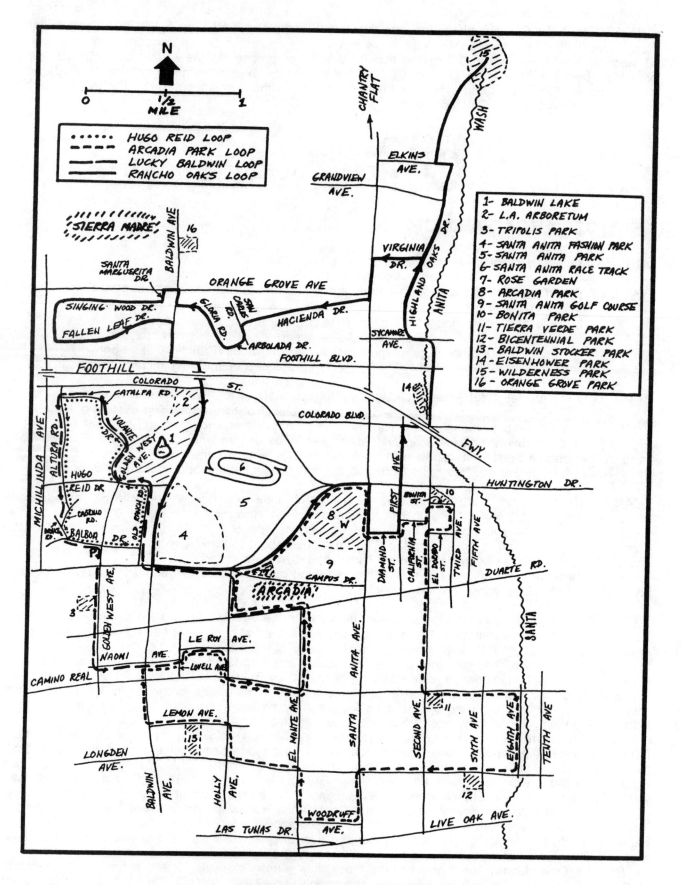

TRIP #32 - ARCADIA LOOP

Dr. (0.8). The path follows that road as it passes the Santa Anita Race Track, the Rose Garden (1.2), and swings north alongside Arcadia City Park which has recreation and picnic areas, trees and grassy rest spots, water and restrooms.

Turn right (south) at Santa Anita Ave. (2.3) and pass an arts and crafts exhibit area. A left turn at Diamond St. leads to a series of jig-jogs which lead to a Foothill Fwy. undercrossing at Colorado Blvd. (3.5). Cruise by Eisenhower Park and a shopping center near Second Ave. and Foothill Blvd., then bike over to Highland Oaks Dr. (4.2). The route goes uphill on a workout grade then heads toward the mountains through a residential area and meets Virginia Dr. (4.7). An option here is to bike about 1-1/2 miles further on Highland Oaks Dr. on a steep, gutsy uphill to rustic Wilderness Park (trees, picnic areas, restrooms, nature trails) -- this is a strenuous to very strenuous workout! The compensations are great vistas and a feeling of accomplishment.

For everyday mortals, the bike route turns left, heads uphill for a short distance, and works its way to some exception-ally impressive residential areas starting south of Orange Grove Ave. and Santa Anita Ave. at Hacienda Dr. (5.2). At Baldwin Ave. (6.7), the bikepath jig-jogs over to Santa Marguerita Dr. and proceeds mostly downhill through some of the most elegant and impressive residential areas in L.A. County. The Singing Wood Dr./Fallen Leaf Dr. area is stocked with mansions and large, elegant homes on huge, immaculately-tended lots.

Everyday reality returns as the path heads right at Baldwin Ave. (8.6) and proceeds downhill to Foothill Blvd. Baldwin Ave. continues about 0.2 mile to the east and soon passes under the Foothill Fwy. The bike route passes one entrance to the L.A. Arboretum just south of Stanford Ave. (9.4) and returns to the starting point (9.9).

Arcadia Park Loop. This 9.7-mile clockwise route starts at Huntington Dr. and Holly Ave. which is reachable from the described trailhead parking area. Other options are to start at one of several parks on the route. This is the flattest route of the group, mainly confined to less spectacular territory than other loops. Most of the route passes through residential areas which are liberally sprinkled with parks.

Bike along Huntington Dr. passing the Santa Anita Race Track, the Rose Garden, and swing north alongside Arcadia City Park. Turn left at Santa Anita Ave. (1.1) and left again in at Diamond St. The route goes through a series of jig-jogs passing Bonita Park (1.9) and heads south on Second St. Then head left at Camino Real and pass Tierra Verde Park (3.2). The path reaches its easternmost edge at Eighth St. (3.7), loops back west on Longden Ave., passing Bicentennial Park (open playground and tennis courts) (4.3).

The bike tour turns left (south) on Santa Anita Ave., passes near the southern Arcadia city limits on Woodruff Ave. (5.4), winds its way north and west on Class II El Monte Ave., and returns to Class III Longden Ave. (6.4). Then it turns right (north) on Holly Ave., left on Lemon Ave., and passes Baldwin Stocker Park (6.9) with picnic areas, restrooms and a playground.

Soon the path turns right (north) on Baldwin Ave. and heads to Camino Real (7.6). From this point, the route shares a path with the Lucky Baldwin Loop. The path jig-jogs north and east, eventually reaching El Monte Ave. (8.9). To return to the starting point (9.7), proceed north on El Monte Ave., left (west) on Durate Rd., and north again on Holly Ave.

CONNECTING TRIPS: There are numerous combinations of possible routes just within the four loops described.

135

TRIP #33 - GRIFFITH PARK

GENERAL LOCATION: Hollywood Hills, Griffith Park

LEVEL OF DIFFICULTY: Griffith Park Dr. Loop - moderate to strenuous
Distance - 8.8 miles (loop)
Elevation gain - single long, moderate-to-steep grade

Zoo Dr. Up and Back Trip - easy
Distance - 8.2 miles (up and back)
Elevation gain - periodic light grades

Los Angeles River Trail - easy
Distance - 3.2 miles (one way)
Elevation gain - essentially flat

HIGHLIGHTS: This is a pleasant ride in a rural setting through one of L.A. County's finest parks. One option is the loop route which includes Griffith Park Dr. and a 1/2-mile strenuous upgrade. (This is the reference option described below.) Another option is to take the Zoo Dr. route up and back, avoiding Griffith Park Dr. completely, or plan a route that includes all but the strenuous upgrade.

There is an option to bike a 3.2-mile trail along the L.A. River. This ride can be used as an option to the Zoo Dr./Crystal Springs return or biked in addition to the basic Griffith Park ride. The trail provides a different perspective of the Griffith Park area, as well as some scenic river bottom and a taste of man's "levee artistry."

Regardless of the option, the tree-lined route passes numerous picnic areas and sightseeing attractions (L.A. Zoo, Travel Town, and the Griffith Park Merry-Go-Round). Griffith Park Dr. is effectively a Class III roadway, while the remainder of the bikepaths are Class II. The Zoo Dr. up-and-back option is a nice family ride for all but inexperienced or very young bikers.

TRAILHEAD: Exit the Golden State Fwy. at Los Feliz Blvd. and turn west. Drive 1/4 mile and turn right (north) at Crystal Springs Rd. Park in the area just off the roadway, preferably in a shady spot.

Bring a light water supply. There is plenty of water in the main picnic areas surrounding Crystal Springs Dr. near the Griffith Park Dr. junction and there are water fountains and restrooms at most park attractions, although bikers must leave the bike trail to gain access.

TRIP DESCRIPTION: **Lower Crystal Springs Drive.** Leaving the parking area, Crystal Springs Dr. starts on a mix of moderate upgrades and flats. In 0.1 mile, pass the Los Feliz Passenger Station, the point of departure for rides on the mini railroad. Continue above and alongside the Golden State Fwy. until it transitions to an area above grassy knolls and horse stables (0.8). The entire Griffith Park area is crisscrossed with great horse trails. Shortly, the roadway passes alongside the Visitor's Center/Ranger Station and, just beyond, meets the junction with Griffith Park Dr. (1.1).

Mineral Wells Picnic Area. Bike straight ahead (north) on Crystal Springs Dr. for the easier family bike route. For the reference loop trip, turn left (west) on Griffith Park Dr. and bike up a short steep upgrade. Cruise past the car roadblock and around the edge of the Cedar Tree Picnic Grounds parking area. Pass above the Griffith Park Merry-Go-Round and a pleasant grassy, shaded picnic area (1.5) which extends for about 1/4 mile.

At the junction north of the picnic area, bear left and pedal alongside the golf course. Pass the Boy's Camp turnoff (2.4), golfer's clubhouse/restaurant, driving range (2.6), and head uphill to the Mineral Wells Picnic Area (2.8), one of the most natural and scenic picnic areas in the park.

The "Roller Coaster." Beyond the picnic area, the route steepens. For the next 1/2 mile, bikers face a gritty uphill that levels off near a developed area. This segment leaves some question as to whether the route is moderate or moderate-to-strenuous. Just beyond the flat, the route twists and winds steeply downhill passing Mt. Hollywood Dr. (3.5) and then leveling out in 0.6 mile.

Travel Town. Just beyond is the turnoff to Travel Town (4.2) with miniature train rides, as well as stationary, life-size steam trains. The roadway continues past Travel Town, makes a turn to the right (east) and becomes Zoo Dr. Zoo Dr. passes alongside the live "Steamer" area (4.3), a small open picnic area (4.5), Riverside Dr. (5.3), and the Pecan Grove Picnic Area (5.4).

L.A. Zoo and the Return Loop. In 0.3 mile is a junction where the bikeway splits. A left turn leads around the edge of the L.A. Zoo parking lot, while the reference route proceeds straight ahead. The

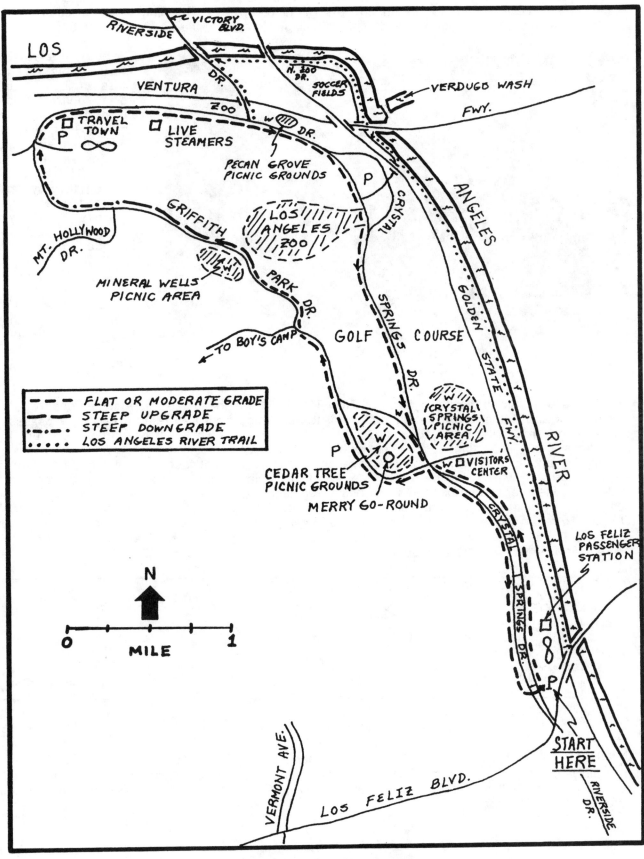

TRIP #33 - GRIFFITH PARK

road passes under a walking bridge (6.1) and continues along a eucalyptus-lined route which passes through two golf courses. In a short distance, pass alongside the eastern edge of the Cedar Tree Picnic Area and later return to the Griffith Park Dr. junction (7.7). The final segment follows Crystal Springs Dr. southbound through a series of small rolling hills back to the parking area (8.8).

Merry Go-round at Griffith Park

Los Angeles River Trail. This 3.2-mile Class I trail can be used as a separate trip or connected to the Griffith Park ride. It is the northern segment of the Los Angeles River Trail. There is an ongoing drive by groups such as the Los Angeles County Bicycle Coalition (LACBC) to, one day, connect this to the southern segment described in Trip #21. In the near term, it is being extended to Glendale Blvd. with the hope of continuing it into the Civic Center area.

The trail entry is on the south levee at Riverside Dr. The night-lighted route cruises east, with nifty Griffith Park and Forest Lawn vistas southward. It pulls away from the Ventura Fwy. and passes the park's soccer fields just before bending south at the 0.5-mile point. Just beyond the Ventura Fwy. undercrossing is a walker/biker entry from North Zoo Dr.

Beyond about (1.2), look across the river and observe the cat faces articulately painted on the water outlet ports which dot the levee face. From this point, which is directly alongside the Golden State Fwy., the river bottom blossoms with heavy vegetation. At (2.5) is an equestrian crossing for riders coming from Griffith Park via a tunnel under the freeway. Los Feliz Blvd. and the end of the segment is at (3.2). To return to the park, turn right (west) and <u>carefully</u> cross three freeway on/off ramps to reach Riverside Dr. in about 1/4 mile. All that remains is for cyclists to turn right again and return to their parked car on what is now Crystal Springs Dr.

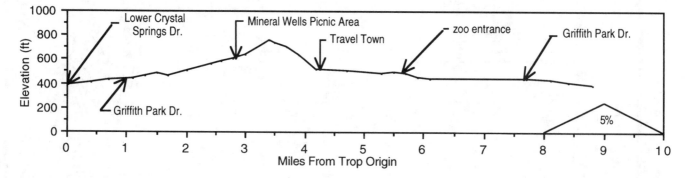

<u>CONNECTING TRIPS</u>: 1) There are other connecting trips in the Hollywood Hills area which are extremely hilly and on Class X roadways. These routes are only for experienced bikers in excellent condition; 2) connection with the Burbank Bikeway (Trip #36) - at Zoo Dr. and Victory Blvd., follow the latter street across the freeway.

138

TRIP #34 - ELYSIAN PARK

GENERAL LOCATION: Elysian Park (Central Los Angeles)

LEVEL OF DIFFICULTY: Loop - moderate to strenuous
Distance - 6.4 miles
Elevation gain - single steep grade

HIGHLIGHTS: Elysian Park provides a natural setting tucked away in the middle of the city of Los Angeles. The trip boasts parks, trees, hills and vistas -- all in a lightly traveled area (barring a major event at nearby Dodger Stadium). The key word is vistas. Few places in L.A. County provide more spectacular views per bike mile. While "gut-busting" on Angels Point Rd., there are rewarding vistas back into the park area, the hills across the L. A. River, the L.A. city skyline, and views to the south that include Dodger Stadium. The price paid is some strenuous hill climbing and an entire route on Class X roadway. There are options to link additional loops and thus expand the trip mileage.

There are numerous additional park service roads and trails for hikers and mountain bikers. Check with the park headquarters to confirm which are open for use.

TRAILHEAD: From the Harbor/Pasadena Fwy., exit at Stadium Wy. and follow that roadway southwest and parallel to the freeway (do not drive up into Dodger Stadium). Continue about 1-1/4 miles past the point where Stadium Wy. takes a 90-degree bend to the northwest. At Academy Rd., drive straight into the park on Chavez Ravine Rd. (do not take the jog to the right, which is the continuation of Stadium Wy.). From the Golden State Fwy., exit at Stadium Wy.. Drive 1-1/2 miles to Academy Rd. and turn right. Just beyond, turn right into the Chavez Ravine Rd. parking area.

Bring a moderate water supply. Bikers will use plenty of water, and resupply is available at several sites within the park.

TRIP DESCRIPTION: **Elysian Park Road (West) and Grace E. Simons Lodge.** Leave a well-treed picnic area with benches, barbecues, playground, restrooms, and water and cycle south along Stadium Wy.. Just across Academy Rd. is a similar picnic area that is slightly more hilly. In 0.1 mile, there is a smaller park area with a blocked uphill entry to Old Lodge Rd.

Just beyond, the route turns right (northwest) and heads uphill on Scott Ave. (0.2). In another 0.1 mile of steep uphill, the path turns right on Elysian Park Rd. and parallels Stadium Wy..

Continue on a moderate upgrade through shaded roadway with views down into the picnic area and cross Academy Rd. (0.6). This is a favorite parking area for folks taking a workday lunch break or just "playing hooky." The path reaches a crest (0.9) and soon passes a small arboretum and picnic area with water. In 0.1 mile, there is a short diversion trip to a nice group picnic area and the Grace E. Simons Lodge. The path proceeds downhill past a small picnic/playground area and returns to Stadium Wy. (1.3).

The "Workout" and the Vistas. The route crosses that street and begins a strenuous 0.9-mile winding grade on Angels Point Rd. This is the toughest part of the trip! The first of several vista points is 0.2 mile beyond with a nice park overlook. Following is a great 180-degree view that includes the "backside" of the L.A. Civic Center (1.7). This is Angels Point where there is access to a lookout kiosk and picnic area. Next are views down into the Police Academy Firing Range and across to the Hollywood Hills (2.0) and, at the crest, a fine overlook of Dodger Stadium and the San Gabriel Mountains (2.2).

Following a flat stretch and steep downhill, the route reaches a junction with Solano Canyon Dr. (2.7). Stay to the left and enjoy the excellent view down into the L.A. River and across to the local hills. In 0.2 mile is another junction. Turn left again and bike on Grand View Dr. to an automobile turnout with an exceptional 180-degree view into the L.A. Civic Center (3.3). Appropriately, this is Point Grand View.

Elysian Reservoir and the "Other" Elysian Park. Grand View Dr. begins a steep, winding downhill, passing the Elysian Reservoir (4.0), and a small shaded park area with restrooms. Soon is a short, steep upgrade that leads to a junction with Park Row Dr. Turn left and cross over the Pasadena Fwy. to the park's southeastern section. There is a short, steep spur trip up Buena Vista Dr. to a tree-walled cul-de-sac on Buena Vista Hill (4.4). For the very determined, there is a steep 1/2-mile spin down Park Row Dr. to the N. Broadway exit. (Take the left fork at the first junction on the downhill and the right fork at the second junction.) Another pleasant diversion is to follow Meadow Rd. over to the Buena Vista Meadow Picnic Area.

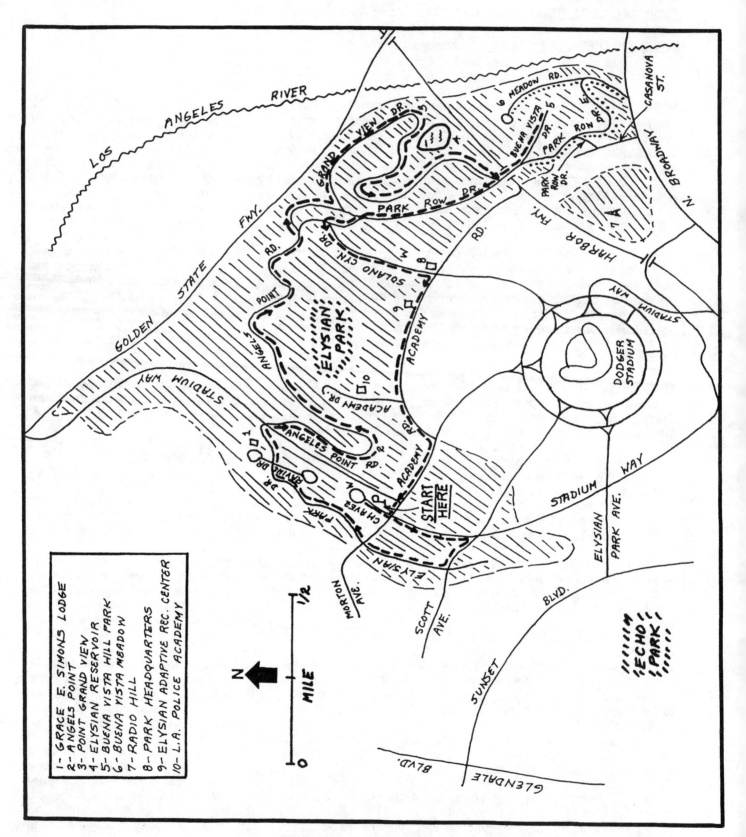

Legend:
1 - GRACE E. SIMONS LODGE
2 - ANGELS POINT
3 - POINT GRAND VIEW
4 - ELYSIAN RESERVOIR
5 - BUENA VISTA HILL PARK
6 - BUENA VISTA MEADOW
7 - RADIO HILL
8 - PARK HEADQUARTERS
9 - ELYSIAN ADAPTIVE REC. CENTER
10 - L.A. POLICE ACADEMY

N ← MILE ½ 0

TRIP #34 - ELYSIAN PARK

Elysian Park with Dodger Stadium in Background

However, our trip returns over the bridge and continues straight ahead on Park Row Dr. on a steep 0.3-mile upgrade. Just beyond the crest, the route reaches a junction (4.9) and bears left, following the arrow pointing to the Solano Canyon Information Center. There is a short downhill to another junction. Turn left onto Solano Canyon Dr. and bike past several plush picnic areas, tennis courts and water fountains to reach the Academy Rd. intersection (5.5). The Park Headquarters is on the east side.

L.A. Police Academy. Turn right (northwest) and pedal up a steep 0.3-mile upgrade past the Elysian Adaptive Recreation Center. Just beyond the crest, pass Academy Dr. and the L.A. Police Academy (5.9). In another 0.2 mile, the roadway turns hard right and descends 0.3 mile further to Stadium Wy.. Proceed across Stadium Wy. to the parking area (6.4).

CONNECTING TRIPS: For those in the mood for further exercise, there are numerous alternate routes within the park, including the Dodger Stadium "spoke."

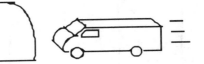

TRIP #35 - GLENDORA BIKEWAY

GENERAL LOCATION: Glendora

LEVEL OF DIFFICULTY: Loop - moderate
Distance - 8.3 miles
Elevation gain - periodic moderate grades

HIGHLIGHTS: This predominantly Class III tour is essentially a loop trip around the South Hills of Glendora. The route has nice views into the local foothills and San Gabriel Mountains, particularly on the northern trip segment. The main route is well laid out and well marked, primarily in residential neighborhoods on lightly traveled roadways and has many potential spurs and connectors which were not investigated by the authors.

TRAILHEAD: From the Foothill Fwy., exit north at Grand Ave., continue about 1/2 mile north to Foothill Blvd. and turn right (east). Drive 0.5 mile to Wabash Ave., turn left and then turn right at Meda Ave. in 0.2 mile. Continue into the Finkbiner Park area and park on Minnesota Ave., subject to the posted laws.
Bring a moderate water supply. There is water at the origin, South Hills Park (spur trip), and some of the schools along the route. (Use the schools only during off-school hours.)

TRIP DESCRIPTION: **The North Segment.** From the park, ride west to Wabash Ave. and turn right. Follow this Class III roadway as it passes through a residential neighborhood past Bennett Ave., Whitcomb Ave. and a market, and reaches Leadora Ave. (0.4). Turn right (east) and begin a steady uphill while taking in the foothills and San Gabriel Mountains to the north. The Class III path continues past Live Oak Ave. and a school (0.9), crosses Little Dalton Wash (1.1) and dead ends at Loraine Ave. (1.4) near the crest.

141

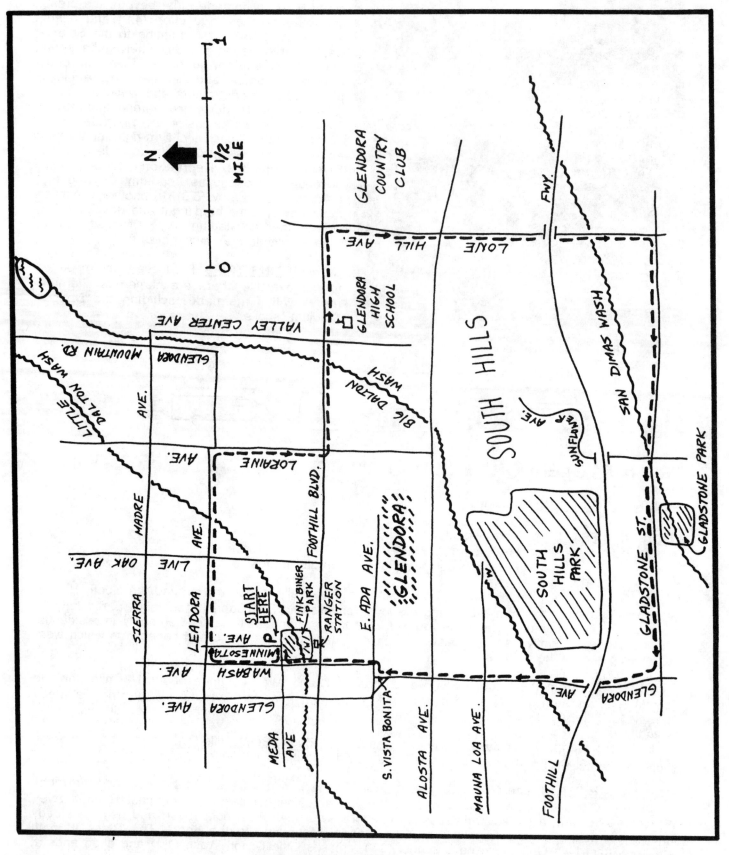

TRIP #35 - GLENDORA BIKEWAY

Turn right (south) and bike on a moderate downgrade 1/2 mile past a school to Foothill Blvd. Turn left and follow a tree-lined and busier roadway on a Class II bikepath crossing Big Dalton Wash (2.4), Valley Center Ave. and passing by Glendora High School (2.5). Start uphill and pedal to a crest just short of Lone Hill Blvd. (3.0). Instead of proceeding up the nasty-looking hill straight ahead, breathe a sigh of relief and turn right at Lone Hill Blvd.

East Segment. Follow a long downhill on a Class III route in a more exposed, more residential area than Foothill Blvd. There is a slight uphill just before Alosta Ave. (3.5) and in 0.4 mile, pass under the Foothill Fwy. There is a San Dimas Wash crossing just beyond and the route is now alongside some large agricultural fields. The South Hills are clearly visible to the right (west) in this area.

South Segment. The bike route turns right at Gladstone St. (4.5) and proceeds on a flat Class II road alongside open fields. In 1/2 mile, cross Valley Center Ave. and again enter a residential area. The bike route crosses Sunflower Ave. (5.5), the San Dimas Wash, Gladstone Park (5.8) and reaches Glendora Ave. in 0.7 mile.

West Segment. Turn right (north) and pass under the Foothill Fwy., cross the Big Dalton Wash (7.0), pass Baseline Rd. and meet up with Mauna Loa Ave. (7.3). A right turn here leads 0.3 mile to South Hills Park and a dead end. There is a small, grassy playground with a restroom, together with lots of local hills to hike.

However, our Class III route heads down Glendora Ave. past Alosta Ave. where the road narrows considerably. In 0.2 mile, the route junctions. Follow the bike sign right to S. Vista Bonita and right again (east) on E. Ada Ave. Pass through a shaded residential area to Wabash Ave. and turn left (7.9). Cross Foothill Blvd., pass the Glendora Ranger Station (8.1), ride across the Little Dalton Wash and turn right on Meda Ave. Ride through the park to the starting point (8.3).

CONNECTING TRIPS: Numerous spurs off our basic trip were observed. Bikepath signs were noted on Bennett Ave., Live Oak Ave., Alosta Ave. and extensions to our basic route were found at Loraine Ave., Foothill Blvd., Gladstone St. and Glendora Ave. Connection with the Baseline Road tour (Trip #45) - at Lone Hill Blvd. and Gladstone St., continue east on the latter road.

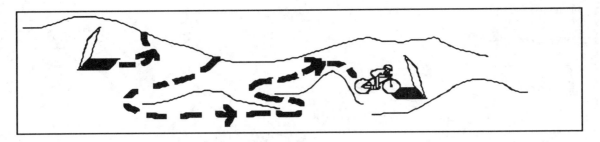

TRIP #36 - BURBANK BIKEWAY

GENERAL LOCATION: Burbank

LEVEL OF DIFFICULTY: Peripheral loop - moderate to strenuous
Distance - 14.8 miles
Elevation gain - continuous moderate-to-steep grades in foothills,
essentially flat elsewhere

HIGHLIGHTS: This 15-mile extravaganza is one of the better inner-city tours in our book. The Burbank Bikeway actually consists of four separate Class III inner loops and a fifth, peripheral loop. The latter loop is described here. The route initially tours the foothills below the Verdugo Mountains in the northeast trip sector; there are several nice parks and excellent San Fernando Valley views. The long and sometimes steep upgrades in this area are also what give the trip the borderline "strenuous" label.

The route drops out of the foothills, passes through "Beautiful Downtown Burbank" and proceeds southwest as far as the L.A. Equestrian Center along the L.A. River. The path follows past the Disney Studios and NBC Television Studios, visits the relaxing, lightly-trafficked residential area on Burbank's west side, then returns to the trip origin via busy Buena Vista St.

TRAILHEAD: From the Golden State Fwy., exit at Buena Vista St. From the northbound freeway exit, turn south on Buena Vista St. (back toward the freeway) and turn left (east) on Winona Ave. Drive several blocks to Keystone St. and find parking subject to the posted parking laws. From the

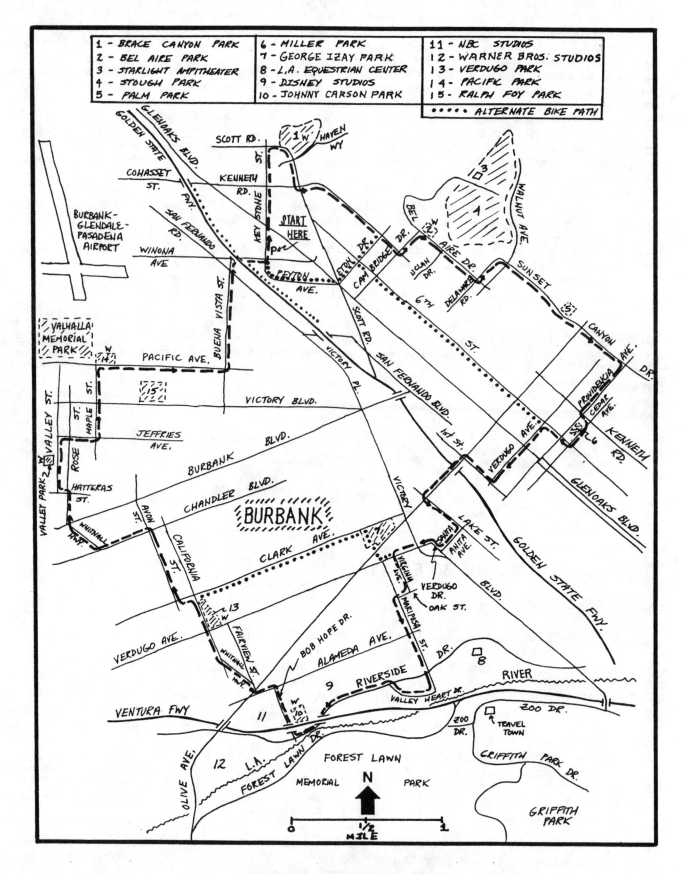

1 - BRACE CANYON PARK
2 - BEL AIRE PARK
3 - STARLIGHT AMPITHEATER
4 - STOUGH PARK
5 - PALM PARK
6 - MILLER PARK
7 - GEORGE IZAY PARK
8 - L.A. EQUESTRIAN CENTER
9 - DISNEY STUDIOS
10 - JOHNNY CARSON PARK
11 - NBC STUDIOS
12 - WARNER BROS. STUDIOS
13 - VERDUGO PARK
14 - PACIFIC PARK
15 - RALPH FOY PARK
••••• ALTERNATE BIKE PATH

TRIP #36 - BURBANK BIKEWAY

southbound exit, turn left upon reaching Buena Vista St. and drive north back under the freeway; turn right on Winona Ave. and continue as above.

Bring a moderate water supply. There are water sources strategically located throughout the trip.

Follow the route map carefully as some turns are not clearly marked (e.g., at the intersections of Kenneth Rd./Providencia Ave. and Santa Anita Ave./Lake St.). In addition, bring a street map as a backup should you lose your way. Because some of the route is tricky, this trip is written with more than the usual number of turns described.

TRIP DESCRIPTION: **The Foothills.** From the Winona Ave. intersection, pedal north (toward the hills) through a shaded residential area on Keystone St. Then proceed on varying grades of uphill for 0.9 mile before reaching Scott Rd. Turn right and puff another 0.2 mile before reaching a level area below Brace Canyon Park.

Just beyond is Haven Way, a diversion route up to the park which has shade, restrooms, picnic area, recreation fields, playground and a mesh of walkways/bikeways. However, our route continues downhill on Scott Rd., turns left on Kenneth Rd. (1.3), curves southeast, and heads moderately downhill to Cambridge Dr. (2.1).

Now the fun begins! Pump up a steep grade 0.3 mile to Bel Aire Dr. A nice lady living at this corner intersection watched us struggle up the hill and offered our tired, weary group of bikers some ice water -- which we gladly accepted! Just across the street is a rest area at Bel Aire Park.

Turn right on Bel Aire Dr. and cruise downhill through this impressive residential area past UCLAN Dr. (Yes,--UCLAN) and then pedal a steep uphill which crests at Delaware Rd. (2.9). Turn left and climb another "gut-buster" 0.3 mile which crests near the junction where Delaware Rd. fuses into Sunset Canyon Dr. Here are scattered views into the San Fernando Valley, particularly on clear days. Bike on a more moderate set of rolling hills through rural territory passing the De Bell Golf Course (3.3), Palm Park (3.7) and reach Providencia Ave. at (4.3).

Burbank-based NBC Studios

Downhill to Downtown. Turn right on Providencia Ave. and bike steadily downhill enjoying the view of the Hollywood Hills and Griffith Park straight ahead. Turn left (east) at Kenneth Rd. (4.6) and right at the next street which is Cedar Ave., skirting pleasant little Miller Park. Turn right at Sixth St. (4.8) and left at Verdugo Ave. in 0.2 mile. The route now enters one of the busier commercial areas of town, passing Glenoaks Blvd. and reaching First St. (5.6). Turn right and bike to busy Olive St., turning left and passing over the Golden State Fwy. on a narrow sidewalk (6.0).

The Southern Segment and The Studios. Ride 0.3 mile to Lake St., turn left, bike to Santa Anita Ave. and then make a right (6.5). Cruise to the end of the street, turn right on Verdugo Dr. and follow that street a short distance before turning left on Verdugo Ave. (6.9). Bike 0.2 mile and turn left on Virginia Ave., continuing to its terminus at Oak St. Turn right, pedal one block to Mariposa St., and turn left on that tree-lined residential roadway (7.4).

The route continues another 1/2 mile through this pleasant residential area and crosses Riverside Dr. where the road narrows significantly. The roadway continues a short distance and ends at the L.A. River at the western edge of the L.A. Equestrian Center. Turn right on Valley Heart Dr. and return to Riverside Dr. (8.4), following that road left (west). The bikeway passes the Disney Studios, goes under the Ventura Fwy. (9.0) and cruises the southern segment of Buena Vista Park. There is a shaded rest area here with water and a views across the L.A. River into Forest Lawn, the Hollywood Hills and Griffith Park.

At the park's edge, go right at Catalina St. and bike back under the freeway to the main body of Buena Vista Park. A creek runs through the park, which has shade trees, restrooms and picnic tables. Across the street are the NBC Television Studios with their KNBC helicopters and television vans nearby (9.3).

The Residential Western Segment. Bike on Bob Hope Dr. to its terminus at Alameda Ave. and turn left (9.6). Pedal almost to the Olive Ave. intersection. However, just short of that junction, use the Olive Ave. pedestrian crossing which leads across to Fairview St. Ride on that street for a short stretch and follow the one-way entry to Whitnall Hwy. as it angles left under the high tension power poles (9.9). Follow Whitnall Hwy. to its end at California St. (10.0), turn right, and cruise by Verdugo Park with the California Swim Stadium and a park with restrooms, tennis courts, barbecue facilities and children's playground.

The remainder of the trip is through lightly-trafficked residential areas with well-marked routes back to the trip origin. The highlights of that segment are provided below.

The route zig-zags its way northward and westward reaching its westernmost point along Valley St. (12.1). At Valley St. and Allan Ave. is Valley Park with shade, restrooms, tennis courts, picnic benches and recreation field. The route then works its way northward on Maple St., reaching Pacific Ave. (13.2). At that junction is a terrific view of Valhalla Memorial Park and its gigantic mausoleum. This area is directly under the Burbank Airport flightpath (an interesting contrast, is it not?).

The Return Leg. The bikepath travels by pleasant little Pacific Park with its shade trees, restrooms, tennis courts and picnic tables (13.3). Cruise through a mix of residential and light commercial zones with splendid views into the nearby Verdugo Mountains and the more distant San Gabriel Mountains. Our route heads north on busy Buena Vista St. (14.0), passes under the Golden State Fwy. (14.6), turns right on Winona Ave. and returns to the trip origin (14.8).

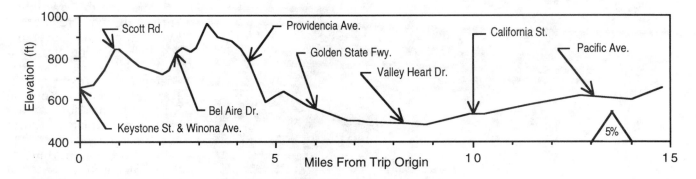

CONNECTING TRIPS: 1) There are numerous combinations of routes just within the five loops mentioned. In addition, there is a linking Class I trail which parallels the Golden State Fwy. between Cohasset St. and Morgan Ave.; 2) connection with the Griffith Park ride (Trip #33) - at Mariposa St. and Riverside Dr., turn left (east) on the latter street, continue to Victory Blvd., and turn left; 3) connection with the Glendale Bikeway (Trip #62) and Verdugo Mountains Loop (Trip #63) - from Sunset Canyon Dr. and Providencia Ave., continue east roughly one mile to the entrance to Brand Park (just beyond Western Ave.).

TRIP #37 - MULHOLLAND DRIVE

GENERAL LOCATION: Santa Monica Mountains

LEVEL OF DIFFICULTY: One way - strenuous
Distance - 13.0 miles
Elevation gain - continuous steep upgrades

HIGHLIGHTS: This roller-coaster tour along the crest of the Santa Monica Mountains provides some of the more spectacular vistas into the San Fernando and San Gabriel Valleys. There are views north across the valley to the San Gabriel Mountains and south to the ocean and the Palos Verdes Peninsula that are breathtaking! A potential drawback of this Mulholland Dr. tour is that it is open and very hilly, i.e., sun-exposed and very physically exhausting. In addition, this Class X, two-lane roadway is narrow in some areas with little or no separate shoulder for biking and some sections are poorly maintained.

The one-way mileage is provided above. This trip can be started from either end. Our tour starts with an up and back of the western Mulholland Dr. segment and covers the region from Sepulveda Pass to the end of the paved section of Mulholland Dr. This up and back is included as a "hint" that it might be wise to test a short segment before committing to the entire trip.

TRAILHEAD: From the San Diego Fwy. northbound, exit at Rimerton Rd. and make a right turn. Continue about a 1/4 mile to the Park and Ride area. From the southbound lanes, exit at Rimerton Rd. and turn left. Drive on the bridge over the freeway to the parking area.

Bring a large water supply and plenty of sun-protection gear. There is water at Coldwater Canyon Park, Vista Point and Laurel Canyon Park, all concentrated in a two-mile stretch. Avoid this route during the week, particularly during the rush hours.

TRIP DESCRIPTION: **Western Segment.** From the Park and Ride area cycle back to Rimerton Rd. and turn left, crossing over the San Diego Fwy. and above the Mulholland Tunnel. Follow the uphill-downhill tour on an upgrade past Curtis School and just beyond, stop and admire one of many excellent overlooks of the San Fernando Valley/Encino area (0.7).

Los Angeles Civic Center from East of Woodrow Wilson Drive

Bike past the Bel-Air Church (note the great view from the north-facing parking lot), and cruise the workout through a lovely residential area to Calneva Dr./Parklane Circle (1.4). The area now takes on a less developed, more rural setting and begins a steady uphill climb for the next 1/2 mile. Near the top of the grade at the Encino Hills Dr. junction is the end of the paved section of Mulholland Dr. (2.1). Beyond is mountain bike territory! Return to the San Diego Fwy. overpass. (The one-way trip mileage starting from Encino Hills Dr. is used in the discussion below.)

Eastern Segment - Skirball Center Drive to Coldwater Canyon Park. Cross back over the freeway and begin a short, steep uphill that is followed by a steep, winding downhill (2.6). Pass Woodcliff Rd.

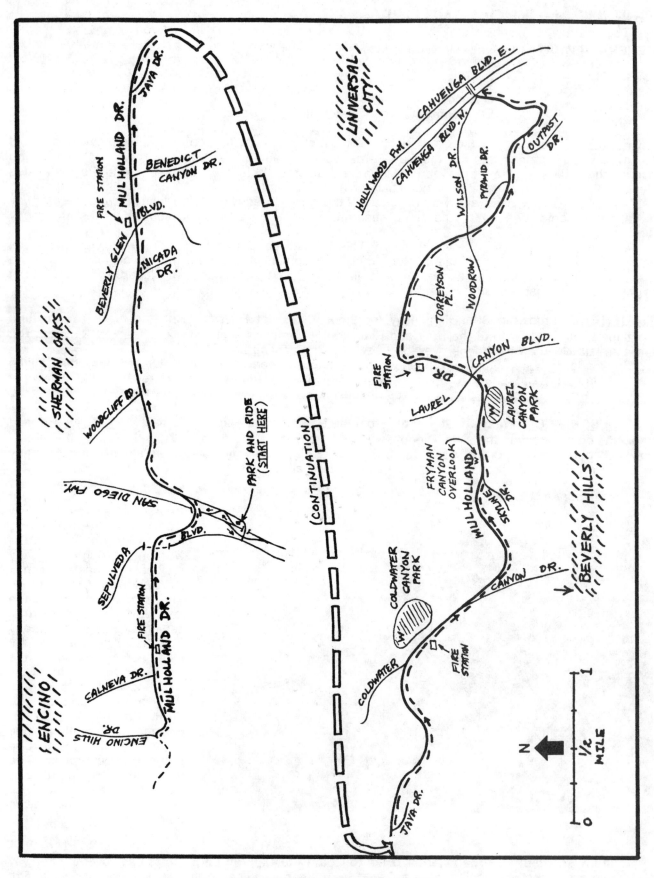

TRIP #37 - MULHOLLAND DRIVE

(3.1), cruise through some moderate rolling hills and pass several overlooks into Stone Canyon Reservoir to the south (3.4). In succession, the tour crosses Nicada Dr. and Beverly Glen Blvd. (4.3).

The journey proceeds uphill for about 1/2 mile, crosses Benedict Canyon Dr. (4.7) and then continues the "rolling hills tradition." There are interesting views into the San Fernando Valley to the left (north) and the canyons and canyon residential communities to the right. In the stretch just beyond Java Dr. is the first of several well-separated "peeks" into the "backside" of central Los Angeles (6.2). The tour heads uphill and soon merges with Coldwater Canyon Dr., and passes near pleasant, shady Coldwater Canyon Park, the home of the "Tree People" (6.5).

Coldwater Canyon Park to Laurel Canyon Park. The bike route continues for about 1/2 mile as a merged roadway; at this point Mulholland Dr. splits off to the left (east, if there is a single direction one can define on this winding road!). The roadway approaches a large radio tower placed high on the hillside and opens up into a view area with a turnout; hike out just beyond the parking area and take in one of the most sweeping, spectacular views of the San Fernando Valley and surrounding mountains (7.6).

There is a short downhill and a flat before reaching another valley vista in about one mile; this is the Fryman Canyon Overlook (and a water stop). Another section of very winding, steep downhill follows leading to pleasant Laurel Canyon Park (9.1) and shortly to Laurel Canyon Blvd. (9.3).

Laurel Canyon Park to Cahuenga Boulevard. Just across this intersection the route starts up a steep, steady, winding grade. Near the crest is an inspiring view of Universal City (10.1). In 1/2 mile near Torreyson Pl. is the official "Universal City Overlook" and another fine view. Head downhill, cross Woodrow Wilson Dr. (11.1) and then start a steep upgrade with views into the downtown Los Angeles area.

At 0.4 mile from the Woodrow Wilson Dr. intersection is a spectacular view into the central Los Angeles area and beyond! The road heads very steeply downhill through a series of curves and switchbacks, recrosses Woodrow Wilson Dr., passes Outpost Dr. (12.3), and meets up with another fine view at the "Mulholland Scenic Vista Turnout" (12.6). The highway snakes its way steeply downward 0.7 mile before reaching the trip's end at Cahuenga Blvd. West.

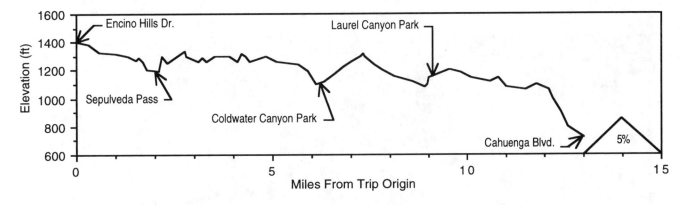

CONNECTING TRIPS: Connection with the Old Sepulveda Hill Climb (Trip #5) - from the Park and Ride area, cross over the San Diego Fwy. at Rimerton Rd.; continue west to the intersection with Sepulveda Blvd.

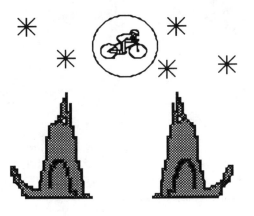

TRIP #38 - SEPULVEDA BIKE BASIN

GENERAL LOCATION: Encino

LEVEL OF DIFFICULTY: Loop - easy
Distance - 9.1 miles
Elevation gain - essentially flat

HIGHLIGHTS: This popular bike route is comprised of two separate loops within the Sepulveda Dam Recreation Area, a 3.8-mile western loop and a 5.3 mile eastern loop. Most of the route is Class I and with use of the Balboa Blvd. bike undercrossings, street travel is restricted to one short 0.3-mile segment. The bikeway tours pleasant tree-lined routes in many areas, cruises around the Balboa Sports Center and several golf courses, and has several open areas with spectacular views into mountains to the east and south. There are several nice "R & R" areas along the route, including Woodley Park.

TRAILHEAD: From the Ventura Fwy., exit north on Balboa Blvd. Cross Burbank Blvd., continue several hundred yards further and turn left into the tree-lined parking area. From the San Diego Fwy., exit west on the Ventura Fwy. and drive about 2-1/2 miles to Balboa Blvd. Continue as above.
   Bring a light water supply. Water is strategically located along the route.

TRIP DESCRIPTION: **West Loop.** Exit the parking lot and head north on a Class I bike route. Directly north is a nice view into the hills at the base of the Santa Susana Mountains. Pedal past a small restroom facility and cruise alongside a large recreation area that is the eastern edge of the Balboa Sports Center. A short distance beyond is a junction with a bikepath segment heading across the recreation field (west) (0.2). Continue north along Balboa Blvd. and in 0.1 mile cross the bridge over the L.A. River. A look into the river reveals bikers on the Balboa Ave. bikeway undercrossing. To the east are views into the Verdugo and San Gabriel Mountains.

Continue north along open fields and turn left at Victory Blvd. (0.7). Pass the USN/USMC Reserve Training Center and enter an open area with a panoramic view south to the Santa Monica Mountains. Bike past the cannon in front of the California National Guard Armory at Louise Ave. (1.3). Next is the San Fernando Valley Youth Center (there are biking activities for youngsters here) and an open agricultural area (1.5). Turn left at White Oak Ave. (1.7) and cross over the Los Angeles River.

Sepulveda Bike Basin Entry Near Balboa Boulevard

   Just beyond, the bikepath shifts over to the west side of White Oak Ave. (Class II) and proceeds 0.3 mile through a residential area to Oxnard St. The bike route turns left and returns to a Class I path alongside a small wash (2.2). This segment continues along open fields to the left and passes the entry to the Encino Velodrome (2.7).
   In 0.2 mile, the bikeway curves to the right (south) and passes a junction with the path which crosses the recreation field (3.0). Cycle past the junction to a picnic/play area with shaded picnic

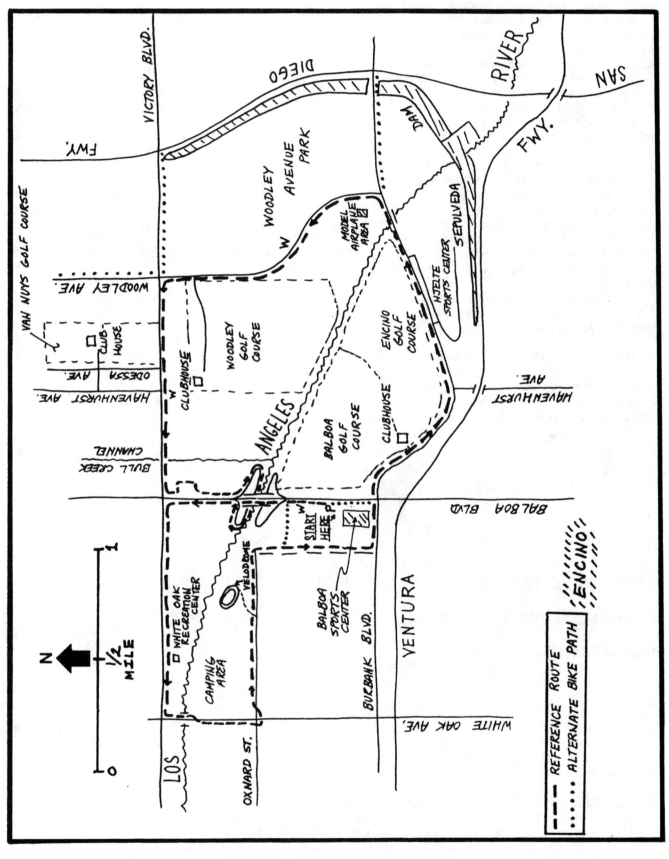

TRIP #38 - SEPULVEDA BIKE BASIN

tables (3.4). A short distance beyond is Burbank Blvd., where the bike route turns left (east) and crosses Balboa Blvd. on a pedestrian cross-walk (3.8).

East Loop. This loop starts along the well-treed Balboa Golf Course, snakes through a parking lot along Burbank Blvd., and passes the Balboa Park Clubhouse (4.2). This is a convenient place to stop for water, food, or any number of "attitude arrangers." Just beyond, the path continues to maneuver between the golf course and Burbank Blvd.

At 0.8 mile from the East Loop starting point, the path crosses Havenhurst Ave. In 0.3 mile is a roadway to the Hjelte Sports Center, an interesting diversion. The reference route continues alongside the Encino Golf Course into an area where there are views into the San Gabriel Mountains (5.3). In another 0.1 mile is a short upgrade just prior to crossing the L.A. River. At Woodley Ave. (5.6) there is an option to continue 0.4 more mile on a Class I path along Burbank Blvd. to the top of the Sepulveda Dam. However, this trip turns left on Woodley Ave. and continues past open fields into an area with an unobstructed 360-degree viewing area (6.0).

In a short distance and to the east of Woodley Ave. is Woodley Park, where there are restrooms, cricket fields and an archery range (6.2). The route passes the entrance road to the Woodley Golf Course (6.8) and turns left at Victory Blvd. (6.9). There is an option to turn east and bike about a half mile to the dam edge. Also, there is a Class III connector on Woodley Ave. which continues about 6-1/2 miles north to Granada Hills. However, the reference route proceeds on a relatively exposed stretch alongside open fields, passing a mini-rest area with water at Havenhurst Ave. (7.3). In succession the path passes a lone rest bench, crosses over the Bull Creek Channel (7.7), and meets Balboa Blvd. (7.9).

Turn left (south) and follow a short path loop that leaves Balboa Blvd. for a short distance (8.1). In 0.3 mile, the route meets the L.A. River. Take the Balboa Blvd. undercrossing to the west side of Balboa Blvd. and backtrack a short distance to the starting point (9.1).

CONNECTING TRIPS: 1) There are numerous spurs off the main route as mentioned in the trip writeup.; 2) connection with the Chatsworth-Northridge-Granada Hills Loop (Trip #55) - at Woodley Ave. and Nordoff St., turn south on the former street and bike 3-1/4 miles to Victory Blvd.; 3) connection with Trip #59 (Woodland Hills-Tarzana Loop) - at the intersection of Oxnard St. and White Oaks Ave., turn right (west) on the former street.

TRIP #39 - CHATSWORTH TOUR/BROWN'S CREEK BIKEWAY

GENERAL LOCATION: Chatsworth

LEVEL OF DIFFICULTY: Loop - easy
Distance - 6.3 miles
Elevation gain - essentially flat

HIGHLIGHTS: This tour explores the Chatsworth area in the western San Fernando Valley. It combines a Class I segment along Brown's Canyon Wash with a Class X tour on lightly traveled roadways. The tour visits two excellent parks, Chatsworth Park North and Chatsworth Park South. There are interesting hills and rock formations there, as well as pleasant, shaded rest areas. There are also fine views into the surrounding hills throughout the trip.

TRAILHEAD: From the Ronald Reagan Fwy., exit south at De Soto Ave. and continue about 1-1/2 miles to Lassen St. and turn right (west). Drive about a half mile to the Brown's Canyon Wash overcrossing and find parking nearby on Lassen St. From the Ventura Fwy., exit north at Topanga Canyon Blvd. and continue about 5-1/2 miles to Lassen St. Turn right and drive about 0.4 mile to Brown's Canyon Wash.

152

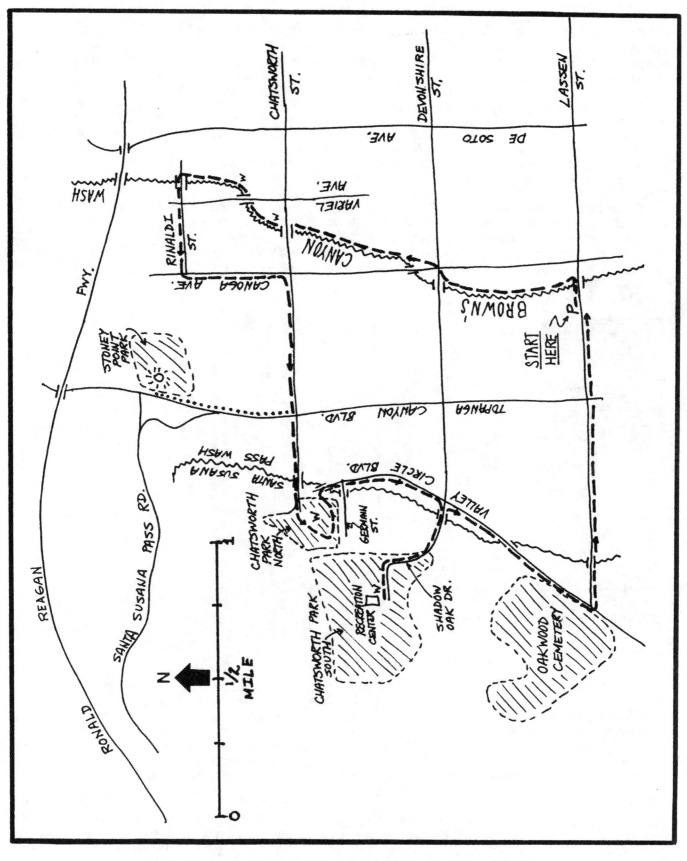

TRIP #39 - CHATSWORTH TOUR/BROWN'S CREEK BIKEWAY

Bring a light water supply. This is a short trip with water along Brown's Creek Bikeway and at both Chatsworth Parks.

TRIP DESCRIPTION: **Brown's Creek Bikeway.** From Lassen St., follow the Class I bikepath which is on the east side of Brown's Canyon Wash. This is the Brown's Creek Bikeway. The path immediately passes a tightly packed group of kennels with a large canine greeting committee. The exposed path continues alongside the backside of a light industrial/commercial area. The bikeway leaves the wash diagonally, crosses Devonshire St. (0.4) and returns to the wash just north of that street.

The bikeway passes a nursery and then cruises through a neighborhood with apartments on the left and homes to the right. There is one section where bikers can pluck citrus off the trees that overhang the bikeway (but don't do it, okay?). Further north is an aromatic area that is surrounded by small pens of farm animals and an area with riding horses (0.9). Shortly, the path crosses Chatsworth St. and proceeds through a residential area. Near Chatsworth St. is a mini-rest area with a bench, shade, and water fountain (1.1). In 0.2 mile, the path fuses with Variel Ave., where there is another mini-rest area (figure this one out!).

Chatsworth Street/Chatsworth Park North. Just beyond the bikeway ends at Rinaldi St. (1.4). The route proceeds left (west) on that wide, lightly-traveled roadway, passes trail-marked hills (foot or bicycle trails) in 0.2 mile, and reaches Canoga Ave. (1.8). There are nice views into the surrounding hills to the west and north in this area. The path turns right on Chatsworth St. (2.4) and reaches Topanga Canyon Blvd in 0.3 mile. Turn right (north) if a visit to Stony Point Park and Stoney Point is on your agenda -- there are some magnificent rocks in this area that attract many climbers and onlookers.

Chatsworth Park South Below the Rock Outcroppings

Our route crosses Topanga Canyon Blvd., passes some horse stables and a parking lot to the left (2.9), and reaches a dead end at Chatsworth Park North (3.0). Follow the bikeway/walkway around the tree-dotted park and investigate the rocky outcroppings at its periphery. There are picnic benches, barbecues and recreation areas, as well as a lovely lush field in the northernmost section of this park. Follow the path past the restroom and ride into the southern edge of the parking area. Just beyond the lot is the terminus (origin) of Valley Circle Blvd. (3.2).

Chatsworth Park South. Follow Valley Circle Blvd. 0.4 mile and turn right at Devonshire Blvd. Bike on that roadway as it changes name to Shadow Oak Dr. This is Chatsworth Park South. This larger park has lighter tree cover, but has nice picnic facilities, large grassy fields, tennis courts, hiking trails into the hills, and a recreation center (4.0).

Return Segment. Return to Valley Circle Blvd. and turn right (south). This segment leads to a more rural area of town and passes alongside the pretty, well-maintained Oakwood Cemetery (5.1). Just beyond is Lassen St., where the bike route turns left (5.3). The tour transitions from rural to light commercial/industrial surroundings and returns to the starting point at Brown's Canyon Wash (6.3).

CONNECTING TRIPS: 1) Connection with the Chatsworth-Northridge-Granada Hills Loop (Trip #55) - the two routes share common roadway in the Chatsworth St. and Valley Circle Blvd. areas; 2) connection with the Santa Susana Pass ride (Trip #56) - from Brown's Creek Wash at Chatsworth St., bike east 1/3 mile to Topanga Blvd. and turn left. In about 1/2 mile on the left (west) is Santa Susana Pass Rd.

TRIP #40 - TORRANCE TOUR

GENERAL LOCATION: Torrance

LEVEL OF DIFFICULTY: Loop -
　　　　　　　　　　　　Distance - 14.3 miles
　　　　　　　　　　　　Elevation gain - periodic easy-to-moderate grades

HIGHLIGHTS: A fine city ride, this 14.3-mile loop tours the periphery of the larger Torrance bikeway system. The tour starts at the Torrance Civic Center, visits north Torrance, cruises the scenic Torrance Blvd. area of east Torrance, then bee-lines south to the Skypark Office Center area. This is followed by a 1.3 mile segment on action-packed PCH and a return via the pleasant residential area along Anza Ave. The tour is of mixed classes, though predominantly Class II.

TRAILHEAD: From the San Diego Fwy., exit south at Crenshaw Blvd. and drive two miles to Torrance Blvd. Turn right (west) and continue one mile to Madrona Ave./Prairie Ave. Turn right and turn right again at the first entry, which leads to a large parking area near the Torrance Recreation Center. From the Harbor Fwy., drive west on Torrance Blvd. 3-l/2 miles to Madrona Ave./Prairie Ave. Turn right and continue as above.
　　Bring a filled water bottle. There is water at the Torrance Recreation Center and at scattered parks which are generally off the described route. There are also numerous gas stations along the way.

TRIP DESCRIPTION: **Northern Segment.** Follow the Class I path on the east side of Prairie Ave. to the intersection, then bike across Prairie Ave. on Class II Torrance Blvd. Pass the stately Marriott Hotel, Hawthorne Blvd., then shift over to the Class I sidewalk path just past Village Ln. Shift back to the Class II Torrance Blvd. path in 0.1 mile and turn right at Anza Ave. (1.0). Bike on the Class II route (the path is shared with parked cars for 0.7 mile) through a residential area. Pass the small shopping center at Del Amo Blvd. and turn right on Class X 190th St. in 0.6 mile (2.3).
　　Pass a larger shopping center and bike on the tree-lined road segment, continue across Hawthorne Blvd., then pass under a railroad bridge. Pedal on the road with generally wide bike shoulder and pass Columbia Park (recreation fields, playground, picnic benches, water, and a few trees). Pass Prairie Ave. (3.6), the Mobil Torrance Refinery entrance, then shift over to the Class I sidewalk path. Follow that path 0.9 mile to Crenshaw Blvd, then return to the Class X path and bike to Van Ness Ave. (5.0).
　　Southbound: 190th St. to Pacific Coast Highway (PCH). Follow the Class III road alongside the Mobil Refinery; there is a wide bike shoulder for most of the Van Ness Ave. segment. Bike through industrial/commercial area past Del Amo Blvd. (5.9) and cruise 0.4 mile to the point where Van Ness Ave. jogs left. Continue straight ahead on little Class X Arlington Ave. 0.1 mile to Torrance Blvd. and turn right.
　　Pedal on the Class II path (which is shared with parked cars) through the pleasant tree-lined residential/light commercial area past Crenshaw Blvd. and a couple of gas stations (6.9). Continue 0.6 mile, turn left on Class X Maple Ave., and bike 0.8 mile south on that lightly-traveled residential street to Sepulveda Blvd. Continue past the shopping center and turn right at the first street, Nadine Circle.
　　Follow Nadine Cr. through the residential area 0.4 mile to 229th Pl., turn right, pass the Torrance and Levy Adult Schools, and turn left on Madison St. (9.0). Continue to Lomita Blvd. and pedal against the traffic on the Class II path; cross Lomita Blvd. (no traffic signal) and rejoin Madison St. by cycling east. Coast past the well-groomed Skypark Office Center, pedal under the Torrance Airport flight path, and follow the 0.2-mile upgrade to PCH.
　　Pacific Coast Highway. Turn right at PCH and follow the Class II path on this busy road across Hawthorne Blvd. (10.2), pass a cluster of fast-food businesses, and go 0.4 mile to Anza Ave. Pass a pair of shopping centers and a donut shop (we could spend a lot of time talking about one of Don's big weaknesses, but we won't). Follow the upgrade past South Torrance High School, then bike another 0.3 mile on the short upgrade just before reaching Calle Mayor (11.4).

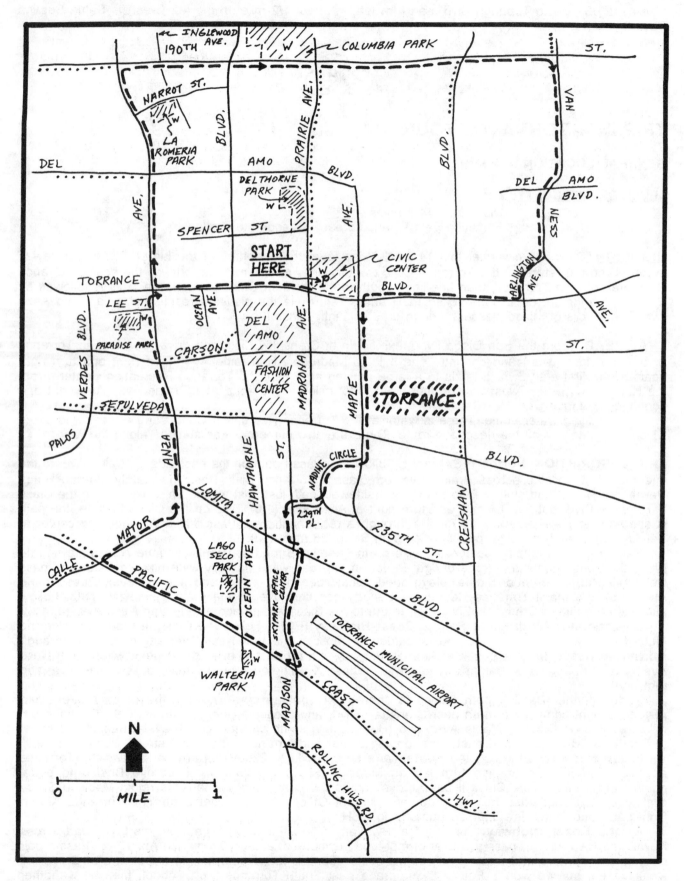

TRIP #40 - TORRANCE TOUR

The Return Segment. Turn right and follow the steep downhill past the shopping center entry. Turn left in 0.6 mile at Anza Ave. and follow Class III road through the residential area to the short uphill segment at Sepulveda Blvd. The route transitions to Class II and continues another 0.7 mile to Torrance Blvd. (13.3). Turn right, veer right again, and follow the small road which parallels Torrance Blvd. In 0.3 mile at Ocean Ave., the bikeway transitions to Class II on Torrance Blvd. and continues across Hawthorne Blvd., Prairie Ave./Madrona Ave., then returns to the trip starting point (14.3).

CONNECTING TRIPS: 1) Connection with the South Bay Bike Trail (Trip #1A) and Palos Verdes Peninsula Loop (Trips #6A and #6B) - at PCH and Calle Mayor, bike southwest on the latter street 1-1/4 miles to Palos Verdes Blvd. Turn north for Trip #1A and south for Trips #6A or #6B; 2) connection with the Gardena/Dominguez Channel ride (Trip #41) - at 190th St. and Yukon Ave., bike north 1-1/2 miles on Yukon Ave. to Alondra Park.

TRIP #41 - GARDENA BIKEWAY/DOMINGUEZ CHANNEL

GENERAL LOCATION: Gardena

LEVEL OF DIFFICULTY: **Gardena City Loop** - easy
Distance - 7.0 miles
Elevation gain - essentially flat

                        Dominguez Channel Round Trip - easy
Distance - 5.2 miles (round trip)
Elevation gain - essentially flat

HIGHLIGHTS: **Gardena City Loop.** A well-marked Class III loop that explores the city of Gardena, this described trip is part of a larger city bikeway system. With the exception of the Van Ness segment, the bikeway is generally on relatively slow-moving residential or light commercial streets. The route is only modestly scenic, but does offer some nice parks which are scattered along the route.
    Dominguez Channel and Alondra Park. There is also a Class I bikepath to the west along the Dominguez Flood Control Channel which is not directly connected to the Gardena loop. This 1.6-mile path starts at 135th St. and Crenshaw Blvd. and works its way south to its terminus at the Alondra Park entrance. There is an excellent Class I park tour beyond this park entry point.

TRAILHEAD: **Gardena City Loop and Dominguez Channel.** From the San Diego Fwy., exit east at Artesia Blvd. and drive 1-1/2 miles to Van Ness Ave. Turn left (north) and drive 2-1/2 miles to 135th St. Continue to 132nd St. and turn right. Find parking near Rowley Park (water, shade, recreation fields, and basketball courts). From the Harbor Fwy., exit west at Rosecrans Ave. and drive 1-3/4 miles to Van Ness Ave. Turn right (north) and drive 3/4 mile to 132nd St., then continue as above.
    Bring a light water supply as there are public water sources at the parks along the trail.

TRIP DESCRIPTION: **Gardena City Loop.** The outer city loop in the accompanying trip map is described below. The western segment starts along narrow and highly trafficked Van Ness Ave., but leaves the busy road and cruises residential territory beginning at 154th St. There is an Army Reserve Center and Freeman Park nearby.
    Once across busy Redondo Beach Blvd., the bikeway passes the civic center area on the 162nd St. southern trip segment. On this stretch is a miniature public Japanese Garden and the Rush Memorial Gymnasium. The eastern trip segment jig-jogs its way north through a residential area and passes near the Victorian-architectured St. John's Lutheran Church (163rd St. and Budlong Ave.). After recrossing Redondo Beach Blvd., the bikeway continues on a tree-lined segment of Budlong Ave. and passes the backside of the Normandie Club (24-hour gambling) near Rosecrans Ave.

157

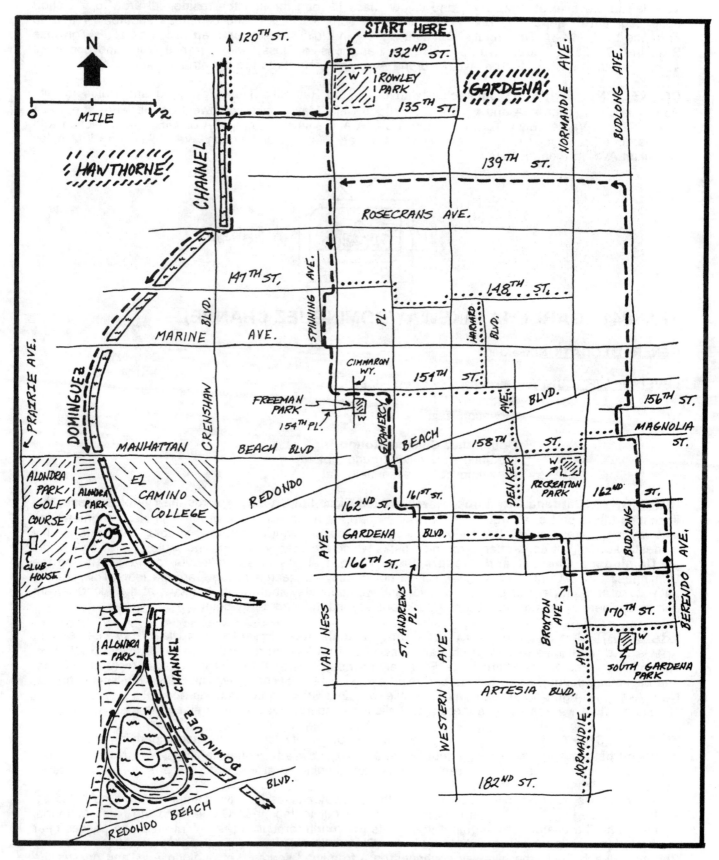

TRIP #41 - GARDENA BIKEWAY/DOMINGUEZ CHANNEL

The route heads west at 139th St., traversing a predominantly industrial area with relatively light traffic and returns to Van Ness Ave. in about 1-1/4 miles. A short 1/2-mile cruise to the north leads back to Rowley Park.

Dominguez Flood Control Channel. From Van Ness Ave. and 135th St., bike west 0.5 mile along the latter street to a bridge just before reaching Crenshaw Blvd. Pass through the entrance gate on the south side of 135th and bike 0.5 mile on the backside of an industrial area to Rosecrans Ave. Cross Rosecrans Ave. to the southwest side of the intersection and switch over to the west levee of the Dominguez Channel. Pedal through a residential area with street crossings at 147th St. (1.3), Compton Blvd. (1.6), and Manhattan Beach Blvd. (2.1). Note that there are roadway dividers on the latter two busy streets which make the crossings relatively easy -- however, keep an eye on the traffic!

Feeding the Fowl at Alondra Park

Alondra Park. Once across Manhattan Beach Blvd., follow the Class I path to the right of the divider fence into Alondra Park. (The gated and locked downhill path to the left leads to the channel floor.). Once inside the park, stay to the left, pass a restroom facility, and follow along the periphery of El Camino College through the green and shaded park. Veer right just before reaching Redondo Beach Blvd. (2.6) and follow the loop around the Alondra Park lake. Bring a few slices of bread and make friends with the ducks and geese! Bike past the large reservoir/swimming pool and follow the loop around the lake's west side, returning to Manhattan Beach Blvd. (3.1). Return to Rowley Park by reversing the incoming route (5.2).

Note: Alondra Park is certainly the tour highlight. An excellent option is to "set up camp" at this park and start the Dominguez Channel ride from there. In addition, the channel ride can be extended one mile north to 120th St. The main concern with this segment is that cyclists must leave the channel and bike to the pedestrian crossings at both 135th St. and El Segundo Blvd.

CONNECTING TRIPS: There are numerous local spurs off the Gardena City Loop.

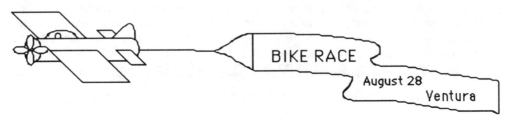

BIKE RACE

August 28
Ventura

159

TRIP #42 - DIAMOND BAR LOOP

GENERAL LOCATION: Diamond Bar

LEVEL OF DIFFICULTY: Loop - moderate
                      Distance - 10.4 miles
                      Elevation gain - periodic moderate grades

HIGHLIGHTS: This pleasant predominantly Class II loop trip starts at rustic Sycamore Canyon Park and proceeds through a mix of flats and rolling hills on Diamond Bar Blvd. through Brea Canyon. Next is a short pump over the Puente Hills and a return via Colima Rd./Golden Springs Dr. There are varied views of the Puente Hills throughout the trip and an excellent view of the valley below and the San Jose Hills from the Brea Canyon Cutoff summit.

There is an interesting workout diversion tour up Grand Ave. which provides a dandy view of Diamond Bar. The Diamond Bar Loop easily can be connected to the San Jose Hills ride if the biker is interested in extending this hillside tour.

TRAILHEAD: The Orange and Pomona Fwys. merge for about a two-mile stretch near Diamond Bar. Exit at Grand Ave., turn right (east) and drive 0.4 mile to Golden Springs Dr. Turn left and continue l/2 mile to the Sycamore Canyon Park entrance on the right and find public parking. The park has restrooms, light tree cover, picnic facilities, children's playground and a baseball field.

Bring a filled water bottle, especially on hot days. We found public water sources at Sycamore Canyon Park and at the Los Angeles Royal Vista Golf Course. There are also gas stations peppered along the route.

TRIP DESCRIPTION: **Golden Springs Dr. Eastbound.** Before leaving the park, investigate the upper segment where there is a hiking trail through a lightly forested area. Turn right onto Golden Springs Dr. and bike on the modest grade which crests and heads downhill to Diamond Bar Village with eateries and shopping. In 0.1 mile turn sharply right onto the wide expanse of Class II Diamond Bar Blvd. (0.6).

Diamond Bar Blvd. Follow this road uphill through the treeless canyon-like setting to the crest at Tin Dr. Coast the downhill past Steep Canyon Dr. to Grand Ave. where all four-corners are filled with shopping centers (1.9). Coast downhill on the long, slight grade past several small shopping plazas, then follow the steeper descent which leads to Mountain Laurel Rd. (2.6). Note the homes on the ridge above---we'll say more about the ridge area in "The Grand Ave. Diversion Trip."

Continue on the mile-long downgrade through a residential setting past Pathfinder Rd., Shadow Canyon Rd. (4.0), the Country Hills Town Center (shopping center) and then bike uphill to the crest at Cold Spring Ln. Just beyond, the road passes Brea Canyon Rd. with a shopping complex and gas stations, then tunnels under the Orange Fwy.; the road name changes to Brea Canyon Cutoff.

Brea Canyon Cutoff. The route passes below the house-bedecked Puente Hills on Class X roadway with a wide biking shoulder. Follow the 3/4 mile workout stair-step upgrade through the exposed canyon past Pathfinder Rd. (5.3). Just beyond at the summit in this more lightly-developed area is an excellent view into the valley below and the San Jose Hills across the valley. Next follow the steep, mildly winding downhill which lets out at Colima Rd. near a small business complex with both sit-down and fast-food eateries (6.9).

Colima Rd - Golden Springs Dr. Eastbound. Turn right (east) and bike on the Class X road with wide shoulder between the two segments of the Los Angeles Royal Vista Golf Course. Continue past the Los Angeles Royal Vista Restaurant and an area of the golf course to the right with a convenient water fountain (7.2). Near Calbourne Dr. is a return to Class II bikeway. Ride on the flat, pass Lemon Ave., and begin the 0.3-mile uphill to an area with fast food restaurants and gas stations. Pass Brea Canyon Rd. (8.5) and ride under the freeway interchange on what is now Golden Springs Dr.

Just beyond is the stair-step upgrade which becomes testy just before reaching Gateway Dr. Here there are both the freeway and lightly-developed hills to the left and commercial complexes to the right. In the next 0.6 mile is a ride on varying degrees of grade which reaches the crest at Grand Ave. at a shopping/industrial complex (9.9). To the north is the Diamond Bar Golf Course and just beyond is the Diamond Bar Country Club. Enjoy the view of the San Gabriel Mountains from this elevated area. In 0.3 mile, turn right and return to Sycamore Canyon Park (10.4).

160

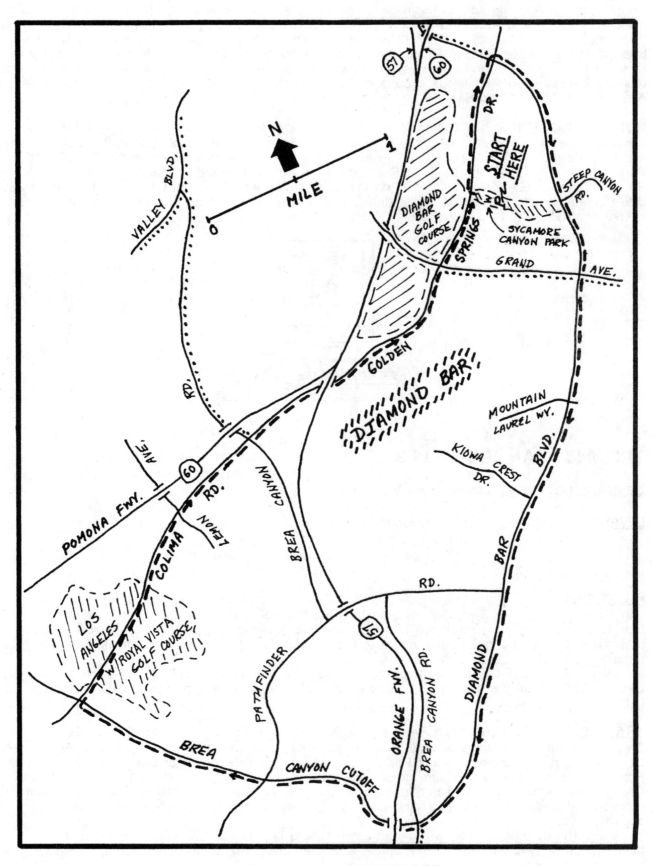

TRIP #42 - DIAMOND BAR LOOP

Grand Ave. Diversion Trip. One look at the street map convinced us to bike up Grand Ave. east of Golden Springs Rd.; the ride on the ridge at the summit appeared to be too good to pass up. So we biked up steep Grand Ave. on a 0.7 mile workout to Shotgun Ln. only to find that the road access to that street is gated -- private property! However, we continued up to Summit Ridge Dr., turned left and biked 0.3 mile to the Summit Ridge Park turnoff. A short distance uphill is the park with water, restrooms, picnic tables and a tremendous view of the surrounding hills and valleys. The total round trip is 2.2 miles. (More-ambitious cyclists can continue north on Summit Ridge Dr. or follow Grand Ave. into the City of Chino Hills.)

CONNECTING TRIPS: 1) Connection with the Hacienda Heights Loop (Trip #27) - at Brea Canyon Cutoff and Colima Rd., turn west at the latter road; 2) connection with the San Jose Hills ride (trip #43) - at Brea Canyon Rd., bike north 1-1/2 miles to Valley Blvd.; 3) connection with the Bonelli Regional Park tour (Trip #44) and the Baseline Road tour (Trip #45) - from the intersection of Golden Springs Rd. and Diamond Bar Blvd., bike north on the latter street, which becomes Mission Blvd. and meets little Humane Wy. in 2-1/2 miles; follow that road to Valley Blvd. and turn left (north) at the first major intersection (Ganesha Blvd.) beyond the Corona Expressway.

TRIP #43 - SAN JOSE HILLS

GENERAL LOCATION: Walnut, City of Industry

LEVEL OF DIFFICULTY: Loop - moderate
Distance - 12.9 miles
Elevation gain - periodic moderate-to-steep grades
(Amar Rd. and Temple Ave.)

HIGHLIGHTS: This is a dandy trip for "hillies." From Nogales St. to La Puente Rd. to the outlet at Temple Ave. and Valley Blvd. (6.7 miles), bikers are treated to a steady diet of ups and downs in the San Jose Hills. The trip is mostly on Class II and Class X roads with plenty of biking room. There are splendid views into the valleys and across to the Puente Hills at the higher elevations. For variety, the remaining half of the trip is in the valley flatlands.

On a hot, smoggy day this workout might budge the strenuous difficulty rating. More adventurous bikers might explore the surrounding hillside, residential communities, particularly on La Puente Rd., Lemon Ave., west Amar Rd. and north Grand Ave.

TRAILHEAD: From the Pomona Fwy., exit at Brea Canyon Rd. and drive north 1-1/2 miles to Valley Blvd., turn right and continue one-half mile to Grand Ave. Turn left and drive 0.6 mile to Snow Creek Dr. and turn right into Snow Creek Park. From the Orange Fwy. south of Diamond Bar, exit at the Pomona Fwy. westbound and turn off at Brea Canyon Rd. Continue as described above. From the Orange Fwy. north of Diamond Bar, exit at Temple Ave. and drive 0.7 mile to Valley Blvd. Turn left, proceed 2-1/4 miles to Grand Ave. and turn right (north). Continue to Snow Creek Dr. as described above.

Bring a filled water bottle (two for hot days). There is water at Creekside Park near the halfway point, which is reached via a testy uphill; however, no easily accessible (on-route) public water sources were found.

162

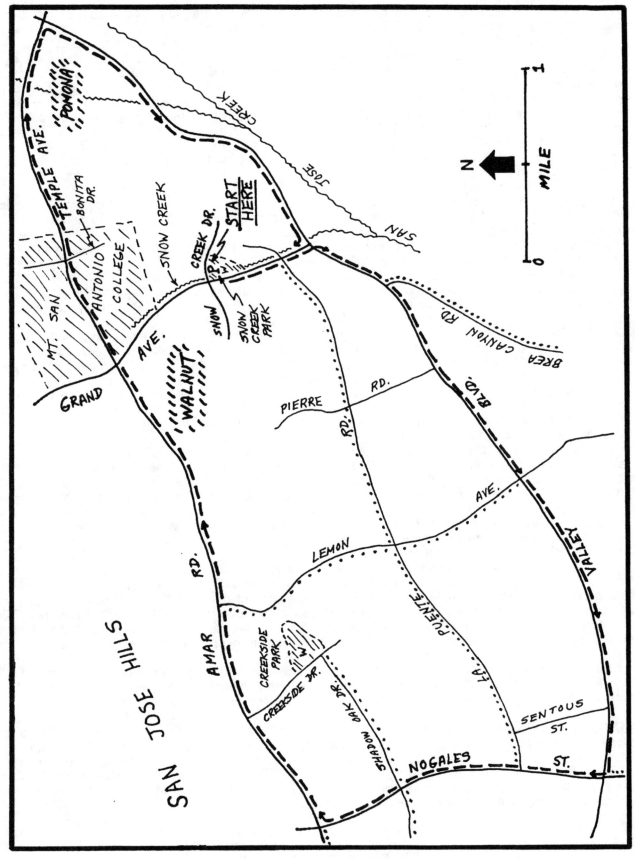

TRIP #43 - SAN JOSE HILLS

TRIP DESCRIPTION: Grand Ave. Explore the well-designed little Snow Creek Park before hitting the road. There are shade trees, picnic benches and a picnicker's pagoda, water, restrooms, sunken baseball field and little Snow Creek on the park periphery. Return to Grand Ave. and bike downhill through the hills. In 0.4 mile pass La Puente Rd., then continue downhill 0.3 mile to Valley Blvd.

Valley Blvd. Outbound. Turn right and bike on the Class X road with wide biking shoulder through the flat and wide valley. The road parallels the Southern Pacific tracks and there is a reasonable likelihood of having a choo-choo for company along this stretch. The area along the tracks has scattered industry for the next several miles - this is part of the City of Industry (surprise!). Ride through varying and sparsely populated and developed areas (mixed residential and commercial) past Brea Canyon Rd., transit a short span beyond Suzanne Rd. where the bike shoulder narrows, and reach Pierre Rd. with its small shopping plaza and gas station (1.8). In 0.7 mile is Lemon Ave. with a gas station, small shopping center and a few rolling hills. Bike past Fairway Dr. and a shopping plaza, Sentous Ave. with a gas station and mini-mart (3.2), then cycle another 0.4 mile to Nogales St. and yet another shopping complex.

Nogales St. So you're wondering -- where are these San Jose Hills? Class X Nogales St. provides the introduction. Bike 1/2 mile in a residential setting to La Puente Rd., using the sidewalk in this stretch if you are nervous about taking up a lane of traffic. However, our trip starts uphill on tree-lined (now Class II) Nogales St., reaching the crest in 0.4 mile. The residential road continues on the flat for a short distance then starts a mild, steady uphill to Shadow Oak Dr. (4.9).

Just 0.4 mile to the left is Shadow Oak Park, while well-equipped Creekside Park can be reached by turning right and biking 0.7 mile on a testy uphill. Our reference route stays on Nogales St. and follows another steady uphill which steepens and continues 0.4 mile to Walnut Plaza (shopping center). Pump another 0.2 mile to Amar Rd. (5.5).

Amar Rd. - The Hillside Tour. Turn right (east) on the Class II road with and pedal through shadeless residential territory. There are barren hills to the left and scattered peeks down into the valley on the right. Follow another steady upgrade which steepens, then reaches the crest at (6.6). For the next two miles to Grand Ave., the route transitions from this steady upgrade to rolling hills.

Bike past scattered residential pockets beneath plush hillside homes and enjoy the periodic views down into the valley. The road passes Lemon Ave. (7.1), then roller coasters through a less-populated area before reaching a little valley with a small, tightly packed community. In a short distance, Amar Rd. reaches the Grand Ave. intersection (8.7).

Temple Ave. and the Downgrade. Pedal by a gas station and continue on the road now named Temple Ave. Pass the Mt. San Antonio College Wildlife Sanctuary, the campus entrance, and follow the steady upgrade alongside the campus. The uphill continues through more open country across Bonita Dr. and the route transitions to Class X with a wide shoulder. What follows is a workout steady uphill to the crest 1.2 miles from Grand Ave. Enjoy the view from the crest, then bike downhill on divided highway through less-developed country. Pass on the periphery of California State Polytechnic University campus on tree-lined (with a short stretch of narrowing) roadway, cross San Jose Creek and bike to Valley Blvd. (10.8).

Valley Blvd. - Return Segment. There is a small shopping center l/4 mile further on Temple St. at Pomona Blvd. However, the reference route turns right onto Class X Valley Blvd. and continues through open and exposed valley country. There are scattered residential pockets along the way with a mix of industry and some farmland. There are also continuous views of the relatively barren Chino Hills to the left. Pass the gas station l.5 miles from Temple Ave. and reach Grand Ave. in another 0.6 mile. Turn right and puff up the workout upgrade 0.7 mile, returning to Snow Creek Park (12.9).

La Puente Ave. Option. On the outbound segment, cyclists can turn west off of Grand Ave. onto La Puente Ave. and enjoy a Class II roadway which continues to Nogales Ave. This alternative is not as flat as Valley Blvd., but more scenic and does reduce the trip length by about a mile.

CONNECTING TRIPS: 1) Connection with the Hacienda Heights Loop (Trip # 27) - at Valley Blvd. and Nogales St., head south for one mile to Colima Rd.; 2) connection with the Diamond Bar Loop (Trip #42) - at Brea Canyon Rd., bike l-l/2 miles south to Colima Rd./Golden Springs Rd. and turn left; 3) connection with the Bonelli Regional Park tour (Trip #44) and the Baseline Road tour (Trip #45) - from the Temple Ave./Valley Blvd. intersection, bike north on the latter road l.7 miles to the first intersection just past the Corona Expressway (Fairplex Dr.) and turn left.

164

TRIP #44 - BONELLI REGIONAL COUNTY PARK

GENERAL LOCATION: San Dimas, Pomona

LEVEL OF DIFFICULTY: Loop - moderate
Distance - 8.9 miles
Elevation gain - periodic moderate grades in eastern side of park

HIGHLIGHTS: A pleasant spin around Puddingstone Reservoir, this tour offers a wide variety of terrain and attractions. As our triathlete reviewer Sally Bond notes, it is also part of the course for one of the Los Angeles County Triathlon series. This is a varied class ride with wide bike shoulder on most of the Class III and Class X segments. The route traverses rolling hills through Picnic Valley, winds along the east shoreline by Raging Waters, visits the North Shore picnic area and beach, cruises by Brackett Field on a flat road, and returns for a hilly tour through the scenic East Shore area. There are numerous vistas overlooking the reservoir. The picnic areas are in a naturally scenic and well-groomed part of Bonelli Park. There are several short grades on this tour which "push" this trip out of the easy category; however, there is an easy two-mile mini loop which circumnavigates Picnic Valley.

TRAILHEAD: From the San Bernardino Fwy., exit north onto Fairplex Dr. Drive 3/4 mile to Via Verde, turn left and continue 3/4 mile to the east entrance of Bonelli Park. Pay the entry fee and drive l/2 mile to the nearest parking. From the Foothill Fwy., exit at Via Verde and turn east. Drive l/4 mile to the west park entrance. Continue another mile and make a hard left into the parking area.

An option is to park in the Raging Waters lot and enjoy some exciting water rides at trip's end. A free option is to park on Via Verde, just west of the Foothill Fwy.

Bring a light water supply as there's water throughout the park. There is a three-mile waterless stretch in the Brackett Air Field - Mountain Meadows Golf Course area. Look out for thorns, particularly off the established roads. Our tour group picked up several of these little devils at unknown locations and eventually had flat tires! (Once the thorns are pulled out, plan on repairing a tube.)

East Shore of Puddingstone Reservoir

TRIP DESCRIPTION: **Picnic Valley.** Bike west on the Class I path near the parking lot which follows along Via Verde. For the next l/2 mile, the route passes a large pagoda, playgrounds and picnic areas.

165

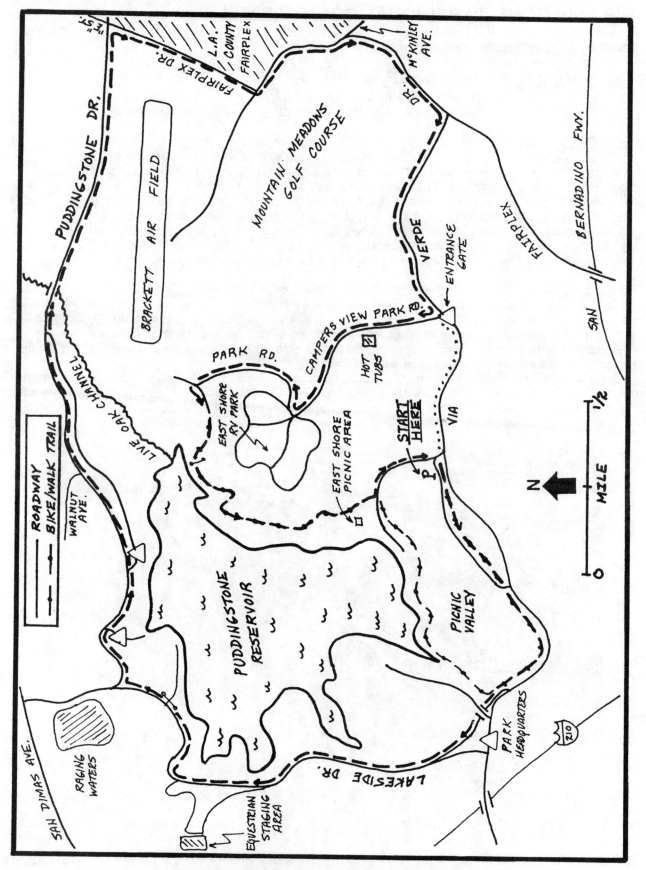

TRIP #44 - BONELLI REGIONAL PARK

The charming grass and treed areas along the path are all part of Picnic Valley and heads downhill. The path crosses under a park roadway and then veers right and heads downhill again along Lakeside Dr. Next it passes above a sailboat launch area where there is an excellent view of the lake and reaches a parking entry where the Class I path ends (1.2).

Raging Waters. Pass the parking entry (stay to the left) and follow the Raging Waters sign to the right at the next road junction. (A left at this junction leads to the Equestrian Staging Area.) Bike next to Puddingstone Reservoir to a picturesque overlook with the reservoir to the right and Raging Waters to the left. Several different water rides can be viewed (and visited), including the ultimate downhill ride, the seven-story high "Dropout" (2.0). At the Raging Waters road junction just beyond, turn right and bike uphill to the powerboat launch area (2.6).

Puddingstone Dr. For the next mile, Class II Puddingstone Dr. passes a series of excellent picnic areas and a site with a miniature sand beach. The road crosses Walnut Ave. (3.2) and begins a short uphill just before reaching the outskirts of Brackett Air Field. Bike alongside the airport and admire the longhorn cattle in the hills to the north, pass the control tower and turn right on Fairplex Dr. (4.5).

L.A. County Fairgrounds and Mountain Meadows Golf Course. Follow the Class I path (west side of street only) one-half mile along the Los Angeles County Fairgrounds and turn left, staying on Fairplex Dr. (A right turn leads to Brackett Field.). Note that there is a nifty spot directly below the flight path in this area. Pedal a Class X stretch 0.3 mile to the Mc Kinley Ave. split and veer right to remain on Fairplex Dr. (5.3). Bike on the mild Class II road uphill along the golf course for l/2 mile, then turn right at Via Verde and follow the steeper upgrade to the Bonelli Park east entry gate.

East Shore. An option is to continue 1/2 mile on Via Verde and return to the parking area. However, this reference ride follows the road right on a steep upgrade which passes the Puddingstone Hot Tubs (public tubs with nice vistas) (6.6); this grade levels in a short distance. Bike into the East Shore RV Park and turn right at the corner market.

Stay to the right and follow the winding downhill into the lower RV park (7.4), turn left at any of the small streets, and follow the road toward the reservoir. Bike below the tent camp area, then pass through the bike entry near the lake edge, and join up with the pleasant Class I path along the lake. This area has one of the premier lake views; it is a particularly nice location from which to watch the powerboats and jet skiers (8.1). Continue uphill on the path to the inviting East Shore picnic area, following the trail inland to the road (8.5), and then turn left. Cycle 0.2 mile to Via Verde, turn right and return to the parking area (8.9).

CONNECTING TRIPS: 1) Connection with the Glendora Bikeway (Trip #35) - follow Via Verde west to San Dimas Ave., turn right and bike 2-1/2 miles to Gladstone St., and then turn left.; 2) connection with the Baseline Road tour (Trip #45) - at Lakeside Dr. and Via Verde, continue west on Via Verde

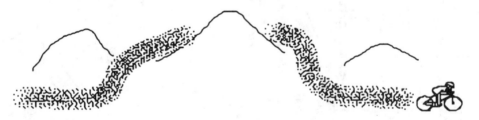

TRIP #45 - BASELINE ROAD

GENERAL LOCATION: San Dimas, La Verne, Claremont

LEVEL OF DIFFICULTY: Loop - moderate
Distance - 22.3 miles
Elevation gain - periodic moderate grades

HIGHLIGHTS: This very scenic loop explores Ganesha Park, Bonelli Regional County Park, cruises the foothills of the San Gabriel Mountains, and visits three fine cities to boot. Most of this tour is on Class X roads with relatively light traffic and with wide biking shoulder. There are hill, valley and mountain vistas scattered throughout this trip. Also, there are numerous interesting diversion trips throughout the loop tour which are identified in the detailed trip writeup.

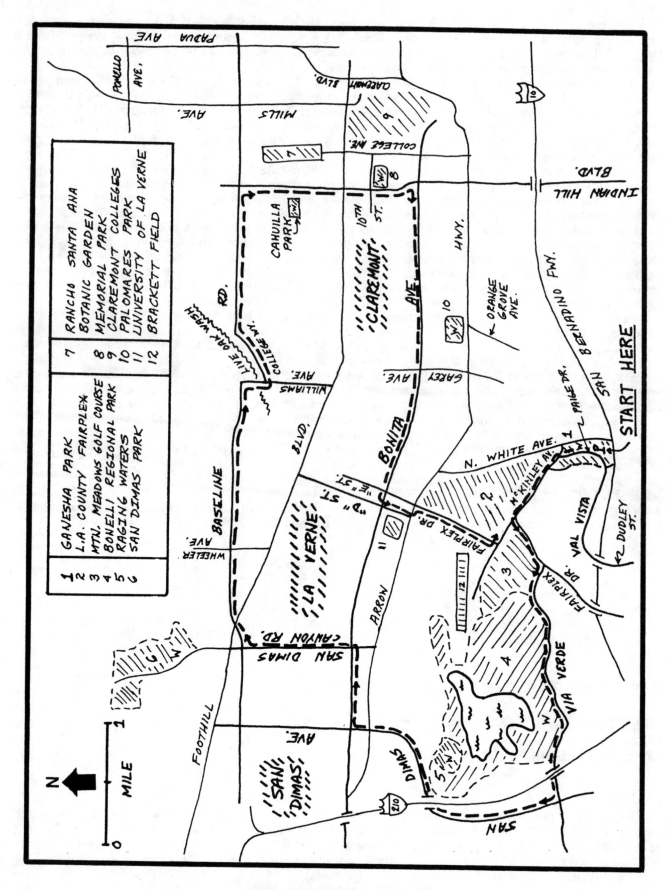

TRIP #45 - BASELINE ROAD

TRAILHEAD: From the San Bernardino Fwy., exit at Dudley St. in Pomona. Turn north and continue as the street changes name to Via Vista Dr. Follow this winding road one mile into Ganesha Park; continue toward the north end of the park on what is now Paige Dr. and find parking. Ganesha Park is a pleasant base of operations. There are dense tree cover, hiking trails, picnic areas, swimming pool, children's playgrounds and restrooms.

Bring a filled water bottle (two if you want to bike without leaving the described route). There is water at several parks which are generally reached with short diversions off the main route.

TRIP DESCRIPTION: **Ganesha Park to Bonelli Regional County Park.** Leave the picnic area near the swimming pool and return to Paige Dr. heading north. Bike uphill about 0.3 mile to McKinley Ave., turn left and pump uphill above the Los Angeles County Fairplex on Class III bikeway. In 0.5 mile on McKinley Ave., the road crests and continues a short distance to Ganesha Blvd. (0.9).

Turn left and bike one-half mile on the mild upgrade on Class III roadway alongside the Mountain Meadows Golf Course. Turn left at Via Verde and follow the steeper upgrade to the Bonelli Park east entrance gate (2.9). Bike in the hills of the large and pleasant park on Via Verde and in l/2 mile reach a spur leading to a parking area. (See the Trip #44 map for more detail.) There are options to stay on Via Verde or to bike the paralleling Class I path through the tree-shaded picnic area known as Picnic Valley. The reference route stays on Via Verde for another 0.9 mile on rolling hills before reaching the park's west entrance gate at Lakeside Dr. (4.4). Continue west a short distance, pass over the Foothill Fwy., and reach San Dimas Ave.

Western Trip Segment. Turn right and bike a 0.4-mile flat to an area with an exceptional view north into the valley area. Follow this Class X road on the steep downgrade with barren hills to the east. Coast downhill past Avd. Loma Vista (5.5) alongside the Foothill Fwy.; the road curves east and passes under that freeway in 0.4 mile. Cycle through the rolling hills in a small canyon and pass an area with a view of Raging Waters. Soon, the road curves back to the north and levels, goes by Ben's Bait Shop (bait and cold liquid refreshments) and then passes a gas station. The route continues across Arrow Hwy. and reaches Bonita Ave. just beyond (7.2).

Turn right (east) and pedal 0.8 mile on this palm-lined road, passing several small shopping plazas before reaching San Dimas Canyon Rd. Turn left and bike on another Class X road with wide shoulder. The road heads uphill through an area with San Gabriel Mountains views directly ahead, crests, then returns downhill and passes Allen Ave. In a short distance is the State Hwy. 30 undercrossing and a more rural area with Baseline Rd. just beyond (9.0). There is a spur-trip option to continue north 0.4 mile to San Dimas Canyon Park for water, restrooms, shade, recreation fields, picnic areas, and a nature center.

Baseline Road. However, our reference route turns right and continues on this Class X road along the base of the San Gabriel Mountains. Bike through the surrounding residential area, pass Wheeler Ave., and navigate through rolling hills to Williams Ave. (11.3). Follow the marked Baseline Rd. detour south and turn left in a short distance at College Wy. Follow this road along the Live Oak Wash and return to Baseline Rd. Bike on a light and steady upgrade which levels near Mountain Ave. (14.4); there is a nifty (and steep) diversion trip on this road into the hillside residential area. The reference tour continues on Baseline Rd. through the residential area 0.5 mile to Indian Hill Blvd.

Indian Hill Blvd. Turn right and follow yet another Class X road through the quiet and tree-shaded residential area. The refreshing downhill leads past Cahuilla Park (water, shade), Claremont High School and crosses Foothill Blvd. shortly (15.9). The road narrows as it continues through the treed, rural residential setting past inviting Memorial Park (water, restrooms, shade, grass, and playgrounds).

Bonita Ave. The return west on this road passes through a residential area up to Mountain Ave., then transitions into a more industrially-oriented region up to the La Verne city limit (17.9). The flat, lightly traveled, Class X road returns to the tree-lined residential area and proceeds to "D" St. (19.9). There is an old fashioned, but well maintained, shopping complex here with a donut shop (Don's weakness!).

The Return Segment. Turn left (south) on "D' St., cruise by the University of La Verne and cycle 0.3 mile to Foothill Blvd. Turn left and right again at the next intersection ("E" St.). Just south of Arrow Hwy., the street name changes to Fairplex Dr., Pedal past the Pomona Raceway between Brackett Field and the west side of the Los Angeles County Fairplex, turning sharply left to stay on Fairplex Dr. Continue 0.3 mile to the McKinley Ave intersection (21.4) and bike straight ahead to stay on that street. Now, simply return to Ganesha Park by retracing the outgoing route. The total tour is 22.3 miles.

Diversion Trips. There are several additional interesting areas to explore in the Claremont area. There is an interesting workout in the Mills Rd.-Pomelo Dr.-Padua Ave. region (Mills Rd. becomes Baldy Rd. and can be continued on the gut-wrenching uphill to Mt. Baldy - expert bikers only!!). There is some excellent tour biking available in the area bounded by Foothill Blvd.-Indian Hill Blvd.-Arrow

Hwy.-Claremont Blvd.; in this zone are Pomona College, Claremont College, Claremont Men's College, Scripps College, Harvey Mudd College and Pitzer College.

CONNECTING TRIPS: 1) Connection with the Diamond Bar Loop (Trip #42) and the San Jose Hills ride (Trip #43) - from the intersection of Fairplex Dr. and Via Verde, bike south 1-1/2 miles on the former road to Holt Ave. Turn right and follow that street as it becomes Valley Blvd. 1-3/4 miles to Temple Ave. Continue south for the San Jose Hills trip and turn left on Temple Ave. to reach Diamond Bar Blvd. and the Diamond Bar Loop trip.; 2) connection with the Bonelli Regional County Park tour (Trip #44) - at Lakeside Dr. and Via Verde, turn north on the former street; 3) connection with the San Dimas Canyon Road tour (Trip # 65) - at the intersection of Sand Canyon Rd. and Baseline Rd. follow the former road north into the foothills.

TRIP #46 - LA MIRADA BIKEWAY SYSTEM

GENERAL LOCATION: La Mirada

LEVEL OF DIFFICULTY: Loop - easy
Distance - 9.8 miles
Elevation gain - periodic easy-to-moderate grades

HIGHLIGHTS: All too often, those little green spots on our maps wind up being wayside parks with some tumbleweeds and a drinking fountain! Not this tour! This is a well-designed route on primarily Class I/Class II bikeways with the trip highlights being Creek Park and La Mirada Park. After cruising a few miles on the city streets, the route follows a natural and refreshing Class I path alongside La Mirada Creek, then visits the green rolling knolls and recreation areas of La Mirada Park. Both inviting parks have their own networks of excellent walking/biking trails.

TRAILHEAD: From the Santa Ana Fwy., exit north at Valley View Ave. and continue 1.8 miles to Foster Rd. (just beyond Rosecrans Ave.). Turn right and drive 0.3 mile to Gardenhill Dr., turn left, then continue 0.2 mile to the parking area in front of the Gardenhill Park Community Center. Gardenhill Park has a playground, trees, picnic benches and barbecue facilities, as well as water and restrooms.
   Bring a light water supply. There is water at the parks and numerous gas stations along the way.

TRIP DESCRIPTION: **The City Streets.** Exit the park and turn right, biking through the residential area a short distance to Foster Rd. and then turn right again. Continue a short distance and turn left (south) on Valley View Ave. Follow the mild stair-step upgrade on this Class II path 0.5 mile to Rosecrans Ave. (0.8). Turn left and cruise through the residential setting past Biola Ave.; a left turn here leads to Biola University.
   Our reference route remains on Rosecrans Ave. and continues 0.5 mile to La Mirada Blvd. (1.8). Turn right and cruise by the La Mirada Civic Theater and the La Mirada Mall. In 0.4 mile, turn left at Santa Gertrudes Ave. where there is a small collection of businesses (including some pleasing eateries). Pass Rosecrans Ave. (3.9) on this Class II route and bike the short workout upgrade to the point where there is a clear view of the Los Coyotes Hills.
   Pedal alongside the La Mirada Golf Course through modest rolling hills, pass Foster Rd. and reach Imperial Hwy. (5.1). Bike 0.3 mile on Class X road and, near the bottom of the first grade, cross the street to the Class I bike entry.
   La Mirada Creek Park. Follow the path through the grassy park alongside La Mirada Creek. The path follows the creek a short distance on both north and south sides. Keep a wary eye for rotating

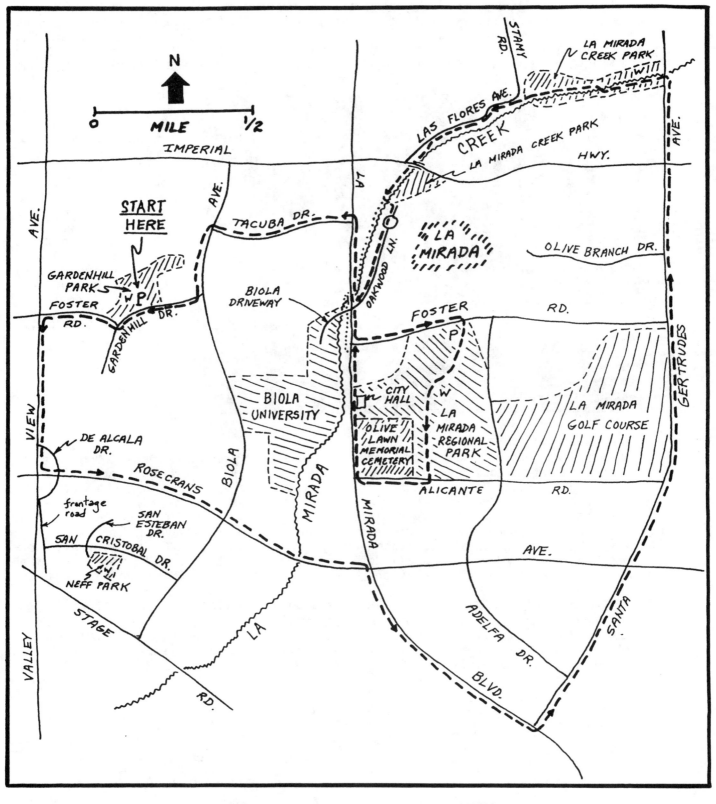

TRIP #46 - LA MIRADA BIKEWAY SYSTEM

sprinklers in this area; Don was thoroughly zapped by one of these gadgets at one of the bridge crossings. (Don never was too bright!) Follow the tree-lined bikeway to the park's edge and transition to Los Flores Ave. There are horse corrals, chicken, geese and even rabbits in this area.

Bike to Imperial Hwy. (6.2); just before reaching this street, follow the dirt path back down to the creek and pass through the short tunnel under Imperial Hwy. This is the southern segment of La Mirada Creek Park. Meander along the creek through this serene environment following the small bridges which cross the creek. At the last creek crossing before reaching the next tunnel, take the paved path to the left up to the residential area. The path leads down to the Oakwood Ln. cul-de-sac and that road leads to La Mirada Blvd. (An option is to stay on the creek path and take the tunnel under La Mirada Blvd. Cross the creek at the tunnel outlet and climb up to La Mirada Blvd. just south of the Oakwood Ln. junction.)

La Mirada Creek Park

La Mirada Park. Turn left (south) on La Mirada Blvd. and bike 0.2 mile to Foster Rd. Turn left and then, in a short distance, make a right, into the parking area (7.4). (Note that there are many paths throughout the park and only a sample route is described. The general rule is to maintain a southerly heading and head for Alicante Rd.) Follow the Class I path that is dead ahead on the short workout upgrade into the La Mirada Park vicinity. There are numerous recreation fields in this green and scenic area.

Follow the path until it passes near Adelfa Dr., then take the junction to the right towards the swimming pool and tennis courts. Near the lowest set of courts, follow that path to the right, turn left at its terminus and cycle down to the small lake. This is a pleasant rest spot with a wide variety of friendly water fowl. Walk a short distance across the grass to Alicante Rd. and turn right (8.1).

The Return Leg. Bike past the well-manicured Olive Lawn Cemetery to La Mirada Blvd. Turn right (north) and follow the rolling hills past the water fountain at City Hall, continuing to Tacuba Dr. (9.1). Turn left and bike on the Class III street through the quiet residential area. Cruise 0.5 mile to Biola Ave. and turn left; follow that Class II route to Gardenhill Dr. Pedal through well-groomed residential territory past Gardenhill Elementary School and return to the Gardenhill Park Community Center (9.8).

CONNECTING TRIPS: 1) Connection with the Coyote Creek Trail (Trip #24) - from the Valley View Ave./Foster Rd. intersection, take the latter road west 3/4 mile to the trail's upper entry; 2) there is also an interesting hilly connecting tour of the Los Coyotes Country Club vicinity which passes through an area of plush residential estates. Continue east on Rosecrans Ave. past the Santa Gertrudes Ave. intersection, turn right at Beach Blvd. and then left at the first street, which is Los Coyotes Dr.

POTPOURRI

First Street Near City Hall

TRIP #47 - SKYSCRAPER TOUR

GENERAL LOCATION: Los Angeles Civic Center

LEVEL OF DIFFICULTY: Loop - moderate
Distance - 10.8 miles
Elevation gain - periodic moderate grades on Beverly Blvd./1st St.

HIGHLIGHTS: At it's best, this is an early Sunday morning tour. Start between 7:00 am and 8:00 am and plan to spend several hours riding and browsing. Traffic during the week is murderous and our recommendation is, "Save it for Sunday." The tour is on a mix of roads with much of the route on Class II or Class III paths, or unmarked roads with a wide, marked car-parking area.

This little beauty provides a fine morning cross-section of the Los Angeles scene. The tour starts at scenic MacArthur Park, then heads into central Los Angeles, visiting the L.A. Convention Center, skyscraperville and the L.A. Flower Market. Next is a short tour through "Street People's Los Angeles," Koreatown and Little Tokyo, El Pueblo De Los Angeles Historic Park and Union Station. The return leg passes through the Los Angeles Civic Center and returns to the trip origin via the rolling hills of Beverly Blvd.

For the truly adventurous, this is a "can't miss" trip.

TRAILHEAD: From the Santa Monica Fwy., exit north at Vermont Ave. and drive 3/4 mile to Wilshire Blvd. Turn right and continue 3/4 mile (past Lafayette Park) to Park View and turn right. Find parking at the west edge of MacArthur Park subject to the posted laws. (There is no parking time limit Sunday and no meter fees -- there is no posted guideline on the latter rule, but we were not ticketed.) From the Harbor Fwy., exit west at 6th St. and drive 1-1/4 miles to Park View. Turn left, cross Wilshire Blvd. and park as above. From the Hollywood Fwy., take the Alvarado St. turnoff southbound and drive 1.1 miles to Wilshire Blvd. Turn left at Park View.

Bring a filled water bottle or two if you do not want to rely on the scattered water sources. There are very few public restrooms along the route. An option is to start the tour from Lafayette Park (Wilshire Blvd. and Hoover St.). This option adds about one mile to the reference tour. Also, some of the inner city roadway is in a rough or torn up state due to Metrorail construction. Road conditions can be checked with the L.A. Department of Transportation.

TRIP DESCRIPTION: **MacArthur Park.** Tour the park before leaving on the trip to the Civic Center. It has a small, but beautiful, man-made lake with water fountains. There are bikeways/walkways throughout the treed park which allow easy access to the park's north side. In this grass-laden hilly park are observation and picnic benches, an outdoor theater, and a mixed array of walkers, joggers, sitters and a few "overnight campers."

Eastward into the Big City. Bike the periphery of the park, heading southeast on 7th St. Turn right on Alvarado St., follow the mild upgrade near 8th St. and cycle on Class II-like bikeway to Olympic Blvd. Note that "Class II-like" is used on this tour to mean unsigned roads with a marked lane for car parking and adequate bike space within the lane. Turn left on Olympic Blvd. (0.6) and pedal on flat Class II roadway through a light commercial section with scattered residences. Bike under the Harbor Fwy. and turn right at the first street, Byram St. (1.3).

Convention Center to L.A. Wholesale Flower Terminal. Turn left again at 111th St. and pass in front of the L. A. Convention Center. There is a view of the civic center skyscraper complex to the left in this area. Turn left onto Class II Figueroa St. and pedal to 9th St. where the marked bikepath ends. Cycle north into the "teeth" of skyscraper country and follow the short upgrade to Wilshire Blvd. (2.2). Turn right and bike on the road that is almost totally shadowed by the surrounding high-rise buildings.

Pass Hope St. and the First Interstate Bank Building, the scene of the deadly and spectacular l988 fire. Bike to the street's end at Grand Ave., turn right, then left again at 7th St. Turn left in a short distance and travel one block north to Pershing Square, listen to a "fire and brimstone" speech from one of the locals (subject is variable), then backtrack to Wilshire Blvd.

Follow the continued Class X road past venerable Clifton's Cafeteria and cruise 0.4 mile to Los Angeles St., where the commercial buildings dwindle in height and the sunshine returns (3.1). Turn right at Maple Ave. and pass the quaint L.A. Wholesale Flower Terminal. This local "flower capitol" bustles at 5:30 am Monday, Wednesday and Friday. Turn left at 8th St., bike a short distance to San Pedro St., and turn left (northeast) (3.3).

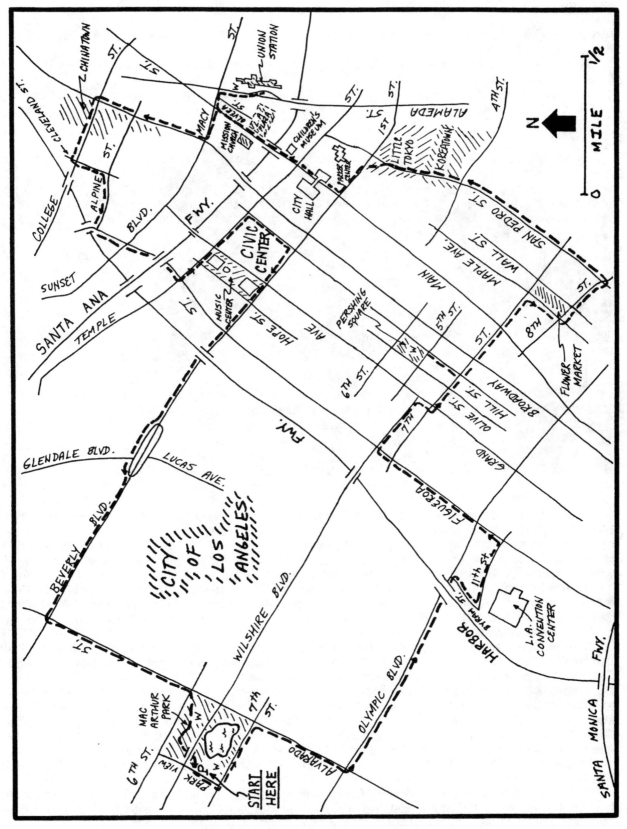

TRIP #47 - SKYSCRAPER TOUR

"War Zone" to Koreatown. Traveling north on San Pedro St. provides a study of poverty and filth (we are providing the "full" L.A. tour!). There is trash everywhere and a large number of folks milling around, many of whom are street people. In 0.6 mile is 4th St. and the southern terminus of Koreatown. The environment transitions to one of cleanliness and order just by crossing from the south side of 4th St. to the north side. At 2nd St. in Little Tokyo, cross the street and follow the diagonal bikeway/walkway through the nifty little shopping center. Stop and observe L.A. City Hall which is framed by the buildings in the mall.

Northward to Union Station. Cross 1st St. and head northwest on Class II bikeway with Parker Center to the right. Turn right on Main St., pass under the City Hall-City Hall East walkway, and continue to the Temple St. intersection (4.4). On the west side is the interesting U.S. Courthouse and to the east, the Los Angeles Mall and pleasant Fletcher Boman Square. Just beyond is the L.A. Children's Museum.

Mac Arthur Park

Cross over the Santa Ana Fwy. and enter the birthplace of Los Angeles. Directly ahead is the expansive El Pueblo De Los Angeles Historic Park which includes the old Mission Church to the left and the charming L. A. Plaza to the right (4.6). Just north of the plaza, paralleling Main St., is renowned Olvera St. Pedal north on Main St. and turn right on Sunset Blvd./Macy St., then right again on Alameda St. Bike a short way to the classic Union Station railroad passenger terminal. Return to Macy St. and bike west.

Chinatown and the Los Angeles Civic Center. Continue west 0.2 mile to Broadway and turn right. Bike through Chinatown on the busy Class X road with two lanes and no bike shoulder -- bike in the middle of the right lane in this stretch all the way to College St. (5.9). Turn left on the Class II bike route and pedal a moderate upgrade 0.2 mile to Alpine St. Turn right and bike the testy upgrade which crests and heads downhill to its terminus at Figueroa St.

Turn left and stare into the L.A. Civic Center, then bike downhill under the Santa Ana Fwy. Turn left at Temple St., pump uphill to the crest at Grand Ave., then cruise by the Music Center complex. Continue downhill to Hill St. (7.1) and turn right. Then bike further downhill over the top of the L.A. subway to 1st St. and turn right again.

The Return Segment. Cycle a short distance on this Class II street and begin the short workout upgrade to a point with views of the L.A. area skyline both east and west. Pass the north side of the L.A. Music Center and bike downhill under the Harbor Fwy. (7.9).

Different from most of our tours, we saved the most testy hills until last. This is a great opportunity to work off all those goodies which were consumed at the landmark sites along the way. Follow the short uphill to the crest from which there is a grand view of three more hills. Just before reaching the Glendale Blvd. overpass, turn right and bike down the paralleling road to Glendale Blvd., cross that street and bike back up to Beverly Blvd. (previously 1st St.) -- trust us, its easier! Climb the steep grade which crests at Belmont Ave. Continue up another shorter upgrade, then pedal downhill to Alvarado St. (8.9).

Turn left (southwest) and bike on Class II-like roadway through the commercial/industrial area. Cycle through light rolling hills past 3rd St. and continue another 1/2 mile to 6th St. and the edge of MacArthur Park. Bike northwest through the park, pass the outdoor theater and pedal through the tunnel to the park's south side. Follow the path up to Park View and return to the starting point (9.8).

CONNECTING TRIPS: Connection with the Exposition Park/USC Campus Tour (Trip #48) - at the intersection of Olympic Blvd. and Figueroa St., turn southwest on the latter street and bike 1-3/4 miles.

TRIP #48 - INNER CITY BIKEWAY SYSTEM

GENERAL LOCATION: Central Los Angeles, Exposition Park, USC Campus

LEVEL OF DIFFICULTY: Loop - easy
Distance - 3.8 miles
Elevation gain - flat

HIGHLIGHTS: **Central Los Angeles.** There is a system of predominantly Class III bikeways spread throughout the central city area, as is shown in the accompanying tour map. The problem is that these routes are so little used by bikers that drivers appear oblivious to the fact that these are shared roadways. This was particularly true on the north-south Hoover St. and Broadway routes. Also, most routes are on busy, fast moving roadways.

We have only biked selected segments of this system, but will generalize: For bikers who are uncomfortable biking with heavy traffic on roadways with limited biking room, use these routes only as connectors to other rides, but not as primary routes. We have included the "Inner City Bikeway System" for completeness.

Exposition Park-USC Campus. There is an interesting and scenic tour available in the Exposition Park-University of Southern California area. The area is shown in the mini-tour map below. Take this tour any time when there is not a major event at either the Coliseum or the Sports Arena. Allow extra time beyond that needed for biking to visit the following: Science and Industry Museum, Museum of Natural History and the Rose Garden in Exposition Park, as well as the USC Campus.

TRAILHEAD: **Exposition Park-USC Campus.** From the Harbor Fwy., exit west at Martin Luther King Jr. Blvd. and turn right (north) in 0.6 mile at Vermont Ave. Drive 0.3 mile to N. Coliseum Dr. and turn right. Find parking subject to posted laws.

Water is plentiful on this tour.

TRIP DESCRIPTION: **Exposition Park-U.S.C. Campus.** A sample Class I peripheral route is shown in the mini-tour map below. However, we recommend a free-form tour which includes many of the scenic interior bikeways/walkways.

Exposition Park. Bike north on Menlo Ave. 0.2 mile and turn right on Exposition Blvd. cycle past one of several treed rest/picnic areas and pass the striking main entrance to the Museum of Natural History. Follow the wide walkway past the north edge of the exquisite Rose Garden (0.4), then continue a short distance to the aircraft displays behind the Aerospace Museum.

Turn right at Figueroa St. and pedal on the walkway passing the IMAX theater and the main entry into the Museum of Science and Industry and the Afro-American Museum. Pass the Sports Arena and turn right at Martin Luther King Jr. Blvd. (1.0). Follow the wide sidewalk to Hoover St. and turn right, left at the next street (E. Park Dr.), and bike alongside the classic Los Angeles Swim Stadium. Turn on Menlo Ave. and cruise along the periphery of the gigantic Coliseum before returning to the trip origin (1.6).

USC Campus. Cross Exposition Blvd. at Watt Wy. and turn left immediately (1.8), pass the Computer Science Center, then turn right at McClintock Ave. Enjoy the varied architectures which are found throughout the entire campus while biking past the Andrus Gerontology Center, Bloom Wy., the

177

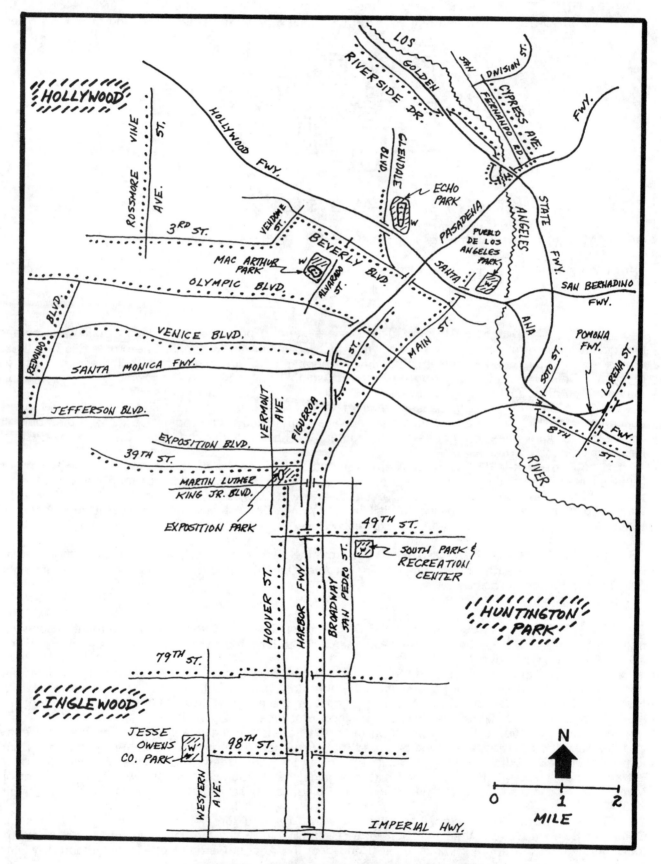

TRIP #48 - INNER CITY BIKEWAY SYSTEM

tennis stadium at Child's Wy., the track stadium, Howard Jones' Field, and the swim stadium, complete with giant hot tub (2.2).

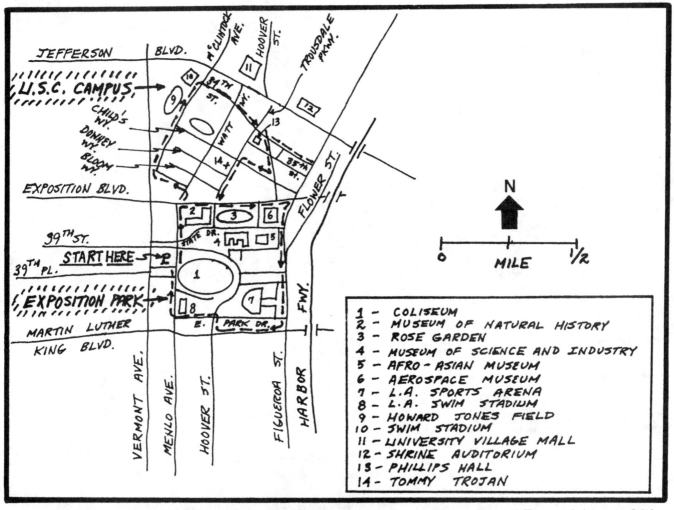

1 - COLISEUM
2 - MUSEUM OF NATURAL HISTORY
3 - ROSE GARDEN
4 - MUSEUM OF SCIENCE AND INDUSTRY
5 - AFRO-ASIAN MUSEUM
6 - AEROSPACE MUSEUM
7 - L.A. SPORTS ARENA
8 - L.A. SWIM STADIUM
9 - HOWARD JONES FIELD
10 - SWIM STADIUM
11 - UNIVERSITY VILLAGE MALL
12 - SHRINE AUDITORIUM
13 - PHILLIPS HALL
14 - TOMMY TROJAN

Rose Garden at Exposition Park

Turn right at 34th St., pedal past the Carson Motion Picture Studio, the water fountain at Trousdale Pkwy., and continue to the end of the street (2.7). Backtrack a short distance and turn sharply left onto Hoover Wy. Pass towering Phillips Hall and follow the picturesque roadway to Child's Wy. (3.2). Turn right and bike through the stately common with its lovely water fountain, then turn left again at Trousdale Pkwy. In a short distance is the popular USC (and UCLA) landmark, Tommy Trojan.

179

Continue pedaling to Exposition Blvd. Cross this road and turn right, then bike just beyond the Rose Garden and turn left. Turn right again at State Dr. and bike to Menlo Ave. Turn left and return to the trip origin (3.8). NOTE: Don is a UCLA graduate, so inclusion of this tour should be considered "beyond the call of duty."

CONNECTING TRIPS: Connection with Tour de Los Angeles (Trip #49) - at the intersection of Trousdale Pkwy. and Jefferson Blvd. (near the water fountain), bike east on Jefferson Blvd., then turn north on Figueroa St. Continue to Venice Blvd.

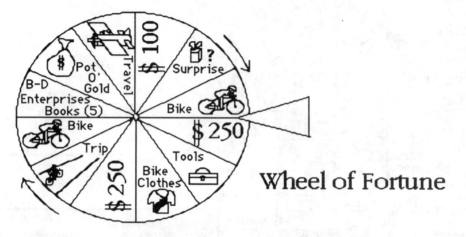

Wheel of Fortune

TRIP #49 - TOUR de LOS ANGELES

GENERAL LOCATION: Ballona Creek, Central Los Angeles, L.A. River, Long Beach, San Pedro, Palos Verdes, South Bay

LEVEL OF DIFFICULTY: Loop - strenuous
Distance - 71.7 miles
Elevation gain - periodic moderate-to-steep grades in San Pedro and the Palos Verdes Peninsula; flat elsewhere

HIGHLIGHTS: This nifty 70-mile plus "looper" cruises Ballona Creek, travels inland into the heart of the City of Los Angeles, then follows the Los Angeles River to Long Beach. Next, the tour visits the scenic Palos Verdes Peninsula before heading north on the South Bay Bike Trail, returning to the origin at Fisherman's Village in Marina Del Rey. For cyclists wanting a true slice of the Los Angeles area, do this tour. Most of the route is on Class I or Class II path. Because of heavy traffic in the Central Los Angeles area, this trip is best saved for weekends.

TRAILHEAD: Follow the Marina Fwy. to its terminus and continue west to Lincoln Blvd. Turn left (south) on Lincoln Blvd. and go about l/2 mile to Fiji Wy. Take Fiji Wy. to the parking area at Fisherman's Village or use the overflow parking lot between the village and Lincoln Blvd.
Bring a couple of bottles of water to minimize water stops even though there is water at several parks along the way. Also bring an automobile roadmap as a backup to cover straying from the described route.

TRIP DESCRIPTION: **Ballona Creek to Central Los Angeles.** The trip description will detail only the new or confusing portions of this loop. Refer to the trip numbers cited in the text for additional detail. This tour starts at Fisherman's Village and continues northeast along Ballona Creek to Kronenthal Park (Trip #4) (6.6). Bike east on National Blvd. which fuses shortly with Class III Jefferson Blvd. In 0.9 mile, turn left at Redondo Blvd. and bike on Class III bikeway with a wide shoulder under the Santa Monica Fwy. Cycle past Washington Blvd. to Venice Blvd. (gas station) and turn right (8.9).
Pedal on Class II roadway through a mixed commercial/residential area, follow the short, mild upgrade and pass under West Blvd. At Crenshaw Blvd. the path transitions to Class III and the bike shoulder varies from skimpy to modest from this juncture to downtown Los Angeles. (This was our least favorite segment of the trip.)

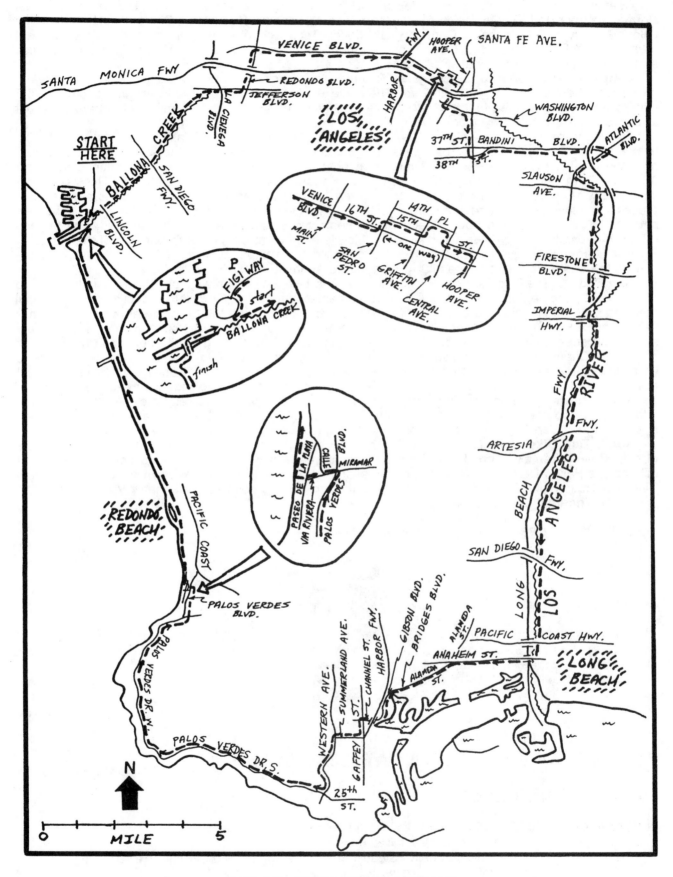

TRIP #49 - TOUR DE LOS ANGELES

Continue through varied areas of residential, commercial, and limited industrial development past Normandie Ave. (11.7). On the northeast corner is Normandie Recreation Center (water, recreation fields). Nearby is the Rosedale Cemetery and Loyola High School---this area is definitely the highlight of the Venice Blvd. segment. Pedal past Vermont Ave., pass under the Harbor Fwy., and cruise through the run-down commercial district to Figueroa St. (13.6).

Central Los Angeles to Los Angeles River. Follow Class X roadway through another 1.8 miles of an old commercial area to Hooper Blvd. The route is Venice Blvd. to Broadway, left to l6th St., 0.5 mile to San Pedro St., left to l5th St., 0.3 mile to Griffith, left to l4th Pl., 0.3 mile to Central Ave., right to l5th St. and 0.3 mile to Hooper Blvd.

Turn right, pass under the Santa Monica Fwy., and turn left (east) at Washington Blvd. in 0.2 mile. In 0.4 mile at Alameda St., the road passes "truck city" where there are hundreds of trucks clustered near the local railway complex. In l/2 mile, turn right at Santa Fe Ave. (16.5) and continue south for 0.7 mile. Turn left at 38th St. which fuses into Bandini Blvd. in a short distance. This is a well-surfaced, wide road which crosses Soto St. and reaches a gas station in 0.4 mile, passes a large meat processing plant (P.U.!), and then crosses the L. A. River. The road parallels the river, continues another three miles to the Long Beach Fwy. undercrossing and reaches Atlantic Blvd. just beyond (20.7). Recross the L. A. River and bike to the bicycle entry point on the southeast side of the bridge.

Los Angeles River. Follow the river 5.3 miles south to Imperial Blvd. (Trip #21), cross over the river to the east levee, and cruise l0.0 miles south to Anaheim St. (Trip #20B) (36.0).

San Pedro. (See Trip #9 map.) Cross the river and bike 2-l/2 miles west on Class X Anaheim St. to Alameda St.; the region is effectively early 20th-century industrial. Turn left and bike one mile until reaching the Los Angeles Harbor area. The street becomes Bridges Blvd., continues another l-1/4 mile to the Harbor Fwy., then turns sharply south on what is now Gibson Blvd. (A Class I path is on the harbor side of the street.) cycle l-3/4 miles to Channel St. and turn right, leaving the harbor area (42.5).

Follow Channel St. a short distance to Gaffey St. and turn left. Pedal a steady l/2-mile upgrade to Class III Summerland Ave. Turn right and bike a series of testy upgrades to Western Ave. There is water at Peck Park to the right, but our route turns left and continues through rolling hills to 25th St. (46.0).

Palos Verdes Peninsula. Turn right and follow 25th St., which becomes Palos Verdes Dr. South, and bike the southern part of the peninsula (see Trip #6C). Follow the road as it turns north and becomes Palos Verdes Dr. West, continuing to Malaga Cove Plaza (Trip #6B) (57.8).

South Bay Bike Trail. (See Trip #1A map.) Go east to Palos Verdes Blvd., turn left and bike 0.9 mile to Calle Miramar. Turn left toward the beach, veer left on Via Rivera, and continue about 0.1 mile across Paseo De La Playa to the beach parking lot. Coast down the bikeway/walkway to the South Bay Bike Trail origin. Cruise north 12.7 miles to the trip starting point at Fisherman's Village (Trips #1A and #1B). The total tour is 71.7 miles.

CONNECTING TRIPS: See individual trip write-ups.

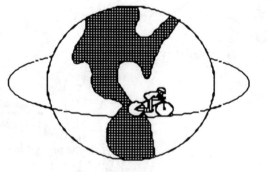

TRIP #50 - AVALON, SANTA CATALINA ISLAND

GENERAL LOCATION: Avalon, Santa Catalina Island

LEVEL OF DIFFICULTY: Loop - moderate to strenuous
Distance - 9.7 miles
Elevation gain - steady, strenuous upgrades on Wrigley Terrace Dr. and Chimes Tower Rd. area

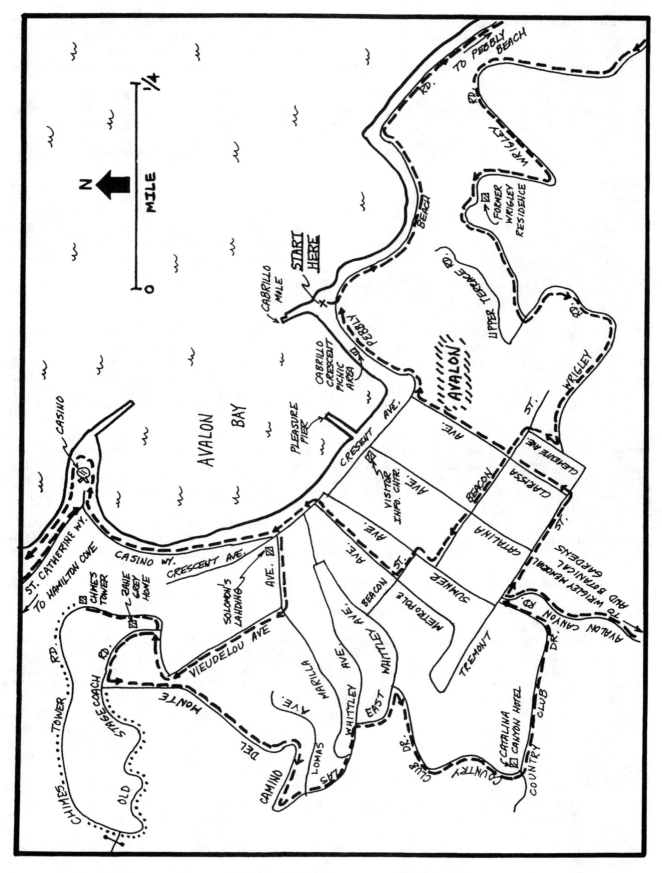

TRIP #50 - AVALON, SANTA CATALINA ISLAND

HIGHLIGHTS: We visited Catalina for this fantastic tour on our wedding anniversary--very romantic! We strongly recommend that you make the trip just for the sake of biking the Avalon area. Visit Santa Catalina Island, bike this scenic route, and return the same day; however, a more relaxing option is to stay overnight and spend the next day telling the locals how you "smoked" the tourist golf-cart crowd with your bikes!

The described tour leaves the channel boat landing and tracks scenic Pebbly Beach Dr. along the coast, then follows an inland road to Mt. Ada, cresting just above the Inn on Mt. Ada (former Wrigley residence). Next is a tour of Avalon proper, a visit to Avalon's Casino, a workout pedal to the Chimes Tower, and a traverse of the hills to Avalon Canyon Rd. From this point is a nifty uphill ride to the Wrigley Memorial and Botanical Gardens and a restful return to the Cabrillo Mole.

TRAILHEAD: Avalon can be reached by several channel boat carriers from San Pedro, Long Beach or Newport Beach, and small air carriers from coastal airports. During summer or holiday periods, make round-trip reservations at least one or two weeks in advance. Bikers can transport bikes on most boat lines for a small fee; check with the line of your choice if interested in this option. Another possibility is to rent a multi-speed bike (18-speed preferred for the trip described) in Avalon proper. Visitors planning overnight trips to Catalina during peak season should not arrive in Avalon without confirmed room reservations.

Bring a filled water bottle. There are abundant public water sources in the flats of Avalon (where it is not needed) and no water in the hillside mountainous areas (where it is needed).

TRIP DESCRIPTION: **Pebbly Beach Rd.** From the Cabrillo Mole, turn left on Pebbly Beach Rd. and bike on the flat road with the ocean immediately to the left and the cliffs to the right. Pass the cruise ship anchorage (many Mexican-bound cruise ships visit Santa Catalina Island), the Amphibian Air Terminal (this mode of travel has fallen off dramatically in recent years), and the Buffalo Nickel Restaurant at Pebbly Beach. This is a 0.9 mile stretch of continuous ocean viewing. Cycle another 0.2 mile to a small residential-industrial complex and, just beyond, branch to the roadway which heads inland and uphill.

The Inn at Mt. Ada (Former Wrigley Residence). Turn right and shift into the "granny gears" on this one-way highway stretch (keep an eye peeled for kamikaze rental golf carts going the wrong way!). The small road progresses on a series of switchbacks through a treed, semi-arid canyon area, follows an uphill, traverses the side of Mt. Ada, then reaches one of several scenic viewpoints in about 1/2 mile. In about one mile from the initial branch point, the road reaches a crest with a spectacular overlook of Avalon and the harbor (2.3).

Just beyond is the private entry to the Inn at Mt. Ada. The majestic former Wrigley Residence is visible at different angles from the street, now named Wrigley Rd. There are additional spectacular harbor views as the narrow (now two-way) street switchbacks down to the City of Avalon at Clemente Ave. (3.2).

City of Avalon. Turn right and immediately left at Beacon St. Cycle 1/4 mile on this residential street to Metropole Ave. and turn right. Follow the mixed commercial/residential road to the Metropole Market Place and turn left (3.7). To the right is the Busy Bee Restaurant, with some delightful outdoor dining under umbrellas and alongside the harbor.

However, our route goes left and passes Solomon's Landing (one of our dinnertime favorites, with a bakery and deli), then proceeds on Crescent Ave. to Casino Wy. Follow this road below the cliffs past the Casino Landing and the Catalina Island Yacht Center. Just beyond is the landmark Casino of Avalon. Turn right and tour the Casino periphery, passing the Catalina Island Museum entrance, the Casino Dock Cafe, and reach the scuba dive area at Casino Point.

Cruise around the Casino and follow the beach pathway to developed Descanso Beach. (4.1). Bike the short uphill to St. Catherine Wy., turn right and follow the testy upgrade through lovely tree-covered Descanso Canyon. We followed the road for a half mile and turned around, although more adventurous bikers can follow the road another 1/2 mile to the deadend at condo city in Hamilton Cove. Return to Solomon's Landing and turn right at Marilla Ave. (5.2).

Chimes Tower. Turn right and pump 0.1 mile up steep Marilla Ave. The reward is a right turn at Vieudelou Ave. and another steep upgrade for 0.2 mile. Pump past Old Stagecoach Rd. and bike on continued steep uphill to a majestic vista point just below the Zane Grey Hotel (original home of Zane Grey). Bike a short distance on continued steep uphill on one-way road to the Chimes Tower and yet another scenic viewpoint. (Note that more ambitious bikers can take the one-way Old Stagecoach Rd.-Chimes Tower Rd. loop and bike downhill to the tower) (5.5).

The Traverse to Avalon Canyon Rd. Backtrack to Old Stagecoach Rd. (Stage Road for short) and turn onto that street. In 0.1 mile at the junction, turn left onto Camino Del Monte. Follow the short workout upgrade, then enjoy a steep downgrade on a tree-lined street with impressive residences. At

184

the next intersection, stay to the right (as with each succeeding intersection up to the Catalina Canyon Hotel.) and proceed on Las Lomas Ave. Pedal downhill past Marilla Ave. and turn right at East Whittley Ave.

Avalon Harbor From Mount Ada

Just beyond, turn hard right onto Country Club Dr., follow the downhill on tree-lined roadway and enjoy the view of the canyon area. At the Catalina Canyon Hotel, follow the road as it proceeds past the spur road to the right (also named Country Club Dr.) and veers to the left (east). Follow the fun downhill past Picture Point (a golfer viewpoint/meeting point), the Catalina Clubhouse, and freewheel to Tremont St. (6.8). Turn right and, in a short distance, turn right again at Avalon Canyon Rd.

Wrigley Memorial and Botanical Garden. Follow the tree-lined uphill road past the north edge of the Catalina Island Golf Course; the 1.2-mile route to the Wrigley Memorial is on steady uphill varying from moderate to testy. This rural road passes the Sand Trap at Falls Canyon Rd. (lemonade, "firewater", and snacks), the Catalina Stables, Bird Park Campground (water, restrooms), and heads past the southern edge of the golf course (7.4).

In 0.2 mile pass the Avalon Canyon Campground (water, restrooms) and follow the steady workout grade to the pay entrance to the stately Wrigley Memorial. Bike riding is prohibited beyond this point. Note that every type of plant life indigenous to the area and a few imported varieties are all classified in the general area (7.9).

The Finale. Backtrack to Tremont Ave. and turn right, biking 0.2 mile to Clarissa Ave. (9.2). Turn left and continue through residential area to the street's end at Crescent Ave. Turn left for the Avalon Shopping Mall (no biking between Clarissa Ave. and Metropole Ave.). However, the reference route turns right, proceeds past the Cabrillo Crescent Picnic Area and returns to the trip origin at Cabrillo Mole (9.7).

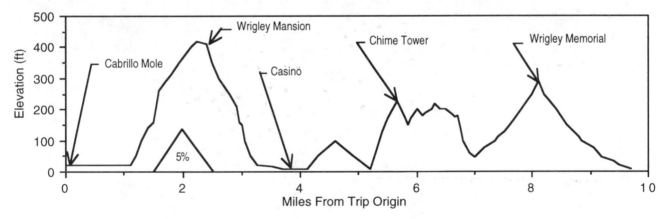

CONNECTING TRIPS: There are no current connector routes. Bicycling into the island interior beyond the gate above Old Stagecoach Rd. requires a permit, which can be obtained at the Catalina Conservancy Office.

NEW TRIPS

Interstate Highway 5 Viewed From Old Ridge Route Road

TRIP #51 - DOMINGUEZ HILLS

GENERAL LOCATION: Carson

LEVEL OF DIFFICULTY: Loop - easy
Distance - 3.5 miles
Elevation gain - essentially flat

HIGHLIGHTS: The major portion of the ride is a tour of the California State University at Dominguez Hills (CSUDH). The trip is broken into a tour of the campus periphery followed by a tour within the main campus complex. Particularly during weekends, this is a pleasant family riding area, well off the major roadways and with little traffic. There is an option to connect this ride with an excursion to nearby, well-stocked Victoria Park.

TRAILHEAD: From the San Diego Fwy., take the Torrance Blvd. off-ramp to Figueroa St. and turn left (north). Drive 1-1/2 miles to Victoria Ave. and turn right, continuing 1-3/4 miles to the CSUDH east entrance area across from Birchknoll Dr. Park on the street Monday through Saturday or in the nearby campus lot on Sunday. From the San Diego Fwy., exit north at Avalon Blvd. and drive two miles to Victoria Ave. Turn right (east) and continue one mile to the east entrance area.
   Bring a light water supply. There are public water sources on campus and at Victoria Park.

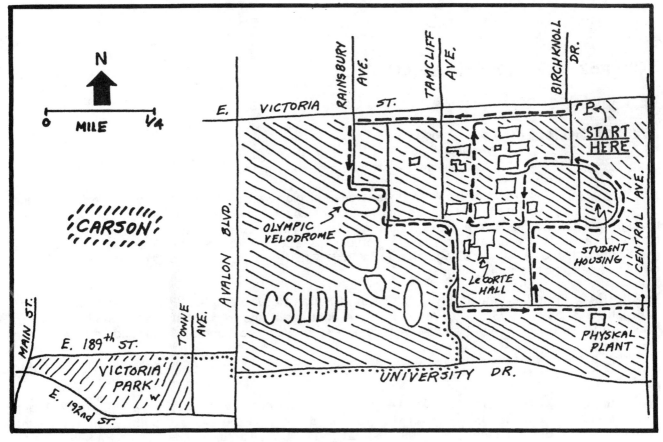

TRIP #51 - DOMINGUEZ HILLS

TRIP DESCRIPTION: **Campus Periphery.** Bike to the east entrance and follow the on-campus frontage road west, paralleling Victoria Ave. Continue to the edge of the westernmost parking area (0.45) and follow its periphery to the next intersecting street. A right (south) turn here leads by the Olympic Velodrome (0.7). Another turn east leads past LeCorte Hall while a subsequent turn south takes cyclists by the tennis courts. Return east at road's end, pass the upper edge of the southernmost parking lot, and bike to an intersection with a sign noting that the "Physical Plant" is straight ahead (1.45).

187

Go straight and reach road's end in an area with at least 50 large greenhouses. Return to the prior intersection and turn right (north) (2.0). Staying on the campus edge at each turn leads bikers through some welcome treecover and alongside the student housing area. The road curves and heads down to an intersection. Right (north) leads towards Victoria Ave., while the main campus complex is straight ahead (2.6).

Main Campus. One of many possible rides might be to keep straight ahead, veer left to stay on the roadway, and turn right into the "Natural Sciences" complex. At the "T"- intersection, turn right, then left again at the Student Union Building (2.8). At the next "T"-intersection, turn right and bike to the frontage road that parallels Victoria Ave. (3.1) Following this road to the right (east) puts cyclists back at the start point in another 0.4 mile. There are numerous other routes within the main campus which can used to explore other areas, as well as to extend the trip mileage.

Victoria Park. It is a short excursion to Victoria Park. An easy way to get there is to take the University Dr. exit out of the south parking lot and turn west. Follow that road 0.6 mile to Avalon Blvd., turn north, and bike a few hundred feet to 189th St. Turn west again and bike past Towne Ave. to the park periphery. There are several Class I paths which tour the park, which makes this segment ideal for all-age family biking. The park also boasts water and restrooms, grass, tree shade, picnic facilities and children's play areas.

 Helmet

 No Helmet

TRIP #52 - AGOURA HILLS LOOP

GENERAL LOCATION: Agoura Hills, Thousand Oaks

LEVEL OF DIFFICULTY: Loop - moderate
Distance - 8.7 miles
Elevation gain - periodic moderate grades

HIGHLIGHTS: This pleasant loop trip passes several nice parks on the way up to the base of the Conejo Ridge, cruises through some scenic "outback," coasts down Lindero Canyon Rd., and returns through the heart of the impressive City of Agoura Hills. The route is generally lightly trafficked and mostly on a Class II bikeway; the Class X portion has a wide bike shoulder. This route also can be combined with the Westlake Village ride (Trip #53) and North Ranch Loop (Trip #54) to provide a myriad of neat bicycle route options.

TRAILHEAD: From the Ventura Fwy., exit north at Kanan Rd. Drive 3/4 mile to Thousand Oaks Blvd., turn right, and continue l/3 mile to Argos St. Turn right again and follow that road a short distance to Chumash Park. This a nice grassy park with some shade, water, restrooms, playgrounds and recreation fields.

Bring a filled water bottle for hot days, although scattered public sources are available on all but the Lindero Canyon Rd. segment.

TRIP DESCRIPTION: Kanan Rd. Bike 0.4 mile back to the intersection of Thousand Oaks Blvd. and Kanan Rd. Turn right (north) on Kanan Rd. and pedal uphill on the Class II path. Pass a shopping center to the left and continue to the crest near Largo Dr. (0.7). To the right is Sumac Park with water, restrooms, picnic area, barbecues and some shade.

Continue through this residential area with a direct view of the hills directly ahead. Pedal on a mild uphill to Fountainwood St., reach a flat, and continue on another moderate grade which peaks near Conifer St. (1.6). To the right is Mae Boyer Park with water, restrooms, tennis courts, a playground and scattered shade.

Start uphill again through this residential area, reaching the top of the grade in 0.3 mile. In a short distance is Smoketree Ave. and a mild upgrade through a thinning residential area. The top of the grade is near Sunnycrest Dr. where the road begins to swing to the left (2.3). The curving roadway

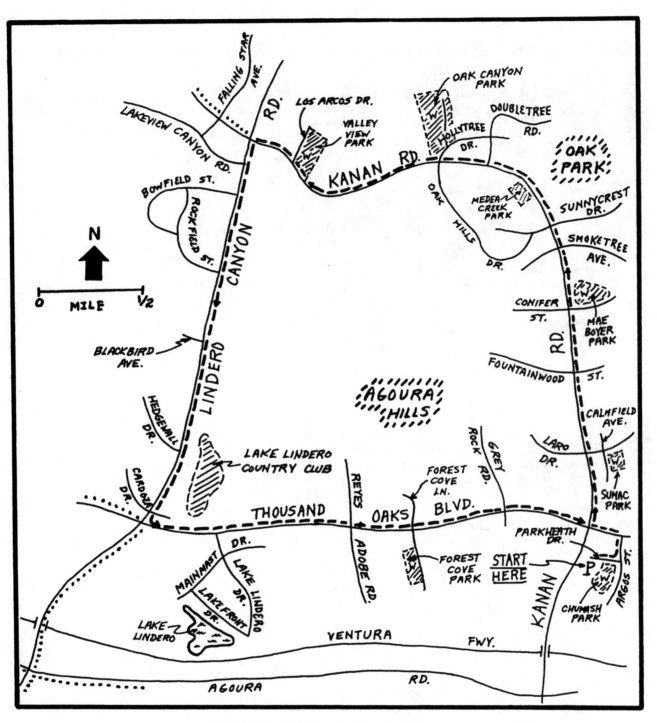

TRIP #52 - AGOURA HILLS LOOP

passes Medea Creek Park (which has a Class I walkway/bikeway that runs from Kanan Rd a little over a mile south, including an entry from Sunnycrest Dr.) and Oak Park High School, now heading west. The hills to the north below the Conejo Ridge are lightly developed in this area (2.7).

Bike downhill to the flat near Hollytree Dr. where the marked bike path ends (the shoulder remains wide). A short diversion north on that street leads to Oak Canyon Community Park (pond, small man-made waterfalls and the core of the park further up with restrooms, paved walk/bike paths, picnic tables and children's playgrounds). Next is a moderately steep upgrade which reaches a crest in a small flat area (3.3). Just beyond, the road rounds a bend and greets cyclists with a view into a valley of upscale residences. Next on the winding road is a short, moderate-to-steep uphill. The road continues through a light residential area, transits alongside Los Arcos Dr. and the entry to Valley View Park (restrooms, sports fields and unshaded picnic areas), then meets Lindero Canyon Rd. and a cluster of small shopping centers in a short distance (4.1).

Medea Creek Park

Lindero Canyon Rd. (return payment for all that uphill). Turn left (south) and continue on the Class II, wide-shouldered roadway past Lakeview Canyon Rd. (4.2). The road passes between a set of small hills, meets Rockfield St. (4.7) and then follows a mild upgrade through a lightly-developed area. An easy downgrade follows, then the road flattens and reaches Hedgewall Dr. (5.5). The path returns to a high-density residential area on a tree-lined street, reaching Thousand Oaks Blvd. and a group of shopping centers (6.2).

Thousand Oaks Blvd. Turn left (east) on the Class II bikeway on a busier road through impressive Agoura Hills. Peek at the Santa Monica Mountains to the south and then follow a mild downgrade past the first of several shopping complexes. Continue on rolling hills past Lake Lindero Dr. (6.5) (Lake Lindero itself is l/2 mile to the south) and return to a residential setting.

Bike through another high-density residential area past Reyes Adobe Rd. (7.0) and follow a 0.3-mile moderate upgrade to a crest with a nice view into the hills to the east. Just south on Forest Cove Ln. is Forest Cove Park with restrooms, athletic fields, scattered shade and children's playgrounds. Coast downhill past Grey Rock Rd. (8.0); there are residence-sprinkled hills to the north and housing tracts on the opposite side of the street. Continue the roller-coaster ride through more high-density residential areas until the route flattens near Kanan Rd. (8.3). Pedal east past this junction to Argos St. and return to Chumash Park (8.7).

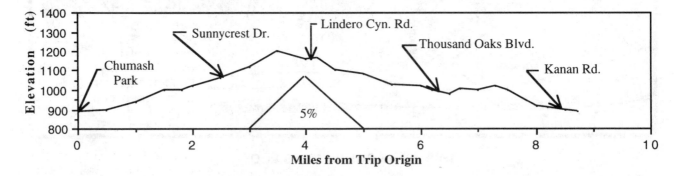

CONNECTING TRIPS: 1) Continuation with the North Ranch Loop (Trip #54) - there are several options, but one of the most pleasant is to bike the extended loop comprised of Kanan Rd., Westlake Blvd. and Thousand Oaks Blvd.; 2) connection with the Westlake Village ride (Trip #53) - at the intersection of Lindero Canyon Dr. and Thousand Oaks Blvd., continue south on the former roadway.

TRIP #53 - WESTLAKE VILLAGE

GENERAL LOCATION: Westlake Village, Thousand Oaks

LEVEL OF DIFFICULTY: Loop - easy
Distance - 9.2 miles
Elevation gain - periodic moderate grades

HIGHLIGHTS: This easy going Class I/II trip is centered around Westlake Lake. The tour begins in a cleverly laid out residential neighborhood, travels across the Ventura Fwy. through a pleasant and massive business and shopping complex, and proceeds along the southern boundary of lovely Westlake Lake. The return segment is through less developed areas with a few light rolling hills. There are several marked diversion routes through the Westlake Village area.

TRAILHEAD: From the Ventura Fwy., exit northbound on Westlake Blvd. and continue 0.5 mile to Cascade Ave., which is the next left turn beyond Thousand Oaks Blvd. Turn left (west) and proceed down Cascade Ave. to its terminus across from a school and Russell Park.

Only a light water supply is needed. Fill up at the trip origin or at other water spots noted in the trip map.

TRIP DESCRIPTION: **Southbound - Westlake Lake.** Leave the cul-de-sac and turn left on Cascade Ave. pedaling 0.4 miles to North Westlake Blvd. Turn right (south) and follow the Class II bikepath across Thousand Oaks Blvd. (0.7). Stop and enjoy one of the many vistas into the surrounding hills, with a particularly nice view into the Santa Monica Mountains to the south. In 1/4 mile, the path crosses the Ventura Fwy. and enters an area of extended and delightful business and shopping complexes. The locale transitions into residential and remains so up to our left turn at Trifuno Canyon Rd. (2.1). Note that there is a mixed Class II/Class X diversion route up to Lakes Eleanor or Sherwood by continuing on S. Westlake Blvd.

Westlake Lake From Trifuno Canyon Road

Pedal another 0.4 mile on an unmarked thoroughfare with a wide shoulder (this entire section rides like a Class II bikeway) to a bridge with a clear view of Westlake Lake. This is a popular "high altitude" duck feeding spot. Continue cruising Trifuno Canyon Rd. with periodic peeks down the lanes into the lake until reaching Golden Leaf Dr. (3.5). This is the open end of the lake with a fine view of the center island and the many small boats, with a tree covered rest area to boot. In 0.2 mile pass "tennis court city" and make a sharp left turn on S. Lindero Canyon Rd.

Northbound - Less-Developed Country. Bike over a bridge which crosses Trifuno Canyon Creek and pass Ridgeford Dr. (or turn onto that roadway for a challenging Class X uphill) (4.0). Pedal 0.1 mile to the top of a knoll where there is an excellent view of the lake's south end. At Lakeview Canyon Rd. (4.6), the marked Class II path resumes. Cyclists can divert left at Watergate Rd. to reach the private entrance to the island at the lake's center. However, the designated route cruises ahead for 0.9 mile to

191

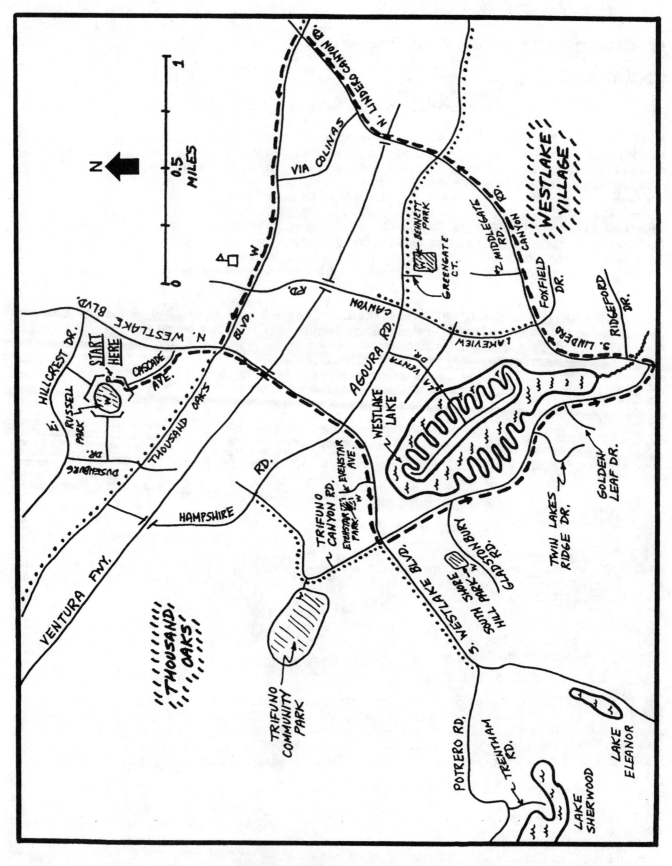

TRIP #53 - WESTLAKE VILLAGE

Agoura Rd. For this trip segment, the bikeway is along a tree-lined roadway. The road is bordered by the walls of the surrounding residential tracts to the west and hillside homes to the east.

In 0.2 mile beyond Agoura Rd. the route crosses back over the freeway and proceeds on a moderate upgrade, reaching Via Colinas and the open fields of the Valley Oaks Memorial Park Cemetery. The upgrade continues to Thousand Oaks Blvd. where there is a shopping cluster (6.6).

Westbound - Rolling Hills. However, our route heads west on the Class II bikeway and continues another 0.3 mile uphill through lightly developed territory. Now begins the roller coaster! First is a free-wheeling downhill to Via Colinas (7.3), followed by a 0.3 mile upgrade. At the top of the grade is the trip premier view south into the Santa Monica Mountains. After a 0.2-mile downhill, the roadway narrows and the path shifts onto the sidewalk as posted (Class I) (7.7).

In another 0.2 mile, the bike route passes just below the Westlake High School baseball fields (there is a drinking fountain near the middle of the complex) and soon reaches Lakeview Canyon Rd. (8.2). In 0.3 mile on the sidewalk route is N. Westlake Blvd. Turn right (north), proceed to Cascade Ave. and return to the trip origin (9.2).

CONNECTING TRIPS: 1) Connection with the Agoura Hills Loop (Trip #52) - at Lindero Canyon Rd. and Thousand Oaks Blvd., turn east onto the latter road; and 2) connection with the North Ranch Loop (Trip #54) - at Cascade Ave. and Westlake Blvd., turn north on the latter road.

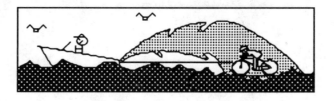

TRIP #54 - NORTH RANCH LOOP

GENERAL LOCATION: Thousand Oaks, Westlake Village

LEVEL OF DIFFICULTY: Loop - moderate
Distance - 10.9 miles
Elevation gain - periodic, moderate upgrades

HIGHLIGHTS: This is a fine rural loop on mostly lightly-traveled roads. Much of the route is on a Class II path or Class X with a wide shoulder. The tour highlights include a visit to the classy North Ranch residential area, a long, mild runout on Lindero Canyon Rd. (paid for with the prior uphill pumping), and a ride by the northern periphery of Westlake Village. This path can be linked with the Agoura Hills Loop (Trip #52) and the Westlake Village ride (Trip #53), sufficient to keep bikers going for a healthy chunk of the day.

TRAILHEAD: From the Ventura Fwy., exit northbound on Westlake Blvd. and drive 0.5 mile to Cascade Ave., which is the next left turn exit beyond Thousand Oaks Blvd. Turn left (west) and proceed down Cascade Ave. to its terminus across from Russell Park.

Bring a filled water bottle. There are limited on-route water sources as noted on the trip map.

TRIP DESCRIPTION: **Westlake Blvd.** Leave the parking area and bike up Cascade Ave. to Westlake Blvd. Turn left (north) and coast a mild downgrade on a road that is tree-lined at the center median. Continue on the marked Class II path through an area with residential pockets on the left and hills to the right. Pass Hillcrest Dr. (0.4) and bike through less-developed territory which is bordered by hills. Bike on a light downgrade past Skelton Canyon Cir. and meet Deepwood Dr. a short distance beyond (1.1).

Pump a 0.3 mile upgrade, enjoy a short downgrade with a canyon view, and pass Valley Spring Dr. (1.7). The marked bike lane ends here, although the wide shoulder continues. Begin another uphill in an area with plush homes to the east and take in a scenic view of North Ranch. In a short distance is Kanan Rd. (2.4).

Kanan Rd. Turn right (east) and bike on the Class II road with a wide bike shoulder. Just off of Upper Ranch Rd. to the right is North Ranch Park (water fountain, open fields, children's playground and a patch of tree cover). The street skirts the northern perimeter of stately North Ranch with the

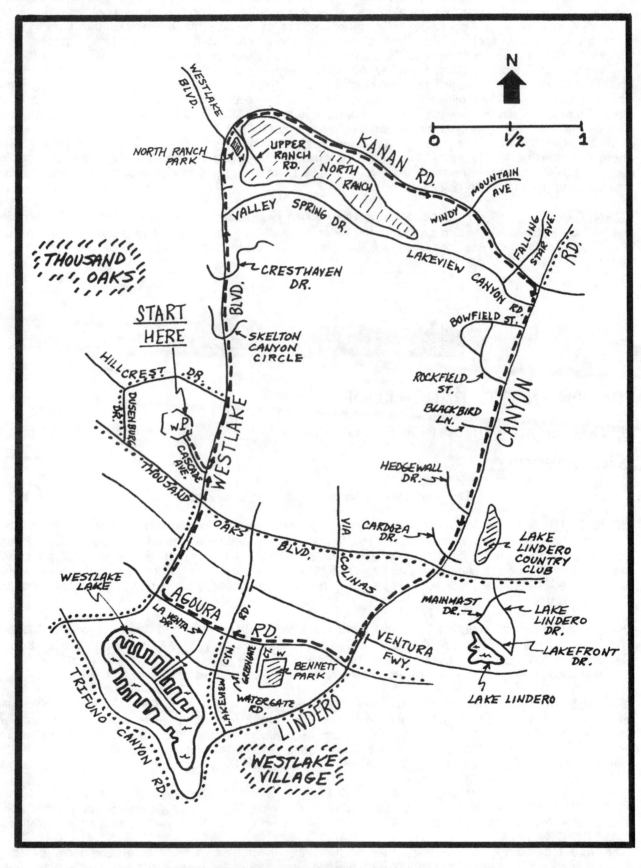

TRIP #54 - NORTH RANCH LOOP

rolling hills of the Conejo Ridge on the opposite (north) side of Kanan Rd. In 0.2 mile, bike a short upgrade which levels near Rayburn St. Follow a half-mile upgrade alongside the North Ranch Golf Course which "gets serious" about 0.2 mile before reaching a crest near Dawn Meadow Ct. (3.5).

Kanan Road In North Ranch Area

Cycle along the eastern edge of the golf course (4.1), pass Windy Mountain Ave., and follow the downhill past South Rim St. (4.4). There are residences on both sides of the road here and an occasional hawk for bird watchers. The road levels near Falling Star Ave. (4.7) and in 0.2 mile, continues to the mall-clustered junction at Lindero Canyon Rd.

Lindero Canyon Rd. Turn right (south) and ride on the Class II, wide-shouldered road past Lakeview Canyon Rd. (5.0). The road passes between a set of small hills, transits Rockfield St. (5.5), and then follows a mild upgrade through a lightly-developed area. A mild downgrade follows, then Lindero Canyon Rd. flattens and reaches Hedgewall Dr. (6.3). The path returns to higher density residential area on a tree-lined street, and reaches Thousand Oaks Blvd. and another group of shopping centers (7.1).

Pass the shopping center at this intersection and follow the downgrade past the open fields of the Valley Oak Memorial Park Cemetery. Continue a moderate downhill across Via Colinas (7.6) and reach the Ventura Freeway in 0.3 mile. Bike another 0.3 mile and arrive at Agoura Rd.

Closing the Loop. Turn right on Class II Agoura Rd. and bike alongside the Westlake Village Golf Club (right) and the northern periphery of the Westlake Village residential area. (Just south at Greengate Ct. is Bennett Park with water, restrooms, children's playground and widely-scattered tree shade.) In 0.3 mile, the street crosses Lakeview Canyon Rd., then cruises along the southern edge of Westlake Plaza. At the end of this shopping center, turn right (north) at Westlake Blvd. (9.6) and pump uphill on Class II road over the Ventura Fwy. (10.0). Bike through an open area 0.3 mile to Thousand Oaks Blvd., then 0.2 mile to Cascade Ave. Turn left (west) and return to the parking area (10.9).

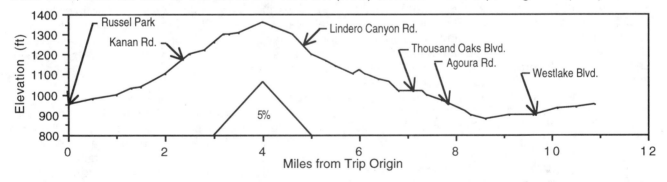

CONNECTING TRIPS: 1) Continuation with the Agoura Hills Loop (Trip #52) - from the intersection of Westlake Blvd. and Thousand Oaks Blvd., bike west on the latter street; 2) connection with the Westlake Village ride (Trip #53) - bike south on Lindero Canyon Rd. from the intersection of that street with Agoura Rd. Also, at the Agoura Rd./Westlake Blvd. intersection, head south on Westlake Blvd.

TRIP #55 - CHATSWORTH-NORTHRIDGE-GRANADA HILLS LOOP

GENERAL LOCATION: Chatsworth, Northridge, Granada Hills

LEVEL OF DIFFICULTY: Loop - moderate
Distance - 28.4 miles
Elevation gain - periodic moderate grades

HIGHLIGHTS: An interesting loop that tours both city and country, this predominately Class X route is definitely for experienced bike riders only. Much of the trip is on lightly-traveled roadway with plenty of biking room. However, there are heavy traffic areas and, for those segments, traffic route options are provided. So why take this trip? This tour originates from lovely Chatsworth Park North, explores the pleasant countryside on the western perimeter of the Chatsworth Reservoir, cruises by the California State University-Northridge (CSUN) campus, and traverses the foothills below the Santa Susana Mountains before returning to the trip origin. There are numerous mountain views. The Chatsworth Reservoir segment is country bike riding at its best! There are plentiful parks along the route for rest-stopping and water bottle filling.

Several alternatives to the basic route are also provided. Their focus is to limit the amount of cycling on the busiest streets, to reduce route length, and/or to visit scenic side streets.

TRAILHEAD: From the Ronald Reagan Fwy., exit south on Topanga Canyon Blvd. Drive past Stoney Point Park and turn right (west) on Chatsworth St. 1-1/4 miles from the freeway exit. Continue to parking just below the road's end at Chatsworth Park North. From the San Diego Fwy., exit west on the Ronald Reagan Fwy. and continue about eight miles to Topanga Canyon Blvd. Proceed as described above. From the Ventura Fwy. east of the San Diego Fwy., turn north on the San Diego Fwy. and proceed as described above. Another option from the Ventura Fwy. is to exit north at Topanga Canyon Blvd. and drive about seven miles to Chatsworth St. Turn left (west) and find parking near road's end.

Bring a filled water bottle on hot days. Water is generally plentiful at parks and some commercial centers, but there are areas such as the west side of Chatsworth Reservoir where none was found.

TRIP DESCRIPTION: **Chatsworth Park North.** Follow the bikeway/walkway around the rustic, shaded park and investigate the rocky outcroppings before leaving. Then follow the path around the restroom and ride into the southern edge of the parking area. Continue just beyond to the origin of Valley Circle Blvd. Follow Valley Circle Blvd. along the Santa Susana Wash 0.4 mile to Devonshire St.

A right turn here leads to Chatsworth Park South (see Trip #39). However, our reference route continues 0.6 mile past the woodsy, pastoral Oakwood Cemetery to Baden Ave. Angle left and follow the rural route through small rolling hills to a dead end at Plummer St. (1.5).

Chatsworth Reservoir/Western Loop. The next 2-3/4 miles of roadway is biker's heaven! The street is a little narrow, but the countryside scenery is terrific. Turn right (west) and follow the short Class I bikepath segment on Plummer St. which gives way to Class X biking. Follow the mildly winding street through a series of rolling hills. In 0.4 mile the roadway mysteriously becomes Valley Circle Blvd. again, which passes alongside the reservoir marshlands, as well as Chatsworth Oaks Park (a lovely shaded park with grasslands, barbecue facilities, playground, hiking trails, nice rock formations, but no water) (2.1).

The route stays on rolling terrain through a quaint rural residential area passing the Log Cabin Mercantile and reaching Box Canyon Rd. (3.0). There is a fine panorama westward into a residential area built high into the foothills. Here Valley Circle Blvd. veers to the south through more rolling hills and meanders alongside the reservoir's west edge. In another 0.3 mile is Woolsey Canyon Rd. Our roadway has hills to the right and the reservoir to the left. The area begins to return to residential near Chatlake Dr. (3.7). The path follows a nifty downhill to Roscoe Blvd. with a complete return to civilization (including a shopping center) at Roscoe Blvd. (4.4).

Southwest Trip Segment. Turn left (east) on Roscoe Blvd., pedal past March Ave. and skirt Orcutt Ranch Park (shade, water). The road widens in this residential area, opening up to a view of the Verdugo Mountains and the San Gabriel Mountains to the east (5.0). After 0.8 mile on Roscoe Blvd., turn right (south) on Woodlake Ave., pass a shopping center and turn left at Saticoy St. (5.8). (Route alternative: Bikers willing to bypass Orcutt Ranch Park can take a more scenic option on March Ave. as noted on the map) Bike on the more restricted path in heavier traffic through a mixed residential/commercial area to Topanga Canyon Blvd. (7.4). Turn left (north) and bike through a

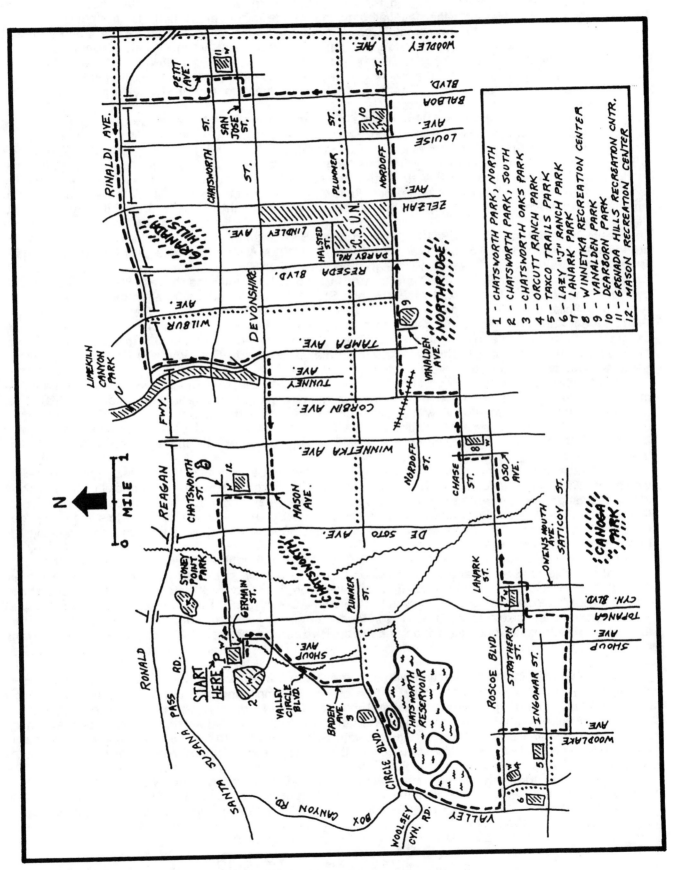

TRIP #55 - CHATSWORTH-NORTHRIDGE-GRANADA HILLS LOOP

commercial area on the heavily-traveled roadway 0.6 mile to Strathern St. A turn east leads along Lanark Park; there's water near the baseball diamond, shade, picnic areas and playgrounds.

Cruise a short distance to Owensmouth Ave. and turn left, bike another short segment and turn right (east) back onto Roscoe Blvd. (8.4). Follow this busy, cramped path through a heavy commercial area, cross Brown's Creek and pedal 0.2 mile past Mason Ave. to Oso Ave. Turn left (north), then right shortly at Chase St. and cycle alongside the Winnetka Recreation Center (water fountain behind the baseball diamond, recreation fields) (10.2). Continue another 1/2 mile to Corbin Ave., turn left and pedal through heavy traffic past several markets.

California State University, Northridge. Bike to Nordoff St. (the east connecting segment of Nordoff St. is north of the railroad tracks) and turn right (east) (11.8). Cross Vanalden Ave. (the turnoff to Vanalden Park) (12.5), pass Wilbur Ave. and Reseda Blvd. (13.1), and in 0.7 mile cruise in front of the CSUN campus. (Route alternative: The tour length can be reduced 10 miles by turning north on Wilbur Ave. and biking to Rinaldi Ave.) There are several nice rest spots and bike paths on campus (see Trip #58). However, the reference route follows a bee-line on Nordoff St. past Dearborn Park at Amestoy Ave. (water, restrooms, sports courts, playground and light shade) (15.1) and turns left in 0.3 mile at Balboa Blvd.

Western Segment. Balboa Blvd. is big and busy! Bike through a commercial area up a short steep grade, pass Lassen St. (16.5) and reach San Jose St. (17.2). A short 0.2 mile pedal east (right) and a left at Petit Ave. leads to Granada Hills Park and Recreation Center (water, tennis, recreation fields). Continue to Chatsworth St., turn left and return to Balboa Blvd. Bike north past San Fernando Blvd., over the Ronald Reagan Fwy. and reach Rinaldi St. (19.5). (Reduced traffic alternate: From Vanalden Ave. (12.5), bike 0.3 mile on Nordoff St. to Class II Wilbur Ave. Turn left and pedal 0.5 mile to Class III Plummer St. Turn right [east] and follow that road 3.4 miles [which includes a traverse of the CSUN campus] to Woodley Ave. Turn left on that Class II roadway and continue 2.5 miles to Rinaldi Ave. Then bike west on that street. This safer alternate makes access to Granada Hills Park less convenient and also adds two miles to the reference trip.)

The Northern (Foothill) Segment. Turn left (west) onto Class II Rinaldi Ave. and bike through a pleasant residential neighborhood on a series of moderate upgrades reaching a flat at Zelzah Ave. (21.3). Just beyond there is a view into Aliso Creek Canyon with the Santa Susana Mountains as a backdrop. The route passes just south and below Porter Ranch and continues on additional mild upgrades to Wilbur Ave. (22.6). Just beyond is a workout upgrade which tops out near Porter Valley Dr., the entry to the local country club.

In 0.3 mile, turn left (south) at a shopping center at Tampa Ave. (23.2). There are some excellent views into Limekiln Canyon (see Trip #57) and the southernmost portion of Limekiln Canyon Park along this segment, as well as mountain vistas to the east and back north. Coast downhill past Chatsworth St. (23.9) and turn right (west) on Devonshire St. Pedal an upgrade on this wide tree-lined street with more mountain views in this area. Just past Corbin Ave. (25.1) the road narrows and the locale becomes more rural.

In 0.6 mile is Mason Ave. and a shopping center. Turn right and bike on a steady, moderate upgrade 0.2 mile to Mason Park and Recreation Center, a grassy, tree-lined park with water, restrooms, and athletic fields (26.2). Just beyond, turn left (west) on Chatsworth St. into an affluent neighborhood with horse paths along the roadway. Cross over Brown's Creek (27.6), pass Canoga Ave. and a group of horse stables, then bike into an area near Owensmouth Ave. with a straight-on view of Stoney Point and its park. The route crosses Topanga Canyon Blvd. and continues 0.3 mile further to the starting point (28.4).

CONNECTING TRIPS: 1) Connection with the Sepulveda Bike Basin ride (Trip #38) - at Woodley Ave. and Victory Blvd., bike north 3-1/4 miles to Nordoff St.: 2) connection with the Chatsworth Tour/Brown's Creek Bikeway (Trip #39) - at the intersection of Valley Circle Blvd. and Lassen St., turn east on Lassen St.; 3) connection with the Santa Susana Pass ride (Trip #56) - at Chatsworth St. and Topanga Canyon Blvd., turn north and bike about 1/2 mile to Santa Susanna Pass Rd.; 4) connection with the Limekiln Canyon Trail (Trip #57) - from the intersection of Devonshire and Tunney Ave., turn north on Tunney Ave. and go a couple of hundred yards to the Limekiln Canyon Trail marker; 5) connection with the California State University, Northridge Campus Tour (Trip #58) - at the Nordoff St./Lindley Ave. intersection, turn north into the campus; 6) connection with the Woodland Hills-Tarzana Loop (Trip #59) - from the Shoup Ave./Saticoy St. junction, turn south on Shoup Ave. and drive to Victory Blvd.

TRIP #56 - SANTA SUSANA PASS

GENERAL LOCATION: Chatsworth, Simi Valley

LEVEL OF DIFFICULTY: One way - strenuous, up and back - strenuous to very strenuous
Distance - 4.1 miles (one way)
Elevation gain - steady steep grade to the summit

HIGHLIGHTS: The ride up to Santa Susana Pass, though short, is a real heart pumper. The tour follows Santa Susana Pass Rd. through a multitude of interesting rock formations in the Simi Hills. The views back into Chatsworth and those of the western mountains from the pass are well worth the effort. The trip can be extended to include a scenic downhill coast into the Simi Valley. However, if you haven't arranged a car shuttle, plan on an equally strenuous ride back up to the pass for the return to the Stoney Point Park trailhead. For cyclists with the time and interest, we suggest a short tour of the base of Stoney Point monolith at trip's end.

Santa Susanna Pass Road Near Iverson Road

TRAILHEAD: From the Ronald Reagan Fwy., exit south at Topanga Canyon Blvd. and drive 1/4 mile to the Stoney Point Park area. There is parking on the east side of the road.

Bring a couple of filled water bottles for rides on hot days, particularly if you are doing an up-and-back into Simi Valley. The only water source for the described trip is at Santa Susana Park, which has restrooms, grass, tree shade and picnic tables.

TRIP DESCRIPTION: The Uphill. Bike north 0.1 mile to Santa Susana Pass Rd. and turn left, enjoying a brief downhill. A modest climb leads through some interesting rock formations on a mild grade and passes Red Mesa Dr. The Union Pacific (UP) tracks can be seen below and to the left. The grade stiffens and the route passes the eastern entry to the Church at Rocky Peak. The road shifts to two lanes (0.8) and winds upward to a point just below the Ronald Reagan Fwy., then shifts east to parallel that thoroughfare.

Just past Oak Valley Farms (1.3) the roadway returns to a single lane. More of the Simi Hills rock formations appear at a distance on the left and there are superb over-the-shoulder views back to Chatsworth and Stoney Point. The winding route takes a sharp turn left and climbs to a flat, passing a fire road entry on the left (2.1). Scenic westward views great bikers as the contour flattens before reaching Rocky Peak Rd. at the summit (2.3). Rocky Peak Park (no facilities) and the Rocky Peak Fire Road entry are across the freeway

The Downhill. Santa Susana Pass Rd. crosses over the unseen UP railroad tunnel near Lilac Ln. and coasts past Box Canyon Rd. (3.1). The road continues to pull away from the freeway as cyclists are treated to mixed views of the Simi Hills, the Santa Susana Mountains and eventually, Simi Valley. Further downhill are views into Twilight Canyon, where the UP tracks reappear out of the mountains. The route flattens, opens to two lanes and passes picturesque Hideout Willies and several other interesting, venerable establishments. Just before reaching a sharp northward road bend is Katherine

Rd. (3.9). (If you cross the railroad tracks, you've gone too far.) Turn left and bike another 0.2 mile to Santa Susana Park.

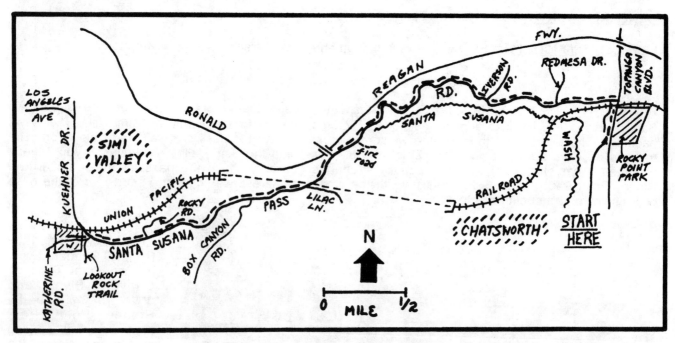

TRIP #56 - SANTA SUSANA PASS

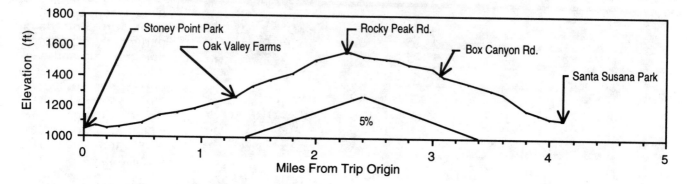

CONNECTING TRIPS: 1) Connection with the Chatsworth-Northridge-Granada Hills Loop (Trip #55) - from the parking area, bike south 1/2 mile on Topanga Canyon Blvd. to Chatsworth St. and turn right; 2) connection with the Chatsworth Tour/Brown's Creek Bikeway (Trip #39) - follow the same directions as above, proceeding 1/3 mile to Brown's Canyon Wash.

TRIP #57 - LIMEKILN CANYON TRAIL

GENERAL LOCATION: Porter Ranch

LEVEL OF DIFFICULTY: Loop - easy

Distance - 3.8 miles

Elevation gain - periodic light upgrades; single short, steep upgrade

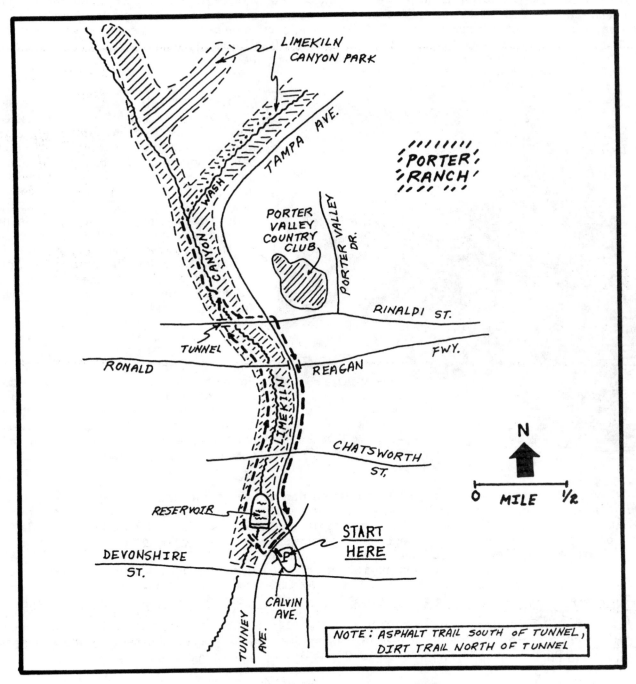

TRIP #57 - LIMEKILN CANYON TRAIL

HIGHLIGHTS: A delightful outdoor excursion in the middle of suburbia, this is a pleasant ride through Limekiln Canyon, alongside Limekiln Creek and through lush bottomland. It is a nice family ride which does have a couple of short "workout" upgrades. The lower 1.2 miles of the trail is paved, while the upper 0.6 mile is graded gravel (bikeable with both thin- and balloon-tire bikes). The graded gravel roadway passes through the most naturally scenic part of the trip and provides a physical creek-crossing to boot!

TRAILHEAD: Exit the Ronald Reagan Fwy. south at Tampa Ave. and drive about 1-1/4 miles to Tunney Ave. Turn right (southwest) and continue 0.1 mile to Calvin Ave. Turn left and find parking in the residential area subject to local traffic laws.

Only a very light water supply is needed for this trip.

TRIP DESCRIPTION: **Lower Trail.** Bike a short distance to Tunney Ave., cross the street, and find the Limekiln Canyon Trail marker a few hundred feet south. Continue up a short steep upgrade to the spillway which straddles Limekiln Creek (0.2). From this point is one of many outstanding views into the Santa Susana Mountains to the north. The meandering Class I trail continues through the canyon with the creekbed to the right and homes on the bluffs above, then reaches a short, steep upgrade just before Chatsworth St. (0.6).

Limekiln Canyon North of the Tunnel

Upper Trail (asphalt). Cross Chatsworth St. and follow a short steep downhill back into the creek bed. Bike another half mile through the lush canyon bottom on a mild upgrade before passing under the Ronald Reagan Fwy. In 0.1 mile, the trail splits, with the left fork heading up the left bank and the poorly maintained right fork paralleling our middle fork route (1.2).

Upper Trail (graded gravel). In another 0.1 mile, the trail shifts from asphalt to gravel and proceeds through a 100-foot tunnel; there is scattered gravel and some glass in the dark tunnel (a chance to walk your bike - hint, hint!). From this point, the trail is on graded gravel - well suited for "balloon" tire bikes and reasonable for "thin" tire bikes. Proceed right (east) to the improved trail segment and bike through the lush canyon bottomland with its many trees and running creek. Cross the creek over a small bridge and bike another 1/4 mile past a small picnic area.

Cross the shallow creek and follow a moderate upgrade to another more modest crossing (1.8). Pump a steeper upgrade to a flat where there is a particularly nice view of the local mountains through the tree cover. In a short distance is a turnaround loop where the reference trip ends. Those with balloon-tire bikes can ford the deeper creek on the spur trail to the right and continue northward.

Return Route. Proceed back almost to the tunnel, then take the trail to the left as it proceeds uphill to Rinaldi St. (2.6). To the west is a series of walking/cross-country bike trails; however, our reference route proceeds east 0.1 mile to Tampa Ave. Bike on the Class X roadway over the freeway (2.9), free-wheel another 0.5 mile downhill past Chatsworth St., turn right on Tunney Ave. and return to the starting point (3.8).

CONNECTING TRIPS: Continuation with the Chatsworth-Northridge-Granada Hills Loop (Trip #55) - from the trip origin, continue south on Tunney Ave. and turn right on Devonshire St.

202

TRIP #58 - CALIFORNIA STATE UNIVERSITY, NORTHRIDGE CAMPUS

GENERAL LOCATION: Northridge

LEVEL OF DIFFICULTY: Loop - easy
Distance - 3.0 miles
Elevation gain - flat

HIGHLIGHTS: This free-form trip is a definite family favorite for weekends or vacation periods. The described route roams the campus periphery, but can also include numerous adventures throughout the picturesque central campus. All routes are unmarked, but traffic is light and there is a great deal of biking room. There are optional routes through adjoining (lightly trafficked) residential areas that can easily extend the total cruise to 4-5 miles depending on the biker's imagination.

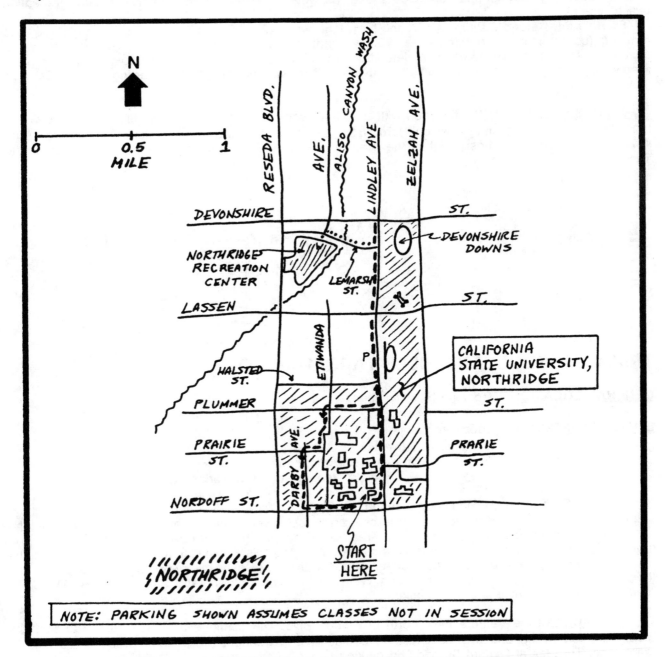

TRIP #56 - CALIFORNIA STATE UNIVERSITY, NORTHRIDGE CAMPUS

TRAILHEAD: From the Ronald Reagan Fwy., exit south at Reseda Blvd. and drive 2-3/4 miles to Nordoff St. Turn left (east) and continue about 0.5 mile to Lindley Ave. Turn left onto the campus, left again into the parking area and continue to the information sign in front of the Drama/Fine Arts Building.

TRIP DESCRIPTION: **North Leg.** Ride east to Lindley Ave. and turn left (north). Cycle past the Student Union Building (0.3), Plummer St. and the fence opening just beyond. Next is a cruise past the Fitness Center (0.7), recreation fields, a baseball field (with a water fountain), and the track and field stadium. Just off to the west are quiet residential streets with generous biking room, a possible later diversion. However, our route continues another 0.2 mile to Lassen St. (1.1).

Cross busy Lassen St. at the intersection and continue to the CSUN North Campus Annex. In 0.3 mile is Lemarsh St.; turn left (west) for a diversion to Northridge Park. In 0.2 mile on our main route on Lindley Ave. is a newly-constructed medical facility, the northernmost point of the route (1.7). On the return leg, cyclists can take a 0.3-mile diversion trip on Lemarsh St. to Northridge Recreational Center. The center has grassy grounds and tree shade, as well as restrooms and water within the recreation facility itself.

South Leg. Return to Plummer St. and turn right (west) (2.8). Cruise 0.2 mile to Etiwanda Ave. and turn left (south) into the parking area. Follow winding Etiwanda Ave. to Prairie St. and turn right, continuing to Darby Ave. (3.6). Turn left and, in a short distance, turn back into the parking area. Freewheel through the lot to Nordoff St. and turn left (east), returning to the starting point in 0.2 mile (4.1).

CONNECTING TRIPS: 1) Continuation with the Chatsworth-Northridge-Granada Hills Loop (Trip #55) - from the trip origin, continue east on Nordoff St.; 2) connection with the Limekiln Canyon Trail (Trip #57) - from the northernmost point of the trip, turn west on Plummer St. and continue l-3/4 miles to Tunney Ave.

TRIP #59 - WOODLAND HILLS-TARZANA LOOP

GENERAL LOCATION: Woodland Hills, Tarzana

LEVEL OF DIFFICULTY: Loop - moderate
Distance - 22.5 miles
Elevation gain - periodic moderate grades;
single steep grade in McFarlane Dr. area

HIGHLIGHTS: This interesting loop ride has both a city face and country face. The flat northern segment traverses an urban-light commercial area for several miles before reaching the highly-developed Promenade Mall/Topanga Plaza area. Once across the Ventura Fwy., the trip returns to a more rural setting amongst the Santa Monica Mountain foothills. This southern segment crosses the hillside community west of Topanga Canyon Blvd. (with some testy hill climbing if you choose) and then tours the elegant rural segment along Wells Dr. The beautifully treed and manicured Wells Dr. "country lane" segment is the trip highlight.

TRAILHEAD: Exit the Ventura Fwy. north at Balboa Blvd. and continue a short distance to Burbank Blvd. Turn left (west) and drive 0.5 mile to Louise Ave. Turn right (north) and proceed 0.6 mile to road's end. Turn left at Oxnard St. and find parking under a shade tree.

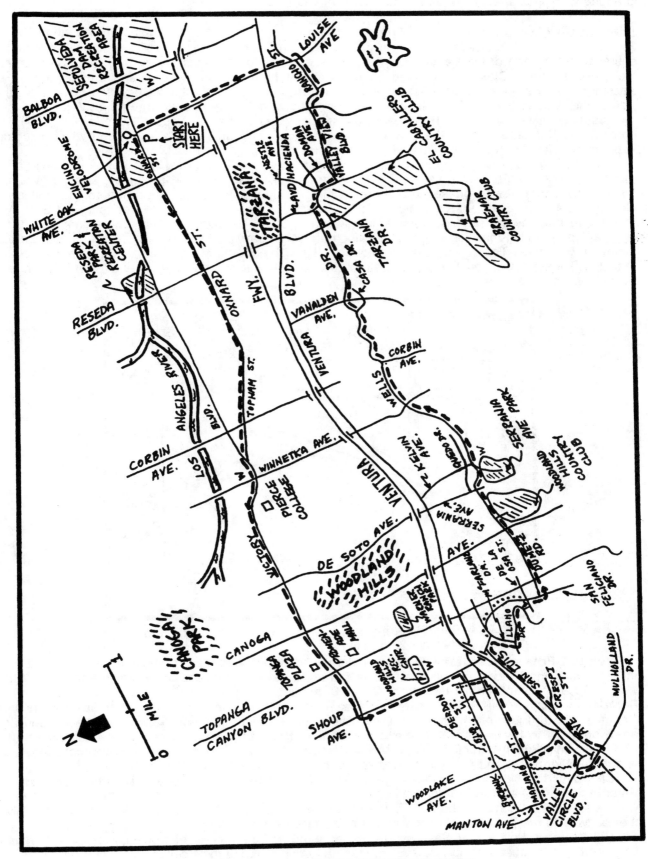

TRIP #59 - WOODLAND HILLS-TARZANA LOOP

Bring a filled water bottle. There are strategically placed water sources along the route, but there is a long waterless stretch along the southern segment.

TRIP DESCRIPTION: Oxnard and Topham Streets. Bike west (away from Balboa Park) along Oxnard St. on the Class I Sepulveda Bike Basin path. Pedal on flat roadway (the trail is relatively flat on the entire segment north of the Ventura Fwy.) past Louise (0.1) to White Oak Ave. (0.7). Across the street, the route becomes Class X. Continue on this road or bike one block north and turn left (west) on Bessmer St. This alternate soon becomes a parallel path named Topham St. which is on the other side of the railroad tracks. (There is less traffic on this I-I/2 mile alternate which ends at Wilbur Ave.)

Just past Etiwanda Ave. (1.4) the path enters a light industrial area, crosses Reseda Blvd. (1.7), and proceeds to Wilbur St. where the surroundings return to residential (2.2). The street, which becomes Topham St. after it bends northwest, ends in I.5 miles beyond Wilbur St. at Victory Blvd.

Pierce College and Shopping Plazas. Turn left (west) at Victory Blvd. and pass the small Larson (baseball) Field. There is water alongside the dugout and shade, reached by turning right at Winnetka Ave. (4.3). The bikeway passes the Pierce College athletic fields, the entrance to the college at Mason St. (4.8), and the Pierce College Farm (open agricultural fields) before reaching De Soto Ave. This is the beginning of a large commercial district (5.3). In a quarter mile is a little shopping center with several potential munchie stops. The traffic gets very heavy in this area - try using the sidewalk for the next 0.5 mile. The route passes between the Promenade Mall (south) and Topanga Plaza, reaching Topanga Canyon Rd. and a return to a residential setting just beyond (6.4). Continue to Shoup Ave. and turn left (south).

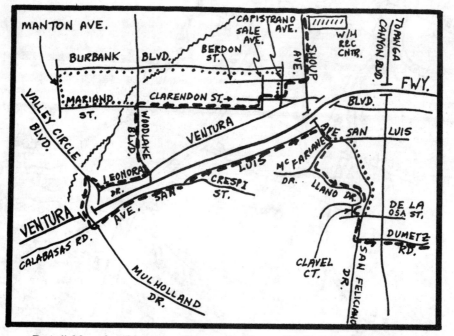

Detail Map for **"Ventura Freeway Crossing"** and **"Hill Country"**

Ventura Freeway Crossing. Bike down tree-lined Shoup Ave. passing Oxnard St. (7.5) and in I/4 mile reaching the Woodland Hills Recreation Center. This is the best rest stop on the trip, with trees, water and a pleasant foothill backdrop. Cross Burbank Blvd. and in just 0.I mile turn right (west) on Berdon St. (8.2); in this quiet residential area is a three-mile marked Class III loop. Bike a short distance and turn left (south) on Capistrano Ave., right on Clarendon St., left on Sale Ave., and right again on Mariano St. (most of this bikeway is marked) (8.5). Continue across busy Fallbrook Ave. (8.8) and in 0.5 mile reach Woodlake Ave. Turn left (south), bike 0.3 mile to Ventura Blvd. (note that there is a gas station here) and follow that roadway to its end at Valley Circle Blvd. (10.0).

Bike over the Ventura Fwy. to the massive shopping area on Mulholland Dr. (10.6). Fill up with water in this area as there are only limited sources for the remainder of the trip. A short diversion to the west leads to the Leonis Adobe and Plummer House. Just south from that area is Park Granada Blvd., the roadway to the plush residential area surrounding Lake Calabasas.

Hill Country. Follow Ave. San Luis (the small street which parallels the freeway) up a short grade to Crespi St. (11.0). Just beyond is a small pedestrian bridge across the freeway. Continue on mild rolling

206

terrain past Fallbrook Ave. (11.5) to Shoup Ave. (12.2), where Ave. San Luis curves to the right and intersects McFarlane Dr. in 0.1 mile.

Now comes the decision point! Turn hard right and start the steep climb up McFarlane Dr. (it gets steeper!) or remain on more moderate Ave. San Luis. The former route offers some nice vistas of the surrounding hills and a short but stout workout. The route continues on a very steep upgrade to Llano Dr. (12.8), bears left on that street, winds another quarter mile uphill, then begins a very steep, winding downgrade to Clavell Court (13.6). Turn left, then left again at De La Osa St., and cycle 0.1 mile to San Feliciano Dr. (The less challenging route goes 0.3 mile on Ave. San Luis to San Feliciano Dr., then turns right (south) onto mild rolling hills in a pleasant residential area, proceeding to Dumetz Rd.)

The bikeway turns left (east) on Dumetz Rd. and heads through a tree-lined residential area passing Topanga Canyon Rd. and a small shopping center (14.1). Next is a 3/4 mile series of rolling hills with a crest at Escobedo Dr., near the Woodland Hills Country Club entrance. Continue to Serrania Ave., where the road bends sharply to the right (south), then curves and resumes its westward track, becoming Wells Dr. Just beyond Serrania Ave. is the like-named park with water, restrooms, grassy knolls and children's play areas. This is the last convenient public water source that we found for the trip's remainder.

Wells Drive Near Kelvin Ave.

Wells Dr. Nearby is the Victorian Westchester County Private Estates (15.7) and, to the right, the entry to Serrania Park. However, our tour stays on Wells Dr. and continues through moderate rolling hills in a well-groomed residential area. The top of the last grade is at Del Moreno (16.2). Follow the steep downgrade past Winnetka Ave., where the roadway narrows and passes through a pleasant grove of trees and continued awesome residential setting (16.7). In 0.4 mile at Corbin Ave. the roadway crests, heads downhill for 0.3 mile, winds uphill again, and reaches Tampa Ave. (17.7).

Just beyond is a junction with Casa Dr. where Wells Dr. winds to the left. The relatively flat remainder of the trip starts by passing a small school recreation area with water fountains (probably locked on weekends) at Crebs Ave. (18.5), and the backside recreation fields of Caspar De Portola Junior High School. Wells Dr. ends shortly at Avd. Hacienda (19.0). Turn right (south) and continue a short distance to Tarzana Dr. (passing the El Caballero Country Club), right again at narrow Nestle Ave., then left at Valley Vista Blvd. (19.7).

The Return Link. This area returns to a classy tree-covered residential setting with the roadway passing White Oak Ave. (20.2), then follows a curve up a moderate grade past several gated properties. The roadway, now named Rancho St., continues to Louise Ave. (20.9). Turn left (north) onto the light downgrade, passing more elegant estates. Bike across Ventura Blvd. (21.3) on a light downhill over the Ventura Fwy. (22.1), and return to Oxnard St. and the trip origin in 0.4 mile.

CONNECTING TRIPS: 1) Continuation with the Sepulveda Bike Basin (Trip #38) - from the trip origin, bike west to the end of Oxnard St. to Balboa Park; 2) connection with the Chatsworth-Northridge-Granada Hills Loop (Trip #55) - at Shoup Ave., bike 1-1/2 miles north to Saticoy St.

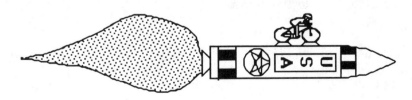

TRIP #60 - HANSEN DAM RECREATION AREA

GENERAL LOCATION: Pacoima, San Fernando

LEVEL OF DIFFICULTY: **Dam ride:** up and back - easy
                               Distance - 4.5 miles
                               Elevation gain - single short, moderate climb to dam

                               Bottomlands ride: loop - moderate (modest off-road biking skills required)
                               Distance - 4.1 miles
                               Elevation gain - periodic moderate grades

HIGHLIGHTS: The primary ride featured is on top of the Hansen Dam itself. A short Class I trail climbs to the levee entry, followed by a flat, 3.4-mile (up and back) segment on the levee's paved surface. The views of the bottomland behind the dam and the more-distant mountain vistas are inspiring.

    A second tour explores the Hansen Dam Recreation Area bottomlands and is best done with a fat-tire bike. It focuses on the western side of the bottomlands, exploring both the area just behind the dam as well as those below the bluffs of the Hansen Dam Aquatic Center and near the Fenton Ave. sports recreation area. There are numerous spurs off the described route for further exploration and the chance for riders to test their sand-riding skills. Also provided is a short diversion trip off the bottomlands tour which leads to the Hansen Dam Aquatic Center

TRAILHEAD: From the Foothill Fwy., exit south at Foothill Blvd. (Osborne St. to the north). Drive one mile to the connecting Osborne St. segment, turn left, and continue a quarter mile to Dronfield Ave. Turn left and drive directly into the upper parking area. From the Ronald Reagan Fwy., continue east to the freeway terminus. Follow the transition route to the westbound Foothill Fwy. and take the first exit south on Foothill Blvd. Continue as described above. From the Golden State Fwy., exit northeast on Osborne St. Drive 2-1/4 miles to Dronfield Ave. and turn right (east).

    Bring a light water supply. The trip is short and the picnic areas have water.

Bottomlands Area Below Aquatic Center

TRIP DESCRIPTION: **Dam Levee Ride.** A pleasant adult or family trip is the easy ride atop the dam. The levee is accessible using a paved trail which starts at the southwestern end of the upper parking lot. The paved trail climbs and parallels Osborne St. just before reaching the parking lot at the levee edge. (This lot is an alternate, easier point of entry.) Pass through the open gate and bike directly onto the levee. The bottomlands behind the dam are below and to the left, while the Hansen Dam Golf Course is to the right. The route passes over the spillway at about one mile and reaches a closed fence and turnaround at 1.7 miles. The full ride is about 4.5 miles. (Note that the levee is a good vantage point from which to plan a bottomlands tour.)

Bottomlands Tour: Southern Recreation Area. Within the upper parking area, bike southeast of the Dronfield Ave. entry (toward the dam) to the entry road (①in the detail map) which heads towards the bottomlands. At the downgrade's end, within the paved lower parking lot, turn right (south at②) and proceed past some grassy play fields and picnic area (0.2). Pass around a locked gate onto a compacted dirt trail which heads directly toward the dam.

    Bike a short distance to a "reference junction" (③); take the path southeast toward the dam spillway. In 0.2 mile of winding through the trees and passing many spur trails is a "T"-junction in an open area. Left leads to the low-water point (Hansen Lake). Our route goes right and reaches the base

208

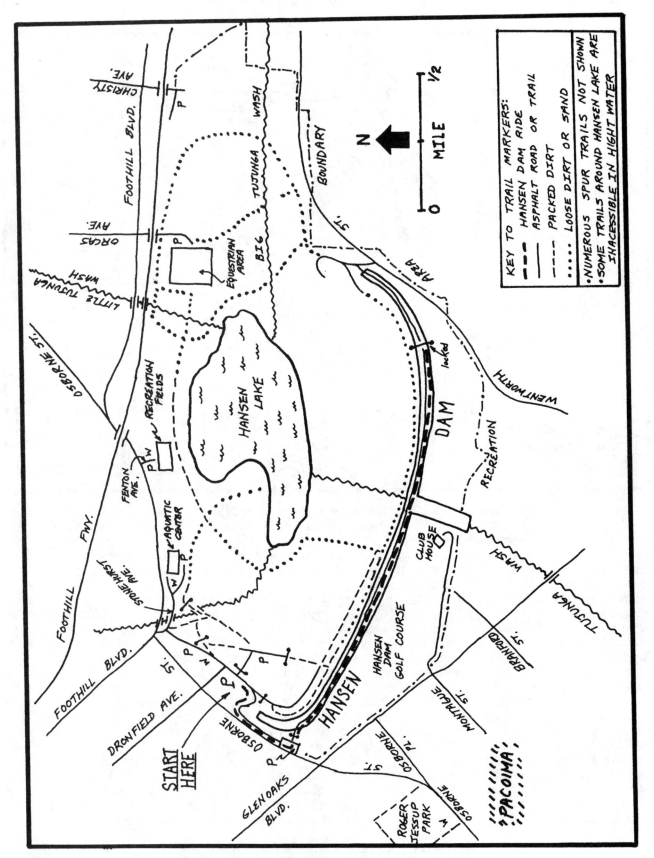

TRIP #60 - HANSEN DAM RECREATION AREA

of the dam in a short distance (0.4). In low water, bikers can turn left and follow a mixed-dirt trail across the spillway entry and along the entire dam base. This is for fat-tire cyclists who love to challenge sand.

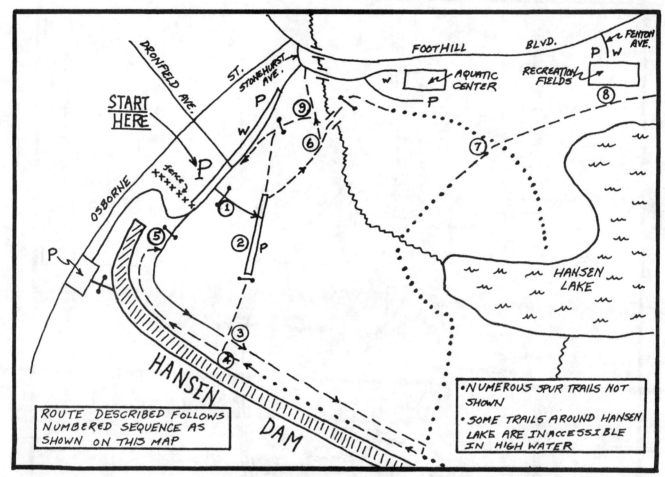

The reference tour goes right along the base through mixed compacted/loose dirt and reaches another junction ((4)). Continue along the dam base and bike almost to the western dam edge. Follow the path towards the southwestern edge of the upper parking lot and take the first major junction to the right (1.1) ((5)). A 0.2-mile stint on paved path returns cyclists to the "reference junction" (1.3). Next, repeat the incoming route, then bike to the northern edge of the lower parking lot and follow the packed dirt horse trail to the northeast (1.9).

Northern Recreation Area. Bike on the horse path past a couple of spurs and follow a short, upgrade to another "reference" junction ((6)). Stay right and pass over a wash, then pass through an open gate (2.1). This route leads cyclists alongside the bluffs below the Hansen Dam Aquatic Center. Follow the wide trail through a mix of hard- and loose-pack and pump 0.2 mile to a "T"-junction ((7)). Right leads to a small rise above Hansen Lake, while the reference route heads left. This hard-pack, wide trail works over to a large recreation area off of Fenton Ave. ((8)) (2.9). There are soccer fields plus picnic facilities, scattered tree cover and restrooms at the north end of the complex.

This is our suggested turnaround point; although experienced and adventurous cyclists with fat-tire bikes can explore the eastern side and make a full loop of the area behind Hansen Dam. A myriad of sandy trails and two major wash crossings are in store for cyclists who opt for this adventure. (Note, however, that we saw few bicycle-tire tracks beyond the recreation area.)

The Return Segment. Backtrack to the reference junction ((6)), turn right (northwest) and bike a steep grade on a mixed-pack dirt surface. In about 100 feet is another trail fork (3.8). Right and steeply uphill is Stonehurst Ave. and the road entry to the aquatic area. Our route left cruises on a shelf which provides some interesting bottomland views. The trail passes through an open gate and follows the next major fork right. A short climb leads back to the upper parking area and an easy glide back to the start point (4.1).

Diversion Trip to the Hansen Dam Aquatic Center. From junction ((9)), climb a 30- to 40-foot rise and bike a couple of hundred yards to Stonehurst Ave., Turn right and pedal through the open gate on paved road. In 0.2 mile is a junction within a large parking area. Going right takes bikers to a bluff which overlooks the bottomlands area. Heading left leads to the Aquatic center with its pool and small manmade lake, complete with self-propelled paddlewheel boats. There are distant views into the Sunland and Tujunga areas from here.

CONNECTING TRIPS: Continue on Osborne St. 0.7 mile past Roger Jessup Park. (The park has grass, shade, picnic areas, water and restrooms). The path becomes Class III at this juncture. Bike another 2.8 miles (under the Golden State Fwy.) to Woodman Ave. There is a six-mile Class III bike ride south on this street.

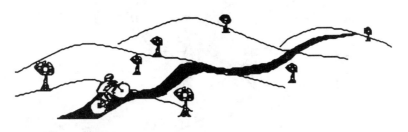

TRIP #61 - EL CARISO REGIONAL PARK

GENERAL LOCATION: San Fernando

LEVEL OF DIFFICULTY: Loop - easy
Distance - 2.2 miles
Elevation gain - single moderate upgrade

HIGHLIGHTS: This dandy little Class I loop trip has some big offerings, particularly as a family bike outing. The route is flat with the exception of one 30-foot downgrade-upgrade. The loop provides two miles of variety, including recreation fields, golf-course, Class X spurs into the Pacoima Canyon Wash, scenic view points, and a well-laid-out park. Bikers can extend the trip mileage by doing the loop several times or by selecting from among many route options within the park.

There is an option to leave the park and bike on lightly-trafficked Class X surface streets 1-1/4 miles to Veteran's Memorial Park. (The route there involves some testy hill climbing.) This exceptional locale is slightly more hilly, but is a delight for family outings in one of the county's most gorgeous and scenic park settings.

TRAILHEAD: From the Foothill Fwy., exit north on Hubbard St. and drive one mile to Garrick Ave. Turn right into the park. Hubbard St. is roughly 3-1/2 miles east of the Golden State Fwy./Foothill Fwy. fusion point and two miles northwest of the Ronald Reagan Freeway fusion point.

Water is plentiful. Bring a light water supply if the trip is to be extended to Veteran's Memorial Park.

TRIP DESCRIPTION: From the parking area near the park's swimming pool, bike southwest towards the tennis courts on the Class I path. Just beyond the courts, turn left and bike alongside the parking area. In a short distance is the Snack and Pro Shop (apparently not open in the winter) (0.2). Cruise through this pleasant and well-manicured park between the baseball diamonds and then veer southeast through a parking area. A short pedal leads to the El Cariso Golf Course Club House (0.4).

Pass the clubhouse and cycle through the parking area on Rajah St. In this area bikers get a glimpse of a small lake within the golf course, as well as a view of the golfers "at work." At Eldridge Ave., turn left (southeast) and hug the golf course periphery on the quality Class I path. Along this entire 0.4 mile stretch, there are opportunities to watch the hackers, whackers, and an occasional veteran golfer.

Hug the edge of the golf course and turn left at Harding St., passing through a small motorized vehicle barrier. In 0.1 mile the path reaches its most southeasterly point. There is a view of the Pacoima Canyon Wash and flood control dam here (for bikers with fat tire bikes, this is a jumping off point to explore the wash) (1.0). Just beyond, the path whips downhill to the floor of the wash; from this area, some of the off-road vehicle play areas in both the wash and the hills are visible.

Bike a short, moderately-steep upgrade to a vantage point with an unobstructed view of the nearby mountains. We watched a hang-glider working the mountain drafts from here (1.3). In 0.2 mile the path

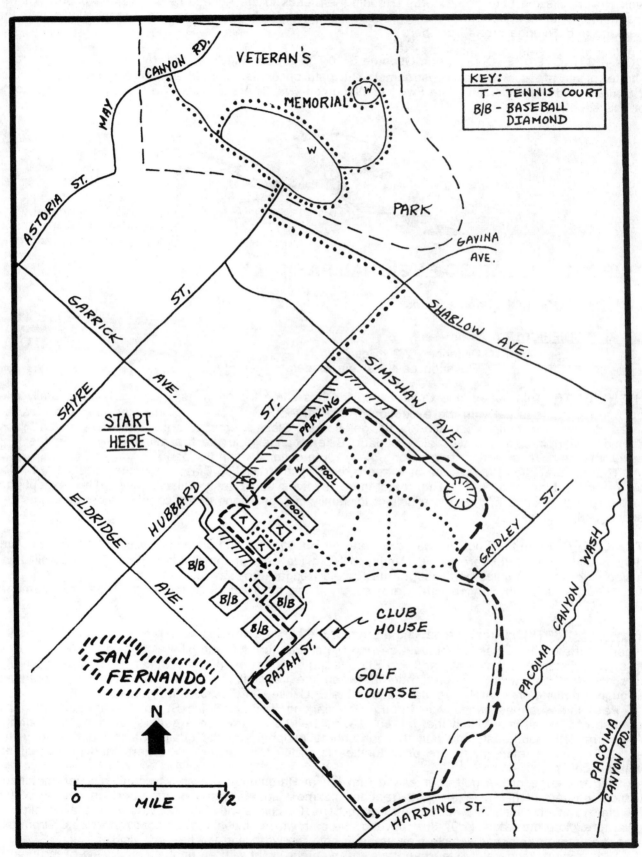

KEY:
T – TENNIS COURT
B/B – BASEBALL DIAMOND

TRIP #61 - EL CARISO REGIONAL PARK

crosses Gridley St., returns to the park and passes through the main picnic area (water, restrooms, picnic tables, barbecues and scattered shade trees). There are numerous paths through the park interior here; our described path keeps to the right on the park periphery paralleling Simshaw Ave. The route passes alongside a group of residences (1.8), crosses a park roadway, and winds its way parallel to Hubbard St. before reaching the trip starting point (2.2).

Middle Area of Veterans Memorial Park

CONNECTING TRIPS: There is an option to bike a short distance to explore Veterans Memorial Park. Follow Hubbard St. 3/4 mile to Shablow Ave., turn left, and continue a quarter-plus mile steeply uphill to Sayre St. Turn right for entry. The park has bikeways/walkways threading most of it's interior plus both sheltered and open picnic facilities, grassy rolling knolls, varied and prolific tree cover, restrooms, L.A. Mission College structures and numerous viewpoints to the valley below. Families might opt to drive directly to the park and spend the day wandering around its intertwining, paved paths.

TRIP #62 - GLENDALE BIKEWAY

GENERAL LOCATION: Glendale, La Crescenta

LEVEL OF DIFFICULTY: One way - moderate; up and back - moderate
Distance - 9.6 miles (one way)
Elevation gain - periodic moderate grades

HIGHLIGHTS: This rewarding tour skirts the Verdugo Mountains, following the foothills from Brand Park in Glendale around to Crescenta Valley Park in La Crescenta. The route includes several excellent parks, provides some scenic views, and is a varied and entertaining ride. When ridden in the direction as described, the return leg from La Crescenta provides a mild but continuous 4-5 mile downhill runout. (Does that say something about the initial leg of this trip?) Though predominately Class X, the quality of roadway, amount of traffic, and available bike shoulder, makes this ride similar to a quality Class III route.

213

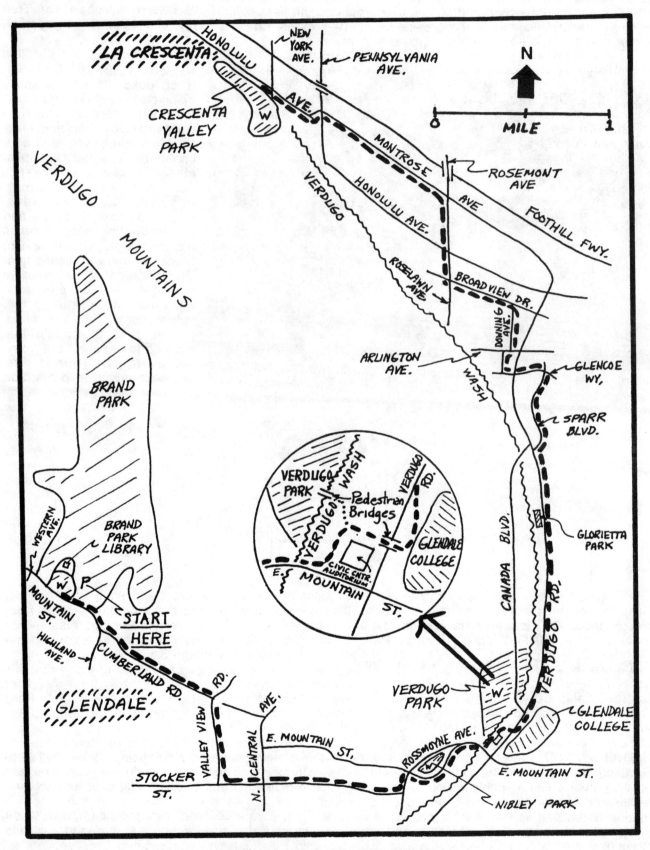

TRIP #62 - GLENDALE BIKEWAY

TRAILHEAD: From the Golden State Fwy., exit east at Western Ave. Drive towards the Verdugo Mountain foothills about l-l/2 miles to Mountain St. Turn right and in a few hundred feet, turn left into Brand Park. From the Ventura Fwy., transition north onto the Golden State Fwy. and proceed as stated above. From the Glendale Fwy., transition west onto the Ventura Fwy. and then transition north in about 2-l/2 miles onto the Golden State Fwy.

There are strategically located water sources at the parks along the route. However, bring a filled water bottle for an up and back trip in the summer.

TRIP DESCRIPTION: Glendale Foothills. Tour Brand Park's grounds before departing, leaving some time to visit the classic and stately Brand Park Library. Once outside the park, turn left onto Mountain St. and bike 0.4 mile through a quiet and stately residential area to the point where the roadway veers right and becomes Highland Ave. At the next intersection, turn left onto Cumberland Rd. and bike another 1/2 mile through light rolling hills to the street's terminus at Valley View Rd. (1.2). Note that any turn towards the foothills in this general area can lead to some challenging uphill adventures for interested bikers!

Brand Park Library

Turn right (south) and follow the steep downhill another l/2 mile to Stocker St. There are scattered views across to the Santa Monica Mountains in this segment. Follow Stocker St. east across busy Central Ave. (2.1) and return to a residential area and a mild upgrade in a short distance. At the end of Stocker St., turn left (north) at Rossmoyne Ave. (2.9) and bike another short upgrade to Mountain St. Turn right and follow the curving road past compact, but delightful, Nibley Park until it veers right and crosses the bridge over the Verdugo Wash (3.7).

Verdugo Road. Just beyond the wash, cross Mountain St. and ride into the parking lot behind the Civic Center Auditorium. In 0.2 mile is a pedestrian walkway (with a ramp entrance on the north side) over Verdugo Rd. Note also that just beyond and to the left is a walkway over the Verdugo Wash which leads to large, well-equipped, Verdugo Park. Follow the ramp (nice view from here) across to the Glendale College Campus, turn left in the parking lot, and pedal to Verdugo Rd. (4.3).

There is no such thing as a free ride! Follow Verdugo Rd. on a steady, slight upgrade that will continue several miles into La Crescenta. Pass a small eatery and market and follow the valley floor past Crestmont Ct. (4.7), Wabasso Wy. (5.0) and reach the top of this grade at Glorietta Ave. (5.7). Pass Glorietta Park and ride about l/4 mile further to Sparr Blvd. just before the point where Verdugo Rd. and Canada Blvd. fuse.

La Crescenta Area. Turn right (east) at Sparr Blvd., pedal uphill through a residential area to Glencoe Wy. (6.7), and turn left. Bike across Verdugo Rd. and pass a small shopping center. Cruise to Downing Ave. (6.9) and turn right (north); follow this road as it jogs right at Arlington Ave. and proceeds on a workout grade to Broadview Dr. Turn left onto a welcome flat and bike 0.3 mile to Roselawn Ave. (Rosemont Ave. to the north) (7.7).

Follow another workout uphill past Honolulu Ave. (There are eateries to the right on Honolulu Ave.) to Montrose Ave. and turn left (8.2). Cross that busy, but flat, roadway through a light commercial and residential area across Pennsylvania Ave. Veer left onto Honolulu Ave. and pedal to Crescenta Valley

Park near New York Ave. (9.6). The most naturally scenic area and best rest stop is at the northern end of the park; lift your bike over the entrance barrier to reach that fenced-in park area.

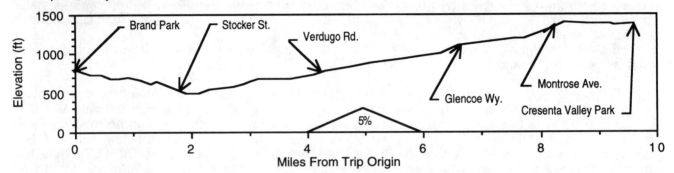

CONNECTING TRIPS: 1) Connection with the Burbank Bikeway (Trip #36) - from the trip origin, bike west on Mountain St. about one mile to Providencia Ave.; 2) connection with the Verdugo Mountains Loop (Trip #63) - at the trip terminus, cycle east on Honolulu Ave. past Crescenta Valley Park.

TRIP #63 - VERDUGO MOUNTAINS LOOP

GENERAL LOCATION: La Crescenta, Tuna Canyon, Burbank, Glendale

LEVEL OF DIFFICULTY: Loop - moderate to strenuous
Distance - 23.9 miles
Elevation gain - periodic moderate grades; single steep upgrade in the
La Crescenta area

HIGHLIGHTS: This grand looper takes a tour around the base of the Verdugo Mountains and includes a canyon visit to boot! The route starts at Crescenta Valley Park, drops down into La Tuna Canyon, returning via Glenoaks Blvd. to the foothills of Burbank (see Trip #36) and Glendale (see Trip #62). The scenic views throughout various sections of this trip are outstanding. Much of the trip is on quality Class X roadways; the exception is that the descent into La Tuna Canyon is on a steep, winding downhill with limited shoulder for biking.

TRAILHEAD: From the Foothill Fwy., exit south at Pennsylvania Ave. and turn right (west) in l/4 mile at Honolulu Ave. Motor about l/2 mile to the Crescenta Valley Park entrance at Dunsmore Ave.
    Bring a full bottle or two of water for this trip. Do not try this trip in the reverse direction unless you are a strong uphill biker! The ride out of La Tuna Canyon into La Crescenta is very difficult and the trip rating changes to "strenuous."

TRIP DESCRIPTION: **Honolulu Ave.** From the park, turn left (west) on Honolulu Ave. and bike uphill to Boston Ave. (0.3), cross under the Foothill Fwy., and begin a steeper uphill just beyond. The route flattens and climbs again before reaching a split in 0.6 mile from Boston Ave. Honolulu Ave. ends. To the right is Tujunga Canyon Blvd.; our route is to the left on La Tuna Canyon Rd.
    La Tuna Canyon Rd. Cruise past the Verdugo Hills Golf Course and sweat out a very steep upgrade alongside the freeway, reaching a flat in 0.8 mile. Pass under the freeway (2.1) and begin a steep, winding descent into the canyon. The road continues through the narrowing canyon past a few isolated residences (3.9), reaching a flattening grade in another 0.3 mile.
    Parallel the La Tuna Canyon Wash, passing a small dam/debris basin and light residential area. Within a mile is a rustic area complete with several mini-ranches. The flat roadway passes Old Buckboard Ln. (5.8) and enters an area where the canyon widens significantly. Within the next mile, the highway returns to civilization, passing more residences in the Wheatland Ave. area and a gas

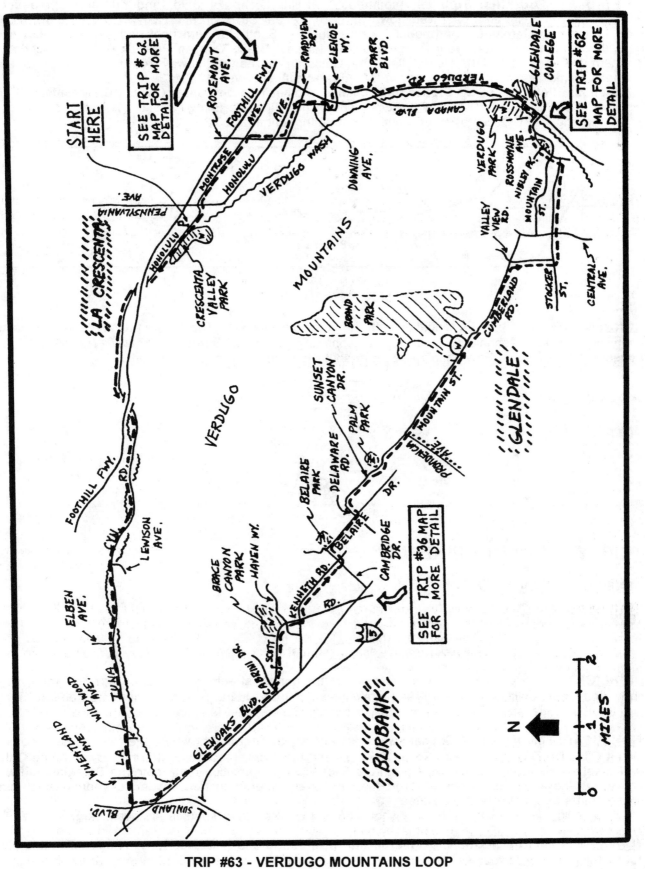

TRIP #63 - VERDUGO MOUNTAINS LOOP

station and other commercial enterprises at Sunland Blvd. (6.8). There are plenty of rest and fuel-up/water stops in this area. Turn left (south) and bike 0.2 mile further to Glenoaks Blvd.

Burbank Foothills. Turn left (southeast) on flat Glenoaks Blvd. and ride through a light commercial/residential area past Nettletown St. (7.5), Lanark St. (8.2), and Hollywood Wy. (8.8). In 0.3 mile, turn left on Carbini Dr. and pedal 0.2 mile uphill to Scott Rd. Turn right and in a short distance pass through the motorized vehicle barricade. Pedal past Brace Canyon Park (9.9), then proceed to Kenneth Rd. and turn left. Now follow the Class III Burbank Bikeway route (Trip #36) to the northeasternmost point at Sunset Canyon Dr. and Providencia Ave. (13.2).

Glendale Foothills to La Crescenta. Continue another mile on Sunset Canyon Dr./Mountain St. to the entrance to Brand Park. Follow the directions of the Glendale Bikeway route (Trip #55) and return to the trip origin at Crescenta Valley Park. The total trip length is 23.9 miles.

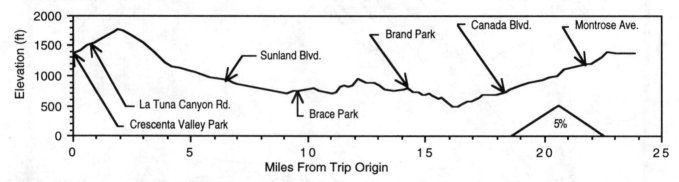

CONNECTING TRIPS: 1) Continuation with the Glendale Bikeway (Trip #62) - the Verdugo Mountains Loop includes the Glendale Bikeway trip; 2) connection with the Burbank Bikeway (Trip #36) - from Sunset Canyon Dr. and Providencia Ave., turn south (downhill) on the latter street.

TRIP #64 - DUARTE BIKEWAY

GENERAL LOCATION: Duarte

LEVEL OF DIFFICULTY: Loop - easy
Distance - 5.0 miles
Elevation gain - essentially flat

HIGHLIGHTS: This easy-going ride tours some of the quieter streets in Duarte, passes several inviting parks and finishes with a 1.7-mile Class I straight-away on the Duarte Bikeway. There are frequent views into the residential-spotted foothills and of the nearby San Gabriel Mountains along the way.

TRAILHEAD: Follow the San Gabriel Fwy. to its end at Huntington Dr., where the road name becomes Mount Olive Dr. Drive 1/4 mile to Royal Oaks Dr. and turn right, proceeding 1/2 mile to the Royal Oaks Park western entry at Vineyard Ave. From the Foothill Fwy., transition north onto the San Gabriel Fwy. and follow the above directions. The grassy park is equipped with tree shade, restrooms, numerous sports courts and a children's play area.

Bring a light water supply. This is a short ride and several water sources are available.

TRIP DESCRIPTION: South and Westbound. Bike east a short distance to Las Lomas Rd. and turn south. Bike on a wide roadway through a residential neighborhood. In about 0.5 mile, at the next street beyond Huntington Dr., is Maynard Dr. Turn right and bike to Crossfield Dr., then turn left and make another right on Central Ave. (1.1) This route takes cyclists on the periphery of a large fenced maintenance and storage complex at the terminus of Las Lomas Ave.

Pedal on Central Ave., a lightly used freeway frontage road, and pass the Otis Gordon Sports Park (portable restroom, sports fields, children's play area) before reaching Mount Olive Dr. Cycle another 0.8 mile to Highland Ave. and Northview Park (playing fields), taking in the San Gabriel Mountains and scattered foothill residences just to the north. Beyond is Duarte High School, then the southern tip of the Duarte Sports Park. (water, restrooms, tree shade, playing fields, courts), just before reaching Buena Vista St. (2.6).

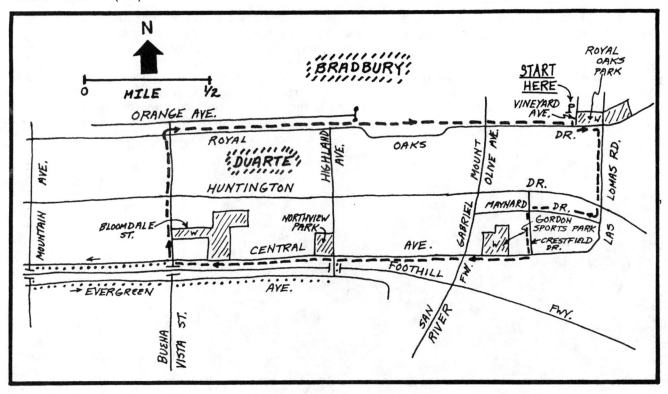

TRIP #64 - DUARTE BIKEWAY

North and Eastbound. Turn right and pedal toward the mountains on a busier street with a wide bikeway. At Huntington Dr. is a small commercial complex and 0.3 mile further is Royal Oaks Dr. (3.2). Across the street, sandwiched between Royal Oaks Dr. and Orange Ave. is the pleasant, tree-lined, Class I Duarte Bikeway. Bike east on the wide bike/walk path enjoying the local flora and an occasional view of the San Gabriels. The 1.7-mile path crosses under the petite Mt. Olive Dr. bridge and then works its way to the Vineyard Ave. terminus. (5.0).

<u>CONNECTING TRIPS</u>: Connection with the San Gabriel River tour (Trip #22E) - from Las Lomas Rd. and Huntington Dr., bike east 1/4 mile on the latter road and look for the entry on the river's east side.

219

TRIP #65 - SAN DIMAS CANYON ROAD

GENERAL LOCATION: San Dimas

LEVEL OF DIFFICULTY: Up and back - moderate to strenuous
Distance - 8.9 miles
Elevation gain - variable moderate-to-steep grade

HIGHLIGHTS: This short canyon ride takes cyclists from the city streets into the foothills of the San Gabriel Mountains. The roadway is narrow and has many blind curves on the upper stretches, although the auto traffic is low speed and sparse. From San Dimas proper, the route climbs modestly past the San Dimas Park and Recreation Center, then steepens as it follows San Dimas Creek up into the Angeles National Forest. The uppermost stretches wind along the canyon's east side above the San Dimas Reservoir, then drop down to the rustic San Dimas Fire Station. The paved road ends at a locked gate just beyond; auto traffic beyond the gate is restricted to cabin owners and fat-tire bikers.

San Dimas Reservoir Dam

TRAILHEAD: From California Hwy. 30 westbound (the western extension of the Foothill Fwy. in San Dimas), exit at N. San Dimas Ave. and turn north. At the next major thoroughfare (Baseline Rd.), turn east (right) and continue 3/4 mile, crossing San Dimas Canyon Rd. Park in this residential area under one of the tall trees. From the east on Baseline Rd., veer right at Foothill Blvd. and drive 1/4 mile to San Dimas Canyon Rd. Turn south (left) and left again at Baseline Rd. for parking. (Baseline Rd. cannot be reached directly from the east by car.)

The above start point allows a full rural tour of San Dimas Canyon Rd., which starts just above Foothill Blvd. An alternate is to start at the San Dimas Park and Recreation Center, which is about 1/3 mile above Foothill Blvd. The park has tree shade, grass, restrooms, picnic facilities, and recreation fields.

Bring a filled water bottle for the climb on hot summer days. The only public water source is at San Dimas Park and Recreation Center.

TRIP DESCRIPTION: **Up to Golden Hills Rd.** Bike across Foothill Blvd. and stare into the local foothills. (Surprise, surprise!) A sign immediately suggests that cyclists on this Class III route use the sidewalk, which disappears a short distance up the road. In 0.3-plus miles is Sycamore Canyon Rd. and the alluring San Dimas Park and Recreation Center. Beyond, the modest climb continues on tree-lined road past Fernridge Dr. (0.8) and passes alongside the San Dimas Canyon Golf Course. The San Dimas Wash is on the right. A short downhill is followed by a bridge crossing over San Dimas Creek (1.8). In 0.2 mile the road narrows further and Golden Hills Rd. comes up on the right. This is the last residential entry of the uphill ride.

On to (Paved) Road's End. The narrow road follows the canyon with San Dimas Creek's abundant greenery to the left . Near (2.4) the overhanging tree shade graces the road and in 0.3 mile, San Dimas Canyon Rd. enters the Angeles National Forest. Just beyond and to the left is a group of Forest Service structures, followed by the first glimpse of the San Dimas Reservoir dam. A set of steep "U"-

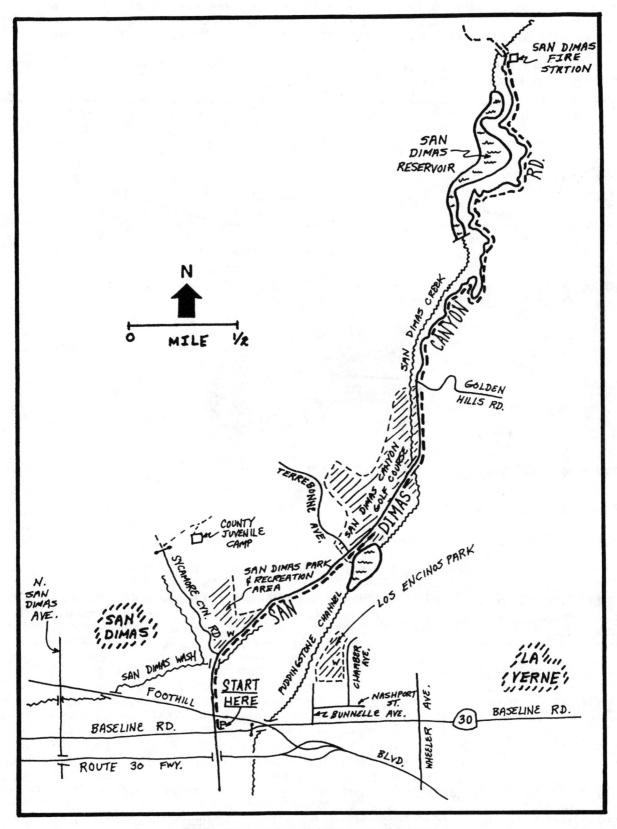

TRIP #65 - SAN DIMAS CANYON ROAD

bends leads up to a more open, exposed area with clearer views of the dam. A flat gives way to a sharp left and a view from above the dam and reservoir (3.2). The next 0.8 mile follows the winding contour of the east canyon wall on ever-narrowing road to the north end of the reservoir. (In this area, it is difficult for two cars to pass, however a single slow-moving car and a biker work out well together.) At about (4.1), the road begins downhill and returns to forested environs, passing the San Dimas Fire Station in 0.2 mile. At 4.4-plus miles is the end of the city-maintained road and a gated access restricted to cabin owners.

   If you have a fat-tire bike, continue onward should your heart desire. Otherwise, all that remains is a short climb and a great runout back to the start point!

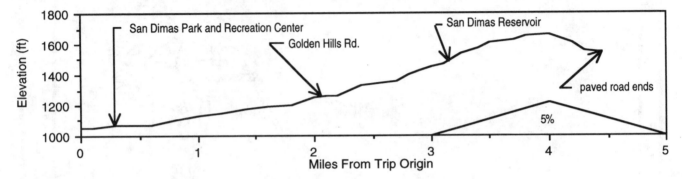

CONNECTING TRIPS: Connection with the Baseline Road tour (Trip #45) - at the intersection of Sand Canyon Rd. and Baseline Rd. follow the latter road east.

TRIP #66 - THOMPSON CREEK TRAIL

GENERAL LOCATION: Claremont

LEVEL OF DIFFICULTY: Up and back - easy
Distance - 4.7 miles
Elevation gain - mild steady grade eastbound

HIGHLIGHTS: This trail is a hidden treasure even to many local area residents. The 2.3-plus-mile route follows Thompson Creek for most of its journey. The well-designed and -maintained trail passes under a varied, light tree canopy for about 3/4 of its length, then transitions into open space for the trip's remainder. Along the way are water fountains, sitting benches, and pastoral Higginbotham Park with a restroom and unique children's playground. Thompson Creek Trail is a light but scenic workout for adults and families alike.

TRAILHEAD: From Baseline Rd., turn north on N. Towne Ave., and drive several hundred feet to a parking area. This is a private entry, normally left open to the public. However, property owners do have the right to deny access. Starting near the trail's western end allows cyclists to do all the climbing on the outgoing leg, which results in a nice coast back to the parking area on the return. There is a public parking area at the east end which is at the intersection of Mills Ave. and Mt. Baldy Rd. To get there from Baseline Rd., turn north at Mills Ave. and drive a little over one mile to the point where Mt. Baldy Rd. originates and veers right. Continue a couple of hundred feet on Mills Ave. to the parking area.

   Well-placed water fountains are available on the trail west of Indian Hills Blvd. The trail is open from 6AM to 10PM.

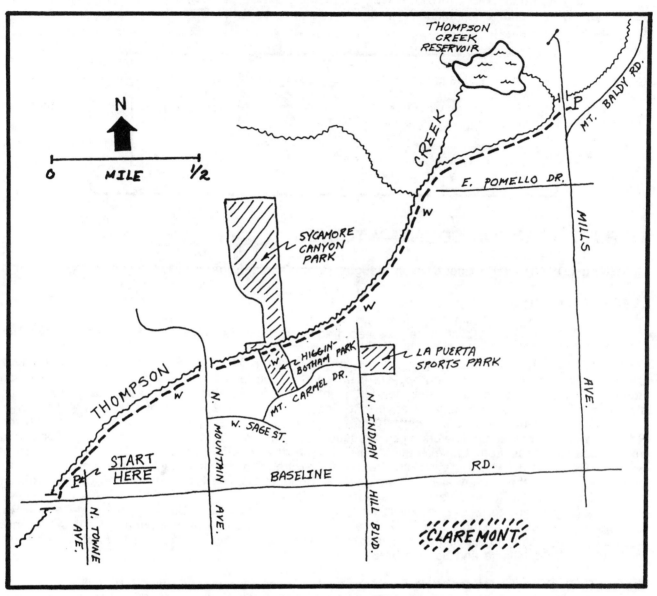

TRIP #66 - THOMPSON CREEK TRAIL

TRIP DESCRIPTION: **Towne Ave. to Pomello Dr.** Join the trail along the concrete channel which is Thompson's Creek and head eastbound. The trailside treecover, foothills to the left and trailside residences on the right are typical of this segment. In 0.4 mile is the first of many walk/bike/equestrian accesses from the residential area. (The equestrians use the dirt trail which parallels the walking/biking trail.) Nearby is the first of three water fountain/sitting bench combinations.

The trail crosses Mountain Ave., the single trafficked street on the route, in another 0.1 mile. Just beyond (0.7) is a trailside restroom on the northern edge of Higginbotham Park; this grassy shaded park has picnic benches and a unique children's play area complete with miniature locomotive, stage coach, southwestern adobe house and other playtime amenities. At (1.0) near another water fountain/park bench is a trail fork. Stay to the left alongside the creek. The last water fountain is just before the trail intersection with the Pomello Dr. terminus (1.6).

Pomello Dr. to Trail's End. The trail stays alongside the creek, but now enters a broad, treeless open space. The climb steepens and heads more northeasterly as the wall of the Thompson Creek Reservoir comes into view. The trail pulls away from Thompson Creek and passes under some power transmission lines near the top of the grade (2.1). In 0.1-plus mile is the trail exit and entry into a large parking area along Mills Ave.

The Return. Coast back to Towne Ave., maintaining a safe pace with the foot traffic in mind. To see the entire trail, continue another 0.1 mile to trail's end at Foothill Blvd., then retrace the path back to the parking area (4.7).

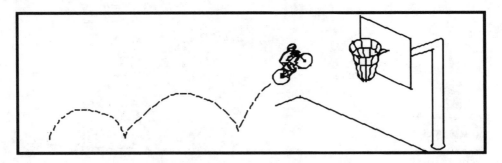

TRIP #67 - CANYON COUNTRY TOUR

GENERAL LOCATION: Bouquet Canyon, Saugus, Santa Clarita, Forrest Park

LEVEL OF DIFFICULTY: Loop - strenuous
Distance - 20.3 miles
Elevation gain - steep grades on Sand Canyon Rd. and Vasquez Canyon Rd.

HIGHLIGHTS: This tour is a canyon lover's delight, visiting Bouquet, Soledad, Sand and Vasquez Canyons in a single loop. The journey starts at comfy Bouquet Canyon Park and mostly coasts on Bouquet Canyon Rd. to the trip's elevation low point at the intersection with Soledad Canyon Rd. The steady moderate climb on Soledad Canyon Rd. includes a 6.7-mile stretch of Class I path, much of which is alongside the Santa Clara River. A turn north leads to a heady summit climb on Sand Canyon Rd. followed by another uphill workout on Vasquez Canyon Rd. Views of both the canyon floors and developed city areas from these summits are well worth the effort. Vasquez Canyon Rd. ends at Bouquet Canyon Rd., where cyclists are treated to a refreshing downhill back to the start point. Note that some parts of the journey are on busy (parts of Bouquet Canyon Rd. and Soledad Canyon Rd.) or narrow (Sand Canyon Rd. and Vasquez Canyon Rd.) Class X road.

There is an option to take a shorter route using a bypass on Whites Canyon Rd./Plum Canyon Rd. Cyclists are treated to a single steep, but scenic, 400-foot-plus climb on the bypass for this 12.8-mile alternative. In addition to reducing trip mileage, this alternative provides some of the better views into the southern Santa Clarita and Saugus areas.

TRAILHEAD: From the Golden State Fwy., exit east at Valencia Blvd. and drive 2-1/2 miles to Bouquet Canyon Rd. Turn left (northeast) and continue 2-3/4 miles to Urbandale Ave. Turn left, drive 1/3 mile to Alaminos Dr., turn right and go four blocks to Wellston Dr. Turn left and drive up to Bouquet Canyon Park at the end of the road. At the park are limited shade, water, restrooms, playgrounds, recreational fields, picnic facilities, and both tennis and basket ball courts. There are also hiking trails and some mountain bike terrain nearby.

Bring a couple of water bottles for hot days. There are several public water facilities on Bouquet Canyon Rd. and Soledad Canyon Rd.; however, Sand Canyon Rd. and Vasquez Canyon Rd. are waterless.

TRIP DESCRIPTION: **Bouquet Canyon.** Retrace the incoming route to Bouquet Canyon Rd. and turn right onto a Class II roadway. Coast past Haskell Canyon Rd. and scope out the massive pipelines of the California Aqueduct in the hills to the left. The Class II path disappears at Alamogordo Rd.; across the street is Central Park -- this massive sports and recreation facility has restrooms) but little shade. On the continued downhill, the route passes one of many shopping centers at Seco Canyon Rd. (2.4). In another 0.8 mile is the trip's low point at the Soledad Canyon Rd. intersection, reached after crossing the Santa Clara River.

Soledad Canyon. Turn left and traverse busy and fast-moving Soledad Canyon Rd. on a steady, 7.5-mile moderate upgrade to Sand Canyon Rd. Our preferred option is to take the Class I bikeway/walkway (the Santa Clarita Trail) on the north side of the street. The initial couple of miles are (relatively) lightly developed, but do include the Saugus Speedway. The Class I path shifts to the

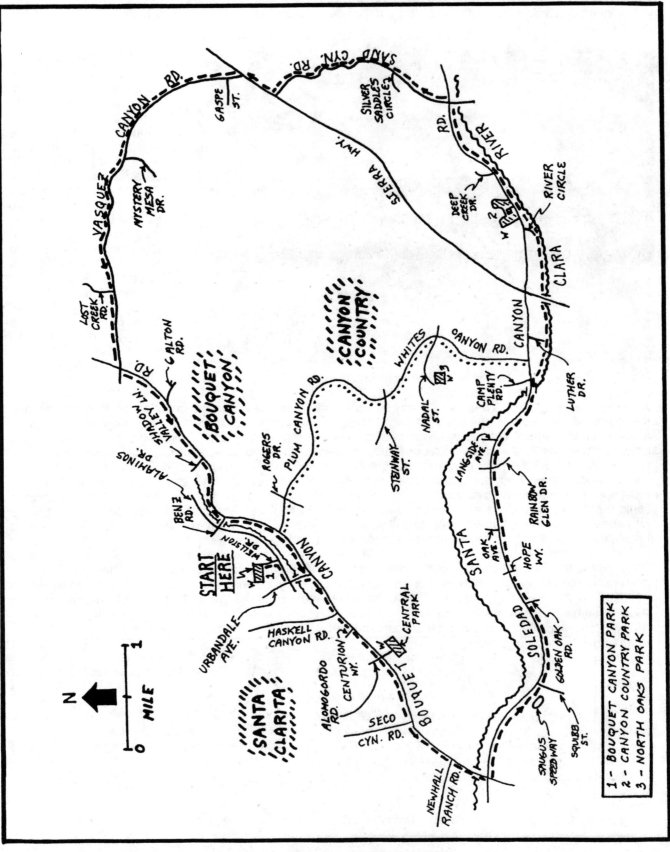

TRIP #67 - CANYON COUNTRY TOUR

south side at Golden Oak Rd. (6.7) and stays alongside Soledad Canyon Rd. to the next Santa Clara River crossing (7.4). At this juncture, cyclists can ride the streets or, better, stay on the bike path. The path swings away from Soledad Canyon Rd., passing alongside a shopping complex, and follows the banks of the Santa Clara River.

Sand Canyon Road Near the Summit

The bikeway tracks east and passes under White's Canyon Rd. (7.7), Sierra Hwy. (8.6) and the Antelope Valley Fwy. (9.5) before reaching its terminus at an outlet just west of Deep Creek Dr. (9.9). (There are also outlets to the first two overpassing streets, as well as one to Soledad Canyon Rd. just east of Sierra Hwy.) Along this stretch are steady views of the wide riverbed. Once back on Soledad Canyon Rd., it is another 0.8 mile to Sand Canyon Rd. on Class X roadway.

Sand Canyon and Vasquez Canyon. Turn left (north) and start a mild grade through rapidly-thinning development and relatively barren landscape, which is typical of the two canyons. The grade steepens and the road narrows as it winds along the contour of the surrounding hills. In 1.3 miles is the summit, where there is a partial view of the lower Mint Canyon area. A swift 0.5-mile downgrade leads to Sierra Hwy. (12.6). A right turn and 0.3-mile flat lead to Vasquez Canyon Rd.

Turn onto that road and pass over the Mint Canyon Wash and cycle through a hill-dotted landscape with scattered small ranchos. A short flat gives way to a 1.1-mile climb to the tour's second scenic crest, where there is a view north into Vasquez Canyon. On the fast downhill, take some time to stop and admire the sculpted rock formations on the left. The route passes Lost Creek Rd. on a moderated grade and reaches Bouquet Canyon Rd. in another 0.6 mile (16.5).

The Bouquet Canyon Return. Turn right and pedal a satisfying downgrade through rural ranchland with the first treeside shade in quite a spell. The route reenters the signed Santa Clarita City limits, passes a small shopping center, where the Class II bikeway begins, and reaches Plum Canyon Rd. in another 0.3 mile (19.1). In 0.5 mile is Urbandale Ave.; right turn leads to the backtrack route to Bouquet Canyon Park (20.3).

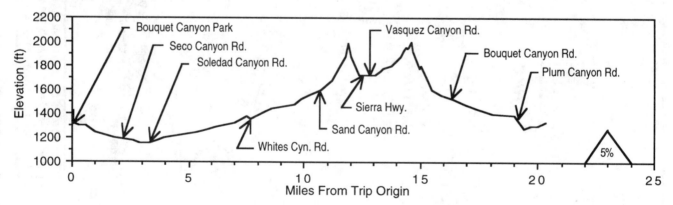

White's Canyon/Plum Canyon Shortcut. A shorter (moderate-to-strenuous) loop involves staying on Soledad Canyon Rd. (as opposed to taking the Class I route junction along the Santa Clara River.) 0.3 mile to White's Canyon Rd. Turn left onto a moderate grade which becomes a serious climb to a false summit in 1.3 miles. Pump past Steinway St. and reach the crest in another 0.3 mile. Take in both the city and canyon views before following a well-deserved 0.4-mile runout through less-developed area on what is now Plum Canyon Rd. Pass Rogers Dr. (3.7) and cycle on flatter terrain 0.4 mile to Bouquet Canyon Rd. Next is 2.6 mostly-downhill miles to Urbandale Dr. and a return to Bouquet Canyon Park. The total tour length with this option is 12.8 miles.

CONNECTING TRIPS: 1) Connection with the Valencia Loop (Trip #68) - at the intersection of Bouquet Canyon Rd. and Soledad Canyon Rd., follow the latter road southwest 1-3/4 miles (the road name changes to Valencia Blvd.) to McBean Pkwy. Turn left and proceed a short distance to Del Monte Dr.; 2) connection with the San Francisquito Canyon and Bouquet Canyons ride (Trip #69) - the trips share a common route below Vasquez Canyon Rd. on Bouquet Canyon Rd.

TRIP #68 - VALENCIA LOOP

GENERAL LOCATION: Valencia

LEVEL OF DIFFICULTY: Loop - easy
Distance - 7.8 miles
Elevation gain - periodic moderate grades

HIGHLIGHTS: This is an interesting Canyon Country tour which travels both the main thoroughfares and residential "back waters" of Valencia. This predominantly Class X ride on wide city streets cruises through pleasant tree-lined sections of Orchard Village Rd. and McBean Pkwy., then diverts to a quiet residential runout just west of the Santa Clara River. There is an option to add two excellent miles to the trip by touring scenic Old Orchard Park and the surrounding residential area.

In addition, just off the main route is the 3-1/2 -mile Class I South Fork Trail which plies the South Fork of the Santa Clara River. Finally, there is a short excursion to William S. Hart Park, which has the Hart Mansion with its knockout vista point, the Saugus Station museum and some inviting natural grounds.

TRAILHEAD: From the Golden State Fwy., exit at Lyons Ave. and turn east. Drive about one mile (near Peachland Ave. on the south side of the road) and park along Lyons Ave. near Old Orchard Park. From the Antelope Fwy., exit at San Fernando Rd. and drive northwest two miles to Lyons Ave. Turn left (west) and drive about one mile to the park. Turn left on Avd. Rotella and left again into the small parking area. The park has trees, grass, restrooms, children's play areas and athletic courts.

Bring a filled water bottle in the summer. There are gas stations and other commercial establishments along the route, although we found few convenient public water sources. Bring an automobile roadmap as a backup should you miss any key roads in the southbound residential leg.

TRIP DESCRIPTION: **Old Orchard Park.** Before starting the main loop, take time to investigate the cozy bikeways within Old Orchard Park (see map insert) and the pleasant surrounding residential area. This is some fine family biking which represents about two miles of Class I trailway. This is a grand example of intelligent community planning!

Main Thoroughfares - Northbound. From near Avd. Rotella and Lyons Ave., bike along Class X Lyons Ave. past Avd. Entrana (0.3) and continue to Wiley Canyon Rd. (gas station) (0.7). Turn right (north) and pedal a moderate upgrade on the Class II path through a residential neighborhood. In a

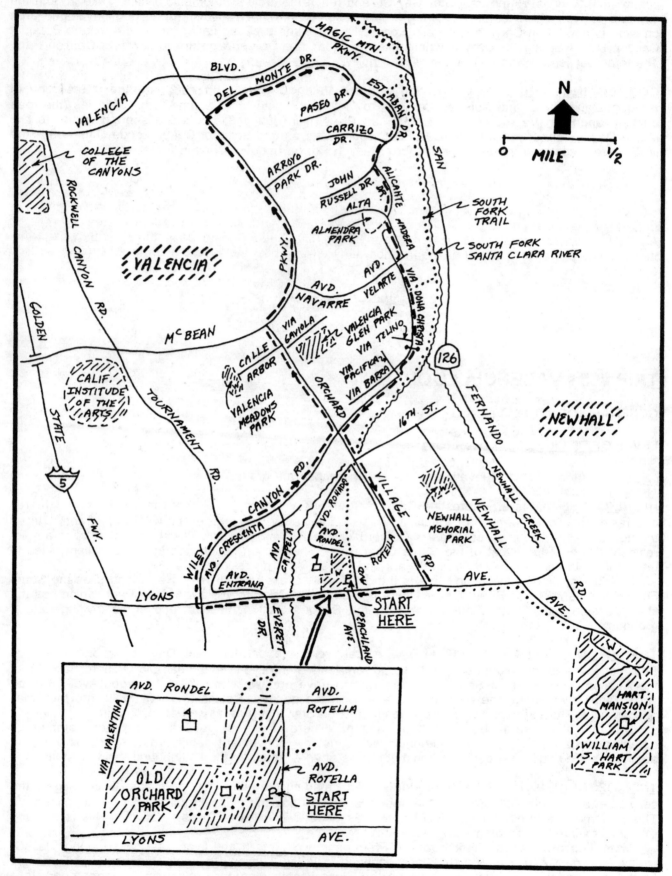

TRIP #68 - VALENCIA LOOP

short distance, follow the downgrade past Tournament Rd. onto a flat area near Avd. Cappela (1.3). In 0.4 mile turn left on Orchard Village Rd. and follow that tree-lined Class X road on a steady and modest upgrade to Mill Valley Rd. (2.0).

In another 0.2 mile is McBean Pkwy. Turn right on that Class X street passing some commercial areas, and bike beneath the roadside tree cover past Avd. Navarre (2.5). In 0.2 mile, near a shopping center, is a clear view north into the mountains. Just beyond is Arroyo Park Dr. (2.9) and 0.4 mile further is Del Monte Dr. The area is relatively open and flat and there is a sweeping panorama into the Santa Clarita Valley.

Residential Streets - Southbound. Turn right (east) on Del Monte Dr. and begin an extended stretch of ride through a quiet residential community. There are scattered community recreation centers with pools, volleyball courts, and other goodies (maybe even drinking water!) in this area. Follow the road 0.8 mile through a wide curve and turn left at Estaban Dr. (4.1). Cruise about 0.3 mile just past Carrizo Dr. and turn left on John Russell Dr.

Follow that road a short distance and turn left again at Alicante Dr. (4.6). Bike along the curved roadway to its end at grassy, open Almendra Park, then turn left at Alta Madera. In short order, make a right at Avd. Velarte and left at Via Dona Christa (5.5). Cycle through this residential area 0.5 mile to Via Telino, transit a walk-through fence and follow Via Dona Christa as it turns right (west) and becomes Via Barra. In 0.2 mile at Via Pacifica, turn left and bike a short distance to Wiley Canyon Rd. (6.3).

Turn right and cruise 0.3 mile to Orchard Village Rd. and turn left. At Avd. Ronada, one option is to enter the residential area and bike on the Class I bike path back to the park. However, our reference route continues south 0.8 mile on Orchard Village Rd. and turns right (west) at Lyons Ave. (7.4). All that remains is a short 0.4 mile pedal back to Old Orchard Park (7.8).

South Fork Trail Excursion. At Estaban Dr., just beyond Sandalia Dr., is an entry to South Fork Park. Other entries along the reference route are at Via Dona Christa just south of Via Flored and Via Pacific at it's south end. From the Estaban Dr. entry, the Class I path follows the west bank of the South Fork of the Santa Clara River 1-3/4 miles north and east to McBean Pkwy. and south 1-3/4 miles to the Orchard Village Rd. Bikers and walkers share this path, which supplies numerous river vista points and a variety of city views. (Additional trail entries are at McBean Pkwy., Valencia Town Center, Valencia Blvd., Magic Mountain Pkwy. and Orchard Village Rd.)

William S. Hart Park. From Orchard Village Rd. and Lyons Ave., bike east 1/3 mile to Newhall Ave. and turn right. In 1/2 mile, just after the fusion with San Fernando Rd., turn right at the marked entry to the park. The expansive lower grounds have the headquarters and visitor's center as well as water restrooms, barbecue facilities, grassy grounds and abundant treecover. The Mason Mansion, the park's highlight, is reached via a small, steep roadway (not open to bicycles) from the lower park. From the mansion area there is a grand 360-degree view of the local environs. The Saugus Station and Museum is at the park's southeastern edge along San Fernando Rd. It offers a historic look at vehicles used for travel in bygone eras.

CONNECTING TRIPS: Connection with the Santa Clarita Valley Tour (Trip #67) - at the intersection of McBean Pkwy. and Del Monte Dr., continue north to Valencia Blvd. and turn right (east).

TRIP #69 - SAN FRANCISQUITO AND BOUQUET CANYONS

GENERAL LOCATION: Santa Clarita, Green Valley, Leona Valley, Bouquet Canyon

LEVEL OF DIFFICULTY: **CANYONS LOOP** - very strenuous
                  Distance - 40.8 miles
                  Elevation gain - several steep-to-sheer grades
                 RIFT ZONE LOOP - strenuous to very strenuous
                  Distance - 22.8 miles
                  Elevation gain - several steep-to-sheer grades

HIGHLIGHTS: Two separate loop trips are provided. The **CANYONS LOOP** follows San Francisquito Canyon, Spunky Canyon Rd. and Bouquet Canyon Rd. in successive order and starts from Santa Clarita. After a mild pedaling stretch, the ride climbs almost 15 miles on the way to Spunky Canyon Rd. Along the way are Powerhouses #1 and 2 and their mammoth hillside penstocks, part of the Los Angeles Aqueduct. Between the two are the remnants of the St. Francis Dam, whose collapse resulted in the single-event, second greatest loss of life in California history. Spunky Canyon Rd. passes through pastoral Green Valley, climbs to a superb valley overlook and flies down to the Bouquet Reservoir. The route shifts onto Bouquet Canyon Rd., follows a last-gasp upgrade, then works its way downhill through serene Bouquet Canyon before returning to the bustle of Santa Clarita. The total elevation gain on this tour is over 3000 feet!

The **RIFT ZONE LOOP** starts from the Green Valley area and plies upper San Francisquito Canyon, Leona Valley and upper Bouquet Canyon Rd. The ride starts from the Green Valley area and climbs to an overlook of Leona Valley on San Francisquito Canyon Rd., then dives down to the valley and Elizabeth Lake Rd. A tour of the rift zone and the town of Leona Valley follows, leading to the Bouquet Canyon junction. An easy-going valley ride gives way to a steep climb to an overlook of Bouquet Reservoir and a swift downhill to that body of water. Loop closure is via Spunky Canyon Rd., which just reverses the route discussed in the loop above. This is a 2000-plus elevation-gain ride.

An option for cyclists in excellent shape seeking a greater challenge is to continue past Spunky Canyon Rd., do the three legs of the RIFT ZONE LOOP and again bypass Spunky Canyon Rd. at the Bouquet Reservoir. The final leg is the Bouquet Canyon Rd. segment of the CANYONS LOOP. (Don't get us wrong. The two loops initially described are side splitters!) This little monster requires over 3500 feet of hill-climbing over the 52.4 miles!

TRAILHEAD: From the Golden State Fwy., exit east at Valencia Blvd. and drive 2-1/2 miles to Bouquet Canyon Rd. Turn left (northeast) and continue one mile to Seco Canyon Rd. Turn left, and motor 1/3 mile to Guadilamar Dr. Turn left and enter the parking area of Santa Clarita Park. The park has tree shade, grass, water, restrooms, picnic tables, sports fields, children's playground and a pool. From the Lancaster/Palmdale area, starting points might be Leona Valley or Elizabeth Lake off of Elizabeth Lake Rd. or Green Valley on Spunky Canyon Rd. Elizabeth Lake itself is a good parking area, as is a spot near the diner or general store in Green Valley or Leona Valley. Note that starting from this direction "saves" the rugged uphill for late in the ride.

Powerhouse #2 and the Penstocks

Bring a couple of filled water bottles or load up at the trailhead. There are few public sources directly on the upper part of the route. However, there are a service station, diner, and market in Green Valley (partial loop) and Leona Valley (full loop) and numerous support facilities in the lower Bouquet Canyon area (both loops). Keep in mind that the trip will be hot and dry in the summer. (Alternately, this can be a very cold ride in the winter!)

TRIP DESCRIPTION: CANYONS LOOP. Santa Clarita to San Francisquito Powerhouse #2. Turn left (north) on Seco Canyon Rd. and climb lazily for 0.8 mile to Copper Hill Dr. In 0.5 mile is Northpark Dr. (to the south)/San Francisquito Canyon Rd. (north), where our route takes the latter street and leaves the dense residential environs almost immediately on a short climb. The road works its way toward and drops near to the bed of the Santa Clarita River, then begins a northerly journey on the east side of San Francisquito Canyon, passing Lady Linda Ln. (on the left) (3.3). In a little over 1.5 miles is the

Angeles National Forest boundary. (What is interesting is that the sparse tree cover to this point thins even further beyond the boundary.)

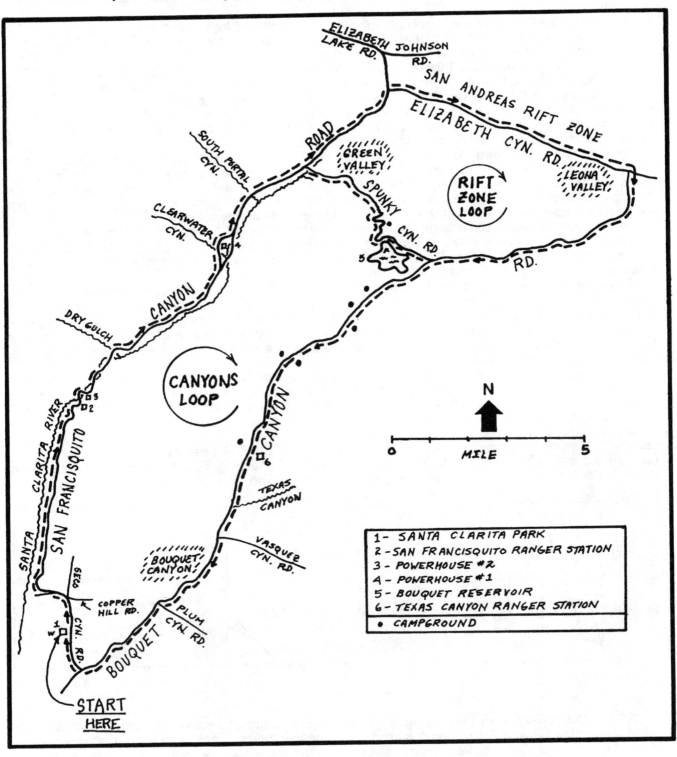

TRIP #69 - SAN FRANCISQUITO AND BOUQUET CANYONS

The two-lane winding road continues further into the narrowing canyon, passing the Drinkwater Flat 4X4 road (dirt) at (6.7). A few crossings over narrow bridges brings cyclists around a bend to view a massive group of penstocks (water conduits to us normal folk) coming down the hillsides to San Francisquito Powerhouse #2 (7.4). This structure is part of the Los Angeles Aqueduct. Just before reaching the powerhouse is an entry to the San Francisquito Ranger Station; stop and read about the

231

1928 St. Francis Dam collapse, an event that resulted in the deaths of 400 people downstream. Another 1.5 miles upstream are large chunks of concrete and steel in the riverbed, the remnants of the old dam.

The Climb to Green Valley. Continue uphill through scattered tree cover, pass Dry Gulch Fire Rd. and cycle by the San Francisquito Conservation Camp (11.8). In another 0.6 mile is the Bee Canyon Ranch turnoff, followed by a steepening grade that takes cyclists to a grand vista area below the penstocks of San Francisquito Powerhouse #1. At the junction with paved, private Pelton St. (13.9), general traffic stays to the left and cyclists follow a downright nasty switchback upgrade, pass dirt Clearwater Canyon Rd. and transit near the penstocks themselves. The grade moderates and lets up near where the power transmission lines cross San Francisquito Canyon Rd. (15.0). A brief coast and renewed climb lead past South Portal Canyon and its namesake road, residences begin to reappear on what is now a flat, and riders meet Spunky Canyon Rd. at (17.0).

Spunky Canyon Road. Turn right (east) on this road pedaling through the tree-dotted town of Green Valley. At Ensenada Rd. are a gas station, general store and eatery (17.9). (None appeared prone to offer restroom facilities except for paying customers.) Pedal to the outskirts of town and pass the Spunky Canyon Campground in another 0.8 mile (tree shade, porta-potties, picnic facilities, but we found no water, as was true of the remaining campgrounds on the return leg.)

Shortly, a very steep climb begins which takes cyclists upward for another 1.5 miles, a segment with great over-the-shoulder views of Green Valley. Beyond the summit is an equally sinuous and steep downhill with excellent Bouquet Reservoir vistas. The road dumps out alongside the reservoir and winds its way eastward to Bouquet Canyon Rd. (23.4).

Bouquet Canyon Rd. and the Downhill. "It ain't over till it's over," because another steep 0.7-mile climb awaits. Beyond the summit are numerous Bouquet Reservoir views as the road bends around that reservoir's contour. The now tree-shaded road heads downhill alongside Bouquet Canyon Creek and passes the marked Bouquet Canyon Recreation Area and a collection of cabins (25.7). Del Sur Rd. and Big Oaks Lodge (29.0) come up and bicyclists pass a dense mixed grove of trees with a palm tree immersed in the middle!

The narrowing canyon leads past the Texas Canyon Ranger Station (32.1) and both Zuni and Las Cantiles Campgrounds (with interesting rock formations nearby), reaching the Saugus Ranger Station at (32.7). In 0.5 mile is the Angeles National Forest boundary and a few scattered ranches, Coarsegold and Lenny Rds., and an area where the canyon widens. Passage by Vasquez Canyon Rd. (35.0) signals a return to a more developed area, with the Santa Clarita City limit reached in 1.7 miles. Just beyond is a small shopping center and the beginning of a Class II bikeway, with Plum Canyon Rd. reached 0.3 mile later (38.0). Glide alongside the myriad of shopping plazas and reach Seco Canyon Rd. in 2.4 miles. All that is left is to pedal a mild upgrade back to Santa Clarita Park (40.8).

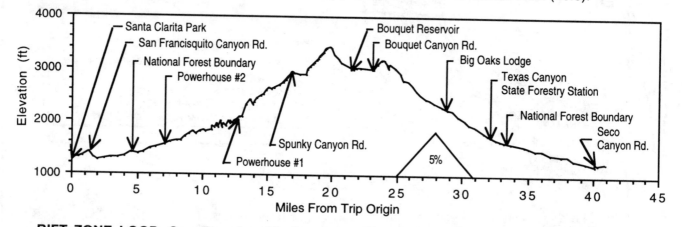

RIFT ZONE LOOP. San Francisquito Canyon Rd. At Spunky Canyon Rd., start a mild climb on San Francisquito Canyon Rd., passing numerous residences on the right hand side. Just above Calle Manzanita, on the left, is San Francisquito Campground (0.5), beyond which the residential development all but ends. The uphill steepens considerably and the road passes the Green Valley Ranger Station (1.5). The summit is reached in 0.7 mile, where there is an impressive view of the extended valley floor below. The exhilarating 0.9-mile downhill through a more barren landscape passes Leona Divide and Tule Divide Fire Rds. before bottoming at Elizabeth Lake Rd. (3.1).

Lake Elizabeth Road. Turn right (southeast) and begin a modest uphill pedal on the rural road through narrow Leona Valley. Though no signs proclaim it, this road lies nearly atop the San Andreas Rift Zone! Cyclists pass a llama ranch early on and enjoy a light rolling terrain on a general downhill which will continue all the way to Bouquet Canyon Rd. At (8.5) is 90th St. W. and a stop sign, which signals the town of Leona Valley's civic hub. There are a market, gas station and a couple of eateries nearby. Another 1.6 miles of this easy going valley pedal leads to Bouquet Canyon Rd.

Bouquet Canyon Road. Turn right (south) and cruise nearly two miles through a wide valley with agricultural fields, ranches and scattered residences, together with occasional fruit and flower stands. Next is a gut-busting 1.5-mile climb through a narrowing canyon alongside Bouquet Canyon Creek. At Lincoln Crest (13.6), the reward is a stunning view of the Bouquet Reservoir below. The winding highway plummets past the Leona Divide Fire Rd. toward the reservoir, then straightens appreciably and meets Spunky Canyon Rd. (16.7)

Spunky Canyon Road. This is just the reverse path on Spunky Canyon Rd. taken on the CANYONS LOOP. The lightly-used road follows the contour of the reservoir for 1.6 miles before turning into the hills and beginning a sweat-it-out upgrade. Now, however, cyclists ride the outside edge over a steep drop-off for a distance before reaching the protective shelter of the Spunky Canyon side, where the road meshes into the hills. At the summit near the 20-mile point, Green Valley is spread out below and to the west. Crane to the east into the hillsides and look for the plush growth of the Spunky Saddle Plantation, a marvelous clustered growth of human-planted trees. A very steep and winding downhill levels near the Spunky Canyon Campground (21.1). An easy ride through verdant Green Valley with its surrounding peaks leads back to the ride start at San Francisquito Canyon Rd. (22.9).

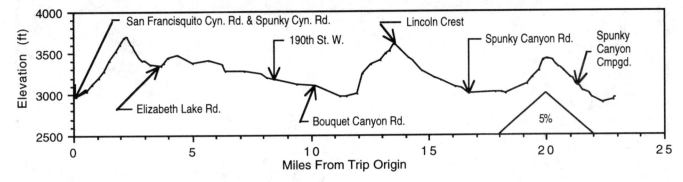

CONNECTING TRIPS: 1) Connection with the Canyon Country Tour (Trip #67) - the trips share a common route below Vasquez Canyon Rd. on Bouquet Canyon Rd.; 2) connection with the Old Ridge Route Rd. tour (Trip #70) - at Elizabeth Lake Rd. on the RIFT ZONE LOOP, turn west on that road and bike to Lake Hughes Rd.

TRIPS #70A-#70C OLD RIDGE ROUTE ROAD

This is a three-part ride that forms an 69-mile very strenuous loop. Riding the full loop is reserved for veteran riders in superior condition. The loop ride involves tackling over 6500-feet of elevation gain! The Lake Hughes Road (initial) and Pine Canyon Road (middle) segments are on sometimes-narrow, winding roadway with light, but periodic, fast-moving traffic. The Old Ridge Route Road (last) segment, though paved, has a 20-mile non-maintained section and is best done on a mountain bike. If using a fat-tire road bike, bring a beefed-up tire patch kit as a precaution. The non-maintained segment is little-used and remote.

For the full loop, bring 3-4 water bottles to see you through the waterless stretchs. Beyond Castaic, we found water only at tiny Lake Hughes at a single small market. If not willing to rely on that water source, consider bringing 5-6 quarts of water.

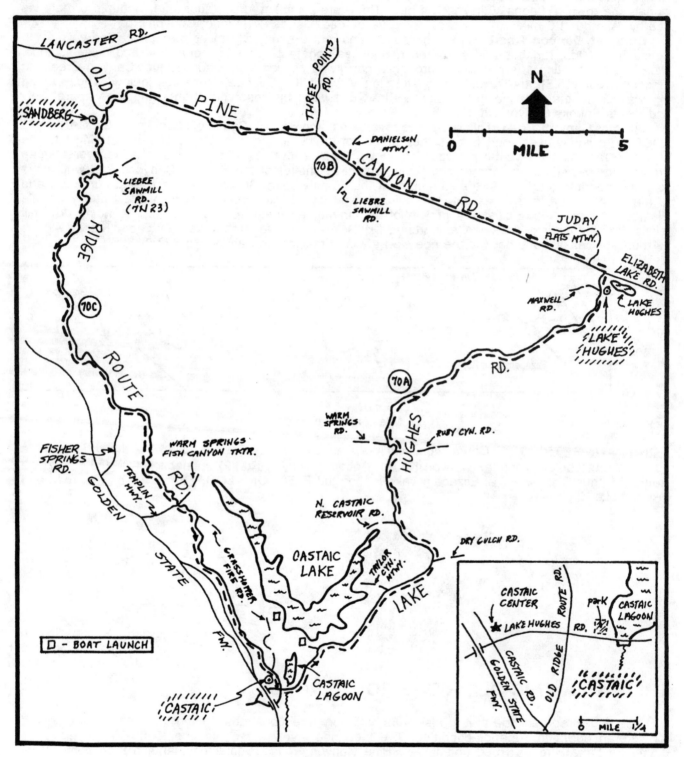

TRIP #70 - OLD RIDGE ROUTE ROAD

TRIP #70A - LAKE HUGHES ROAD

GENERAL LOCATION: Castaic, Lake Hughes

<u>LEVEL OF DIFFICULTY</u>: One way - strenuous to very strenuous
Distance - 23.5 miles
Elevation gain - several long, moderate-to-steep grades

<u>HIGHLIGHTS</u>: This segment follows Lake Hughes Rd. from its origin in Castaic to its end at the small town of Lake Hughes. There is over 3000 feet of climb as the road works its way above Castaic Lake, plummets into the outlet of Elizabeth Lake Canyon and follows that canyon as it winds its way 13 miles and 1300 feet to Lake Hughes. On the way, there are superb Castaic Lake vistas and sporadic looks beyond the canyon walls to other distant canyons which pepper this region. Auto traffic is light and the traffic speed is low on the (generally) sinuous portions of the route; however, some drivers do push it in the straighter sections of roadway, requiring that cyclists stay vigilant and ready to hug the road shoulder.

<u>TRAILHEAD</u>: From the Golden State Fwy. in Castaic, exit east at Lake Hughes Rd. Park at Castaic Lake, then turn left at the next intersection, Castaic Rd. Several hundred feet up the road is the Castaic Center mall, with plenty of parking. An option is to start from the Castaic Lake Recreation Center, which is on Lake Hughes Rd. about 1/2 mile from the Castaic Rd. intersection.
   Bring 2-3 water bottles to see you through the waterless stretch between Castaic and Lake Hughes. Note that there is a Ranger station near the mid-point, should cyclists need emergency assistance.

<u>TRIP DESCRIPTION</u>: **Castaic to Warm Springs Road.** Return to Lake Hughes Rd. and turn east, passing Old Ridge Route Rd. (the full-loop outlet) and Castaic Lagoon and the Castaic Recreation Area just beyond (0.5). In 0.4 mile is the start of a steep climb above Castaic Lake. There are numerous lake vistas on the way up, which continue up to the Elizabeth Lake Canyon inlet. Pass the marked "Main Launch Ramp" at (2.3) and continue climbing through sage-brush-covered hillsides, reaching the Angeles National Forest Boundary in 0.8 mile. A short downhill gives way to a two-mile climb, which crests, then drops to the Dry Gulch Rd. junction (7.1).

Lake Hughes Road Above Castaic Lake

Lake Hughes Rd. climbs again for a mile, pulling back towards Castaic Lake, then begins a well-deserved downhill. Two miles into the downgrade is the N. Castaic Reservoir Rd. junction (10.1), reached shortly after a distinct entry into Lake Elizabeth Canyon. The road follows the canyon contour back uphill to a crest (11.6), then transits a relatively flat area, passing Ruby Canyon Rd. and reaching Warm Springs Rd. in 0.6 mile (13.2). There is a Ranger Station here, private camp facilities and other local amenities, all off the main road.

Warm Springs Road to Lake Hughes. Lake Hughes Rd. follows the winding canyon on a sustained uphill for the next ten-plus miles. For most of the way the road is not far above creekbed level. The route passes seasonal campgrounds at (14.8) and (19.6) and enters a forested zone. In another 0.3 mile is the private Canyon Meadows Baptist Conference Center, followed by the Forestry Nursery (Lake Hughes Unit) (20.0) and a couple more private campgrounds. In another 1.7 miles starts a series of small roadside ranches and the outskirts of the tiny community of Lake Hughes. At 23.5 is the junction with Pine Canyon Rd., complete with a small market and roadside tavern. (Note that tree-surrounded Lake Hughes itself can be reached with a 1/4-mile diversion east on Elizabeth Lake Rd. and a turn right (south) at Norblett Dr.

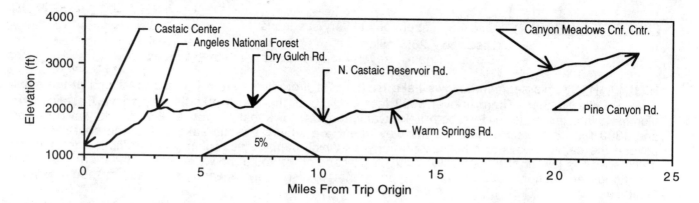

CONNECTING TRIPS: 1) Continuation with the Pine Canyon tour (Trip #70B) - turn left (west) at Pine Canyon Rd. at the Lake Hughes Rd. northern terminus; 2) continuation with the Old Ridge Route Road ride (Trip #70C) - turn left (north) at Old Ridge Route Rd. in Castaic; 3) connection with the San Francisquito and Bouquet Canyons tour (Trip #69) - at the Lake Hughes Rd. terminus, turn east onto Lake Elizabeth Rd. (Pine Canyon Rd. to the west).

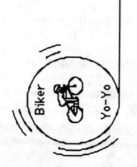

TRIP #70B - PINE CANYON ROAD

GENERAL LOCATION: Lake Hughes, Sandberg

LEVEL OF DIFFICULTY: One way - strenuous
Distance - 17.2 miles
Elevation gain - periodic moderate-to-steep grades

HIGHLIGHTS: The Pine Canyon Road segment is a 17-mile countryside ride through tree-bedecked rolling hills, much of it straddling the San Andreas Rift Zone. There is close to 2000 feet elevation gain with several sustained moderate-to-steep grades. The first 9.3 miles is on a countryside lane with scattered residences and sporadic, fast-moving traffic. The remainder of the trip (beyond Three Points Rd.) is very lightly traveled and is more typified as having well-separated ranches. If your joy is solitude and a countryside setting, the latter portion of the ride is road biking at its best.

TRAILHEAD: From the Lancaster/Palmdale area, take the Antelope Valley Fwy. and turn off westbound at Elizabeth Lake Rd. (County road "N2") and drive 14 miles to the Lake Hughes Rd. intersection. (Note that the road name changes to Pine Canyon Rd. just beyond.) Turn south onto Lake Hughes Rd and find parking near the market or tavern. From the Golden State Fwy., exit east at Lancaster Rd. (State Hwy. 138), and drive 21 miles to Three Points Rd. Turn right and continue five miles as it veers left and merges into Pine Canyon Rd. In another 9-1/2 miles is Lake Hughes Rd. Park as described above.

Bring a couple of water bottles to see you through this "dry" route on hot days. If the plan is for an up-and-back tour in the heat, add water to suit your needs.

Pine Canyon Road Near Sandberg

TRIP DESCRIPTION: **Lake Hughes to Three Points Road.** Start on this two-lane country road under a scattered tree canopy. Relish the thought that, unlike the Lake Hughes Rd. portion, this is typical of most of this segment. Start a 4.5-mile moderate climb that peaks, then drops to Kings Canyon Rd. Along the way are scattered residences and a creekbed alongside the road. Near the summit are a private church grounds and a wedding chapel at Tweedy Ln. (6.1).

A refreshing downhill that ends just beyond Kings Canyon Rd. is followed by a modest 1.7-mile climb. The road then passes scattered residential pockets on a long, blow-it-out downhill that bottoms at Three Points Rd. (9.3).

Three Points Road to Old Ridge Route Road. Cyclist that blink will wind up heading north on Three Points Rd. since a hard left is required to say on Pine Canyon Rd. A modest climb takes cyclists beyond the scattered residential pockets, past Seccombe Rd (10.4) and into an area dotted by small ranches. This area of rolling hills is well-treed both away from and alongside this winding road. After a nice downhill is the Rancho Corona del Valle Ranch, one of the larger in the area (14.8). The ride finale is a steady 1.6-mile upgrade which leads to the Pine Canyon Rd. terminus at Old Ridge Route Rd. (17.2). (The skinnied-down track across Old Ridge Route Rd. is a private drive used by Sandberg residents.)

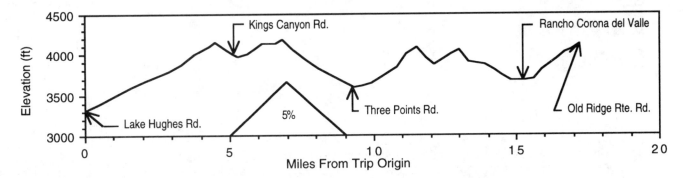

CONNECTING TRIPS: 1) Continuation with the Lake Hughes Rd. tour (Trip #70A) - turn south at the trip origin at Lake Hughes Rd.; 2) continuation with the Old Ridge Route Road ride (Trip #70C) - turn left (south) at Old Ridge Route Rd. at the terminus of this ride.

237

TRIP #70C - OLD RIDGE ROUTE ROAD

<u>GENERAL LOCATION</u>: Sandberg, Castaic

<u>LEVEL OF DIFFICULTY</u>: One way - strenuous (north to south); very strenuous (south to north)
Distance - 28.0 miles
Elevation gain - periodic moderate to steep grades (north to south);
periodic steep-to-sheer grades (south to north)

<u>HIGHLIGHTS</u>: Being both on-road and off-road cycling book authors, this ride is a charmer for both groups! Much of the ride is on paved, but non-maintained, Forest Service Road 8N04. It is doable with any fat-tire bike that has good tire tread, but is best done on mountain bike tires. There is little road traffic north of Templin Hwy. (read that as few vehicle nuisances, but also that it is remote) and the route transits high-desert scrub with minimal tree cover.

The north-to-south ride described has nearly 4000 feet of drop, yet still offers some challenging climbs (1500 feet total) with some mixed perspectives of the great, relatively-undeveloped outdoors together with the downlooking vistas of the bustle of Interstate Hwy. 5. There are remnants of the grand days of the Old Ridge Route Road, including the old Tumble Inn, together with many looks at the stratified geology and plant life of this high-desert arena. The varied canyon, Castaic Lake and even developed City of Castaic vistas along the way are awesome. The peace and quiet of the natural northern trip section, combined with the rewarding downhill blowout on the more-developed southern section give this ride the best of both worlds!

Old Ridge Route Road Above Fisher Springs Road

<u>TRAILHEAD</u>: From the Golden State Fwy. exit at Lancaster Rd. (State Hwy. 138) and drive east 8-1/2 miles to County Hwy. "N2." Look for the sign noting "Old Ridge Route Road." Turn right (south) and climb two miles to the Pine Canyon Rd. junction. From the Lancaster/Palmdale area, take Ave. "D" westbound, continuing as it becomes Lancaster Rd. At six miles west of 300th St. W., turn left (south) at Hwy. "N2" and follow the directions above.

Bring a couple of water bottles to see you through this waterless and remote segment, more on hot days. Ensure that your tire patch kit and repair tools are packed -- it could be a long walk out otherwise!

<u>TRIP DESCRIPTION</u>: **Trailhead to Reservoir Hill.** Climb 1/2 mile on paved road to a flat where the maintained road ends. The surface transitions to a mix of broken asphalt and concrete with scattered seams of dirt and then returns to a modest climb above Liebre Gulch (to the west). At (1.6) is a level, where there is a distant peek at Pyramid Lake. The first downhill leads past a marked turnoff (Forest Service Road 7N23) to Bear Canyon and Sawmill Canyon Campgrounds (3.1). Shortly is a shift to an eastern exposure, one of a myriad of view changes that will occur on this ridge ride.

A mild uphill leads past a rock wall and the site of the old Tumble Inn (4.4), followed by some ups and downs and a passage through a narrowing slide area (6.4). A downhill takes cyclists on the first of several passes below transmission lines to the start of an extended saddle (7.1). A tough 1.4-mile, 400-foot climb leads to a crest below the Reservoir Hill summit, where there is a majestic view into

Cienaga Canyon to the east (9.1). This is the most challenging upgrade for the north-south Old Ridge Route Rd. transit.

Reservoir Hill to Templin Highway. The road quality improves somewhat on the downhill as bicyclists pass a road closure gate and reach another saddle, where there is a brief first glimpse of Interstate Hwy. 5 (10.8). Soon is a passage through another slide area and a nice winding downhill with open Hwy. 5 vistas, followed by a transit under a pipeline-supporting suspension bridge (12.3).

Beyond a low saddle is a climb past Forest Service Rd. 6N43 and the first Castaic Lake vistas just beyond the summit (16.8). A refreshing downhill takes cyclists on a sweeping turn to a southeast heading and over the Angeles Tunnel of the West Branch of the California Aqueduct (18.0). The road continues past a roadside ranch with trailer homes in the lower reaches in another 0.5 mile. From here to trip's end, the ride is on quality asphalt roadway. A one-mile climb leads to a flat and an exposed area with steep drops above Castaic Lake's upper bay. Just beyond is the first stop sign and the junction with paved Templin Hwy. (20.2).

Templin Highway to Castaic. Bike straight ahead on a short steep climb to a flat (diverting either direction on Templin Hwy. will require a steep return to this junction) and follow the winding road past an out-of-place trailer home situated on a lake overlook (21.3). What follows is a refreshing 6.3-mile, 1800-foot runout to Lake Hughes Rd. in Castaic. The road passes a small cluster of homesites, dives down toward and parallels Hwy. 5 from above. There is a minuscule climb at (24.5), followed by more downhill and an entry into a residential pocket above Castaic Lagoon in about two miles. The trip's second stop sign looms at (26.7), followed by the Lake Hughes Rd. intersection (27.6). A turn west (right), and a second right at Castaic Rd. returns cyclists to the Castaic Center shopping complex (28.0).

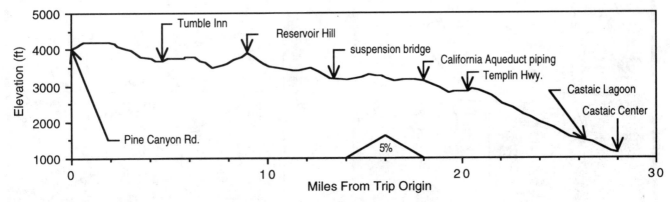

CONNECTING TRIPS: 1) Continuation with the Lake Hughes Rd. tour (Trip #70A) - turn east on Lake Hughes Rd. in Castaic; 2) continuation with the Pine Canyon Road ride (Trip #70B) - at the trip origin, take Pine Canyon Rd. east.

TRIP #71 - CALIFORNIA AQUEDUCT

GENERAL LOCATION: Llano, Baldy Mesa, Hesperia

LEVEL OF DIFFICULTY: One way - moderate; up and back - moderate to strenuous
(difficulty rating is dependent on weather conditions)
Distance - 27.5 miles
Elevation gain - essentially flat

HIGHLIGHTS: This tour is a desert rat's dream. There are grand mountain views in the distance and relatively undeveloped desert landscape close-up throughout the entire 27-plus mile tour. Those who revel in peace and solitude will find that the route is lightly used for most of the year. The nearby flora and fauna are generally undisturbed, i.e., left to be enjoyed by those quietly passing through.

TRAILHEAD: From State Hwy. 138 west of Pearblossom and near Llano, turn south on 165th St. and drive two miles to the California Aqueduct. Park on the east side of the street away from the entrance area. There is a portable restroom here. Another option is to start from Hesperia near the intersection of Amargosa Rd. and the aqueduct. From State Hwy. 395, turn west at Main St./Phelan Rd. and turn right (north) at Key Pointe Ave. Drive to a "T"-intersection and turn right on Amargosa Rd., following that frontage road 1/4 mile to the aqueduct.

The route is waterless, exposed and relatively remote, although there are scattered residences off some roadways which cross the aqueduct. Bring 2-3 water bottles on hot days as a contingency, or bike this route in the <u>cool</u> of winter. (It does snow at this 4000-foot elevation!) Temperatures of 100-degrees F-plus are not uncommon in the May-October period and high winds are a staple in this high desert area. In addition to the normal repair tools and tire patch kit, bring some sunscreen -- there is no tree cover and minimal shade from any source. Sunglasses are a must! Finally, stay out of the aqueduct! The walls are steep and can be slippery, making it extremely difficult to get back out.

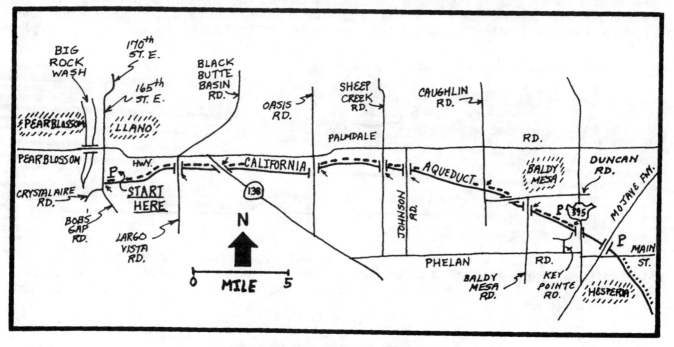

TRIP #71 - CALIFORNIA AQUEDUCT

TRIP DESCRIPTION: Start by reading the sign at the entry gate which reads, *Walk-in Fishing Only, No Bicycles, No Vehicles*, then observe the *Bike Trail* sign further in. (Oh, well!) Slip through the walker/biker entry on the north side and cycle on a rough asphalt surface, characteristic of the entire tour. The route is flat with a few little ups and downs. To the right (south) are the San Gabriel Mountains with Mt. Baldy and sister peaks prominently on display in the distance and a chain of foothills in the foreground.

Observe the yucca trees and mixed desert scrub to the north. Both the mountain vistas and high-desert landscape are characteristic of the scenery on the entire tour. Also, plan on visits from numerous crows, a few hawks and other of natures desert creatures. We saw a couple of large dogs (or possibly coyotes) from a distance on the far eastern segment actually working their way out of the water.

On the ride east are unmarked road crossings (both paved and unpaved) requiring cyclists to dismount, pass through an entry gate, cross the road and reenter through the gate on the opposite side before resuming the tour. Luckily these distractions are well-spaced and can serve as welcome breaks for the "backside." Street names are stenciled on the sides of the overpasses which face the aqueduct. Major cross streets are Largo Vista Rd. (4.3), Hwy. 138 (6.5), Oasis Rd. (11.3), Sheep Creek Rd. (15.9), Johnson Rd (17.3), Caughlin Rd. (21.4), Duncan Rd. (22.5) and Baldy Mesa Rd. (23.7).

The mountain panorama changes slowly as bikers find themselves nearly north of the Cajon Summit on the eastern segment of the trip. The San Bernardino Mountains are to the southeast. The ever-plentiful yuccas seem to come in every shape and size. There are pockets of residences near some of the road crossings, becoming more preva-lent in the Baldy Mesa locale. Near trip's end, bicyclists stare directly at the high-speed traffic of State Hwy. 395 and soon reach Amargosa Rd. (26.2)

California Aqueduct West of Oasis Road

CONNECTING TRIPS: Connection with the aqueduct segment eastbound out of Hesperia: cycle from the trip end point south to the Key Pointe Rd./Phelan Rd. intersection and turn left (east) onto the latter roadway. Bike 1-1/2 mile on what becomes Main St. to the aqueduct crossing and look for the marked entry on the east side. The trail follows some modest ups and downs, then essentially flattens for the remainder of the ride, which ends in 6.6 miles at Ranchero Rd. Intervening cross streets are Maple Ave (3.9), Mesquite St. (4.3) and Cottonwood (5.2).

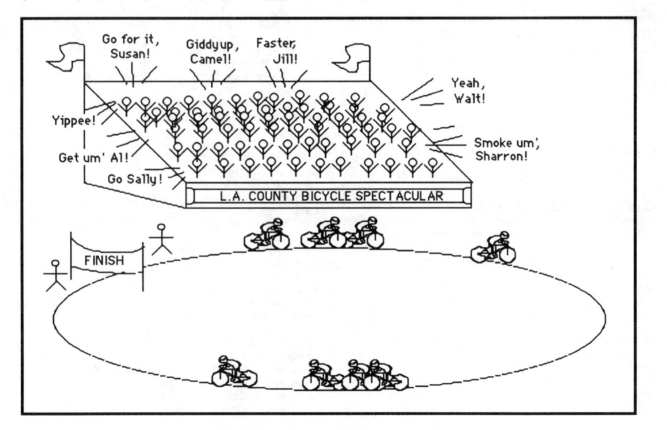

INDEX

(Trip Number Noted Below)

BICYCLE RIDES: LOS ANGELES COUNTY

B-D Enterprises Books

Nothing to It!

B-D Enterprises books are available at better bicycle stores, both walk-in and on-line book stores, recreational outlets and from the publisher. For additional information about our books, write us at 122 Mirabeau Ave., San Pedro CA 90732 or e-mail us at <bnyduk@aol.com>.

All cycling books have a master county map(s), master trip matrices, detailed trip maps, elevation contours, a detailed index and numerous photos. Prices noted in the book summaries which follow are suggested retail prices. The cost may vary in individual stores.

BICYCLE RIDES: LOS ANGELES COUNTY

Published 4/89; second printing (revised) - 8/91;
third printing (revised) - 5/95
Completely revised/updated edition 6/00
ISBN 0-9619151-8-8
Library of Congress Cat. Number 99-097150

8-1/2 " X 11" Format; 244 pages; $12.95 $13.95
71 Trips and 85 Individual On-road Rides

Sample Book Contents by Section:
   • **The Coast** - South Bay Bike Trail, Palos
Verdes Peninsula, L.A. Harbor, Long Beach
Shoreline Park, Santa Monica Mountains, PCH
Coastal Century
   • **River Trails** - Upper Rio Hondo, Lario Trail,
San Gabriel River, "Big Banana", West Fork of
Upper San Gabriel River
   • **Inland** - Whittier Narrows, Arroyo Seco Trail,
Kenneth Newell Bikeway, Griffith Park, Elysian
Park, Mulholland Drive, Sepulveda Bike Basin,
Diamond Bar, San Jose Hills, Bonelli Park
   • **Potpourri** - L.A. Civic Center, Tour de Los
Angeles, Santa Catalina Island
   • **New Trips** - Agoura Hills, Santa Susana
Pass, Hansen Dam, San Dimas Canyon, San
Francisquito & Bouquet Canyons, Old Ridge
Route, California Aqueduct

BICYCLE RIDES: ORANGE COUNTY

Published 9/88; second printing (revised) - 4/90;
third printing (revised) - 8/93; fourth printing
(revised) - 11/96
ISBN 0-9619151-2-9
Library of Congress Cat. Number 88-071407

8-1/2 " X 11" Format; 154 pages; $9.95
35 Trips and 42 Individual On-road Rides

Sample Book Contents by Section:
   • **The Coast** - Huntington Central Park,
Sunset to Newport Beach Strand, Upper Newport
Bay, Laguna Beach, Laguna Niguel & Del
Obispo Bikeways, Doheny/San Clemente Bike
Route, Newport Beach/Corona Del Mar, San
Clemente to San Diego
   • **River Trails** - Santa Ana River, San Diego
Creek, San Gabriel River, Coyote Creek
   • **Inland** - El Cajon Trail, Carbon Canyon,
Orange/Irvine Park, Santiago Canyon Road,
O'Neill Park, Aliso Creek Trail, Mission Viejo
Bikeway
   • **The "Big Guys"** - Western & Eastern County
Loops, Orange County Century

BICYCLE RIDES: INLAND EMPIRE

Published 4/90; second printing (revised) - 4/94
ISBN 0-9619151-4-5
Library of Congress Cat. Number 89-091606

8-1/2 " X 11" Format; 154 pages; $8.95
30 Trips and 37 Individual On-road Rides

Sample Book Contents by Section:
- **Riverside County**
    - Riverside City: Upper Santa Ana River, Tour de Riverside, Lake Perris, Pigeon Pass
    - Western Interior Valleys: Perris & Temescal Valleys, Badlands & Fault Lines, Temecula Wine Tour, Lake Elsinor
    - Coachella Valley: Upper Whitewater Rvr., Palm Springs, Coachella Bikeway, Indio Hills
- **San Bernardino County**
    - San Bernardino/Redlands Cities: San Antonio & Cajon Canyons, Prado Park, Timoteo & Live Oak Canyons, Sunset Drive, Oak Glen
    - Mountains: Big Bear Lake, Lytle Creek
    - Desert: Joshua Tree National Park, National Trails Highway (Old Route 66)
    - Colorado River: Parker Strip, Needles-Bullhead City Loop
    - California Aqueduct Bikeway

BICYCLE RIDES: SAN DIEGO AND IMPERIAL COUNTIES

Published 6/92; second printing 6/97
ISBN 0-9619151-5-3
Library of Congress Cat. Number 90-093234

8-1/2 " X 11" Format; 218 pages; $11.95
62 On-road Rides

Sample Book Contents by Section:
- **The Coast**
    - Metropolitan San Diego: Mission Bay, Balboa Park, San Diego Bay, Point Loma, La Jolla, Old Town, Scenic Drive, Techolote Canyon, Imperial Beach, San Diego River, Otay Lake, San Diego to San Clemente
    - North County: Rancho Santa Fe, Lake San Marcos, Vista Lagoons Loop, Oceanside
- **Inland**
    - Urban: El Cajon, Santee Lakes, San Pasqual Valley, Escondido to Sea, Fallbrook, Ramona, Mount Helix, Blossom Valley
    - Mountains/Backcountry: Mount Palomar, Julian, Laguna Mountains, Pala Mission, Lake Morena, Bonsall Canyons, Crest-Dehesa. Barona Valley, Bear Ridge Loop
    - Desert: El Centro, Salton Sea, Borrego Springs, Great Overland Stage Route
    - Colorado River: Winterhaven

BICYCLE RIDES: SANTA BARBARA AND VENTURA COUNTIES

Published 9/94; second printing - 7/98
ISBN 0-9619151-6-1
Library of Congress Catalogue Number 94-094025
6 " X 0" Format; 274 pages; $10.95
68 Trips Including 15 Best Mountain Bike Rides

Sample Book Contents by Section:
* **Santa Barbara County**
    - City of Santa Barbara: Santa Barbara City, Hope Ranch, UCSB Campus, Mountain Drive, Goleta, Carpinteria
    - East County: Gibralter Road, Romero Canyon, East & West Camino Cielo, Upper Santa Ynez River, Refugio Pass, Paradise Road, Wine County Tours, Solvang Century, Figueroa Mountain
    - West County: Jalama Beach, Casmalia & Solomon Hills, Los Coches Mountain, Point Sal, Oso Flaco Lake, Cuyama River
* **Ventura County**
    - The Coast: Port Hueneme, Ventura-Ojai, Ventura-Santa Barbara, Coastal Century
    - Inland/Urban; Agoura Hills, Westlake, Thousand Oaks, North Ranch, Simi Valley, Rocky Peak, Potrero Road
    - Mountain/Backcountry: Sycamore Canyon, Ojai-Santa Barbara, Sisar Canyon, Sulphur & Pine Mountains, Lockwood Valley, Mount Pinos

BY DON AND SHARRON BRUNDIGE

MOUNTAIN BIKING L.A. COUNTY (Southern Section)

Published 9/96
ISBN 0-9619151-7-X
Library of Congress Cat. Number 95-094085
6 "X 9" Format; 241 pages; $11.95
66 Trips and 100 Individual Mountain Bike Rides

Sample Book Contents by Section:
* **Santa Monica Mountains (SMM): East** - Franklin Canyon, Dirt Mulholland, Sullivan Canyon, Trippet Ranch/Eagle Rock, Will Rogers/Backbone Trail
* **SMM: Central** - Redrock Canyon/Calabasas Peak, Crags Road/Malibu Creek, Bulldog Loop, Paramount Ranch, Puerco Canyon, Castro Peak, Zuma Ridge, The Edison Road, East Los Robles Trail, Conejo Crest
* **SMM: West** - Sandstone Peak, The Grotto, Sycamore Canyon, Guadalasco Trail, Rancho Sierra Vista/Satwiwa, West Los Robles Trail
* **Mountclef Ridge/Simi Hills** - Mountclef Ridge, Wildwood Park, Lynnmere Trail, Cheeseboro & Palo Camado Canyons
* **Santa Susana Mountains** - Rocky Peak, Limekiln & Aliso Canyons, Mission Peak/Bee Canyon
* **Verdugo Mountains/San Rafael Hills** - Brand & Beaudry Mtwys., Summit Ride, Hosteller/Whiting Mtwys.
* **Puente Hills** - East & West Skyline Trails
* **Potpourri** - Walnut Canyon, Bonelli Park, Palos Verdes Peninsula, Santa Catalina Island

BY DON AND SHARRON BRUNDIGE

SANTA MONICA MOUNTAINS
SANTA SUSANA MOUNTAINS   SIMI HILLS
VERDUGO MOUNTAINS/SAN RAFAEL HILLS   PUENTE HILLS
PALOS VERDES PENINSULA   SANTA CATALINA ISLAND

OUTDOOR RECREATION CHECKLISTS
A Unique Book Concept With the Multi-Activity Outdoorsperson in Mind

Published 11/98
ISBN 0-9619151-9-6
Library of Congress Cat. Number 96-095421

5-1/2 " X 8-1/2" Format; 422 pages; $14.95
Predominantly All Major Outdoor Activities Included

Why pay the price to buy a book for every outdoor activity that you plan to explore? *Outdoor Recreation Checklists* provides exhaustive equipment checklists and extensive gear discussions and tradeoffs for a wide range of activities. This four-season book covers both land and waterborne adventures ranging from camping to remote mountaineering to self-guided or chartered rafting or fishing trips. Just check the book's front cover (shown at upper right) to be convinced. There are over 70 checklist pages and over 160 photographs.

How is anyone qualified to write such a book? Don and Sharron Brundige, with 25 years of outdoor recreation experience and authors of nine Southern California on-road and off-road bicycling books, have collaborated with a group of grizzled veterans in a broad range of outdoor activities to create this wide-ranging work. *Outdoor Recreation Checklists* is unique on the market. Literature searches conducted over the two years of book development prove this convincingly.

Why is the book so useful for all of the activities covered? Just read a few reasons noted on the book's back cover (shown at lower right). Besides, having all these checklists and tradeoff discussions in one book assists you in identifying gear that is useful for more than one activity. This may save you money and/or affect your gear investment strategy.

What's in the book that is useful to bicyclists? There are four sections dedicated to cycling; two are for on-road biking (daytime and multi-day) and the other two for off-road biking. The book has general discussions on trip planning/preparation, safety, respect for the territory and logistics/communication. There is a detailed discussion of the classic "Ten Essentials," that gear needed for survival contingencies. There are general-use sections on first-aid kit needs and on outdoors meal planning, with many mealtime suggestions. Finally, there is a separate section identifying gear which is common to multiple outdoor activities. This matrix-formatted section may assist you in prioritizing the investment of your hard-earned bucks.

B D Enterprises
Bicycle Books